£3.00

GEORGE MACLEOD

*By the same author available as
a Fount Paperback*

CHASING THE WILD GOOSE
THE IONA COMMUNITY

GEORGE MACLEOD

Founder of
the Iona Community

RONALD FERGUSON

*

COLLINS
8 Grafton Street, London W1

William Collins Sons & Co Ltd
London · Glasgow · Sydney · Auckland
Toronto · Johannesburg

First published 1990
© 1990 Ronald Ferguson
ISBN 0 00 215297 5
Set in Linotron Plantin
Made and Printed in Great Britain by
Billing & Sons Ltd, Worcester

Dedicated to

LORNA, LADY MACLEOD
(not a hero, just a saint)

*who lived the truth
that goodness need not be boring*

Contents

Contents

List of Illustrations

Preface

Biographers, said Auden, are gossip writers and voyeurs calling themselves scholars.

But he would, wouldn't he?

Researching and writing this book has been a dauntingly exciting task. The claim that George MacLeod is one of the greatest living Scots has been made so often as to be a cliché. That does not make it any less true: yet, at the same time, he is an elusive, complex man who has inspired great loyalty and much opposition in the course of a long and controversial life.

I accepted this commission from Collins with much gladness, because I admire George MacLeod and believe his story to be worth telling. (I declare this at the outset, so that the reader may deduct points for bias. Beware biographers who conceal their assumptions.) Before I got to know George MacLeod, I was, like many people, in awe of him. After I became leader of the Iona Community, I learned to love the man. Latterly, I have been close to him at vulnerable points in his life, and I was privileged to conduct the memorial service for his wife, Lorna, to whom this book is dedicated. In my time as leader, he was immensely supportive and personally kind. At the same time, I recognized early on that I would have to resist his powerful embrace if I was to remain my own man: from then on we understood each other and got on well. Admiration need not dull one's critical faculties, and this book is, as it should be, a critical biography.

The first obligation of the historian – and indeed of the minister of the gospel – is to the truth, insofar as the truth itself is ascertainable. I like Desmond MacCarthy's observation that the biographer is "an artist under oath". George MacLeod and his family have never wished it otherwise. Although I have been given unrestricted access to all papers, I have never been put under any pressure to act as family retainer. In Auden's terms, there is gossip in the book – why not? – and some may even claim to detect the odd hint of voyeurism, depending on the definition of terms. I would simply agree with Paul Roazen, biographer of Freud, who observed that "it is impossible to establish a man in history without compromising his privacy". It is how it is done that matters.

My brief was to write a book which would be historically well grounded and comprehensively researched, yet would also be readable and widely accessible. The original sources which emerged turned out to be a historian's dream. Letters, journals and diaries from early days were discovered in tea chests and dark corners, most of them searched out by the indefatigable Maxwell MacLeod, whose enthusiastic and uncompromising engagement in the "quest for the historical George" helped make the investigation such an adventure. So many legends have surrounded George MacLeod and the founding of the Iona Community – several of them created by the old Celtic spellbinder himself – that the tracking down of the historical reality behind the holy smokescreen became an intriguing detective story.

Researching the MacLeod dynastic story – which, surprisingly, has never been fully told – took me into the realms of Scottish church history over the past two and a half centuries: and the span of George's own long and full life coincided with vast changes in ecclesiastical, social, economic and political life in Britain. I am especially grateful to Alec Cheyne, Emeritus Professor of Ecclesiastical History in the University of Edinburgh, for his enthusiastic encouragement at various stages in the manuscript's life.

The research included not simply the study of documents, but interviews and correspondence with many, many people. Devotees and critics alike were prepared to give up hours to the task. In many ways, the story of George MacLeod could have been told by way of his impact on countless people, and to keep that important dimension of his life and work to the forefront, I have interspersed the historical narrative with verbatim accounts by living eyewitnesses.

The need to hold together academic thoroughness and readable prose – and how could it be otherwise in a study of a man who both searched the theological depths and sought to make his message relevant to ordinary people? – has led to one necessary compromise. In order to keep the narrative flow as untrammelled as possible, I have held footnotes to a minimum. The text itself usually indicates the source: reminiscences are contributed by the people named, either through correspondence or interview, accounts of General Assembly debates are from the verbatim records unless otherwise stated, and letter writers or recipients are

Preface

named in the text itself. All of these sources, many of which have only come to light in the last few months, are being collated and catalogued, and will be placed in the MacLeod archives. (To avoid confusion, I have spelt MacLeod throughout with a capital L: there was no consistency of spelling within the dynasty until George's father settled the issue.)

It is impossible to name the many people who have helped with this project, but I would particularly like to thank Iain Maciver, assistant keeper of manuscripts in the National Library of Scotland; the staff of the Mitchell Library, Glasgow; Harry Reid, deputy editor of *The Glasgow Herald* and the *Herald*'s library staff; Janet McBain of the Scottish Film Council; Rev. Johnston McKay of BBC Religious Broadcasting; Rev. James Weatherhead, Principal Clerk to the General Assembly of the Church of Scotland, and his secretary, Chris Brown; Lawrence Marshall, secretary of the Iona Cathedral Trustees; Lt Col. A. W. Scott Elliot of the Argyll and Sutherland Highlanders; Peter Finch, secretary of the Nutfield Local History Group; Councillor Iain Thornber; Rev. David Roberts; Rev. Kathy Galloway; Rev. John Sim; and Teresa de Bertodano, Senior Editor, Collins Fount.

Acknowledgments are also due to the Iona Community for permission to print extracts from *We Shall Rebuild*, *Only One Way Left*, and *The Whole Earth Shall Cry Glory*; to Hodder & Stoughton, for permission to quote from *The Years of Fulfilment*, *The Glimmering Landscape*, and *John White*; to John Murray for permission to quote from *Clayton of Toc H*; to Methuen for permission to quote from *Govan Calling*; to SCM Press for permission to quote from *Speaking the Truth in Love*; to Hutchison for permission to quote from *Laughter in Heaven*; to the Handsel Press for permission to quote from *The Kilt Beneath my Cassock*; to the BBC, for permission to quote from recorded materials; and to *The Glasgow Herald*, *The Scotsman* and the *Scottish Field*.

On a more personal note, I would like to express my thanks to George Mackay Brown, that great Orkney *seanachaidh*, for his encouragement to me in my writing, both fiction and non-fiction, and to my wife, Cristine, for her loving support.

RON FERGUSON

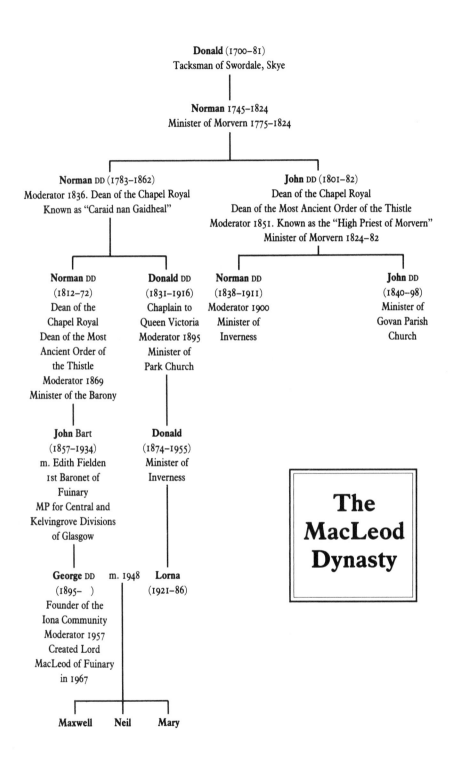

Donald (1700–81)
Tacksman of Swordale, Skye

Norman 1745–1824
Minister of Morvern 1775–1824

Norman DD (1783–1862)
Moderator 1836. Dean of the Chapel Royal
Known as "Caraid nan Gaidheal"

John DD (1801–82)
Dean of the Chapel Royal
Dean of the Most Ancient Order of the Thistle
Moderator 1851. Known as the "High Priest of Morvern"
Minister of Morvern 1824–82

Norman DD
(1812–72)
Dean of the
Chapel Royal
Dean of the Most
Ancient Order of
the Thistle
Moderator 1869
Minister of the Barony

Donald DD
(1831–1916)
Chaplain to
Queen Victoria
Moderator 1895
Minister of
Park Church

Norman DD
(1838–1911)
Moderator 1900
Minister of
Inverness

John DD
(1840–98)
Minister of
Govan Parish
Church

John Bart
(1857–1934)
m. Edith Fielden
1st Baronet of
Fuinary
MP for Central and
Kelvingrove Divisions
of Glasgow

Donald
(1874–1955)
Minister of
Inverness

George DD   m. 1948   **Lorna**
(1895–)   (1921–86)
Founder of the
Iona Community
Moderator 1957
Created Lord
MacLeod of Fuinary
in 1967

Maxwell   **Neil**   **Mary**

The
MacLeod
Dynasty

Frontispiece

This day I begin the memoir of my beloved John. Oh my God and his, guide my pen! In mercy keep me from writing anything false in fact or sentiment. May strict Truth pervade every sentence! May I be enabled to show in him the Grace of God, so that other scholars in Thy school may be quickened and encouraged to be followers of him as he was of Christ! I feel utterly unworthy to undertake this memoir, or of any of even the least of Thy saints, but Thou who hast given me this work in Thy Providence, and called me to preach the unsearchable riches of Christ, wilt enable me, I doubt not, to show the riches of Christ as displayed in a poor sinner.

NORMAN MACLEOD OF THE BARONY
September 6, 1852

Prologue

The old Mull shepherd has seen them coming from a long way off, far down the barren glen. The sleek red car is moving quickly in the bright sunshine. He calls swiftly to his dogs, encouraging them to bring the huge flock across the road before the car arrives.

The weather is hot for August, and the shepherd has had a hectic day. His work has been constantly interrupted by the stream of cars returning from the big event on Iona. In a moment, the red car is upon him, the driver tooting his horn impatiently as the car is surrounded by sheep and dogs. The passengers notice that the shepherd is about to shout abuse, when he suddenly catches sight of the old man hunched in the front passenger seat. The Mull man stops, tears off his hat, and waves the vehicle through as the sheep scatter. A moment later, the car is speeding down the glen.

The elderly man in the front of the car is George Fielden MacLeod, also known as the Very Reverend, the Lord MacLeod of Fuinary. In his 94th year, he is frail and tired. Scotland's most eminent living churchman is being driven from his beloved Iona for what, he has announced, is the last time.

The 1988 celebrations on Columba's isle have been to mark the fiftieth anniversary of the founding of MacLeod's Iona Community. The high point of the week was the dedication of the MacLeod Centre, an international centre of reconciliation for young people and families – set across the road from the living quarters of Iona Abbey which were rebuilt by George MacLeod and his community. The new building was opened free of debt after a wide-ranging international appeal – many of the donations coming as a thank offering for the inspiration of the man after whom the centre is named.

As with most public events in his highly public life, the dedication has been marked by controversy. Protestant extremists held aloft banners, in front of the television cameras, proclaiming MACLEOD IS A FALSE PROPHET and, when the elderly man shuffled forward on his sticks towards the lectern to take a prayer, a shout was heard in the silence, "Turn to Christ before you die, Doctor

Prologue

MacLeod". At the end of the ceremony, Lord MacLeod almost danced into the new building, holding on to the arm of Mrs Leah Tutu, wife of the Archbishop of Cape Town. George's voice, singing a South African hymn, "Marching in the Light of God", sounded to those near him like that of a child.

When he left the island with which his name has been so profoundly associated, many people felt that he was going home to die, his life work complete. There were tears on Iona jetty when he left.

The car speeds through the glen. The impatient driver, Lord MacLeod's son, Maxwell, wants to get his father back home to Edinburgh as quickly as possible. His father, as usual, has other ideas. At Fishnish, waiting for the ferry, he turns to his two retired secretaries, Nan MacKenzie, who had been with him for over sixty years, and Mary Macgregor, who had come out of retirement to help with the MacLeod Centre campaign.

Over there is Morvern, he tells them, the land of his forebears. When they get to the other side, Maxwell will drive them to his house at Fuinary and they'll light a fire and have tea. He hasn't been there for years.

The passengers remonstrate quietly. Surely Dr MacLeod wants to get home? He is not to bother. Another day perhaps. Maxwell pleads with him: the old house is dilapidated, there is no tea, not even water.

No, says the old man, he must go there.

At Lochaline, the car turns in the direction of Fuinary. Moving more slowly now on the single-track road, they pass the old graveyard. George points out the family tomb, where seventeen of his ancestors sleep.

Four miles on, they swing to the north up a steep track, overlooking a beautiful Hebridean bay. Fuinary manse stands bleak and ghostly, in four wooded acres.

A hard shove on the door gives them entry. "My God, you've let this place get into a hell of a mess," the old man mutters.

Maxwell, who is by now convinced that his father has chosen to come to Fuinary to die, helps him to a chair in the only one of the twenty once-elegant rooms which is remotely habitable. To the old man's amusement, his son produces a gunmetal flask that George had used in the First World War, and pours a stiff dram into a cracked mug. He then goes out and carefully adds a few drops of cool water from the Fuinary burn.

Prologue

In front of the crackling fire, father and son talk of their Morvern ancestors, while the ladies make a discreet tour of the grounds. The old house seems filled with the spirits of bygone MacLeods.

Then the old man closes his eyes and falls asleep. His son lays a coat upon him, and checks his pulse.

In a deep sense, George Fielden MacLeod is home.

PART ONE

*

DYNASTY

1

The Big Men of Morvern

A thousand, thousand tender ties
Accept this day my plaintive sighs
My heart within me almost dies
At thought of leaving Fuinary.

DR NORMAN MACLEOD
"the Highlander's Friend"

I should like to be at the head of everything!

DR NORMAN MACLEOD OF THE BARONY

George Fielden MacLeod, that Presbyterian equivalent of a turbulent priest, was born in 1895 into one of Britain's most formidable ecclesiastical dynasties.

The powerful MacLeod house, which has now given more than 550 years of ordained service to the Church – producing six Moderators of the General Assembly of the Church of Scotland, and amassing seven Doctorates of Divinity, two Deanships of the Chapel Royal, two Deanships of the Thistle, and four royal chaplaincies – shaped and moulded George, even at the points at which he dramatically tore up the family script.

It is nicely ironic that such a well known pacifist should trace his descent from a Highlander who was deeply engaged in beating ploughshares into swords.

The Isle of Skye cradled the early MacLeods, nurturing a Celtic mysticism and poetry and passion which has marked the family ever since. Donald MacLeod, "tacksman" (gentleman farmer), lived in the mid-eighteenth century at Swordale, a few miles from Dunvegan Castle, ancient seat of the Clan MacLeod.

Descended from one of the earlier Chiefs, Donald was armourer

3

to the Chief of the Clan MacLeod. In addition to making excellent weapons, he is said to have been the first to introduce family worship to the district. In 1763 the Synod of Glenelg granted bursaries of £6 a year to several hopeful young men intending the ministry, among them Norman, "son to Donald MacLeod, tacksman of Swordale". Norman graduated at Aberdeen in 1767 and for a time was tutor at Dunvegan Castle, where in 1773 he met Dr Samuel Johnson and James Boswell.

At the age of thirty, Norman MacLeod was presented to the parish of Morvern by the Duke of Argyll in 1775. It was said of him when he sailed from Skye, accompanied by his one-eyed servant Rory, that "a prettier man never left his native island." His commanding presence was much commented upon – he was more than six feet in height – and he was described as having a noble countenance which age only made nobler.

Morvern, in the western Highlands opposite the island of Mull, was Jacobite territory. When Bonnie Prince Charlie raised the standard of revolt in 1745, not a single man from Morvern joined the loyalist Argyll militia. The hilly grassland of Morvern was "wasted" by reprisals.

Norman MacLeod had been chosen for political reasons. A stout Presbyterian and Hanoverian loyalist, he was said to have done more than anyone to reconcile the people of Morvern to the final collapse of their Jacobite hopes, and to lead them from episcopalianism into the established Presbyterian church.

Thus was founded a great Scottish Levitical house. As Lord Sands put the matter quaintly in his description of the first General Assembly of the Church of Scotland attended by Norman in 1777: "The young minister of Morvern, who was thus introduced to the General Assembly, carried in his loins no fewer than five Moderators of that venerable body."[1] His great-great-grandson was destined to make the figure six.

The young minister did not have an easy time to begin with. His grandson, Norman, who immortalized his grandfather and the parish of Morvern in his evocative *Reminiscences of a Highland Parish*, set the scene.

"When the minister came to his parish, the people were but emerging from those old patriarchal times of clanship, with its loyal feelings and friendships, yet with its violent prejudices and intense clinging to the past, and to all that was bad as well as good in it. Many of his parishioners had been out in the '45, and were

Prince Charlie men to the core. These were not characterized by much religion – one of the predecessors of our minister had been commanded by this party not to dare in their presence to pray for King George in church, or they would shoot him dead. He did, nevertheless, pray, at least in words, but not, we fear, in pure faith. He took a brace of pistols with him to the pulpit, and cocking them before his prayer began, he laid them down before him and for once at least offered up his petitions with his eyes open."[2]

The minister of Morvern's charge covered 130 square miles, with a seaboard of 100 miles, and he ministered to the spiritual needs of 1800 people. He and his family lived at Fuinary (sometimes spelt Fiunary) manse, rebuilt for him in a lovely situation overlooking the Sound of Mull.

Norman MacLeod won the people over by his personal qualities. At a time when there were more than a few rogues in the ministry, his devotion, learning and pastoral care made him both revered and loved. He had a small stipend and a large family. The sixteen manse children learned to love the open seas and the hills, the nearby waterfall roaring in its dark gorge, and the hunting and fishing. In the winter evenings, young and old gathered round the fireside where songs and laughter mingled with graver discussion. Not infrequently, the minister would tune his violin and call on the lads to lay aside their books and the girls their sewing, and get them to dance. Family worship, conducted in Gaelic, ended the day.

The two churches in Norman's care were not much more than barns, yet the site of one of them, Keil Church, (short for Cill Columcill – the Church of Columba) was said to have been chosen by St Columba of Iona in the sixth century. The awareness of nearby Iona island, one of the great cradles of European Christianity, was strong in Morvern, and must have appealed to the romantic MacLeod mind. It was Norman's uncle, Neil MacLeod of Kilfinichen in Mull, who showed Johnson and Boswell round Iona and was described by Dr Johnson as "the clearest headed man I met in the islands."

Norman MacLeod ministered in Morvern for fifty years. His grandson graphically described his last Communion service in 1824.

"When he entered the pulpit, he mistook the side for the front; but old Rory, who watched him with intense interest, was immediately near him, and seizing a trembling hand, placed it on the book-board, thus guiding his master into the right position for addressing the congregation. And then stood up that venerable man, a Saul in height among the people, with his pure white hair falling back from his ample forehead over his shoulders. Few, and loving and earnest, were the words he spoke, amidst the profound silence of a passionately devoted people, which was broken only by their low sobs, when he told them they should see his face no more. Soon afterwards he died."[3]

Before he died, the MacLeod patriarch had the pleasure of seeing his youngest son appointed his assistant and his successor.

John MacLeod's ministry was at least as distinguished as his father's. Despite attempts to lure him away, he remained as minister of Morvern from 1824 until 1882, the combined ministry of father and son in the same parish being 107 years.

John MacLeod became one of the Kirk's most outstanding ministers. He was made Dean of the Most Ancient Order of the Thistle and Dean of the Chapel Royal, as well as being granted the degree of Doctor of Divinity by Glasgow University. He was elected Moderator of the General Assembly of the Church of Scotland in 1851.

Doctor John's bearing was even more imposing than that of his father's. Standing six feet seven inches, with a powerful athletic frame, he was nicknamed "The High Priest of Morvern".

John MacLeod presided over a period of rapid social change in Morvern, and in the end became the last remaining link with the old order. Cattle had originally been the basis of the West Highland economy, but the steady increase in population, combined with a climate which put the Highland farming at a disadvantage, put severe pressure on the situation. When it was discovered in the Borders that certain strains of sheep could survive all the year round on pasture that had only been grazed in summer by cattle, the scene was set for the Highland Clearances, the hardship of which lives on in bitter memory.

John MacLeod's soul was disquieted as he saw his beloved community altered beyond recall. No revolutionary, yet concerned for the poor, the minister was torn between love for his parishioners, and his understanding of the economic realities of his day. He became a tragic and lonely figure.

The other great controversy in which he was involved was that leading up to and surrounding the Disruption of 1843, when more than a third of the established Church of Scotland ministers and lay people separated to form the Free Church of Scotland. This grievous sundering of Presbyterianism, in which the Auld Kirk (the national, established church) lost many of its most able people, was one of the most divisive events in Scottish history. The immediate issue was that of the power of patrons, mainly landed gentry, to appoint ministers to charges.

The patronage issue brought to the surface divisive theological controversies which had been simmering for a long time. For many years the Church of Scotland had been dominated by the Moderate party – clergy and leading laymen who were suspicious of religious enthusiasm. Influenced by the rationalistic philosophy of the day, they were more in tune with English fashions, on the side of law and order, and were generally at home with the landed gentry. The more urbane Moderate clergy were strong on culture and morality, weak on dogma.

The Evangelical party represented the more popular movement, but they were less well organized and were prone to schism. Their faith tended to be personal, dogmatic, clear-cut and enthusiastic, and they were less than impressed by continental philosophy. They stood firmly by the Westminster Confession of Faith, that pillar of scholastic Calvinist orthodoxy.

In the decade before the Disruption, the Evangelicals gained the ascendancy in the Kirk's General Assembly. The leading Evangelical figure, Dr Thomas Chalmers, was a man of deep personal piety and great intellect. His followers argued that congregations should be free to "sit under" a minister of their own choosing. The landed gentry had no desire to surrender their right to choose ministers for the parish churches which they endowed and supported. Patronage was an important weapon of social control. The last thing many of the powerful heritors wanted was a zealous Evangelical minister on the doorstep!

Behind the theological arguments lay the emergent economic realities of Scotland. A thrusting merchant class, based in the growing cities, came into conflict with the old inherited order. The rising tide of an Evangelicalism shorn of the harsher aspects of traditional Calvinism and emphasizing self-help and personal responsibility, met the spiritual needs of the new, confident Scottish bourgeoisie. Patronage became the battleground, as the old and new forces took up their positions.

John MacLeod stood firmly with the established Kirk of the land and defended it with vigour. When the agitators came down to his part of the country, he met them almost single-handedly. The general verdict is that it was largely his influence which kept people loyal to the Church in the district, when many other parts of the Highlands opted for the Free Kirk.

The controversy, which divided Christian brother from Christian brother in Presbyterian Scotland, was not without its amusing side. John built another church at the far end of the parish. He offered two local men the chance to build the track to the new church. As they were taking off their coats, one of the workmen asked whether it was to be a Free church or an established church? When told it was the Auld Kirk, he put his coat back on saying he might be poor, but he wasn't about to help anyone get into the established Kirk. John won them over when he said, "Come here up the brae and hew out the track down the way – so you can help people get *out* of the established Church!"

Dr John's extensive ministry in his beloved Morvern made him one of the Scottish Kirk's best known characters. When Tennyson visited the district in 1853, he worshipped at Keil Church. The Poet Laureate was much struck by Dr MacLeod ("such a well-borne head!" he exclaimed) and the two men sat up far into the night, swapping stories.

When he died in the manse of Morvern in 1882 in his 83rd year, the oldest minister in the Kirk, *The Scotsman* paid a tribute to the man they called the "Father of the Church of Scotland".

"To look at him, one might have supposed he had been brought up in kings' palaces rather than in the humble manse of a remote and mountainous parish . . . To have sat with him in the evening opposite the door, overlooking the waters of the Sound of Mull, and heard his wonderful stories of Highland life and character afforded a reminiscence not likely to fade from the memory of any who enjoyed the privilege . . . The spectacle of an open-air communion in Mull, with the tall, white-haired figure towering over the assemblage, and moving them by his words as the trees are stirred by the wind, was one which, once seen, could not readily be forgotten. No man in the Highlands was better loved or more widely respected; and as his influence was great, so will the remembrance of his manly Christian character be enduring."[4]

John MacLeod's oldest brother, Norman, was one of the greatest Gaelic scholars of his day. He had Gaelic schools established throughout the Highlands, and prepared Gaelic school books for the children. After his translation to the Lowland parish of Campsie in 1825, he spent much time devising schemes for the benefit of the Gaelic-speaking people, starting a monthly Gaelic magazine and preparing a definitive Gaelic dictionary. In 1836 he accepted a call to the Gaelic Chapel, Glasgow, afterwards known as St Columba Church. The same year he was chosen Moderator of the General Assembly of the Church of Scotland, and his alma mater conferred upon him the degree of Doctor of Divinity. He was also appointed Dean of the Chapel Royal and one of Queen Victoria's chaplains.

Like his brother, he actively supported the established Kirk during the ten year controversy which led up to the Disruption. While the bulk of the Gaelic-speaking people followed the Free Church, the St Columba congregation remained loyal. Dr Norman, who died in 1862, earned himself the soubriquet "Caraid nan Gaidheal" – the Highlander's friend.

In one particular regard, the MacLeods made things difficult for their successors. The coathooks were placed so high up in the hallway of Fuinary manse, that subsequent incumbents found it difficult to hang up their coats.

The MacLeods of Morvern were big men.

If it is difficult to place George MacLeod without knowledge of the Morvern patriarchy, it is impossible to understand him without a more than passing acquaintance with his grandfather, the leading Scottish divine of his day.

Norman MacLeod, born in 1812, was the eldest son of "Caraid nan Gaidheal". At the age of 12 he was sent to board with the schoolmaster of Morvern, and spent many delightful summers there. He remembered Fuinary as "the Garden of Eden without the serpent".

Norman's grandfather and father would doubtless have been surprised had they known that the boy would come to be known throughout Scotland simply as "Norman", or "the great Norman". For the young man was more interested in stories than in scholarship, in mimicry and in theatre than in earnest conversation. When he went off to Glasgow University, his parents were worried about him, and wrote anxious letters about his conduct.

The elder Norman asked his boisterous son to conduct himself with calmness and seriousness on the Sabbath day, and "cease your buffoonery of manner in tone of voice and distortions of countenance, which are not only offensive, but grievous. You carry this nonsense by much too far, and I beg of you, my dear Norman, to check it . . . You, even already, seldom use your own voice or gestures or look – all is put on and mimicked; this must cease, and the sooner the better."[5]

His biographer, his brother Donald, reassured his readers that the youthful Norman had not gone too far in his student days.

"His moral life was at the same time pure, and his religious convictions, though not yet as strong as they afterwards became, were yet such as prevented him from yielding to the many temptations to which one of his temperament and abounding, as he did, in animal spirits, was greatly exposed. Next to the grace of God, his affection for home and its associations kept him steady."[6]

Two factors gave Norman a more serious bent. The first was the death of his younger, and more earnest, brother James, and the influence of Dr Thomas Chalmers, whose theological lectures at Edinburgh University gave new direction to his life. He decided to become a minister. In 1834, Chalmers arranged for him to become tutor to the son of a Yorkshire gentleman, and they spent a year at Weimar in Germany. Norman loved the exchange of ideas on the continent, and the social life appealed to him as well. Donald reassures Norman's admirers again:

"He may, indeed, have often given too great a rein to that 'liberty' which was so congenial to his natural temperament, but it is marvellous that the reaction was not greater in one who, brought up in a strict school, was suddenly thrown into the vortex of fashionable life. He was passionately fond of music, sang well to the guitar, sketched cleverly, was as keen a waltzer as any attaché in Weimar, and threw himself with a vivid sense of enjoyment into the gaieties of the little capital."[7]

His mother wrote telling him to concentrate on reading his dead brother's bible, and to keep the deathly image of James before him in times of temptation. Imbibing Coleridge, Goethe and Wordsworth, and coming under the spell of a local baroness, Norman struggled to find a form of faith which could co-exist with a love of life. What was happening in Weimar was the making of an unpuritan divine who would lead a revolution in the Kirk.

In 1838, Norman was inducted to his first parish in Loudoun, Ayrshire. Two days before he became a proper preacher, he attended his last ball – and felt very sad. He wrote in his journal:

"I have returned sick at heart. It is my last ball! And I heard the German waltzes played, and my brain reeled. I shut my eyes. I was once more with my old Weimar friends; when I opened them the faces were the faces of strangers, and I could stand it no longer, but left at twelve. I alone seemed sad. The louder and more cheerful the music grew, the more deeply melancholy I became."[8]

The young preacher poured his energies into the task of ministering to the needs of his Ayrshire parish. It was Covenanting territory, with its history of bitter struggles against the imposition of episcopalianism. He was summoned to meet one old deaf woman who was a leading light among the Covenanters. She sat in the midst of her supporters, holding her ear trumpet.

"Gang ower the fundamentals!" she instructed the young minister. Norman bawled the main themes of Protestant theology into the ear trumpet, until the lady was satisfied. He had passed the test.

The young minister – tall, attractive, full of life – became a popular figure in the community, and his preaching filled the church with attentive hearers.

The Disruption of 1843 – preceded by ten years of damaging controversy – weighed heavily upon him because of its divisiveness. He detested party spirit and intolerance. The roots of his breadth of outlook went back to his home.

"Christianity was a thing taken for granted, not forced with a scowl or a frown", he wrote of the influence of his parents. "I never heard my father speak of Calvinism, Arminianism, Presbyterianism or Episcopacy, or exaggerate doctrinal differences in my life. I had to study all these questions after I left home. I thank God for his free, loving, sympathising and honest heart. He might have made me a slave to any 'ism'. He left me free to love Christ and Christians."[9]

The General Assembly of 1843 – famous in the annals of Scottish ecclesiastical life – was a deeply depressing event for Norman. When more than a third of the Assembly walked out, many leaving the security of manse and stipend, they were met by cheering throngs in the streets of Edinburgh. It was an exciting and glamorous movement. For Norman, it was just as much a sacrifice to stay in; he felt it would have been a relief to join the processions outside.

"I cannot incur the responsibility of weakening the Establishment – that bulwark of Protestantism – that breakwater against the waves of democracy and of revolution – that ark of a nation's righteousness – that beloved national Zion, lovely in its strength, but more beloved in the day of its desolation and danger," he wrote to his best friend, John Mackintosh, who sided with the Dissenters.[10]

The national Church of Scotland, which had once commanded the allegiance of the bulk of the people of Scotland, was by 1843 reduced to one Presbyterian denomination amongst several. Its recovery by the end of the century was due in no small measure to the leadership of Norman MacLeod.

He was called to be minister of the Barony Kirk, Glasgow in 1851 – the same year in which he married Catherine, sister of the beloved John Mackintosh, whose biography Norman wrote.

The Barony, next to Glasgow Cathedral, had some of the worst slums of the city in its parish. In a flurry of activity, the energetic minister organized district meetings for adult education, founded the first Congregational Penny Savings Bank in Glasgow, set up a refreshment room where people could get cheap food, and established a reading room. New recreational facilities were organized, the mission staff of the church was increased from one to five, the congregation held parish missions, six new churches were erected in the parish.

People crowded into the Barony to hear Norman preach. His biggest concern was that the poor were excluded because they didn't have proper clothes to wear or couldn't afford the seat rents; his solution was to hold special evening services at which people who were respectably dressed were turned away. Fourteen hundred people, all dressed in working clothes, regularly filled the church; and some of the people in the congregation were members of the Glasgow upper class who had dressed down for the occasion. Moleskins borrowed from their servants helped them slum their way in.

Norman MacLeod was the talk of the town. Attractive, engaging, humorous, loquacious, droll, exuberant, he was a natural leader in a Kirk which had to win back lost territory.

Doctor MacLeod – he was made a Doctor of Divinity by Glasgow University – was much loved by the city's poor. He visited them, prayed with them, and defended them against attacks by others. It is said that when the child of one of his poor members was stricken by fever, she called out the Free Kirk Minister, who prayed over the contagious child. When asked why she had not called out her own minister, the worthy parishioner replied that she didn't wish to expose the beloved Norman to the danger of such serious infection!

It was not only the poor of Glasgow who heard the great Norman gladly; his ability to communicate with all kinds of people was widely commented upon. He became a great favourite of Queen Victoria, who regularly summoned him to Balmoral. His first sermon at Crathie in 1852 was noted by the Queen as follows:

"We went to Kirk as usual at twelve o'clock. The service was performed by the Rev Norman MacLeod of Glasgow, son of Dr MacLeod, and anything finer I never heard. The sermon, entirely extempore, was quite admirable, so simple and yet so eloquent, and so beautifully put . . . Everyone came back delighted; and how satisfactory it is to come back from church with such feelings! The servants and the Highlanders – all – were equally delighted."[11]

After the death of the Prince Consort, Norman spent many hours counselling the Queen.

As the Queen's favourite chaplain, Norman admired Victoria and could say to her what was in his heart – "She always strikes me as possessed of singular penetration, firmness and independence, and very real; she was personally singularly kind, and I never spoke my mind more frankly to anyone who was a stranger and not on an equal footing" – even when what he had to say was not what Her Majesty wished to hear. A story handed down in the MacLeod family suggests that Norman was chosen to inquire delicately into the nature of the Queen's relationship with her ghillie, John Brown, and that he got a royal flea in his ear for his trouble. The story adds that the next day the Queen asked him to plant a tree with her as a gesture of reconciliation. There is, understandably, no record of such a conversation; but his grandson, George F. MacLeod, noted in his diary as a young man how he looked for and found the tree in the place where the records said it was.

When the Duke of Edinburgh advised Norman to preach for twenty minutes, the minister pulled himself up to his full, considerable height and – as he wrote to his wife – "told him I was a Thomas a Becket, and would resist the interference of the State, and that neither he nor any of the party had anything better to do than hear me. So I preached for forty-seven minutes, and they were kind enough to say they wished it had been longer."[12] His grandson was to have similar sharp conversations with a future Duke of Edinburgh.

Despite the controversies, Norman MacLeod was a much loved

figure at Balmoral, and his journal shows how the Queen would sit spinning contentedly at the wheel while her favoured chaplain read Burns' poems to her.

Life in Glasgow Presbytery was not so calm, and when the bold Norman spoke for three and a half hours on the Sabbath question, all hell broke loose.

The issue, in 1865, was the proposal to run Sunday trains. Should it be allowed? The Presbytery said no, and issued a letter to be read from the pulpits within its bounds. The minister of Barony refused. In his peroration saying why he had declined to read the missive, Norman argued that the Jewish Sabbath had been superseded by the Lord's Day, which was a day of freedom. The speech resounded throughout Scotland, and Dr MacLeod immediately became the nation's most controversial personality. In an era when the doings of leading churchmen took up many column inches in the press, the Barony minister was either national hero or villain. He was hissed by fellow ministers in the streets of Glasgow, vilified in correspondence and mocked in newspaper cartoons.

The Barony minister did not lack courage, and he might well have sung the words of the popular hymn he himself composed:

Courage, brother! do not stumble
Though thy path be dark as night;
There's a star to guide the humble;
"Trust in God, and do the right",
Let the road be rough and dreary,
And its end far out of sight,
Foot it bravely; strong or weary,
Trust in God and do the right.

In his attack on the traditional Scottish sabbath, Dr MacLeod was further prising the Kirk free from the puritan embrace – much to the fury of his opponents, who found it difficult to deal with such an able, devout, humorous, tobacco-puffing, popular preacher. Glasgow Presbytery restricted itself to an admonition, and the Kirk's General Assembly declined to censure him. It was a turning point for the Church of Scotland. Puritanism was well and truly in retreat.

Norman MacLeod was a great Victorian – preaching to Florence Nightingale, spending earnest hours in conversation with David Livingstone, reading Burns to the Queen herself – who was leading the Church of Scotland out of bondage to its own past and marching it towards the next century.

In his attacks on ultra-Calvinists – "They won't enjoy life; they won't laugh without atoning for the sin by a groan; they won't indulge in much hope or joy; they more easily and readily entertain doctrines which go to prove how many may be damned than how many may be saved" – he was echoing the views of yet another distinguished member of the MacLeod family, the brilliant theologian John MacLeod Campbell, who was deposed for his insistence that Christ had died for all and not just for the elect. Emotionally, Norman was with his grandfather back in Morvern, playing his violin for dancing in the manse. When he heard that the old songs and tales had been put under clerical ban in some areas, he was heard to exclaim, "What next? Are the singing birds to be shot by the kirk sessions?"

Such sentiments did not endear him to puritans, but the Auld Kirk steadily reclaimed old territory and even broke new ground as the Dissenting bandwagon slowed down. His unanimous election as Moderator of the General Assembly of the Church of Scotland in 1869 confirmed his standing as a leader of a revolution which had strong popular backing.

Yet despite his successes and apparent confidence, his journals reveal more than a touch of Celtic melancholy and self-doubt. They also shed light on the struggles of a Christian man trying to come to terms with the conflict between his high animal spirits and the expectations people had of a Victorian clergyman.

His labours had taken a steady toll of his energy, and a trip to India as convener of the Kirk's India mission nearly finished him off. When he rose to speak at the General Assembly of 1872, many of the commissioners felt they were seeing him for the last time. He spoke for an hour and a half about the Church's mission to India, arguing for a wider ecumenical view, and despairing over the fact that missionaries were exporting Scottish ecclesiastical differences – "Is it not monstrous to make the man they ordained on the banks of the Ganges sign the Westminster Confession of the Church of Scotland or the Deed of Demission and Protest of the Free Church?"

When he died a few weeks later, he was mourned by the great. Queen Victoria, who described him as "minister of all Scotland", was distraught. Dean Stanley wrote that Norman "represented Scottish Protestantism more than any other single man. Under and around him men would gather who would gather round no one else. When he spoke it was felt to be the voice, the best voice of Scotland." Gladstone, who made a special study of Norman, said it was because the Scottish Church had been able to rear Dr MacLeod and men like him that she had been able to brave all the storms and retain her national position.

No one mourned Norman more than the poor who packed the streets of Glasgow for his funeral.

Norman was not the only son of "The Highlander's Friend" to distinguish himself in the Kirk. His brother, Donald, was minister of Park Church in Glasgow, Chaplain to Queen Victoria, and Moderator in 1895.

John MacLeod of Morvern's son, Norman, was minister at Inverness and became Moderator of the General Assembly in 1900. Another son, John, was the pioneering minister of Govan Parish Church.

The MacLeod house not only represented power in the Church of Scotland, but also a particular – and very influential – ethos. The distinctive MacLeod style was marked by attractiveness, tolerance, breadth, humour and gaiety. Theologically it was broadly evangelical, inclusive and ecumenical. Politically it was sympathetic to the establishment, yet concerned for the poor. Combined with Celtic romanticism and poetry, skilled oratory, confidence in the presence of all ranks of people and a popular touch, the MacLeod style was bound to be a potent force for change in the Church.

It was this developed, confident MacLeodism which Norman the Third's grandson, George Fielden, inherited in full measure. When George was pursuing a loquacious career as the darling of the Edinburgh ecclesiastical establishment in the 1920s, the young preacher's father was asked if the mantle of the great Norman had fallen on George?

"Yes," replied Sir John MacLeod with characteristic geniality, "the gas mantle!"

George Fielden MacLeod was his grandfather's son.

2

The Blessing and the Curse

We English are everlasting children in an everlasting nursery.

H. G. WELLS

Every man of ambition has to fight his century with its own weapons. What this century worships is wealth. To succeed, one must have wealth. At all costs, one must have wealth.

OSCAR WILDE

The MacLeod mantle could be a blessing or a curse.

To bear the name of Norman MacLeod and to be the first-born son of the great Norman of the Barony was to carry a burden which required broad shoulders. Norman the Fourth was no Norman the Conqueror. He could not wear the crown, but he bore the cross. After a spell in commerce in Liverpool, he went out to Canada, beaten by alcohol, living the life of a down-and-out, pursued by creditors.

The torch was passed to the second son, John Mackintosh, named after his uncle, the Free Kirk minister whose biographical memoir was written by his dear friend Norman of the Barony. Born in 1857, young Jack MacLeod decided that rather than be a mediocre minister he would be a good accountant. Educated at Glasgow Academy and in Germany, he started work in an Edinburgh accountant's office, becoming in 1880 a member of the Edinburgh Society of Chartered Accountants. Two years later he settled in Glasgow.

By all accounts, young Jack MacLeod was a popular and hardworking professional. Being a son of Norman of the Barony did him no harm, and he easily made the kind of contacts necessary to rise in the Glasgow accountancy world. All he needed was a pretty wife who would be good at socializing: if she also had money, then so much the better. One such candidate was Edith Fielden.

The Fielden dynasty was to cotton and wealth what the MacLeod dynasty was to the Kirk. Edith's grandfather, "Honest John' Fielden of Todmorden in Lancashire, was one of the largest cotton manufacturers in the world. He was a millowner with a conscience, a man with a mind of his own. Brought up a Quaker, he became an active Unitarian. He went into politics and promoted the "Ten Hour Bill" which reduced the number of hours children could work in factories.

His son, Joshua, had his father's business acumen and money, but not his radical views. In 1863 he moved to the huge Nutfield Priory in Redhill, Surrey, having been elected Conservative MP for the Eastern Division of West Riding. Set in rolling countryside, the neo-Gothic Priory had two towers, a vaulted cloister, three dining rooms, thirty bedrooms, and a Great Hall with organ and minstrel's gallery. It was a real "Upstairs-Downstairs" situation. When guests came, they brought their own servants with them, and the home and visiting servants sat at table in the butler's dining room downstairs in exactly the same formation as the masters and mistresses upstairs.

Joshua made Nutfield the kind of place to which anybody who was anything would want to be invited. Musical recitals were particularly sought after, and the Fielden children would perform gracefully for the appreciative company. As a Unitarian, Joshua was not involved with the local Church of England parish church, though he did contribute to its restoration fund and the records show that his wife and daughters played their part.

The Fieldens were very rich, but they also had a strong, and even austere sense of duty. A vivid picture of the household is painted by Joshua and Ellen's grandson, Lionel.

"Life at Nutfield was held firmly in a framework of habit and ceremony. As the hands of the grandfather clock which stood beside the organ moved towards eight in the morning, doors would softly open upstairs, the sound, followed by that of rustling skirts, percolating through the gallery of the Great Hall. The descent of the staircase would be made by the family and guests. Arrived in the Hall, they stood; no one said good morning, no one spoke. As the clock struck eight, my grandmother's door, in the centre of the gallery, opened; and presently she floated down to us. She smiled but did not speak, continuing past us through the Gothic arch beyond the organ, and entering the morning room. We followed, and arranged ourselves on small gilt chairs round the walls. Then the servants, who had been waiting at the green baize door in strict order of precedence, headed by the cook and the butler, filed in. I suppose there were about twenty of them. Grandmamma read prayers – brief – from a book which she had printed for these occasions. Then she rose, and wished the servants good morning: they filed out. She would then make some optimistic remark about the weather, and we went into the dining room, where breakfast was set at a huge circular table in the window-embrasure, overlooking the immense view."[1]

Lionel also provided an unusual insight into his "handsome and bad-tempered" grandfather.

"When, as a child, one of my aunts bit her small brother, he told her: "True, if you do that again I shall bite you!" She did it again and heard his heavy footsteps approach. Slowly he raised her and bit her arm to the bone."[2] Clearly not a man to be trifled with.

When John Mackintosh MacLeod met Edith Fielden at Cannes – she was playing tennis at the Fielden villa there while John was on holiday in the area – he knew who he wanted to be his bride. Edith agreed. The only problem was Father. When John wrote to Joshua Fielden in June 1886 for his daughter's hand, the answer was a firm No. The young Glasgow accountant was not of sufficient standing. The fact that he had Moderators and royal chaplains in his family did not cut much ice with the socially conscious entrepreneur. The daughter of Joshua Fielden could do better.

John was distraught, but wisely did not confront a man whose bite was worse than his bark. Edith's sister Mabel encouraged him not to accept defeat, and she arranged illicit meetings in Scotland.

Whether Joshua would have relented or no is not known; he died in March 1887, the victim of an earthquake while in Cannes for a health cure. Edith and Jack became engaged in July 1887. It was a real Victorian love match.

"My beloved," wrote Edith in October, "It is a great mercy that we are so at one on all essential points . . . As I look on every side I can see nothing but blessings."

The engaged couple were certainly at one politically. John's Tory views were strengthened by Unionist opposition to Gladstone's plans for Ireland, and in 1895 he publicly opposed the voices calling for the disestablishment of the Church of Scotland.

"Oh how wicked the Radicals are," wrote the granddaughter of

George MacLeod

Honest John Fielden. "As for Gladstone," she commented on the prime minister who had been so impressed by her beloved's father, "I quite agree with you that no word is bad enough for him."

On Christmas Day the Fieldens entertained the men of the village at Nutfield Priory. Edith hid away all her jewellery as she knew there were some Radicals among the men.

"When I think that if God wills, this time next week you will be with me – no, darling, I can't write of it," she told her beloved. "It seems almost too much happiness and what shall I say – perfection – for any mortal to have here on earth. God bless and keep you and bring you safe to the arms of your beloved Edith."

January 4, 1888. The first entry in Edith's journal. "My wedding day, John Mackintosh MacLeod and I were married at two in the afternoon at St Michael's, Chester Square, London. It was a great disappointment that Dr Donald MacLeod was not allowed to take any part in the service, he being a Presbyterian." The bride was wearing half-mourning for her father.

A Presbyterian minister, even one as eminent as Dr Donald MacLeod, was not validly ordained in Anglican eyes in 1888. The Scottish Presbyterian MacLeod reputation counted for nothing in England.

The well-to-do couple lived comfortably but not ostentatiously in Glasgow. They travelled regularly – no passports required – in the secure world of the Continent. It was an era when progress was felt to be inevitable and the clouds of war seemed very distant.

1890. Florence and the Rhine.

1891. John Mackintosh Norman (at first called Ian, then Norman) is born.

1892. Move into a three-storied house at 4 Park Circus Place, Glasgow.

1893. Ellen – named after Edith's mother – is born.

Then the entry in Edith's journal. "1895, June 17, George was born at 11.30 am. The other two children went to Nutfield for five weeks."

George Fielden MacLeod was named after his father's brother, Professor Sir George MacLeod, who succeeded Joseph Lister as Professor of Surgery at Glasgow Medical School in 1869 and became Senior Surgeon-in-Ordinary in Scotland to Queen Victoria. When he died in 1892, the *Scottish Standard* said of him that there could be no doubt that the rapid advance of Glasgow University as a medical and surgery school was largely due to his unwearied efforts and to his knowledge of continental science.

In the year of George's birth, Sigmund Freud founded psychoanalysis, Röntgen discovered X-rays, Marconi invented the wireless, and Auguste and Louis Lumière introduced the cinema. There were as yet no aircraft, motor cars or gramophones.

Britain was the greatest nation in the world. Queen Victoria had been on the throne for nearly sixty years, and during her reign Great Britain had grown to have dominion over a quarter of the world – "the empire on which the sun never set". British heavy industry was very strong, and the formidable Royal Navy patrolled the high seas, ensuring the safe passage of goods, values and missionaries.

The upper class and the upper middle class could afford to travel regularly on the Continent, especially if they had staff to look after the children at home. The MacLeods went abroad most years. Edith said it was her ambition to paddle in every sea in Europe.

It was a comfortable, urbane existence. Awareness of poverty or hardship did not appear to obtrude. Income tax was only 8d in the pound. Estates were passed intact from father to son. The upper classes were very secure indeed, and felt free to exhibit their wealth ostentatiously. Jack, a keen Mason, was rising steadily in the accountancy world, knowing the right people, giving the correct handshakes. He had formed a new partnership and business was good. He was well liked and respected, and was treasurer of several charitable trusts. The only fly in the ointment was the steady flow of letters from Canada indicating brother Norman's erratic alcoholic progress.

There were several servants at Park Circus Place. The cook and the maids were in the basement, and were summoned by bells. The children were attended to upstairs by the nanny.

George's earliest memory was of being driven, at the age of two, in carriage and pair at Nutfield on the occasion of Queen Victoria's Jubilee. He also remembered the announcement of the relief of Mafeking.

Another early memory was of standing in his room on the day of Queen Victoria's funeral in January 1901. His nurse, an Aberdeen lady who sang the children to sleep with evangelical hymns, was having an argument with Edith. The sun was streaming in, and Aberdeen was firm that all the blinds should be drawn as muffled church bells clanged the hour of the royal committal. Mrs MacLeod asserted that the Queen was probably glad to be gone to her Prince Consort, and that these things did not matter anyway. She won – until she left the room. Then Aberdeen pulled down one of the three blinds.

The next door neighbour was the first in the street to have a motor car, with a chauffeur. Generally, the only sounds to be heard were the clip-clop of the hansoms in the street.

The peace deepened on Sundays. George was later to describe that special day in the MacLeod household.

"Somehow before eleven o'clock we were always sitting in the same chairs, my father reading the *Spectator*, my mother writing a letter and the rest of us silent 'with a good book'. As the quarter struck, my father gave a cough, peculiar to the day, my mother stamped a letter, and we rose. As we left the house, synchronized doors noiselessly emitted other strings of human sausages till they slowly converged on the broad steps of the church on the corner."[3]

The preacher at the corner church, Park Church, was the Rev. Donald MacLeod, D.D., Moderator of the General Assembly of the Church of Scotland, chaplain to the sovereign, brother of Rev. Dr Norman MacLeod of the Barony.

It was a stable universe. Father would come home at 5.30 pm from the office or the Western Club, and would relax in the smoking room with a whisky and soda and cigarette, before changing for dinner (two maids in attendance, written menu). He and Mother would entertain guests. Jack was a jovial and kindly man, with a reputation as a good raconteur. Mother was quieter, deferential to her husband, yet with something steely about her.

The children generally played upstairs in the nursery with Victorian building bricks and a wooden Noah's ark. A favourite game was "Church Services". Ellen and Norman were the office-bearers, George the minister, and Mother and Father and guests the congregation. When the offering plate was passed round, the congregation pretended to put something in. On one occasion, an uncle put in a pound. When the little minister – as he became known – shook hands with the departing congregation, he gave the uncle back his money, saying, "Your change, sir!"

Norman, handsome and extrovert, was the favourite. A keen reader, he would invent games to keep George and Ellen quiet. When they played Boer War games in the nearby Kelvingrove Park, Norman was always the captain. George never took part in these military clashes and revolver charges, preferring to hold on to Nanny's hand. The three children were very close, living and playing and learning in a secure, essentially Victorian, environment.

Family holidays each summer were memorable. Many of Jack's clients were rich, and when they died his firm had to look after their property. Holidays at Tavool, on the shores of Loch Scridain in Mull, stood out. Father commissioned a 15-ton steamboat, and the trips to Staffa and Iona were much enjoyed.

Religion took its place naturally in the MacLeod household. Religious values were simply assumed, and churchgoing was mandatory. Jack was a devoted churchman, as keen as his father on uniting the disparate strands of Presbyterianism, and resisting those who wished to see the Church of Scotland sever its links with the state as a precondition for such unity. As Hon. Treasurer of the Glasgow Church of Scotland Defence Association, and as vice president of the Knox Club (a pressure group formed to safeguard the Protestant succession to the throne), he gave public lectures on the history and constitution of the Kirk and her privileges, and organized petitions to Parliament. He was also clerk to the managers of the MacLeod parish church, which had been erected in Barony parish as a memorial to his father.

The religious ethos of the MacLeod household was centred on the notion of duty. It is best summed up in a scroll which John MacLeod gave to Norman and George at Christmas, 1901. Headed "Do Your Duty", it said:

> Come wealth or want, come good or ill,
> Let young and old accept their part,
> And bow before the awful Will,
> And bear it with an honest heart.
> Who misses, or who wins the prize?
> Go, lose or conquer as you can;
> But if you fail or if you rise
> Be each, pray God, a gentleman.

The scroll was in the handwriting of John MacLeod, whose personal seal was accompanied by the seals of George's grandfather and great-grandfather. It was as if the message of a great, broadly evangelical house had been reduced to a simple command: Be a Gentleman. It was a message that was to remain deep in George

MacLeod's being: there is a sense in which he has remained all his life a Victorian gentleman.

It was to further his training as a gentleman that George was packed off to Prep School in Edinburgh at the age of eight. He most of all hated to leave his nanny, who was his chief source of emotional warmth at 4 Park Circus Place.

Cargilfield School for Boys was in Barnton, and had a good scholastic record. Young George didn't particularly enjoy it, and looked forward to returning to Glasgow at the end of term.

One family memory of him as a lad was of George buying up all the "lum" hats at a jumble sale: he then proceeded to put them down the centre of the hall and jump on them!

"You must not expect me to win any races in the sports," he wrote to his mother in 1908, and the first indications of a lifelong obsession with shifting furniture around came at the same time – "I hope that you have not arranged our top room, because if you do not mind I would rather like to do it when I come home. I am looking forward to next holidays. Only 5 more days! Hurrah! Your loving George."

On one occasion, George had to sing a solo at a recital. The family had a meal at an Edinburgh hotel, and George ate a bad egg. The family story is that when he sang the line, "I waited for the Lord" from Handel's Messiah, he vomited.

George struggled with French grammar, Latin and Greek, and did what he could to avoid sport. He was always keen to get back to the security of 4 Park Circus Place. It was, of course, a privileged existence, and he did not question it till later.

"Delicious days they were – for the privileged," he was to write. "We did not know of Disraeli's other nation, the underpaid and the unemployed. True, there was a mystery one evening when every area was seen from our top windows to be filled with waiting and submerged police. The Lord Provost lived round the corner and a hunger march was expected to protest outside his door. Either it never materialized, or we were packed off to bed, to sleep unknowing."[4] No doubt drifting off to sleep to the accompaniment of evangelical hymns.

There were many beggars in the Glasgow streets. On one occasion, John MacLeod told George to give a penny to a blind man. When the boy returned, his father remonstrated with him because he had not touched his cap.

"But father, he's blind!" said George.

The Blessing and the Curse

"Yes, but he may be a fraud!" came the reply.

In 1909, at the age of fourteen, there came the next stage in the formation of a Victorian-Edwardian gentleman. George MacLeod, top hat in its box, was on the train for Winchester.

"Manners Makyth Man" was the motto of the famous College of St Mary, Winchester. The task of this most illustrious English public school was to train not just gentlemen, but leaders. The college was founded in 1387 by William of Wykeham, whose scheme of education also embraced New College, Oxford. The quadrangles, and the fine chapel, tower, hall and cloister spoke of tradition, history and inspiration.

The Winchester tradition had always been to treat the boys almost as adults, and from the age of fourteen, the young Scot would have been encouraged to speak, behave and dress like an English gentleman – complete with top hat, stiff collar, waistcoat, and fob watch. The time at Winchester represented the Englishing of George MacLeod.

He described his first morning in his diary entry of September 16, 1909.

"Went to Chapel and walked up and down meads, walked round cloisters while bells tolled. Was pushed by an eager hand into a seat in Chapel where I could see nobody and hear nothing . . . went to Dr Sweeting, was engaged for Glee Club and Chantry."

Young George's first letter home to his mother from Culver House, Winchester, four days later, described being out for a walk down by the river with only his top hat to shade him from the sun. After the fashion of grandfather Norman, the letter had a drawing of George in top hat. He went on:

"Well, my darling, it was sweet of you writing me those letters. But as they are putting a new organ into chapel, the cloisters are a sort of workshop, filled with all manner of things – pipes, blocks of wood, ladders, stones, bricks, plaster, etc – so it is not quite enchanting at the present minute but I hope the organ will soon come and then I am sure it will be very beautiful."

Every boy, George tells his mother, receives a shilling a week, called "Battlings" – an allowance given to every man by his house, originally given to provide food for fast days. He has to do six hours exercise – "ekker" – each week, and preparation begins each evening at 7 pm. The letter concludes:

This is my last Sunday of 'grace'. Next Sunday I will be *Brew Cad*!! Boiling the kettle, setting the tea, buying the

25

cakes, fetching the milk, eating the remains and washing up!! Well, my darling, I suppose I must say farewell. Thank you for the umbrella. I am reading Arsene Lupin, it is thrilling. Farewell. Give my best love to Father and to yourself. Your loving George."

George's second letter gives an account of his first exposure to the Roman Catholic tradition. He and his brother went to Westminster Cathedral.

"It was wonderful – the tremendous hall in the centre and the little chapels round it," he told his mother, "but when we left, neither Norman nor myself were converted! Much the reverse indeed."

The main religious influence on George was that of the Anglican tradition. He was a member of the Chantry choir, and attended Chapel every day. His letters home, however, tended to be concerned with matters physical rather than spiritual. One order was for 1 pressed tongue, 2 boxes of sardines, four pots of jam and a towel for drying plates.

As a "junior", young George had to perform tasks for the prefects, and to do various "sweats" like brewing tea. He didn't particularly enjoy sports, and indeed loathed cricket. He enjoyed forays into London. He was present among the huge crowds at the Guildhall for the royal proclamation of the accession of King George V to the throne after the death of Edward VII in May 1910.

"The clock struck 12 and the trumpet sounded and there was – to most people – a proclamation read, but to me there was silence," he wrote home. "Then the band played 'God Save the King' so I presumed that the ceremony was over. Then the procession marched forward and I thought I might as well get back as best I could. But the crowd behind me thought differently and I had to march on."

One of his Winchester contemporaries was Oswald Mosley, who was to become famous, or notorious, as the founder of the British Union of Fascists. George remembered him as a "dull chap" who was bullied a great deal. George claimed in later years that he himself was one of those who bullied young Mosley, and used to say that Mosley's violent activities in the 1930s represented his way of working out his grudge against society. (The thesis that Sir Oswald Mosley rampaged through the streets with his fellow blackshirts because he had been thumped around the ear as a boy by the pacifist-to-be George MacLeod is a delicious one, but is unfortunately a little too fanciful to sustain).

Visits home to Glasgow were always a highlight, and young George looked forward to them very much. No need to be "brew cad" at home, where the servants took care of everything. Life at 4 Park Circus Place was structured and secure.

Family outings were highlights. On one occasion John MacLeod took the boys with him on a shooting expedition to Rannoch Moor. The cold lunch was brought out, with the appropriate alcoholic refreshment. The only problem: there were no bottle openers. Father had dinned into the boys two things: never forget to say your prayers at night, and never forget bottle openers on a picnic. Fearing his terrible wrath, they watched frozen as he leaned back in the heather with the look of resignation of one about to experience martyrdom. Norman and George were amazed when he sat up quickly – he had put his hand down on a rusty old bottle opener! The gratitude of the boys was profound, but it did not match their father's. He later took them out on the moor with a large box of bottle openers, which he proceeded to scatter at various remote locations.

Father was engaged in good works – he had been auditor of the Glasgow International Exhibition in 1901 and was now honorary treasurer of the Association of Fine Art and Music, as well as being deeply involved in Park Church and the Presbytery of Glasgow – and his business career was prospering. He was a member of the Carlton Club in London – the only Scotsman not an MP so to be honoured – and his deepening political involvement was reflected in his election as chairman of Glasgow Conservative Club and his appointment as convener of the Western Division of the Scottish Unionist Association. Genial Jack MacLeod was popular, dependable and well-connected, and by 1911 was an indispensable figure in the Scottish Unionist establishment. He was very much at home in the peaceable and prosperous Edwardian years, when Great Britain was at the pinnacle of empire building, industrial development and naval power.

Mr MacLeod believed in the natural order of things. The upper class did not need to work and lived well in the big houses, on the grouse moors, and at Ascot and Wimbledon. Many of the upper middle class, like himself, could afford servants, and could engage in hunting, shooting and fishing in the relatively unspoilt countryside.

Of Britain's population of 45 million in 1910, more than 75 per cent belonged to an impoverished working class. Poverty, under-nourishment and slum living led to rickets, tuberculosis and scurvy. Britain's position as the "workshop of the world" was founded upon the long hours of men whose wages were low. To be unemployed, to be a seasonal worker or simply to be ill in a society which had no social security system was to be forced to rely on the Salvation Army or the workhouse. Drunkenness was endemic. The Liberals did try to alleviate the situation; the Provision of Meals Act of 1906 enabled many schoolchildren to have free school meals, and in 1908 old age pensions were introduced for the first time. Lloyd George's controversial "People's Budget" of 1909 raised money by new taxation to help the poor, but it met furious opposition from the Conservatives. In 1910, labour exchanges were opened to help people find work.

These reform measures were important, but for some they were not enough. New trade unions were formed to protect the rights of workers, and in the Edwardian era there were several damaging strikes as workers sought a share in the nation's evident prosperity. The interest in trade unionism was matched by the growth in the newly formed Labour Party, which sent 40 MPs to the Commons in 1910. Cracks in the Victorian-Edwardian structure were begin-ning to show. The Irish problem generated more heat and violence, and the suffragette movement became more demanding.

John MacLeod was not unsympathetic to the plight of the poor, and was aware of the debate going on within the Kirk about the issue. Indeed his own cousin Donald, of Park Church, called for better housing conditions, and increasing numbers of ministers of the Church of Scotland supported social welfare. Thomas Chal-mers' dictum, "We leave to others the politics and passions of this world", was no longer acceptable as the evangelical spirit gave way to a passion for social reform, and new social theologies were worked out. Strikes were seen by some ministers as legitimate forms of action by which to advance the kingdom of heaven. Jack MacLeod was sympathetic to the "deserving poor", but he was utterly opposed to socialism, which he saw as an undermining force.

Winchester College was a bulwark of the social order which Jack MacLeod wished to defend. Norman wrote home to report joyfully that not a single person could be found to speak for a socialist motion at the debating society, and someone had to be brought in from outside to do the honours.

George absorbed the Wykehamist ethos without question. God was in his heaven, and all was well in a world stewarded by a leadership class to which Winchester contributed generously. In accent, manners, dress, assumptions and behaviour he was, like many sons of the Scottish gentry, an English public schoolboy through and through. Along with his peers, he was confirmed at Winchester by an English bishop as a member of the Church of England. What the ancestral MacLeods of Fuinary would have made of all this is an interesting question.

George enjoyed Winchester, without making a great impression on the place. He once "raised books", which meant that he was top of his division academically. He was never a prefect or in any position of leadership. His letters and diary show an enjoyment of London and the theatre. The frequent travel, stays in London hotels and visits to restaurants and theatres made him a self-assured and independent young man who appreciated his place in the scheme of things. On reaching his London hotel on one occasion, he thought at first that he had forgotten his wing collars – "I had awful thoughts of coming down more like an American dentist than a MacLeod" – but all turned out to be well.

Top hat (no jumping on lum hats now), wing collars, being called "sir" by the porters, mixing with the sons of the Scottish and English aristocracy, the housemaster's port; it all contributed to an assurance which might well have become uncontrolled arrogance had it not been for the tempering influence of a Christianity which was assumed rather than argued. Young George MacLeod was not only born to rule but born to serve. But in what sphere? He determined to become a lawyer, and so, in October 1913, he set out for Oriel College, Oxford, to study law.

George was a fairly earnest student at Oxford, and most of the time was spent working or rowing. He did get caught up in one student event which earned him a 4/6d college fine.

"Condash it, there was I, a gentlemanly son of a British gentleman walking gentlemanly along with another gentleman in gentlemanly dress," the 18-year-old student wrote home in a letter which could have come straight from the pen of his grandfather, "when a cad of a proctor with three cads of assistants ('bulldogs') and also 5 cads of policemen were also walking caddishly along about 30 yards in front, behind us was an interminable good crowd, when suddenly the caddish proctor with three caddish bulldogs and two caddish policemen turned caddishly round and like cads began to walk straight for a gentlemanly son of an English gentleman accompanied by a gentleman. Behind was an interminable crowd. In front was an interminable crowd. Like a gallant gentleman we saw escape was impossible, so rising to our full height before that howling crowd (they were howling silently!) we nobly and calmly awaited the end."

The young student's letters to his mother describe a busy life of hard work and a strong interest in religion, which he said was "seething" in Oxford.

When Bishop Henley Henson preached a 55-minute sermon attacking the Church of England's isolationist position, George was jubilant.

"He quoted Maclean and Inverness Norman and showed magnanimously the Kirk was willing to give way a bit, and said it was for the English Church now to give way her half, but that she would not do it etc. Why? Because they were bigoted, narrow, unchristian, heathen, canting. He took episcopacy and hurled it to the ground and for 55 minutes he knocked about all the Bishop of Oxford's views.

"The funniest thing was to watch the high church dons and missionaries down below (the undergrads sit in the gallery). First of all they sneered at the quiet little man who was knocking them about merely by words and logical reasoning, then they looked at the gallery where their young hopefuls were leaning more and more forward and showing more and more interest, then they began to get angry as H. H. went on and as the gallery got more and more silently appreciative. Then they got white with rage as H. H. obviously got the whip hand, oh it was killing. H. H. was so beautifully straight and neat. At one remark a man in the gallery laughed for sheer joy! The men below were quite perturbed."

This is the first indication of enjoyment of religious controversy on the part of a man whose name was to become a byword for ecclesiastical provocation north of the border and who, like Henley Henson, could turn normally unperturbable churchmen white with rage. In that first year at Oxford, George MacLeod began to appreciate the power of stimulating ideas, especially when delivered with conviction and style.

Family holidays continued to provide much enjoyment. Norman and George had inherited their parents' love of continental travel –

The Blessing and the Curse

"George loves abroad," Ellen used to say – and they enjoyed a vacation in the south of France. Ellen was shocked when her father went to gamble in the casino on a Sunday. When she asked why, as an elder of the Kirk, he could do that, he became very angry with her, saying she was "just a silly girl" who "didn't understand".

Poverty in Britain and gathering tensions abroad do not appear to have impinged upon the consciousness of a young man whose enjoyment of his own developing powers was increasingly evident. The confidence in the country at large was mirrored in George's assumptions about his own guaranteed place in the divine scheme of things. Indeed, the words "God" and "England" – like his Wykehamist peers, George learned to name the whole of the United Kingdom "England" – could be uttered very comfortably in the same breath. When George reached his 19th birthday on 17th June, 1914 he was very much looking forward to the next session at Oxford and to enjoyable things to come.

On 28th June, 1914 the famous shot rang out in Sarajevo. On 4th August, Germany invaded Belgium, and Britain was in the war. Two days later British troops were sailing for France.

It was generally believed that the fighting would not last long. The British officer class, trained at the great public schools, would surely lead the country to a speedy victory.

Men would need to be recruited. Who better to head up that recruitment in the West of Scotland than that worthy citizen and rising politician John MacLeod?

George, gentlemanly son of an "English" gentleman – officer material of course – knew what to do. He went to Stirling Castle and enlisted with the Argyll and Sutherland Highlanders, the natural choice for a man with Morvern in his blood.

It was his duty, condash it. And it would be a bit of an adventure, too, wouldn't it?

3

All Out for Boche Blood

Good morning! Good morning! the General said
When we met him last week on our way to the line.
Now the soldiers he smiled at are most of 'em dead,
And we're cursing his staff for incompetent swine.
'He's a cheery old card,' grunted Harry to Jack
As they slogged up to Arras with rifle and pack.
But he did for them both by his plan of attack.

SIEGFRIED SASSOON

George had a good war. He served in three battalions, saw a fair bit of action, was decorated for bravery and, above all, survived.

His father was proud to see him do his duty for king and country and join up with the 12th Battalion, the Argyll and Sutherland Highlanders. It was part of "Kitchener's Army" – volunteers recruited to back up the small British army and help stop the crucial German campaign plan of rushing through Belgium to take Paris.

Both sides thought it would be over soon. The German plan was to smash through the undefended neutral Belgian frontier, take Paris within six weeks, then turn east to face the slower moving Russians. Both sides reckoned on a war of dramatic movement which would be over by Christmas. The officers and men who went cheerfully off to France as part of the British Expeditionary Force in August 1914, looked forward to the excitement and a bit of glory. At the battles of Mons and the Marne, the German advance was slowed down, being finally halted at the first battle of Ypres in November. What had started as temporary hiding places in the mud became semi-permanent trenches, as the two sides faced each other in stalemate.

George went for training at Tidworth and Codford, learning about marching, drilling and use of the rifle. When he became a

Second Lieutenant, it was his turn to teach the new recruits how to aim and fire their rifles. His letters home, often asking for food, papers and clothing, were full of public schoolboy phrases like "ripping", "top hole", "topping", "deuced clever", and "frightfully", and he announced that he was "awfully pleased to get the pistol".

In January 1915, George moved to Sutton Veney Camp at Warminster. Digging trenches, route marches, rifle practice and mock battles formed the weekly routine.

The mud, the rain, the routine and the lack of action and, above all, the news from the front depressed George – "Oh, these German devils are worth beating; by Jove they're good!" – and his diary shows fluctuations of mood. It was dawning on him that war killed people, and his friends were not exempt. The death of one of his teachers particularly disturbed him.

"Got a letter from mother to say that poor old Birch had died for his country. Who dies if England lives? What a ripping fellow he was. I used to worship him as a boy, and as a man I don't wonder I worshipped him. A gentleman."

As more news of deaths came in, the patriotic young officer tried earnestly to find a framework for thinking about such matters.

"Three Wykehamists killed today, and I knew them all," he wrote to his sister Ellen. "All this story about things never being the same strikes me as being very true, but I believe that is the entire reason for the war, to have a jolly good spring cleaning – not in lives, but in money, thought, luxury, etc., and until the countries jolly well do change this war is not going to stop . . . About every 100 years humanity, unless it is checked, triumphs in the fact that it is running itself so well without any divine aid, or it imagines it does and then when the limit is about reached there's a jolly good smash-up and we happen to be living in it, that's all!"

The young George MacLeod's God was above all a moral deity with a special purpose for "England". His was an inherited theology of moral duty, linked to a purposeful patriotism.

George's father had no apparent qualms about the war. He was given special permission to go to France to see what was happening, and after his visit to Ypres he wrote to George in very optimistic terms. He wished that he were in charge of the war, he said, because the Germans, "besides being the vilest race the world has ever seen are the stupidest".

In the West of Scotland, John MacLeod was clearly a man to be reckoned with. Pipe bands accompanied him to West of Scotland towns to appeal for recruits, and he encouraged munitions workers to produce more in order to "rain hell on the Germans". He busied himself with good works. He helped to run the Glasgow Red Cross, and was elected president of the Sons of Ministers Society of which he had been secretary for 28 years. As an elder of Park Church, he was active in Glasgow Presbytery and in the General Assembly of the Church of Scotland.

Edith MacLeod was involved in the war effort as well. Thanks mainly to her efforts, a hostel was opened near Park Circus Place "for the reception of Belgian refugees of the better class". Her husband's sister also took a public role in the war campaign, advocating the introduction of compulsory war service.

It was only a matter of time before Jack became an MP, just like two of his wife's brothers. In July 1915, he was unanimously adopted as Unionist candidate for the Central Division of Glasgow, and he won the by-election fairly comfortably.

By September 1915, George was reading press cuttings of his father's speeches while crouching in a trench in France. With the war of movement over, both sides on the Western Front eyed each other across the barbed wire. The occupying German army strengthened its defences and invited the Allies to attack. It was clear that no side could win the war without attacking and bearing massive losses: since the Germans were in occupied territory it was necessary to drive them out.

Many volunteers had responded to Lord Kitchener's recruiting drive, and the British Expeditionary Force had been swelled in numbers from the ranks of the two million men who had joined up. The numbers were needed, since the basic British strategy was to throw bodies at the barbed wire and hope for a breakthrough.

In his first letter from the front line trenches, Lt MacLeod, now a platoon commander, told his beloved sister about a visit to the front.

"I had a look at the Boche – his trenches, through a periscope – a most uninspiring sight. But if you stood up on the parapet – Ping from one of these trees and . . . well, don't stand on the parapet. If we send a bomb over they send 50 back and it isn't really worth it . . . These shells either get a man or miss him, and no amount of dodging can help anyone!"

Life in the trenches was grim. What had begun as protective ditches had by now become home for millions of men. The front line trenches, each protected by barbed wire – often draped with stinking, rotting human remains – faced each other across a muddy no man's land of several hundred yards.

The men lived in dug-outs, like animals in burrows. When the heavy rains came, conditions became intolerable.

Conditions like that led to complaints such as "trench foot" – swollen and painful feet which could sometimes only be dealt with by amputation. All the men had lice, and diseases such as dysentery and cholera were rampant.

The British strategy was expensive in men. By the end of 1915 more than three million men had left mothers, wives and families to take the "King's Shilling" in an atmosphere charged with patriotic fervour. Men who did not volunteer had white feathers pinned to their clothing. The cry for conscription became ever more clamant. The John MacLeods of the world were doing their work well.

By the end of the year, the 12th battalion was on the move: destination, Salonika. The plan was to despatch British and French divisions to Salonika to bring relief to the embattled Serbians and to check the German influence over Greece.

In his letters home, George did his best to present a cheerful front, and he was also good at keeping up the spirits of his men. Yet the incessant digging, the lack of action, the persistence of the omnipresent rats – "went after rats with a revolver, no good" – and the sense that the war could last for years dispirited him. He kept telling himself that there was no point in becoming depressed. The bouts came most often when he heard of the death of friends: he looked to his faith to help him.

"It's in cases like these," he told Ellen, "that you thank your stars that there is a God and something bigger than this funny, unbalanced, illogical life – as it seems to us. The question 'Why, Why, Why' is very apt to creep up, and the sooner we learn to take the answer 'just because' in questions like these, the better we will be . . .

"After the first selfish pang of having been unfairly treated, there's an immensely glorious feeling of one's friend having done something really worth doing; as if the sorrow – bad enough in all conscience – is outweighed a hundred times by the other side of it – the only 'lasting' side of it. To me it does not matter one bit the fact that all these brave fellows were lost at Gallipoli and now we have retired; after all, when they died they were doing their utmost for the cause, which they represented; and there, as far as the individual is concerned, the matter ends. Whether or no that particular 'charge' was a success or failure; whether or no that or this general made a mistake; whether or no a whole expedition is a failure; that man has been ordered to do a thing and has proceeded to do it, and so far as he is concerned his job is done and well done. The person says 'think of the poor people who have lost their relatives there', but to put it shortly, is it the man's fault that his division went to a 'Failure Field'? No! All these lives are a stepping stone to something infinitely great and are very literally the further salvation of the world."

Really?

"The more one sees of other countries, of other interests, and of the ideals of other people," he said in the same letter, "the more one realizes what a splendid type the *Britisher* is. I don't say we as a nation are Britishers for too few of us are. But to these people we meet elsewhere, the man who comes from Britain is apparently a man to be trusted, and always to be looked up to as a Sportsman – that's because of Britishers, who have made the name for us, and when you come here you see what a life we have to live up to if we are to maintain that name and incidentally our position in the world, as a nation. I must say the Britisher is a reputation worth having; no superficiality, just *genuine* and there's nothing finer in the world than 'the real thing'. Yes, those of us who live after this war have our job cut out for us."

Well played, Winchester!

One trait the Britishers needed to acquire, suggested George MacLeod – who told his father that his speeches in the House of Commons were splendid – was that of hitting the enemy really hard. Having already condemned the "mouse eyed conscientious objectors", he said of the Germans – "their doctrine of war is 'Hit, hit hard wherever and however you can' and, by heaven, they at least live up to it. I wonder what our doctrine is! It's more like 'Spit, spit genteelly and don't make a mess of the carpet at any price'. We always seem to lack that priceless acquisition of going the 'whole hog' when we go at all – we so often go a little bit, when the only way to do it is full tilt!"

The only thing at which George could go full tilt was Grecian mud. Dig, dig, dig. For week after boring week.

The handsome young lieutenant also entertained two Scottish nurses "to whom we gave tea for Scotland's sake (if you had seen them you would realize how strong our love for Scotland must be); one was fat, small and wore specs, the other was long, thin and wore specs likewise. The first about 23 and the latter 32; the first was very Scotch and I should think intellectual – the type that in pre-war days walked down Sauchiehall Street in a tartan blouse with Gibbon's 'Decline and Fall of the Roman Empire Vol. 1' under her arm; one of these unfortunate people who rarely venture on a remark and when they do, attract so much attention that they are far too frightened to finish it coherently – a type I am usually heartily sorry for but this one, my dear Ellen (worthy though she may have been, I am sorry to have to say it) had clammy hands and that is one thing that – however, the other did all the talking, the type that always does the talking and belonged to that legion of Scotch women who find it a physical impossibility to differentiate between tea and mouthwash, and who cannot end a sentence without adding fresh saliva to their already moist lips."

The truth is that despite the apparently confident demeanour, the amusing but fundamentally earnest young George MacLeod was awkward in the company of the opposite sex. Having lived a good proportion of his 20 years away from home in all-male residential situations, he was not practised in conversational arts with women – apart, that is, from his sister Ellen with whom he maintained a very lively and deeply affectionate correspondence.

In the summer, the troops moved out to dugouts in the hills, the better to cope with the heat and the flies. On 17th June, 1916, George celebrated his 21st birthday with champagne drunk out of a tin cup. His war diary shows that the day began with breakfast at 4.45 am, followed by a route march in very dusty conditions: sleep in the heat of the afternoon: concert at night.

There were depressive feelings in the hot afternoons. George called these times "losing the war". He was usually "winning the war" by the evening. "When the sun has gone down and you lie listening to the gramophone with a cigarette in your mouth, everyone is winning the war, no matter what disaster the official communique may have reported."

While lying on his bunk in the heat, his thoughts turned to Iona, and the regular holidays the family spent there.

"Oh how I would love to be at Iona with you all in August. It ought to be just ripping. The weather wouldn't matter – if it's wet, how glorious to sit in a wee house by a fire and read till tea, then have a big tea (on top of no exercise), and perhaps a 'drench walk', just to get up an appetite for dinner, and then read another nice book, by a nice fire, and next day do the same thing – just a real proper unhealthy existence – but oh how glorious!"

There is something touching about young George MacLeod, sweating in the Salonika furnace, yearning to be in a drizzle on the island whose name was to become inextricably bound up with his.

George's mood of frustration after six months of "waiting and gossiping" changed when he became acting adjutant, a job which required administrative and organizational skills. Saying that he inherited his father's love of doing something worthwhile, he admitted to being "ever so bucked with life".

"I love running a show (however rottenly) like everyone else," he confided to Ellen excitedly. "As a second in command, you're running someone else's show, and that's most riling."

The action didn't last long.

War diary, August 31, 1916. "Saw my face in the mirror. Losh, it was a nasty shock. This must be the devil of a disease if you don't take care."

Dysentery certainly was a devil of a disease. It could kill. His weight dropped to eight stone. After a spell in casualty he was on the hospital ship bound for Malta.

The spell at Imtarfa hospital was not a happy one. Different diets were tried, but he could not shake off the disease. He mooned around, listening to the gramophone in the ward, waiting for letters from home, looking at photographs of Iona.

"The Western Isles have a great call for me," he wrote, "and I always feel I could write poems about them. The very vision gets me on to a sort of poetic plane and my first lines are splendid . . . but I never get any further!"

The fact that his eyes turned yellow caused great alarm, but he improved enough to be sent home. On November 16, 1916 Lt George F. MacLeod was met at St Enoch Station, Glasgow by his father.

The sickly wanderer had returned home.

It was great to be reunited with the family, with whom George had maintained such a regular correspondence. Four Park Circus Place was alive with the exchange of news, and stories from the trenches.

George's first social engagement was to have lunch with the Rev. Allan Murray, the minister of Park Church, who had just become engaged to sister Ellen.

He did the social rounds. Tea at new Cranston's restaurant, visits to the theatre, riding lessons, driving lessons, golf, shooting duck. He went through to Edinburgh and had a long chat with Dr Norman Maclean, former minister of Park, who was now minister of St Cuthberts. The well-known divine, seeing the potential in the young man, gave him encouragement and suggested that he write a book.

When his health improved, he was not sent back to Salonika, but was transferred to the 11th Battalion of the Argylls in order to serve again as part of the British Expeditionary Force on the Western Front. The stalemate war was devouring men, and four million or so volunteers were needed to replace the dead. Indeed the number of volunteers was not enough, and in 1916 compulsory military service had been introduced for the first time in British history.

The 11th Battalion had lost many officers on the Western front, and George was pleased to find some old 12th colleagues transferred to fill the gaps. He was also pleased to see some Cargilfield and Winchester chaps.

George was delighted to be made a fully fledged adjutant in July 1917. His role was to act as staff officer to the commanding officer; he was in receipt of a continuous flow of information, and had to be on top of what was happening, as well as controlling supplies and ammunition. As a natural organizer, he loved the work and the concentrated attention it demanded.

Concentrated attention to detail kept his mind off the wider war for most of the time. George said he couldn't bear to read the newspapers because of what was happening in Russia, and because of the number of casualties.

"When you think that next week will bring in the fourth year of the War – now and again one almost feels hopeless," he wrote to Ellen, "but that is usually just before breakfast, or some other such unprintable time – after dinner one realizes that there must be something that is going to turn up, somewhere, somehow, which will clear the clouds away. I have heard it said that a man comes out of this war with a very real religion or no religion at all. That is a very common saying here, nowadays – personally I think that any man who sees this war must come out with a very real religion or cut his throat!"

It was thinking like this which eventually led George to full-time service in the Church.

His immediate destination, though, was Ypres, which could turn out to be a shortcut to the nearer presence of God.

There had already been two important battles at Ypres, which was situated in a very dangerous salient. General Haig, commander-in-chief of the British armies, had decided to break out in an attempt to reach the Belgian coast. The Third Battle of Ypres had begun on 7th June, 1917, when a million tons of British explosives were detonated under the German trenches with a noise that was heard in London. In that first day of battle, the German armies lost 25,000 men and the British 17,000. The British plan was to push through the German ranks to Passchendaele, but the soldiers became bogged down in the rain and mud.

"Had hot time in the afternoon – had to be relieved at midnight – are now resting in four inches of mud – rained pretty solidly since 3 o'clock yesterday, and still pouring at 4 o'clock – everybody soaked to the skin, blessing Johnnie Walker, cursing the Hun and amazingly cheerful," wrote George of the famous 31st July offensive. He sent home a sample of Flanders mud as a souvenir.

Eight days later, he was writing to his father, describing the battle of Ypres at that stage as a victory. The reality was that the British had lost 30,000 men in the first week and the whole battlefield was a quagmire. Horses, guns and men were simply sucked under.

General Haig insisted that the men continue to push towards Passchendaele. George's battalion was detailed to take the Heights of Frezenberg, a ridge about a mile and a half away from the ultimate destination. The Germans were in a strong position, occupying farm houses on the hill fortified by concrete pillboxes, and able to mow down the "ladies from hell" – as the kilted Highland regiments were described.

George's adjutant notes for 21st and 22nd August, 1917 reveal that communications all day were precarious. "Heavy shelling of Frezenberg Ridge. Capt. J. H. Porteous, being in the front line for the first time, was killed by a sniper . . . Line was composed of almost 40 rifles and six Lewis guns under Lts Cameron and Mackay. The line was reorganized with the greatest gallantry by these officers under incessant fire and consolidated with a view to possible counter attack."

He described parts of the battle in a letter home.

"At 4.45 the bombardment burst and over they went. At the same time the Boche opened a much heavier fire than was expected, and apparently had the door to headquarters marked off, by a machine gun and snipers. The telephone was disconnected three minutes before the show. The first two orderlies we sent out with messages got sniped, and for 6 hours we had to send all our messages by homer pigeons. Two officers came in wounded to headquarters within ten minutes of the start, and a 4 inch shell landed on headquarters, wounding 5, all of whom came into our part of headquarters – a room about 6 ft by 12, with 2 inches of water on the floor – to be attended by a doctor, who had been held up by the Boche barrage and could not get forward, till too late. All this just to give you some idea of what a joyful morning you can spend if you like to look for it."

It was for his part in this battle that George Fielden MacLeod was awarded the Military Cross. When his commanding officer was killed, Adjutant MacLeod took over and led the reorganization. Fifteen out of 20 officers were lost, and 330 men out of 400 failed to return. The official citation said the Military Cross was awarded "for conspicuous gallantry and devotion to duty as adjutant, volunteering to go out and do duty in the hastily-organized line of defence when no company officers remained. He carried out his duties as adjutant as well, and was of the greatest assistance in keeping cohesion."

George simply wrote to his mother three days later saying, "We have just come through another show, and had a pretty wretched time," and a few weeks later said, "Off hand, I got the thing for the Ypres show, which I told you of – though where the conspicuous gallantry and devotion to duty came in I don't know – I think it is more due to the particularly poor shooting of the Boche on that day!"

In the same letter, George told how he and the CO walked through the ruins of Ypres as members of the last battalion to leave the line. They crossed the canal – "the west boundary of the vile place" – stopped for a moment, looked at each other, and spat into it – "the most venomous spiteful spit I ever spat!"

Thus did he turn his back on Ypres, the hellish crucible which had claimed the lives of so many of his colleagues and friends, and from which he was desperately lucky to walk out alive. The tragedy is that when Canadian troops finally took Passchendaele on 6th November, 1917, it was hardly worth taking. A quarter of a million British soldiers had died in order to advance seven miles.

What made the strongest impression on George was the spirit and courage of the ordinary soldiers at the front. He particularly appreciated the humour of the rough and ready Glasgow men. Having shared terrifying danger with such men, he could no longer simply accept the social assumptions he had taken for granted at home and at school.

As the miserable slaughter continued, hardly a family in Britain was left unscathed. It seemed only a matter of time before the dread telegram would arrive. "Missing, believed dead" was a bleak message: the pain was not assuaged by the fact that such grief was commonplace.

It was an anxious time for John and Edith MacLeod as they waited for news of their sons. Jack, who had played such an important part in encouraging young men to enlist for glory, only to see them sucked into a mass muddy grave, could not allow self-doubt to take root, nor dwell on the possibility that the next death message might be about Norman or George. He instead turned his anger on those who were sowing seeds of doubt in the nation. The chief targets in his sights were conscientious objectors and socialists.

John MacLeod attacked the "serious menace" of the growing Socialist Sunday Schools when he addressed the General Assembly of the Church of Scotland. He said they were materialistic, and encouraged people to become conscientious objectors. Commenting on a report which lamented the large decrease in the numbers attending the Kirk's Sunday Schools, he said that every Christian church must organize in all districts of the country more Sunday Schools and foster to the utmost Boys' and Girls' Brigades, scout troops and foundry boys' associations (applause).[1]

Mr W. H. Hamilton of Barrhead replied to Mr MacLeod in the columns of *The Glasgow Herald* in a style which could hardly have been bettered by the Rev. George MacLeod of Govan twenty years later.

"The Gospels are a largely used text book in such Socialist Sunday Schools, and the words and principles of Jesus are most earnestly studied and taught . . . It proves nothing, except to prejudice, that some conscientious objectors to military service have been brought up in such schools – unless it proves that the teaching of Jesus has had a large place in their training there. One need not reopen that vexed question further than to urge that men may so object not in a spirit of desiring exemption but in a spirit of fidelity to moral conviction and idealism derived from the Gospels."

By 1917 food shortages were causing great problems as the German U-boat strategy of cutting off supplies to Britain took effect. Edith MacLeod spoke at meetings of the Patriotic Food League, urging people to be economical with food. When a cookery exhibition and demonstration was held in Partick, a crowd of 2000 rioted, objecting to ladies from the West End telling them how to spend their earnings.

Mr and Mrs MacLeod's exhausted son wrote home requesting oatcakes, tongue, herrings in tomato, cheese, creme de menthe sweets, jam (juicy), homemade cakes, pickled onions, French mustard, cocoa, soap, and papers such as *Tatler*, *London Opinion*, *Wykehamist*, *Life and Work*. All this while writing notes requisitioning guns, bullets, shells, mules and spades, in the midst of flying shells.

"Tonight 2 trench mortars had the effrontery to land almost at our front line. I rang up the Artillery Liaison Officer and told him I wanted retaliation on it. I happen to know him, and he is absolutely fed up with the war. He said 'I'll see what can be done' and immediately let fly sixty 18 pound shells on the position!!! I believe the poor dear Hun who was working the trench mortar was last seen somewhere near Frankfurt, still going strong. Long live the munition workers!"

By March 1918, George was cheerier. He wrote approvingly of the men who were "just as great as ever – no cover – bitterly cold at nights – very little prospect of a clean up – but all there every time – and lord how they hate the Boche." In one attack his battalion did well – "Boche casualties were AWFUL. I will tell you all about it some day. You can imagine it was a great day for me" – and in another raid his men took 30 prisoners and gained three Military Crosses. He added: "So we are all very bucked, and the men are cheery as sandboys, and all out for Boche Blood, which is meet and right, as the prayer book (Christian) says."

When Colonel Mitchell, his commanding officer, died of pneumonia, his devoted adjutant was shattered. Saying that he was "without doubt the best man I ever met", George recalled how he had, trying to draw his superior out, expressed the view that this was a religious war, pure and simple. Mitchell let George speak for three minutes, then said: "MacLeod, I have often read your bunkum and signed it too, but I have never heard you talk it before!"

It was in a time of despair after Mitchell's death that George asked another senior officer, "What's all this bloody business about?" The response he got from his friend was a warning that another similar question would see him on his way home with a guard.

He was horrified on one occasion to come across one of the quieter sergeants in the battalion lining up six German prisoners of war to shoot them. He asked him what he was doing, and found the man had a glazed look in his eyes: he too was a casualty of war.

In the Spring of 1918, the Germans made a great offensive. Thanks to the Russian collapse, they were able to reinforce their troops on the Western front and mount new attacks. The exhausted Allies had to retreat, and the fighting was desperate. The 11th Battalion suffered so many casualties that it had to be amalgamated with the 8th Battalion, and Lt MacLeod was gazetted to the 8th Battalion with the rank of adjutant and captain.

There were many men from Morvern in the Eighth, a romantic Battalion with a great tradition. Very much Argyll-based, it had been dominated by the Campbell aristocratic line. Men had traditionally joined up at the request of their chiefs, and a summons from such as the Duke of Argyll would not be refused. George earned kudos with the men by his knowledge of Morvern personalities.

George certainly knew how to drink in the army: and how to gamble. The officers played cards to pass the time, and the money and cigarettes soon changed hands – "our great game at nights is 'vingt et un', and after a week's play and endless excitement and laughter you find yourself in or out about 5 francs". His cure for the rampaging influenza was whisky.

"The Signalling Officer and Intelligence Officer both went down with it, which left me and the CO on our lonesome," he told Ellen. "Then I promptly had symptoms of it, with a throat, legs that became familiar with one another, a temperature and a hatred of all mankind. But as there was no one left I simply said 'George,

my lad, Christian Science' and put on all the warm things I could
find and with lavish aid from Johnnie Walker DROWNED IT."

The half bottle of whisky, drunk neat, cured the 'flu, and he was
fighting fit.

By the end of July, not only George but the Allies were "winning
the war". American troops were by this time in Europe, and the
Germans were suffering terrible casualties. The Allies were now
working in a much more concerted fashion, and were at last able to
go on to the offensive. On 3rd August, 1918 the 17th French
Division and the 15th Scottish Division, including the 8th Battalion, Argyll and Sutherland Highlanders, prepared a co-ordinated
attack on the steep heights of Villemantière and Buzancy.

An eyewitness of the events, Lt René Puaux of the French
Army, described the battle, in which the kilted Scots made the first
assault, with the French behind.

"The ground over which the Scottish had to attack was extremely
easy for the Boche to defend, because the positions of Villemantière
and Buzancy were on heights dominating the valley, with steep
slopes. It must have needed superhuman courage on the part of the
Scots to scale the heights. Also, many brave men had fallen, and
their corpses lay there, spread out on the ground, showing by their
position the different phases of the attack and of the victory.

"At eight o'clock in the morning, the Scottish troops, headed by
their pipers, came marching through the ruined village, straight
from the field of battle. It was an astonishing sight for us
Frenchmen. The ranks had been sadly thinned; companies showed
but the strength of platoons, but the men were magnificent."[2]

The French were so moved by the courage of the Scots that they
built a monument with the materials at hand. George helped with
the construction. The inscription, made by Lt Puaux with hammer
and pocket knife, had a symbolic Scottish thistle encircled with
French roses, and read:

> Here shall flourish forever
> The Glorious Thistle of Scotland
> Among the Roses of France.
>
> From the 17th French Division
> To the 15th Scottish Division

The French Government was moved, too, and captain George
Fielden MacLeod, who claimed lightheartedly to have swallowed

eight tons of gas in four days, was one of several brave Scots to be awarded the *Croix de Guerre avec palmes.*

With the Allies now breaking through and chasing the enemy to the Belgian coast, and the Turks and the Austrians surrendering, life in the officers' mess was much more relaxed. At the Brigade horse show, George was asked to ride a huge mustang in a "Five Furlong Scurry". He was not reassured when a soldier who had been a professional jockey told him he would not ride a horse with such eyes. He sent home a full description of the race.

"The starter happened to drop the flag at the same time as my horse let go, and I got a romping start," he later wrote. "I was still there (I am told) after the sunken road, and I had some idea that I was leading. A fast aeroplane overhead seemed to be slowly going backwards, and hey presto! we were at the corner. I took it very wide (at least two men had advised me to do this and I suppose the horse heard, because my pulling with all my strength on the left rein had never made any difference before) and I realized that a black form had taken the corner close, and was riding neck and neck with me. All I could see was this other horse, going like Hell, and myself exactly level – a yelling mob of about 1000 on either side, and an open space at the end. I realized I was talking to the horse and telling her to 'go like the devil, Betty' and she did. Someone in the crowd said, 'You're going ahead Mac' (as if I had anything to do with it) and she did, and in I came first. The Divisional General congratulated me on the splendid win, as I patted the dear beast where horses are accustomed to be patted. It was only then that I realized I had forgotten to bet on the damned thing!"

Starvation in Germany, combined with strikes, riots and muti- nies brought about the collapse of the government and the flight of the Kaiser. On November 9, 1918, the new German government sued for peace. The armistice began at 11 am on 11th November, 1918. In London, cheering crowds danced in the streets as the church bells pealed.

At the front, Captain MacLeod's men took things very quietly – "an unconscious feeling of deep thankfulness, far deeper than any hilarity could express." George wrote home on Armistice Day: "Tonight the boom of the guns is gone! But then there wasn't a sound to be heard last night, so I'm afraid we were frightfully unromantic – the only excitement I had today was when my host got so enthralled with his story of what a Boche officer did in his house that he seized me by the throat in lieu of Boche officer, and nearly throttled me – and then apologized profusely."

Thus ended a slaughter which killed 10 million men and left another 20 million wounded. It was the "war to end all wars".

At least, that is, until the next time.

PART TWO

*

QUEST FOR
THE HISTORICAL
GEORGE

4

The Celtic Spellbinder

'My immediate desire is religious freedom, but my long-range goal is to get into real estate'.

New Yorker cartoon of one Puritan to another, stepping off the Mayflower.

I never travel without my diary. One should always have something sensational to read on the train.

OSCAR WILDE

There is a field of New Testament studies known as the "Quest for the Historical Jesus", in which scholars attempt to strip away the many layers of tradition surrounding Christ and recover Jesus of Nazareth as he really was in the flesh. It has proved a stubbornly difficult task, since the life of Jesus is embedded in interpretive theology from earliest times.

The "Quest for the Historical George" is hardly of the same scale, yet there are some similar problems. George MacLeod is a legend in his own lifetime, and further confusion is added by the fact that one of the principal myth-makers is the subject himself. A crafty Celtic wizard who knows a good story when he tells one, George observed that the trouble with the more prosaic English, as opposed to the wildly imaginative Celts, was that they couldn't distinguish between facts and truth. The MacLeod view of history is a wildly romantic one, and while rightly spellbound by the "truth" of the vividly narrated story, the listener has to keep at least one foot on the ground and ask steely questions about the facts.

Here are three widely believed theses:

George MacLeod

George MacLeod was so sickened by the carnage of the First World War that he emerged as a crusading pacifist.

George MacLeod was so affected by the plight of the men under his command that he became a crusading socialist.

George MacLeod's radical socialist-pacifist views were formed under the influence of his Quaker mother.

What unites these three theses is that, however attractive, they are untrue. They have been repeated so often in oral tradition and in newspaper articles and books over many years that they have become the bedrock of the received interpretation of the life of George MacLeod.

While it can be safely assumed that seeds of doubt about the MacLeod family's political and military certainties were sown during the First World War, it was a considerable time before they flowered. What is clear from the evidence is that the beloved picture of Captain MacLeod, MC, emerging from the war with a totally new religious, political and philosophical manifesto is part of the "myth of George incarnate". As for his radical Quaker mother, she simply did not exist. There had been Quakerism in the Fielden family two generations before Edith, but her father had adopted his father's Unitarianism – an undogmatic form of Christian thought which rejected the doctrines of the Trinity and the Divinity of Christ – and Edith had been involved with the local Church of England parish. Her political views were at least as conservative as her husband's, and her support for the war effort was strong.

George did come out of the war a changed man in one major aspect: he was now determined to give up his legal studies and become a minister of the gospel. His theology was still very much morality and duty-based – although his patriotism was of a more chastened variety – and he felt the primary post-war task was one of moral and spiritual reconstruction. Furthermore, it was a task which would require as many sacrifices as the war itself had done. As a survivor of a conflict which had offered platoon commanders an average life-expectancy of three weeks, he felt an obligation to his colleagues who had made the supreme sacrifice.

He had not been overmuch impressed by religion as he had encountered it in the army. His diary has several unflattering references to church parades, such as "rotten service and sermon", "a most dismal affair", "sermon about carnage – bunkum", and he condemned one minister as a "guess-I-think-so preacher". (He exempted from these strictures the Rev. G. A. Studdert-Kennedy – "Woodbine Willie" – whom he heard speak at the end of the war and whom he considered to be an exceptional man). As he chafed in the makeshift pew, the great Norman's grandson reckoned he could do much better: the man who condemned the British for waging a half-hearted war against the enemy had decided that he wanted to go full-tilt at the atheists.

Much later, in a television broadcast entitled "Why I Believe", George recounted a conversion experience he had had towards the end of the First World War. He said that once, returning from a particularly hectic leave, he had realized that he was "going to hell in a hurry". In addition to gambling, he reckoned he was going through half a bottle of whisky and 50 cigarettes a day. He had knelt down in the railway carriage in which he was travelling and surrendered his life to Christ.[1]

As an essentially private person, it was unusual for George to speak in such a personal way about his own interior experience. His diaries and letters make no reference to such a life-changing happening and certainly give no indication of such excessive living: yet, allowing for later MacLeodian dramatization and even exaggeration, it is clear that something happened to push him in the direction of the ministry.

Much of it, of course, ran in the blood. Every male of the MacLeod dynasty was compelled by the weight of family history to consider full-time service in the Church. There is so much of Norman of the Barony in George: the energy, the love of life, the passion, the humour, the idealism, the personal attractiveness – and also the melancholy dissatisfaction with the way life is actually being lived. The times of depression noted in George's war journals came when he was less than fully stretched. He was, and is, by temperament, an all-or-nothing man. And like his grandfather, he saw life as a conflict, much of which was waged within his own being. Disgust with some aspects of his way of life in the army – he used to tell his family in later years that he gave in to all the sins except sexual ones – would give way to idealistic commitment. The puritan and the passionate wrestled each other within him.

★

The time after the Armistice had been boring and frustrating, and Captain MacLeod, rather than exulting at the end of the fighting, was restless and sometimes ill. The guddle over demobilization arrangements, created by his superiors, made him angry, and he lost his temper on more than one occasion. Nothing enraged him more than incompetent superiors: he usually felt he could do the job better himself.

The returning soldier disembarked from a US navy ship at Southampton on April 24, 1919, and was back at 4 Park Circus Place, Glasgow five days later for a great family reunion. There was much to catch up with. Ellen and Allan were now married, and brother Norman was there with his new Italian wife, Isa Brusati, whom he had married in Egypt while serving with the RNVR.

John MacLeod had retired from the Central Division to provide a safe seat for Bonar Law, Chancellor of the Exchequer – a gesture which did not go unappreciated by his political masters at Westminster. In the General Election in December 1918 he had stood as Coalition Unionist candidate for the Kelvingrove Division of Glasgow, winning a comfortable victory over his Liberal opponent. The election was a personal triumph for Lloyd George, who now headed a Unionist-dominated coalition with a large majority. He promised a "land fit for heroes", and in the immediate post-war euphoria, people believed that a new world order might be created.

The Church of Scotland had a difficult task in the immediate post-war era. Things were far removed from the days of Norman MacLeod, when the principal choice for many Scots was which branch of Presbyterianism to belong to. The rise of the new scientific world view, the impact of biblical criticism and the changed urban social patterns had combined to undermine the Victorian religious consensus. The Evangelical ideology could not bear the weight of the changing intellectual and social conditions.

The response had been twofold – a new social theology, and a drive towards reunion. In the early part of the twentieth century, the main focus of theology had shifted from individual salvation to the kingdom of God on earth. Confidence in individualism had waned, and the search was on for more collective solutions. New social theologies stressed the corporate nature of faith in the world, and sought to sketch out patterns for a Christian life with justice and concern for the poor at its heart. This thinking in turn led to alliances with those seeking political change, and the new socialist movements were felt by some churchmen to be congenial.

This *rapprochement* between some parts of the established Church and the new political movements collapsed during the First World War. The strikes on Clydeside were condemned by the Kirk, and the Bolshevik revolution in Russia sent shockwaves through the establishment. Socialism was a dangerous business. The newer social theologies already looked dated, and the deaths of some of the most able theologians denuded the movement of leadership. The theological issues thrown up by the war were difficult to answer satisfactorily, and there were very uncomfortable questions about the Church's almost jingoistic and uncritical support of the war effort. The alienation of intellectuals and working class people put the Church into a defensive and unconfident position.

Despite the growing secularization of society and the steady erosion of the Church's position in the civil and political life of the country, considerable numbers of people still attended public worship and identified themselves with some branch of the Church. After the decline in membership and involvement in religious organizations since the late Victorian times, church membership had actually increased during the war.

The undermining of confidence in the Church's message as a whole had, however, contributed to the desire for the reunion of the different branches of Presbyterianism. The Free and United Presbyterian Churches had joined forces in 1900, and a great deal of the energy which had gone into the social concerns of the earlier part of the century was channelled into the ecumenical movement. What was becoming clearer in the immediate aftermath of the war was that an embattled Church was going to have a hard job in a society which questioned the old order in religion, morals, politics and the place of women, and which had new distractions in the form of mass sport, the radio and the cinema.

It was in such a Church that George MacLeod would exercise his ministry.

The war hero was restless at home. In the comfortable ambience of 4 Park Circus Place, it was as if the war had never been, or at least was past history.

It had been decided that Oxford students who had studied before war service would be given a BA, to make space for all the post war students who wished to enrol. It was also indicated that two years' study in theology would be sufficient for the ministry. George enrolled at Edinburgh University in September 1919.

While he enjoyed his two years' study there, he found a lack of fellowship and excitement after his time in the trenches. He appreciated biblical studies, but was not a man to be a devotee of any one theologian: in fact, he was not a great reader of systematic theology at any time. He enjoyed flirting with ideas and communicating them in exciting and vivid language, but although he was clever, he was not a scholar in the sense of disciplined and systematic study. ("Attended Old Testament class and got the 4th class prize. Gee the others must have been bad!" he wrote in his diary.) He made an impression on Professor W. P. Paterson, who noted in his diary for 21st November, 1919; "I had a second batch of first year students to tea. Among them was a grandson of Norman MacLeod, who rose to be Adjutant. He seems to be a chip off the old block – in respect of stature, geniality and humour."[2]

Professor Paterson, who held the chair of Divinity, was a scholar who liked to make his students think. He was regarded as one of the most able exponents of the "just war" theory: the view that war could be justified theologically under certain well-defined circumstances. Wherever George MacLeod got his pacifism from, it was certainly not from his Divinity professor.

George shared a flat on the Mound with other students. After visits to the cinema or theatre they would sit up late smoking, playing bridge or putting the world to rights. Life was not all serious, by any means. The First World War veteran, used to the sound of artillery fire in the Flanders fields, constructed a spring-loaded cannon which fired oranges on to dismayed pedestrians in Princes Street Gardens below.

He enjoyed boxing, tennis and watching rugby, as well as fishing and shooting. The week before he was due to be licensed as a preacher of the gospel he went with a cousin to the Grand National.

"I did not know the name of a single horse in any of the races," he later wrote to a friend, "but I put £1 a race on the horse that took my fancy *and won on every race*. Travelled back first class and never gambled since. But God knew he was on a winner."

His grandfather would have understood perfectly.

What attracted George most of all was work with youngsters in the poorer parts of Edinburgh. Poverty and tuberculosis were rife. Many of the youngsters were malnourished and literally dressed in rags. ("After lunch, visited parishioners in Pleasance," George noted in his diary. "Awful houses, some clean, some messy".) He could not help but contrast the situation with his own privileged upbringing, and his strong sense of duty ensured that he would do what he could for these lads. For the rest of his life, George would have a burning compassion for underprivileged youngsters.

Towards the close of his two-year term at Edinburgh University, George accepted the offer of a postgraduate fellowship to Union Theological Seminary in New York. It was to prove to be an exciting and enjoyable experience.

The voyage itself was not without its moments. Setting out on the TSS Cameronia from Ireland on 12th September, 1921, the ship rolled and George's cup gently slipped off the marble mantelpiece of the smoking room into the lap of Irving Berlin. The composer was furious.

New York, with its skyscrapers towering over the church spires, was impressive. George went to theatre on Broadway, and enjoyed the Ziegfeld Follies. The sense of excitement, the exaggerations, the talk of the taxi drivers and the display of wealth amazed him. Once installed in the Union residence on Broadway, he was invited out to wealthy county estates for golf and dinner. The confident Scot, brought up to be at ease in any company, was much sought after. "After supper, we told many stories – anything Scotch goes down, and when you are hard up, an English story told in Scotch brings the house down." Like his grandfather, George was a good mimic, whose *joie-de-vivre* was infectious. He enjoyed golf on the millionaire courses.

Study? Oh yes. It was good, too. He chose to major in preaching, public worship, religious education and New Testament theology. Union was a liberal theological college, accepting the results of the "Higher Criticism" of the Bible, a place where ideas circulated freely. Professors E. F. Scott, H. E. Fosdick, Hugh Black and Sloane Coffin were big names on the theological circuit, and George enjoyed their teaching without becoming a disciple of any one of them. "I have to read a paper on the prophetic idea of the Remnant in the Old Testament, and if their idea of it was as vague as mine, I will have some difficulty in writing it," he told Ellen.

America fascinated George. As an old Winchester and Oriel man, he was disturbed and thrilled by the lack of formality, and he mocked the American use of the English language. (He loved to quote the wife of the Mayor of New York who, in response to the Queen of Belgium's compliments, was reported to have said, "Gee, Queen, you've said a mouthful!".) Yet the sense of possibilities, the internationalism, the egalitarianism and the free circulation of ideas excited him. 1921 was the beginning of a life-long love affair with the United States of America.

As a clergyman, he was able to travel on public transport for half price, and the Scotsman took full advantage of the concession. He went to baseball and football matches, enjoyed the big cinemas with their orchestras, and saw a bit of the country. He snake-danced with 80,000 people after a football match at Yale, throwing his hat over the crossbar, went to hear Harry Lauder sing, dined with contacts in New York and Boston, and attended recitals. He even spoke at meetings on subjects he knew little about – "I am becoming an expert at beating them at their own game of Bluff!!!"

Study continued to excite and puzzle. He told his father that they "wallow in Modernism and lean towards Pragmatism and are happy at the points at which these two mysteries meet." Observing that there was not a Professor at New College who would be happy about the Westminster Confession of Faith, he said of Union: "Though there are dangers in the whole thing, I believe that it is tending to produce 'thinking' men, as opposed to children fed on outworn theories, which if still preached to an educated congregation today, will alienate them, because they can't believe them, and who therefore jump to the erroneous conclusion that they can't believe Christianity." This was happening at a time when William Jennings Bryan, the populist politician, was stomping the country, attracting big crowds with his diatribes against Charles Darwin and the theory of evolution.

George spent Christmas with a wealthy Bostonian family, and attended midnight communion at the packed Episcopal Cathedral – "none of the officiating clergy had American accents, which in my eyes – though not I suppose in the eyes of the Almighty – does make a difference." He was taken to meet the former US ambassador to Belgium and Japan.

"He had a perfectly huge house, and a perfectly beautiful one," he told his mother. "He seemed a perfect ass, but in the middle of the conversation said he was sure that I would like a whisky and soda. It sounded so funny, and he so obviously wanted one himself, that I said Yes, and the 15th footman brought it. My dear, you never saw such a thing, roughly the size of a goldfish bowl, and with the whisky and soda already poured in to the brim, and very strong – literally about the size of three glasses, and I hadn't touched whisky for weeks . . . on the drive home my conversation was brilliant."

One of the reasons George had gone to the States was to do his early preaching free from the shadow of the MacLeod reputation. It was not to be. He found that Scots were the backbone of many of the big Presbyterian Churches, and Dr Norman MacLeod's reputation was well established. When he stayed with the bishop of Massachusetts, his host took down the biography of Norman of the Barony from his shelves and started to read from it. At another dinner party he sat next to the editor of the New York Times, who had brought along a cutting from a Chinese newspaper, all about Norman of the Barony. At meetings he was due to address, he was introduced as the grandson of one of Scotland's greatest orators. There was no escape from the great shadow.

There was no escape from what was in the genes, either. For George MacLeod in New York, read Norman MacLeod in the Weimar.

The social whirl went on and on. English tea at Harvard. Bridge parties, with marriageable daughters brought out. Recitals – "a young conductor, who conducted for three hours without any music in front of him, I think that some day he will be famous, by name Stokowski". Visit to Philadelphia. Visit to Atlantic City – "quite the vulgarest and most enjoyable place you could imagine". And so on, and so on, to Weimar music, transmuted into the Charleston tempo of the jazz age which appalled and excited the sensuous, puritan Scot with the same kind of high "animal spirits" as his celebrated grandfather.

The exciting news from home, in January 1922, was the announcement that Mr John MacLeod, MP was to retire as representative of Kelvingrove Division at the end of parliament. He continued to be active in benevolent work, and chaired a meeting to support an appeal for £50,000 to erect and endow a Scots church and college in Jerusalem. His services were recognized in May, when he was appointed a Deputy Lieutenant of the City of Glasgow, and was awarded the degree of Doctor of Laws of Glasgow University.

The MP's son's interest in politics was growing apace. He sat up late at night with his fellow students discussing American politics, which he found absorbing. He was not impressed by one of the lecturers at Union, who was a socialist, but he became caught up in the debate about postwar reconstruction and about how future wars might be avoided. George was in favour of President Woodrow Wilson's proposals for outlawing secret diplomacy and the establishment of a League of Nations with powers. Although not a pacifist, he favoured disarmament and the resolution of disputes by international agreement. Along with other Union students, he spoke at meetings on this line.

The impressionable young Scot was fascinated by American wealth – "poverty here does not denote the lack of a car, it merely means that they only have one: only bankrupts (undischarged) have none" – but was equally impressed by American generosity. He marvelled at the giving of church members and noted how ministers would lay before the congregation the financial requirements of the time, and expect these needs to be met.

In March 1922, there came a meeting with the man who, more than any other human being, was to be his example and mentor.

P. B. ("Tubby") Clayton, founder of Toc H, visited New York to raise funds. Clayton, an army chaplain in Flanders, had established a hostel in 1915 in the Ypres salient, named Talbot House (motto: "Abandon rank all ye who enter here"), which had ministered to the needs of half a million men. After the war, some officers and men had got together to see if they could perpetuate the spirit of co-operation among all classes, which they had seen at Talbot House. Thus Toc H (The Morse signal for the Talbot House initials) was born. The postwar plan was to collect young men of all classes and denominations to meet together in Christian fellowship, to set up hostels as a base for small Christian communities, and to recruit young men for voluntary service.

George had been very impressed by the work and reputation of Talbot House in Ypres and had signed up as a member of Toc H. In facing front-line dangers during the war, he had felt denominational differences to be irrelevant, and he liked the way in which Toc H provided a base for people of all Christian traditions. They were serious, yet not pompous, about their faith, and they had an ability to communicate with the ordinary "Jock". It was his kind of movement, and it was to prove very influential in the thinking which led up to the establishment of the Iona Community.

Tubby Clayton recognized the great potential of the young Scot, and earmarked him for future work. George accompanied him on his visits, and gained a unique insight into the work of one of the most admired figures of the British church scene in the 1920s and 30s.

"He is a most amusing fellow – rather a typical Oxford don type, and very casual in a way," wrote George. "The result was that he always wanted me to take him round to see people, as he thinks so much he never knows what direction he is going in – which does not suit New York! He gives the impression of being lackadaisical, but as a matter of fact is a terrific worker. His interviews with some of the big Anglican men here were screams. They are all typically New York – very busy, and want to settle a job in about 15 minutes. He knows perfectly well that if he meets them by only talking to them for 15 minutes, they will forget all about it, as soon as he is gone. So he nearly always stays an hour in each place – yarning away about his work, usually sitting on the edge of a chair, without saying anything very definite, about what he wants. After 20 minutes they get rather fidgety and blurt out, 'That's all very interesting, but what do you want me to do . . . do you want money, or do you want me to arrange a meeting for you to address?' to which he replies, 'Neither, that is to say, both' in a slow Oxford way, followed by an irresistible laugh, and then goes on yarning (always in a charming way). After about 35 minutes they (or rather the American clergyman, for they are all individual interviews) suddenly get really interested and they keep the conversation going, with questions of real interest, and he finally leaves them, having been personally conquered by him, with an indelible impression of what he really wants from them – which is a real interest in the movement. It was a beautiful thing to watch this invariably happening wherever we went – especially as he is a most unprepossessing figure, being quite as round as he is tall."

Thus were laid, in New York in 1922, the foundations of the highly successful fund-raising strategy for the rebuilding of the monastic buildings of Iona Abbey between 1938 and 1967.

Before Tubby Clayton left, he told George that Toc H must be started in America. Would he be prepared to be acting secretary of the movement? George agreed – "this Clayton man is a wonder . . . he is one of these people to whom 'No' is out of the question" – and the two men sat up till quarter to two in the morning, "while he hurled papers, propaganda, letters and addresses at me". Commanding officer and adjutant.

George MacLeod

George was always much more impressed by men of action than by theologians, and his style, if not his profile, became more and more Tubbyesque. This MacLeod man was always to be a wonder . . . one of these people to whom "No" was always out of the question.

George organized meetings and dinner parties. He persuaded a wealthy patron in 5th Avenue to hold a dinner on behalf of Toc H. It was not reminiscent of a Flanders trench meal.

"We started with cocktails, had sherry with the soup, white wine with the fish, champagne for the remaining eight courses, and liqueur brandy with the coffee – and thereafter I was most enlightening on the whole question of Toc H to my next-door neighbour, young Rothschild, who became very interested in the movement, but I couldn't find out if he was a Jew or not, and have never been able to find out since, which is unfortunate, as I understand that that family has money!"

As his time in America drew to a close, George was undecided about his next step. Professor Hugh Black offered him an extension in his scholarship for another year, and Dr John Kelman, one of the great Scottish preachers in New York, pleaded with him to be his assistant.

Tubby Clayton wanted him to open up Toc H's work in Glasgow – "If anything comes of the movement in Scotland," wrote George to his father, "it would eventually be a feather in my cap for the Church, as it is the only movement that I can see that is actually doing anything big for the wandering boy in the city." There were also overtures from St Giles' Cathedral, Edinburgh, about an assistantship. Being sought after made life very confusing – "I do envy the blokes in the Old Testament times when there was always a sporting chance of writing on the wall, but the wall in my room is the most prosaic thing you ever saw." At any rate, he was due to spend three months in a rural parish at Nakusp on the side of Lake Arrow, British Columbia.

He decided against staying in America, but set off for Canada with his future plans still unresolved. Little did he think that he would return many times – and that nearly seventy years later he would go back to New York to be honoured by Union Theological Seminary for his services to the World Church.

★

The Celtic Spellbinder

The time in Canada was refreshing and interesting. Again, he thought it would be a good opportunity to test his preaching skills out of reach of the MacLeod legend. He might have known better.

First preaching engagement, Toronto: "They had written me up in the Toronto Globe on the Thursday before, and to my horror the assistant minister went through a panegyric of Grandfather's preaching capabilities before the congregation, before I entered the pulpit!! I nearly left the building. However, it was great to think that Grandfather had preached there 70 years before, and I got through the thing somehow. After the morning service it was very moving, delightful and intensely tiring – at least 30 people came in to shake hands with me – men who had heard him preach – men who had been christened by him – men who had seen his funeral – and men who had never seen him but knew all about him."

Nakusp, British Columbia, was fruit-growing and lumber territory. There were Scots – "occupied mostly in the lumber mills making telegraph poles and losing their thumbs": English yeomen – "they believe passionately in Hell and strong tea, and glower at you all through the sermon": and English squires – "all gloriously happy, and gloriously bankrupt". The glamorous young Scots minister, who took three different services each Sunday, was something of a sensation. The Presbyterian superintendent warned him not to dance or smoke in Nakusp, at least not in public; George, ever his own man, wrote back to say that he never danced in private and that he intended to smoke both in private and in public.

George's priority was that of survival. He lived alone in the wooden manse, and he had never really had to fend for himself before – there had always been a maid or a cook or a batman to cater for him. Breakfast was a problem to the handless bachelor minister – "to scrape or not to scrape is the burning question of the day," he told Ellen – but he usually managed to eat out with his parishioners and their marriageable daughters. The former Wykehamist liked the democratic and unconventional spirit of Canada.

"So much of the silly part of old-time convention is gone. . .no one ever wears gloves," he wrote in amazed tones. "Then again it is real democracy – everyone really knows everyone else – the doctor, the blacksmith, the policeman and the minister have a four at tennis and it is quite natural – no effort on anyone's part – no one calls anyone else Sir."

The energetic young minister visited his flock regularly, ran dances for the teenagers, taught youngsters to swim, held ecumenical services and, typically, dashed off a letter to his superiors telling them how the mission work should be run. He did things at a pace which surprised the more lethargic residents of Nakusp. They were sorry to see him leave.

On 3rd October, 1922, George MacLeod left Canada on the SS *Princess Patricia*. He was returning wiser, invigorated, more confident – and full of ideas and New World slang. He was heading for an assistantship at the most prestigious church in Scotland, the High Kirk of St Giles, Edinburgh.

The Scottish ecclesiastical world was at the feet of yet another dazzling MacLeod.

5

A Sense of Two Nations

*The works which are counted good before God . . . to
save the lives of the innocent, to repress tyranny, to
defend the oppressed.*

THE SCOTS CONFESSION, 1560

God will not always be a Tory.   LORD BYRON

The assistantship at St Giles' Cathedral had been arranged by the
minister, the Very Rev. Dr A. Wallace Williamson, with a little
prompting by John MacLeod, who was anxious to see his son lay
the foundations of a good career in the Church. What better place
to begin than the High Kirk of Edinburgh?

Set firmly in the Royal Mile, in the heart of the old town of
Edinburgh, St Giles' was the nearest thing Scotland had to a
national pulpit. While Presbyterianism did not allow for bishops,
the minister of the Cathedral, which had played such a colourful
part in Scotland's kaleidoscopic history, had a special status. The
Cathedral's liturgy, music and preaching were expected to be of a
high standard. Assistantships there were much sought after by
aspiring churchmen.

In the 1920s, St Giles' stood in the midst of some of the worst
housing in Scotland. Poverty was rife, and tuberculosis was a killer
in the overcrowded slums. In one close, 157 people lived on top of
one another, and that was not exceptional. It was not uncommon
for more than twenty people to use the same water tap, and most
people shared an outside toilet. Malnutrition was common, as was
drunkenness. Many of the lads were messenger boys whose working career would end at sixteen, when their places would be taken
by cheaper labour from the schools. Few of them went to secondary
school or evening classes, and the crowded street was their play-
ground. Crime was a constant temptation.

George MacLeod

It was this aspect which most interested George MacLeod. He would have liked to work with Toc H, but it had not yet been possible to set up a full-time job and to arrange the necessary church approval. He knew from his student experience, however, that the job at St Giles' would bring him into contact with many young people, and that he would be able to set up Toc H branches in an informal way.

George MacLeod's impact was enormous. One young man who testified to the power of his personality was Harry Whitley, who was working as a clerk in an Edinburgh brewery by day, while trying to run a boys' club in the Pleasance at night. One Sunday, he and the lads were sitting on the pavement, keeping an eye out for policemen, when round the corner swept a tall, commanding figure dressed in a dark suit and white collar. He stopped, sat down beside the boys on the pavement so that his long legs dangled in the gutter, then at the end of the conversation said: "Why not come to church? I'll make a bargain with you. If you come I'll meet the gang of you next week and take you up the tower of St Giles' Cathedral, and give you fish and chips afterwards." Then he sprinted off towards St Margaret's Parish Church, Dumbiedykes, where he was helping out his friend, the Rev. Bruce Nicol, that evening.

"We followed in a sheepish sort of way," recalled Harry, "knowing that we were not dressed for church – in fact, most of my companions had never been in church. Boldly, however, I led them in through the main door and quickly spotted an empty pew right at the back – it had cushions on the seat; perhaps that's why I chose it! No sooner were we seated than an elder moved up and loudly whispered in my ear: 'You can't sit there. This pew belongs to – ', and he mentioned some name. I refused to move. Again I was reminded that we were trespassing, and this time I answered, 'Well, if we can't sit here we won't sit anywhere.' So up we got – I think we were all delighted to have an excuse for escape – and out we trooped.

"I don't think we were pleased with ourselves, for we wandered back to our stance, and when eventually the congregation scaled we stood our ground and waited for the preacher. Along Prospect Street he came like a commanding officer descending on some disobedient troops. He gave us it good and hard for not keeping our word, and then I explained the reason. Instead of approving our action, he condemned us all the more. It rather looked as if

66

our fish and chips and the tower of St Giles' were out. Then he laughed and said: 'All right. I'll see you next week outside the north door of St Giles' – my name is MacLeod.' This was my first and memorable meeting with George MacLeod – the most controversial minister in the Church of Scotland these last three decades. We had our visit to St Giles' and afterwards an hilarious supper in a fish and chip shop in the High Street. We were all MacLeod men from that moment. Bit by bit he was to lead me to a decision."[1]

Thus began the colourful and stormy ecclesiastical career of the Rev. Dr H. C. Whitley, who was later to climb the St Giles' tower in his own right, as minister of the Cathedral. His call to the ministry is typical of many such examples of the influence of George MacLeod, who had seen the potential in the young man. As with Tubby Clayton, it was difficult to say No to this man MacLeod.

The St Giles' assistant took him under his wing, and encouraged him each step along the difficult way to the ministry. Nor was the encouragement merely spiritual. Among George's papers, there surfaced recently a faded letter from the headmaster of an English "crammer" school, asking George if he would continue to pay the fees for young Whitley so that he could have another go at his exams – "can you let him have another try? He is such a good fellow that we should love to have him back for another term. He does us good. He is easily the most popular man in the school." George helped Harry at different times in his ministry, preaching for him when he was ill or away, marrying him, baptizing his children, and eventually burying him. Stories of this kind of individual challenge and commitment could be repeated many times; it was this mixture of toughness and personal kindness which, as much as anything, makes George MacLeod's name revered by so many in Scotland today.

Another person who first met George when he was at St Giles' and was profoundly influenced by him was Roy Sanderson, then a schoolboy, later to become a distinguished Moderator of the General Assembly of the Church of Scotland.

"I remember that I was immediately impressed by his exuberance and outgoing personality and what I might call his expression of a hearty kind of Christianity," he recalled. "I found the same reaction to him among my contemporaries when George preached in school chapel, and equally among teenagers from the more populous areas of Edinburgh or Glasgow when he visited a boys' club or spent a night with them in camp. But, then, so were the old ladies in their drawing rooms and professional men in their exclusive clubs impressed by him. As a young and 'favoured' minister he was much sought after, and he certainly had a great influence on a wide circle of people both through his preaching and his general attitude."

The work was demanding and exhausting, and George was refreshed by holidays on his beloved Iona. He learned a great deal from his "bishop". When Dr Williamson had been called from St Cuthbert's to St Giles' in 1910, it was said that it was by the voice of the whole nation. Made Dean of the Thistle and of the Chapel Royal in 1914, he was an outstanding preacher and leader. He taught his assistant a great deal about the conduct of public worship.

George had everything going for him: a well-known family, a privileged upbringing, private means, a distinguished war record, a handsome appearance, an oratorical streak and, above all, that confidence and sense of ease which so often went with aristocratic (and expensive) *breeding*. If the number of young ladies attending public worship – at a time when the officer class of men had been decimated – increased somewhat, their motivation might not have been entirely spiritual. The 27-year-old eligible bachelor was uncomfortable in the presence of beautiful young spinsters, and could only deal with those who tried to form a close spiritual relationship with him by being more than a little brusque or detached. What waste! What challenge!

MacLeod junior's appeal was not lessened by now being the son of a Baronet. Stanley Baldwin had written to John MacLeod to say that His Majesty the King was pleased to express his willingness to confer upon him the dignity of a Baronetcy of the United Kingdom. Jack wrote Baldwin a personal letter, saying: "I cannot let the moment pass without sending you personally my sincere thanks to you for all the great trouble you have taken in this matter", and saying he would be happy to be of use in the future.

Visiting the high flats looking north from High Street, the St Giles' assistant minister began to get a sense of "two nations", especially when he found that quite a few old folk had never walked along Princes Street, on which they looked down! It wasn't "for the likes o' them". Nor was the Church for that matter. The gulf between the poor and the respectable classes, and consequently between the poor and the Church, was a large one, and it troubled George. He felt that the Church as a whole was not facing the implications of the gulf, even while preaching the message of Jesus of Nazareth whom the common people "heard gladly".

For George MacLeod, the existence of "two nations", rich and poor, was an offence against the notion of community which he had found in the trenches, and which he had hoped would be a central feature of the post-war reconstruction. The divisions in society were still very deep, and he felt the Church, of all bodies, should exhibit a new kind of community and thus should provide leadership for the rest of the nation.

The sad fact was that the Church of Scotland, which had made so many promising noises about moral reconstruction and social justice at the end of the war, had largely turned its back on the working class movements for social and political reform. The pre-war social theologies had given way to more timid neutrality. During the war there had been high hopes that a united Church would play a key role in reconstruction, yet it failed to rise to the challenge. The Committee on Church and Nation, under the convenership of Rev. Dr John White, a conservative in ecclesiastical and political matters and a good friend of John MacLeod, restricted itself to fairly safe issues. The working and unemployed classes of Scotland, whose hopes had been raised by earlier pronouncements, knew that they need look no more to the Church for support. They would entrust their future to the socialists. The big strikes of 1919, and John Maclean's agitation for a Scottish Socialist Republic, merely widened the gap.

Was *anyone* facing the implications of the gulf?

Yes, Toc H. And Tubby was on his trail.

Clayton was still keen to open up Glasgow to the work, and he was even more sure that George MacLeod was the man. By this time, he had got the funds together for a full-time appointment. There were two questions in his mind: would George MacLeod, having tasted the high ecclesiastical life, take a step off the career ladder and work full-time for Toc H? And would the Church of Scotland provide backing? The Church of England had sponsored Toc H south of the border, and its chaplains were Church of England clergy. Clayton saw that if the work was to open up fully in Scotland in the 1920s, it would need to be endorsed by the national Kirk, and would need to be spearheaded by an ordained Presbyterian.

Despite his father's reservations, George agreed to do the job. The problem was that ministers in Scotland were normally only ordained to work in congregations to which they had been called. For the first time, and certainly not for the last, George MacLeod was a problem for the Kirk, someone who did not fit the system. The General Assembly considered the matter carefully, and decided that he should be ordained by the Presbytery of Glasgow to the full-time appointment of Toc H Padre. The ordination took place in Park Church, Glasgow, on September 21st, 1924.

"I leave this kindly place with a hundred jobs left undone and a sore heart," George wrote from St Giles' to his friend, Dr Milorad Petrovitch, a Serbian refugee who was a protégé of Lady Mac-Leod's, "facing very much the unknown with plenty of genial friends telling me that I am ruining a promising career by the fool scheme . . . be that as it may, I have at least the guts to try it out and I can't believe God laughs at such efforts, even though outwardly they may be failures."

Toc H described itself as "an aristocracy of comradeship drawn from the schools, universities, offices and factories". It had received a Royal Charter in 1922, and the Prince of Wales was one of its patrons. In the Royal Charter, its aims were described thus: to challenge the younger men of each generation with the Christian ideal of brotherly love, beyond the confines of class and denomination, and to inspire unselfish service in and through its members. The movement was organized in branches, one of whose officebearers was known as the Jobmaster. His job was to receive and, as far as possible, to meet requests for service. Each branch possessed a lamp, which was used in a ceremony of light at the beginning of branch meetings. One of the questions in the ceremony of light was "What is service?", the response being "the rent we pay for our room on earth".

Its appeal for George MacLeod was evident. Toc H stood for living religion, simple doctrine, doing rather than saying, fellowship which broke through class barriers, and working together. It did not talk about the gulf between the classes, it acted. There was a hearty, practical simplicity about its life and fellowship. For George, Toc H embodied the future as it should be.

He threw himself into the work with characteristic gusto. Living at 4 Park Circus Place and basing himself at the new club room of the Glasgow branch, he started new boys' clubs and organized mountaineering trips for the lads. For the first time, he became acquainted with the Glasgow underworld of poverty, homelessness and vice, and was understandably horrified. Four Park Circus Place had known nothing of it, but it soon did. George brought back various scruffy urchins, one of whom was George Adie.

"I first met him when I was fifteen," he recalled. "I was in a boys' home in Argyle Street, because my father used to beat me. Toc H sent visitors to the club, and they used to help us.

"One night I was standing shivering under the canopy in Gordon Street, drookit as a rat, when I felt a hand on the back of my neck. It was George MacLeod. He took me to his house, and got the cook to make me a meal at ten o'clock at night. He contacted the Church of Scotland and got me a job in the market garden.

"He was great fun. He wore a homburg hat all the time, and he used to kick it right downstairs then put it on his head! He used to sit down at the piano and sing songs with the men at the Pitt Street club. When he saw me on the streets, he would give me money for accommodation."

George kept up contact with many of the lads as they grew up, and continued a personal interest in what they were doing.

In his first report to the Home Mission Committee of the Church of Scotland, George MacLeod said that Toc H was "an attempt to perpetuate among men who served in the war, and to hand on to the younger generation, that great spirit of fellowship and mutual sense which was the only thing that kept men sane in time of war, the dulling of which in times of peace was so great a disappointment to many who came back."

Many of those who came back were disappointed in a Church which seemed to have done little about the causes of poverty.

Sir John MacLeod, an influential member of the Church and Nation Committee, had his own views on poverty in Glasgow. Chairing a meeting of the Glasgow Benevolent Society for the Relief of the Destitute Sick and Poor, he was reported as saying that Glasgow's housing was not as bad as was made out. It was the case, he said, that there were parts of the city which were very bad, but he asserted that these places were very largely due to the immense immigration which had been going on for years and years by those of alien blood attracted by the industrial activity of Glasgow. They remained, and left behind them children and grandchildren in increasing numbers. "They seem to know how to multiply families," he said. In due course, they became naturalized Scottish people and Glasgow people, but always they retained to the full "their alien blood and outlook".[2]

This fairly crude anti-Irish broadside met with a popular response, at a time when anti-Catholicism in Scotland was at its height. The Church and Nation Committee in the 1920s fuelled the anti-Catholic feeling, especially after Clydeside returned social-ist MPs in the 1922 General Election. The magisterial John White referred to the Irish as an "inferior race", and his committee said that the Scots were being driven out by immigrants who made much less satisfactory citizens. It said that the Irish Roman Catholics were responsible for a high proportion of crime in Scotland, and attacked "the general thriftlessness of the Irish people and the readiness with which they seek financial relief.

"Such are the people who are gradually taking possession of our native land," said the committee, which urged the government to take immediate action.

Was this an example of the Christian reconstruction which was to take place after the great war? The tragedy is that the Church of Scotland, rather than offering a new vision for a reconstructed nation, was supporting a rather mean-spirited view of national identity and was turning its energies upon itself: this at a time when the scientific, cultural and political trends were running away from the Church. People badly needed a spiritual vision which helped them interpret the new situation: what they found was a Church which had largely surrendered the central intellectual, political and cultural ground and, in the main, left them to their own devices.

The "roaring Twenties" offered many distractions and crazes as the new popular culture took hold among the "bright young things". The radio, cinema and mass-circulation papers competed for popular attention as one craze succeeded another, and fashions in dress, music and morals changed. The Bloomsbury set produced satirical literature which helped form the "modern" spirit: Lytton Strachey's debunking found a ready hearing in the country. Pessimistic voices such as T. S. Eliot's conjured up the image of a wasteland.

The notion of reconstruction had gradually given way to disillu-sion. Stanley Baldwin's motto of "safety first" characterized a government which had gone back to pre-war thinking and practices.

Sir John MacLeod continued to be active in good works. He raised big sums of money for various organizations, rejoicing in being called "beggar" like his father before him. An invitation to 4 Park Circus Place for black tie dinner was something to be sought after. His brandy and stories were good, as was the food, well prepared in the basement. Lady Edith became less mobile when she fell and injured her hip: Sir John had installed for her benefit the first domestic lift in Glasgow.

George loved the Toc H work. He told the Kirk in his report that meetings of Toc H – "which needs to perpetuate the spirit which made the war, despite the killings, a grand experience" – rarely finished before 11 pm. That comradeship existed among all classes was proved, he said, by the group which gathered one evening to hear a miner talk about the coal crisis.

"There were in the room a Colonel of the Regular army, a Captain of Territorials; three Fascists, two Socialists; two men who had seen the inside of a prison, an ex-Borstal boy sitting beside a policeman; several unemployed, a clerk from the Unemployment Bureau quite near them; a Cambridge man actually on the same form as an Oxford man; a padre and several who rarely go to church; and the rest from offices, shops and works. The incidental fact that the coal miner failed to make an appearance did not deter the above-mentioned prosaic gathering from discussing something else for two hours and singing songs together for half an hour."

Though the work in Scotland was expanding, thanks to the efforts of its charismatic padre, all was not well with Toc H. The burning question was the extent to which the movement was for all Christians, and how this affected the issue of intercommunion. In Flanders, the "upper room" in Talbot House had been for all denominations: when All Hallows church in Barking became Toc H's spiritual home, it was announced that there would be holy communion for confirmed Anglicans, and that others would go to a Free Church for the sacrament. For the Glasgow padre, this was an outrage. Either they all sat at the one table at All Hallows, or they separated communion from the movement.

George was infuriated by what he saw as Anglican exclusivism. He shared his family's indignation that his great uncle, the Rev. Donald MacLeod, had not been allowed to share in the conduct of the wedding of George's parents since, in Anglican eyes, a minister of the established Church of Scotland was not properly ordained. Was Toc H to be basically an Anglican movement which excluded others from the holy table? He had been excited by Toc H because it promised to break down class and denominational barriers in the spirit of wartime co-operation. He hoped it would be in the frontline of denominational change. What he saw happening was to him a denial of the kind of community necessary to give a lead to the nation.

George got little support from other Toc H padres, who were mainly Anglican. His chief opponent was a fellow Scot, Peter Monie, the honorary administrator of the movement, who complained to Clayton:

"George MacLeod and I have quite different ideas of Toc H. I regard it as fundamental that Toc H should include all sorts of Christians and I am certain that this cannot be realized unless Toc H stands clear of ecclesiastical disputes, is scrupulously careful to leave such matters to the Churches, and avoids attempting to help the cause of unity by 'gestures' etc. of its own devising. The people who talk most about unity aren't necessarily the people who do most for it. Some of us believe that for the present, prayer is the straightforward and only effective way of helping . . . what you have to choose between is a Toc H which does include 'all sorts' and a Toc H which is out to back a particular solution."[3]

The battle lines were drawn up. Monie was arguing that George's preferred solution, open communion, would split the movement and destroy ecumenical co-operation; indeed, he accused George of working openly for a "Pan-Protestant Toc H" which would exclude Anglo-Catholics. George felt that the exclusive ecclesiastical positions adopted by some Churches were part of the Christian problem in the twentieth century, and he had hoped that Toc H would be embodying new solutions rather than restating old problems. It was a classic "priestly versus prophetic" struggle.

"I was in London from Monday to Wednesday," George wrote despondently to Petrovitch, "arguing with Anglican ecclesiastics on the necessity of intercommunion among friends in a temperature of 80 degrees (the argument I mean!) . . . I am desperately depressed at the Church in many of its phases just now – and am beaten back in all my endeavours to break the bonds."

Clayton was grieved by the problem.

"Foolish as I am," he wrote to George, "I am too wise to meddle with a thrust in tierce exchanged between two terrible Scots minds, both lambent with the love of God."[3] What Tubby did not know was that, at the time of the controversy, Monie was contemplating becoming a Roman Catholic, while hoping to remain as administrator of Toc H.

When it became clear to George that he did not have support among the other padres, he resigned his post on 11th January, 1926. Clayton referred the matter to the Central Executive of Toc H. They accepted his resignation with "the very greatest regret – a regret which we know will be shared by the members generally." The Executive endorsed the recommendation of the Padres that "it is not expedient that intercommunion services should be arranged in connection with Toc H festivals and conferences", arguing that issues such as intercommunion were matters to be decided not by them but by the Churches concerned. The Executive added that while they respected George's convictions, "they cannot agree to commit the Society to the policy he has advocated, and thereby compel a considerable number of members to choose between their loyalty to Toc H and their loyalty to the Church."[4]

George was deeply hurt by the decision. He had invested a great deal of himself in the movement – in a sense, it was his first real Christian love. As an all-or-nothing man, as a young man in a hurry, he was impatient for change. If the postwar world was to be renewed, the postwar Church would have to lead the way – but who would change the Church? If a progressive movement like Toc H would not meet the issue of intercommunion head on, who would? George knew the despair of every impatient idealist who finds the world stubbornly refusing to bend to his will.

There is a sense in which George MacLeod could only justify his own survival amidst the carnage of world war by becoming an agent of postwar change. Underneath the social gaiety and charm, there was a deadly serious purpose, overlaid by a driving sense of duty – even of guilt. He was not a MacLeod for nothing. He was a surviving MacLeod for something.

The Toc H crisis is revealing, because it shows a great deal of the character and personality of the young MacLeod. He earns high marks for idealism and commitment, low marks for political skills. He had not prepared the groundwork for change in Toc H, but had made a cavalry charge on his own. Already, while some saw him as a prophet focusing single-mindedly on the hard issues, others saw him as a menace with an egotistical capacity for division. His MacLeodian self-confidence certainly encouraged him in the belief that he could do better if he were at the helm, as he had often felt in the Argylls.

George was depressed by the dispute, and by what he perceived to be lack of vision. If Toc H would not pick up the banner of radical change, who would?

Maybe the established Church could be the cradle for the kind of community he yearned for? An invitation came from the congregation of the fashionable St Cuthbert's Church in the West End of Edinburgh to become collegiate minister, in succession to the scholarly and witty preacher, Dr R. H. Fisher. He accepted, and took up his appointment on 23rd February, 1926.

Why did he accept? Tubby Clayton used to say that one of the reasons George left the Toc H job was that his father was pressurizing him to settle down to a "proper" job in the Church. Though nothing like the whole story – George would have continued with Toc H had the intercommunion issue been resolved to his satisfaction – there was a kernel of truth in the remark. Sir John was not displeased when his son left the backwater of Toc H to return to the heartland of the Edinburgh ecclesiastical establishment.

At the age of 30, George was remarkably young to gain such a prestigious appointment, and St Cuthbert's would be the perfect launchpad for an ecclesiastical career. It was impossible not to be noticed there, at a time when the sayings and doings of prominent churchmen still took up many column inches in the newspapers, and it would only be a matter of time before yet another gifted MacLeod would wear the Moderatorial lace.

The Glasgow Herald, edited by his father's friend, Sir Robert Bruce, had no doubt about the significance of the appointment of so young a man to "one of the great congregations in the Church of Scotland.

"What the future has in store for him is not for the writer to say more than this. Mr MacLeod has in exceptional degree the persuasive pulpit gifts of the men of his family, who made the name of MacLeod in past generations a household word in Scotland. But he is essentially of the new generation in religious outlook and sympathy. A student, a soldier of combatant rank, a missionary, a pastor among the poorer denizens in the High Street of Edinburgh, a guide and friend of ex-servicemen in Toc H – Mr MacLeod has had much of the preparation needed for the great work to which he has been called. The Church of Scotland will follow his further career with the keenest interest. Granted health

and strength and the loyal and discerning interest of his parishioners, he must in time become a powerful influence in the religious
life of the capital."[5]

So it was to be. The glamorous war hero packed them in. On
Sunday evenings, people queued for forty-five minutes to be sure
of a seat when MacLeod was preaching – 1800 people crammed
into the auditorium, with some sitting up the pulpit steps. George
would arrive for worship in his open-topped three-seater Citroën
sports car – his silk hat sticking up through the roof – and dash,
frock-coated, down the stairs to the church.

As at St Giles', there was a notable increase in the number of
young ladies attending public worship. Hanging breathlessly on
every word – one does not have to be a disciple of Freud to have
some inkling of the sexual dynamics of a situation in which a
handsome young preacher of impeccable pedigree was uttering
public words of love – they were referred to, not unkindly, as "the
Band of Hope". George became known as "the Rudolph Valentino
of the Edinburgh pulpit". One slightly dotty lady used to lie down
on the road in front of his sports car. Edinburgh's West End has
never been quite the same.

The young preacher rented a house at 8 Charlotte Square, after
a spell in Eglinton Crescent, using a room as his office. He shared
the house with a number of friends, including Nunky Brown
(pioneer of the probation service), Harry Whitley, Dr Milorad
Petrovitch (the Serbian protégé of Lady MacLeod's), and the St
Cuthbert's assistant minister. It was an informal Christian community, welcoming many people for food, discussion and worship
in the chapel room upstairs.

By this time George had a former army batman, William Fallon,
and his wife Dinah, to look after his needs. Fallon, a gruff Irishman
who had won the Military Medal while serving with the Black
Watch in the First World War, was George's handyman, butler
and protector (assisted by his fierce dog, "Jimmy"). A former coal
miner, Fallon was not a man to be trifled with. (When his previous
employer complained that the coffee which he had carried up three
flights of stairs was not hot enough, he poured the coffee down the
stairwell, and threw the cups down after it.) Mrs Fallon did the
cooking: she used to "read" tea leaves and cards for friends and,
fearing George's disapproval, would hide the cards down the side
of the settee when she heard his footsteps.

Thus, in 1926, George MacLeod was setting his mark again on

the Edinburgh Establishment. As one elderly lady put it: "He held the West End in the palm of his hand."

All was not to be plain sailing, however. But with George MacLeod, it never was.

Darling of the Establishment

We are here on earth to serve others . . . but what the others are here for, the Lord only knows.

THE VICAR OF MIRTH,
(A POPULAR GRAMOPHONE RECORD OF THE
1920S)

My preaching is a failure if it can charm but not change.

THOMAS CHALMERS

There are those who claim that George MacLeod's ministry at St Cuthbert's was the real high point in his life: that his preaching at that time was evangelical, dynamic and pithy (whereas later, on this view, it became obsessive, garrulous and repetitive): that his theology was orthodox without being simplistic (whereas later it became suspect): that his sympathies were broad and his interests many (whereas later they became distorted by his intense commitment to pacifism and socialism).

Did St Cuthbert's represent the time before the Fall?

George was certainly never more like his grandfather than while collegiate minister at St Cuthbert's. The crowds attending worship testified to his popularity, and his ability to communicate with all classes was marvelled at. His preaching was rooted in the Bible but it was adapted to the jazz age: little wonder the BBC singled him out as the coming man in Scotland for radio preaching.

When religious broadcasting had started in earnest in 1923, many churchmen regarded it with great suspicion. John Reith, the formidable Scottish Calvinist at the head of the BBC, had invited the Rev. Dick Sheppard, rector of St Martin-in-the-Fields Church, London, to broadcast, and when Sheppard gave what he called his first "cry in the dark to over two hundred thousand people", the response was overwhelming. The more popular religious broadcasting became, the more the ecclesiastical protests rolled in. One outraged cleric protested that if a church service were broadcast, a man might listen to it in a pub – and with his hat on! A resolution was presented to the Church of England Synod, calling for the prohibition of religious broadcasting, which was seen as at best vulgar and at worst blasphemous. Such was the rapport between the preacher and his listeners that a huge listeners-in social was held in the Albert Hall ("The owner of the voice meeting the owners of the ears," said Reith, who was delighted by the success of the broadcasts).

Like Dick Sheppard, George MacLeod had a burning passion to communicate the gospel to ordinary people and he saw radio broadcasting as a God-given opportunity. After all, in one broadcast he could reach more people than John Wesley had preached to in his whole life! The richness of his aristocratic voice, his phrasing and timing, his ability to create vivid word pictures and his gift of expressing orthodox doctrines in economic contemporary language made him a natural communicator on radio. "What do you consider the ideal length of time for a sermon?" he was once asked. "Three minutes if it's a bad one," he replied.

As the Scottish Dick Sheppard, he was regarded by some ministers as a showman – which he undoubtedly was. He enjoyed being centre stage and he had the gifts to command attention: but those who dismissed George as merely a showman did not know their man. Like his grandfather before him – he had the great Norman's panache as well as his orthodoxy, his humour as well as his seriousness – the celebrated young public preacher had private melancholic misgivings about his own gifts, and the adulation he received made him feel both exuberant and guilty. Some of his more modest critics had much to be modest about, and their jealousy increased when they had to change the times of their evening services because their congregations wanted to hear MacLeod on the radio!

Ronald Selby Wright, another future Moderator who came under his spell, remembers him at that time as "inspiring, charismatic, respected and liked. He came like a great whirlwind into Edinburgh and everybody greatly admired him – if he'd stayed on, he would have swept Edinburgh off its feet. Everywhere he went he carried this great fire of enthusiasm with him, which made it so much easier to 'believe'". Asked on one occasion how he would help a man who wanted to believe in God but could not, he replied, "I would tell him to 'make-believe' in Him – act always as if God were alive. He would, by experience, come to know Him."

Selby Wright never forgot his first encounter with George MacLeod.

"He had just come to St Cuthbert's, which was filled to capacity each time he preached, and continued to be so until he went to Govan some years later. My brother and I decided we would go to hear him preach one Sunday in the morning at St Cuthbert's, and he preached on the text 'If I had not come, you would not have had sin'. We were both so thrilled with the sermon that we decided we would both go and hear him again that evening when he happened to be preaching in Inverleith. Much to our surprise, and I must admit, our pleasure, we heard him preach again from the same text. It so happened that I arranged to have tea with him and meet him personally for the first time that coming week. He had a beautiful double flat in Eglinton Crescent, and he was looked after by Mr Fallon and his wife. Fallon, to those who didn't know him well, was at first rather a forbidding figure, and he ushered me into the study since his master had not yet appeared. When the master did appear he looked at me and said, 'Ah, if you had not come I would not have had sin, because nobody would have known that I had preached the same sermon twice on the same Sunday!' As I say, we had never really met before and yet he had noticed in the two packed churches individual people in them. I don't need to say any more about George MacLeod and the great influence he was and has been on so many young people in Scotland."[1]

Much encouraged by George, Selby Wright began the St Giles Boys' Club in 1927. It later became the Canongate Boys' Club, and was the foundation of a long and memorable ministry in the Canongate. People such as Nunky Brown, Ronald Selby Wright, George MacLeod and Harry Whitley acted as unpaid probation officers for boys who were in trouble with the police, and they saved many lads from further difficulty at critical times in their lives. And not a few men were led into the ministry as a result of such work.

Roy Sanderson had heard George preach at Oriel College, Oxford, in 1927 – "I recall how disappointed I was that he proved to be rather nervous on the occasion, and not so sparkling as I had hoped" – and when he got in touch with the St Cuthbert's minister at the end of term, George drove him in the famous touring Citroën to visit a boys' club.

"As we approached the club, George suddenly jammed on his brakes – traffic was not so dense in those days – and stopped two boys crossing the road. 'Why are you not at the club?' he asked them: and they hung their heads in silence. 'What have you got there?' he then said, and immediately they held up jam jars with tiddlers in them and began to tell George where they had caught them, and so on. As we drove away, George turned to me and said, 'You see the mistake I made? I first rammed my interest down their throats and they had nothing to say: but when I asked them about something they were interested in they were ready to talk.' I have always remembered that, and have found it a bit of most useful advice."

The troubled awareness of "two nations" was never far from George's consciousness. The General Strike in 1926, which the owners had seen as a triumph, but which had increased the bitter polarization of classes in the country, worried him deeply. Walking along Princes Street at the time, he had to run with the frightened crowd as mounted police made a charge. His army experiences had given him a sympathy for the plight of ordinary working men who were struggling to make a decent living for their families, and his knowledge of the circumstances of the poor youngsters of Edinburgh fired him with a desire to see a more equitable society. Communist groups thronged the Mound, and the St Cuthbert's minister enjoyed hearing the soapbox orators outline their vision of the new world. He liked to quote one exchange:

"When the great revolution comes, I shall be there to lead you," roared one diminutive speaker.

"You? Ye havenae the strength to lead a wicked life," came the rejoinder which convulsed the crowd.

The part of the work at St Cuthbert's which he enjoyed above all else was the parish mission work in Freer Street, situated in the densely populated tenement area of Fountainbridge.

The Freer Street mission was one of the main parts of St Cuthbert's outreach towards the poor. A wide range of activities was organized for all ages. In addition to the collegiate ministers, St Cuthbert's had an assistant minister, a student assistant, an honorary minister and a parish deaconess. Set in a cul-de-sac with a pub at one corner and a pawn shop at the other, the mission attracted large numbers of poor people, many of whom couldn't afford to go to the cinema. George poured his energies into the mission. He started a men's club, and got in dressmakers to help the women. He organized concerts, and liked nothing better than to sit at the piano and sing songs like "a lum hat wantin' a croon". His extrovert nature thrived on banter with Edinburgh's poor and in participating in the kind of working class repartee which he had enjoyed in the trenches. He was greatly loved by the mission people, who regarded him as a "real toff". One young tenement baby was baptized George MacLeod in honour of the St Cuthbert's minister!

More than a hundred volunteers from the congregation were involved in the mission, but there was still a gap between Freer Street and the West End. St Cuthbert's was "no' for the likes o' us, Mr MacLeod". He started a youth group called The Knights of St Cuthbert's – which the young people disconcertingly called the Night Club – and encouraged the members to attend worship at St Cuthbert's. To mark their first anniversary, a banner was woven, and it was agreed to dedicate it at the Armistice Day celebration in the church, provided the boys agreed to meet George outside the west door of the church twenty minutes before the service. As they saw the evening congregation pour in and realized they were soon to march up the aisle together behind the flag, they sneaked away into the darkness, one by one. The wildest boy of the lot, seeing George's concern, plucked his sleeve and announced, "Dinna lose hairt, Mr MacLeod. If they a' desert ye, I'll stand by ye: Ah'll come and carry the bloody banner on my ain!"

George became more and more involved with Toc H again, recognizing the continuing merit of its work and concerns. As honorary chaplain of the Edinburgh branch, he gave a lot of time to the movement. He did not allow the experience over intercommunion to sour him, and he retained the respect and affection of most of the senior people. At meetings in the Outlook Tower and Candlemaker Row, George helped to make Toc H a centre of social life among young people in Edinburgh. It was also a great centre of social work: eight out of the first 12 boys' clubs in Edinburgh were started by members of Toc H.

The young minister was also concerned with what the now flourishing Oxford Group, started by the American pastor, Frank Buchman, called the "up and outs". He started a young men's group called the Venture Club – based on the schoolboy howler, "a certain man drew a bow at a venture, but he missed the venture and hit Ahab" – which met in the common room at 8 Charlotte Square. It provided a mixture of discussion, worship in the house chapel, work for the community, and outdoor activities.

"Will you risk it with us?" George wrote in a pamphlet distributed to the young men in the parish. "We can promise you one thing: a good deal of laughter before it is half gone through. And there are other things we are bound to promise you, if indeed this Venture would succeed – just a few tears. For that is the odd way this world is made." The Venture Club attracted the young professionals in the congregation, and provided a few recruits for the ministry.

Eight Charlotte Square was a haven for waifs and strays and professional men and students. Roy Sanderson often went round for cocoa and biscuits after a hard night's work at the boys' club.

"The household gathered together for this lighthearted supper-meal and some hilarious times we had with George in the centre playing the fool," he recalled. "He was in that sort of relaxed mood: and then, when the time came, we all went upstairs to the chapel and had family prayers – a perfectly natural transition and yet one which greatly impressed someone unsophisticated like myself. George has always had a genius for fusing quite naturally the secular and the sacred: and his gift of prayer has been quite outstanding, both in its phraseology and its aptness. I remember much later, when I was in Glasgow, George writing me about my own personal devotional discipline, about which I had been consulting him, and saying, 'Prayer is really good fun, can become good fun, and the future of our Church is going to be funny until we can write that sentence.'"

Bill Rogan, who would later become minister of Paisley Abbey, remembered the atmosphere at 8 Charlotte Square, where he lived while assistant minister at St Cuthbert's. The discussions were vigorous – no mention of pacifism at that time, though – and the young lawyers, teachers and accountants who participated were also deeply affected by the MacLeodian preaching style on Sundays.

"His preaching was very distinctive," Bill Rogan recalled. "He had a tremendous command of language, and had a great ability to get across to young people. He could express sublime thought and theological argument in such distinctive terms that you had to sit up and take notice. His preaching was very direct."

Another young man impressed by George's preaching at St

Cuthbert's was a student called George Reid, another future Moderator of the General Assembly of the Church of Scotland.

"The first time I clapped eyes on him was at a Scottish Schoolboys camp where I was an officer. He addressed us briefly and was vociferously applauded by some four hundred schoolboys. Not a word he said do I remember, but I retain a vivid memory of the impression he then made on me – the most vivid and virile personality I had ever seen encircled by a dog collar, addressing us with the awesome authority of an English public school accent."

It was this magnetism which drew crowds to St Cuthbert's. Mrs Annis Frackleton, who was deeply involved in the life of the congregation and of Freer Street mission, said of George's preaching: "One came away heading for the mission field every Sunday night. He was formidable, riveting. There was no microphone in the church in those days, but the congregation hung upon every word, and didn't mind how long he preached. And what a great breaker of hearts he was in those days – very handsome.

"His preference was for the underprivileged. When my grandmother died, his first thought was to hold a service for the maids."

Part of George's appeal was his deep concern for individuals. Nan MacKenzie, a twelve year old girl who had been ill and was in a plaster jacket, had carefully polished apples and put them in a basket for the church. George observed her struggle, and preached on the trouble she had gone to. This personal affirmation was profoundly important to her, and she later worked for many years as George's secretary at the Iona Community office.

George MacLeod was at ease with all sections of the St Cuthbert's congregation, which included many from the upper echelons of Edinburgh's civic, business and professional life. On one occasion, he had to visit the Lord Lyon, King at Arms, who was in hospital. The only problem was that the patient was very deaf. The young minister determined that the best thing he could do was to bawl the Lord's Prayer into his ear. When he had done so – the patient nodding away all the time – the Lord Lyon roared with laughter as he took George's sleeve and said, "My, George, your jokes are as good as ever!" How George delighted to tell that story against himself!

George started popular "People's Services", and instituted a Christmas Eve service, one of the first of its kind in a Presbyterian Scotland which tended to regard such things as Popish. (Aberdeen had led the field, holding the first in Scotland nearly forty years previously.) The Anglican influence of Winchester and Oxford had left George with a liking for such things, as well as an appreciation of such "Catholic" practices as observance of the Christian Year. He also organized a complete redecoration of the church and the halls. The energetic man-in-a-hurry was something of a whirlwind: and also something of a pain in the neck to his senior colleague, who was none other than his former parish minister, the Rev. Dr Norman Maclean.

Dr Maclean was a Highland mystic who was greatly interested in the afterlife. Before going to St Cuthbert's he had been Dr Donald MacLeod's successor at Park Church. Dr Maclean remembered vividly a service in 1913, and the young man who sat in the pew next to Mr John M. MacLeod, who had asked that his father's hymn, "Courage, Brother" might be sung.

"I suddenly realized the reason: that his grandson might sing it. But it was the rapt look in the eyes of this lad that so affected me that I felt, as the sermon went on, that I was preaching to that one worshipper alone. I remember the text of that sermon: 'I will pour out my spirit upon all flesh, and your young men shall see visions and your old men shall dream dreams' . . . I never heard a word regarding that sermon, but the face of young George MacLeod was a mirror reflecting every shade of thought."

The next day, accompanied by Ellen, young George had gone to see Dr Maclean and asked him questions about how well the churches were attended in the industrial areas of the city. The Park Church minister told him that attendances were poor, and that the Church badly needed a new vision.

"My visitors were shy and soon departed," noted Dr Maclean. "But thereafter I never lost sight of George MacLeod."[2]

There were times at St Cuthbert's, to which he had gone in 1915, when Dr Maclean wished he could have lost sight of George MacLeod. The heartiness, energy, exuberance and popularity of the young man sometimes grated on his senior colleague. George attended Norman's evening services, but the senior man did not return the compliment. This led to one amusing consequence. One evening, George took as his text, "The veil of the temple was rent", dwelling on its literal disaster. The next Sunday evening Norman, oblivious, took the same text and opened with the shattering sentence, "Only someone of very limited intelligence would imagine the veil was really rent."

Dr Maclean was a stiffer, more formal figure than his relaxed colleague – it would be difficult to imagine Norman singing "A lum hat wantin' a croon" at the Freer Street Mission – and he did not have the same appeal for young people. Hence the natural jealousy. Not only that, the reformist, activist, all-or-nothing younger man lacked tact: and as adjutant he always felt he would have done better as commanding officer. It is little wonder that the senior man sometimes bridled: yet he always admired George's gifts and vision, and whenever there was any crisis in the Maclean household, it was George MacLeod who was sent for.

"Norman Maclean is jealous of me nursing the heart of the congregation while he has been away," George wrote to Harry Whitley. "This is sin, and is exceeded by a quite definite sin of pride on my part that St Cuthbert's responds to my nursing!"

In the same letter, he told Harry, who was now on the St Cuthbert's staff, that he should be himself.

"If you become diffident, dutiful, obsequious and sane, I shall undoubtedly sack you. This means that if you are to stay on, in the nature of the case, you must occasionally expect me to kick you."

Maclean and MacLeod each had their own beadle. Each beadle was loyal to his own man, and would lead him in procession at the beginning of the service. The beadle was a powerful figure in the old Scottish Presbyterian system. His role was much more than that of verger or caretaker or church officer: he was the minister's own "man" who would take care of him, robe him, protect him and lead him in to worship.

Dr Maclean's beadle, Robertson, had been butler to the Duke of Argyll, and was a well known character. When asked by George why sermons had become shorter, Robertson, who had a perpetual drip at the end of his nose, replied: "Pairfectly simple. In the real old days the meenister aye stairted by pitting the hale congregation into hell – and it took him at least another twenty minutes to get them oot again: you young'ns spoil it a' by stairtin' in the middle." Robing an extremely rotund dean of an English cathedral who came to preach, Robertson gave him the silk rope that was to encircle him and said with deference, "D'ye mind haudin' on to this wee bit ropie and I'll be roun' ye and back in a minute or twa". George, in narrating these stories, liked to add that the ecumenical movement was not noticeably advanced by that sally.

The tremendous demands on George's time and energy took their toll. There were times when he simply had to withdraw. An aunt of his, Miss Polly, a daughter of Norman, used to take him in. She would put him to bed, confiscate his clothes, and refuse to let him up until such times as she deemed he was ready. The tiredness brought with it melancholy feelings in a man who was impatient to reform the Church, if not the world.

Miss Polly was rewarded by trips in the Citroën. It often broke down, and she would be deposited at someone's house while her handless nephew phoned for a mechanic. (George's relationship with the combustion engine was ever a curious one. Like his father, he would refer to the engine as "the boiler thing up front". He once had the workings of a car explained to him, but as he didn't anticipate understanding a word, he paid no attention. On a later occasion, his car radiator sprang a leak. He flagged down a car. He was told that if he put an egg in the radiator – he had groceries with him – it would find the leak and seal it. Unfortunately, he failed to let the water cool before he broke the egg, resulting in a radiator filled with bits of poached egg. Using lateral thinking, he projected the notion further, pouring in oatmeal. By the time the car was towed into a garage, it required the ministrations of a cleaner as much as a mechanic.)

Although George was making a name for himself in Scotland, much of his father's ambition was focused on Norman. He arranged for his elder son to be made one of the Company of Archers, the monarch's bodyguard in Scotland, and for Isa to be presented at court (much to the chagrin of Ellen who, as a mere daughter, did not rank as highly as the wife of a favourite son in the MacLeod hierarchy). The attractive and gifted Norman went into his father's firm, though he never felt as fulfilled in his work as a Chartered Accountant as he did in his amateur dramatic ventures.

Because he had tuberculosis, Norman spent six months every year in Italy or in a sanatorium in Switzerland. The rest of the year, he and Isa lived in a big house outside Glasgow.

If the second MacLeod son was not transforming the Church, it was certainly changing by itself. On 26th May, 1929, the Moderator of the General Assembly of the Church of Scotland and his counterpart from the United Free Church greeted each other, and led a long procession of the two assemblies, numbering over 2,000 ministers and elders, to be welcomed at the west door of St Giles' Cathedral by its minister, the Rev. Charles Warr. As the packed crowds sang psalms, no one had reason to feel prouder than Sir

Darling of the Establishment

John MacLeod, whose father had been so grieved by the Disruption of 1843, and had longed for a reunion of Presbyterianism in Scotland. Sir John was one of the architects of the reunion, having helped with the necessary earlier legislation in the House of Commons. One of his closest colleagues and admirers was the Rev. Dr John White, who was to play a significant part in George's subsequent career.

The reunion of the two main strands of Presbyterianism into the one national Church of Scotland – albeit with a much more tenuous relationship with the State – may have come about partly through the churches' recognition of a decline in their status, but it was a genuine cause for rejoicing. Nevertheless, it was achieved at a cost. The churches' energies had been diverted from the urgent task of post-war reconstruction, and their social influence had been greatly diminished in the process.

Underneath the success of lively, well-attended churches like St Cuthbert's, more corrosive influences were undermining the Church's foundations. When the International Missionary Council met at Jerusalem in 1928, its first volume of reports observed bleakly: "No student of the deeper problems of life can fail to see that the greatest rival of Christianity in the world today is not Mohammedanism or Buddhism or Hinduism or Confucianism, but a world-wide secular way of life and interpretation of the nature of things."

It was against this secularism – a humanistic view of life which saw no need to bring in notions of God to explain the world – that the Church had to wage battle: the history of the Church in Europe in the twentieth century is the story of a largely unsuccessful attempt to stem a tide which would reach its full flood in the 1960s.

Nineteen twenty-nine was a crucial year in many ways. A minority Labour government came to power under the leadership of Ramsay MacDonald: and the crash in Wall Street, which had stockbrokers jumping from their windows, brought severe recession to Britain. The Labour government's response was to cut unemployment benefits. The brave new world was no more.

It would be expected that a man of George MacLeod's gifts would fairly soon be offered a senior charge of his own. The name of Edinburgh's rising star was at the head of any list when a prominent church became vacant. In May 1929 he received an intriguing request from the vacancy committee of Govan Parish Church in Glasgow: would he consider becoming their minister? He took the approach seriously, pacing round Charlotte Square with friends, but came to the conclusion that he still had work to do at St Cuthbert's. ("You will regret it whichever you do," John White told him. "Try to work out which you will regret longest.")

"Had I gone to Govan," he wrote to Harry Whitley, "deep down would have been the feeling that we had relegated St Cuthbert's and its ilk as for ever impossible of conversion. Could we do this? Is it only slums that can be got going? Must all the West End and middle class be handed over to fashionable preachers and superficial Christianity for ever . . . I think we have a little temptation to relegate the well-to-do as hopeless and concentrate our vision on the poor, perhaps because we can 'put it across to the poor' and so get satisfaction at seeing it work. The prime difficulty is to be as much a 'monk' in Charlotte Square as in the more dramatic background of Govan Cross."

George suggested that his close friend, the Rev. Bruce Nicol from St Margaret's, Dumbiedykes, would be the ideal man for the job. Govan took his advice, and Mr Nicol was duly inducted on 4th September, 1929. George MacLeod's friends and admirers in Edinburgh breathed a sigh of relief.

Within six months, Bruce Nicol was dead, of tuberculosis. Govan came back for George MacLeod. His answer this time was in the affirmative – provided certain conditions were met.

Thus did the young prince of Scotland's preachers set out westwards on a journey that was to change his life, and the lives of many people ever since. In the process, the darling of the establishment was to become the unholy disturber of the Kirk's peace.

Was George MacLeod's four year ministry at St Cuthbert's the high point of his career? Exactly that point was put to him in later years by Mrs Jean Small, the wife of one of George's distinguished successors at St Cuthbert's, the Very Rev. Dr R. Leonard Small.

"Of course," replied MacLeod laconically, "I wasn't preaching the gospel then."

PART THREE

*

FROM BREAKDOWN
TO BREAKTHROUGH

7

The Pope of Govan

The gates of hell will not overwhelm the Church; it has opened up its own gates to hell too often. It zealously inveighs against the harm done to Joseph and the sheep, but it has made its arrangements with the upper classes and serves as their spiritual defender. It bristles at see-through blouses, but not at slums in which half-naked children starve, and not, above all, at the conditions that keep three quarters of mankind in misery.

ERNST BLOCH

A man becomes a theologian by living, by dying and by being damned, not by understanding, reading and speculating.

MARTIN LUTHER

It was in grimy Govan that the roof of the old privileged superstructure finally caved in on the confident young preacher. His life was never to be the same again.

George MacLeod went into Govan like a whirlwind. But why did he go at all?

The answer is to be found in history, in the desire to experiment, and in guilt.

The historical connections, as with so much in George MacLeod's life, went back to that manse of Fuinary. The Rev. John MacLeod of Fuinary's son, also called John, was called to be minister of Govan Parish Church in 1875. His was an outstanding ministry, and had it not been for his premature death in 1898 at the age of 58, yet another MacLeod would undoubtedly have been decked out in Moderatorial lace.

Dr John MacLeod, made a Doctor of Divinity by Glasgow

University, was a formidable and somewhat intimidating man. Of similar stature to his father – a journalist told how a curious crowd followed the "High Priest of Morvern" and his two sons around Glasgow, amazed by the height and distinguished appearance of the three men – John was described as "like a sea king, with the drooping moustaches of a Scandinavian chieftain".

It was no ordinary Presbyterian minister who went to Govan in 1875. A student at Glasgow University at the age of 13, John served 12 years as minister of Duns, in Berwickshire. These were the days when the Auld Kirk was regrouping, and reforming its life in response to the traumatic Disruption, and there was considerable debate about what exactly the established Church stood for. In England, the ideas of the Oxford Movement had nourished the Anglo-Catholic wing of the Church of England, and the same ideas had found ready acceptance among a minority of clergy north of the border. The advocates of what became known as the Scoto-Catholic Movement stressed priestliness, the mystery of holiness of worship, the centrality of holy communion, the observance of the Christian year, and the importance of doctrinal teaching.

John MacLeod became an enthusiastic proponent of these Catholic ideas. John, unusually, also became a member of the Catholic Apostolic Church, without surrendering his Kirk membership. Led by the mystic Edward Irving and founded in 1832, the Catholic Apostolic Church represented a heady mixture of Catholic ritual and Pentecostal manifestations such as speaking in tongues.

The Church of St Constantine, otherwise Govan Parish Church, was one of the most historic places of worship in Scotland. There had been Christian worship on its site since the days of its Celtic patron saint in the sixth century, and druidic worship before that.

Situated on the south bank of the river Clyde, Govan in its early days had been more important than the fledgling village of Glasgow. Govan parish had long-standing links with the University of Glasgow, which was within its bounds; its ministers held the office of Principal of the University until the eighteenth century. When John MacLeod went to be its minister, Govan parish encompassed more than two hundred thousand people. It had several daughter churches, and the parish minister was responsible for recruiting clergy and supervising the whole work of the parish.

Dr MacLeod set about his task with prodigious energy. An outstanding preacher – for preparation he would lock himself in a darkened room and emerge with a few pencilled jottings – he preached for an hour every Sunday morning and evening. His sermons were uncompromisingly doctrinal. He increased the number of communions, introduced observance of the Christian Year, visited assiduously, and built more churches. He decided that the Govan Parish Church building was inadequate, arranged for it to be transported stone by stone to a site within the parish, and had a new one built to his specification. The handsome stone building – opened in 1888 – was like a Cathedral, with long nave, side chapel and chancel with central communion table.

In his 23-year ministry at Govan, John MacLeod stamped his presence on the area, earning himself the popular epithet of "Pope John of Govan". When he died, three years after the birth of George MacLeod, *The Glasgow Herald* said that "though sometimes a little brusque in manner, he was kind and affectionate at heart".

This was the daunting historical legacy inherited by George MacLeod. Yet there had been many changes since the days of Pope John. The union of the churches in 1929 had led to a redrawing of parish boundaries. The area encompassed by Govan Old Parish Church, as it was now called, was reduced to a fifth of its previous size and took in some 10,000 souls – a far cry from the near quarter of a million for which Pope John had overall responsibility before God. The Govan community had grown prosperous on the development of the shipbuilding industry, but the recession of the late 1920s had led to many men being laid off.

Govan had always been a proud community. Many Highlanders had gone to live and work there after the Clearances, and Govan had a family sense which Glasgow itself lacked. Although now officially within the city boundaries, old Govanites did not see themselves as Glaswegians. Govan also had an aristocratic work force. Clyde-built ships were regarded as the best in the world. The recession and consequent poverty and wastage of skill was demoralizing for the independent-minded Govan community.

Govan Parish Church had also suffered decline, along with the Kirk in general. Its minister had declared in 1920, "The work of Reconstruction may be slow but it is sure, and we believe the outlook for 1920 is distinctly promising. The new epoch has begun. The new world is coming. Human life will never again be the same as it was before the Great War. This is God's world, and we have faith in God's overruling Providence – 'God's in His heaven – All's right with the world!'"

The bitter disillusionment which followed was reflected in the life of the Church in Govan which, like the Kirk elsewhere at the time, to a large degree turned in on itself while trying to come to terms with the reality of declining influence in a baffling and changing world. The successful moves towards Presbyterian reunion had masked, in Govan as elsewhere, a retreat by the Church from the centre of public life and influence, defiant rhetoric notwithstanding. God may have been in his heaven, but He appeared to have lost control of His world. By 1929, when the parish minister left, broken in health, there was something of an air of defeatism around. The church building itself was grimy and grey, and obviously needed quite a bit of attention.

At the beginning of the century, Lady Pearce, widow of a wealthy Govan shipbuilder, had gifted to the people of Govan a new community centre. As a mark of her admiration for John MacLeod, she had placed the Pearce Institute under the management of Govan Parish Church. Situated very close to the church building, it was used both as the centre of church activities and as a resource for the wider community. This unique partnership had a great appeal for George MacLeod: it was like having the Freer Street Mission in the grounds of St Cuthbert's. Here was the chance to make a bold experiment in the life of the Church.

When Govan came, for the second time, George spelt out his conditions in what must be one of the most uncompromising letters ever written to a church vacancy committee. In it, the St Cuthbert's minister said that he believed it was imperative to return to the notion of a territorial ministry. He was prepared to be minister for those who were resident in the parish and to those outside the bounds who were active members, but he was not prepared to minister to those who lived outside the parish and who were not involved in the life of Govan Church; they should be encouraged to attend their local parish church. He would see those who were already members as his co-workers in reaching out to the many people in the parish who had no church connection.

Despite the reduction in the parish area, he wanted to keep the same number of staff and to try to have a more permanent staff. He also proposed not to live in the manse, which was outwith the parish area, but to live with his staff in the top flat of the Pearce Institute, "the better to visualize our real problem and to centralize organization in such a way as to reduce it to a minimum."

George told the vacancy committee he had studied the deed of constitution of the Pearce Institute, in which Lady Pearce had stated that the work of the Institute should be carried on along with and as part of the work of Govan Parish Church, and he proposed to make the P. I. his base of operation for parish work.

"Stated in a sentence," he concluded, "if your present desire is for a minister to the 3000 souls at present on your roll more or less regardless of parish areas and parish responsibilities, then I believe you would be better served by another. If, however, you are prepared to embark on a venture along the above lines which (it is useless to deny) will mean a certain measure of reorganization and new attitudes to the work of Govan Parish in general, I shall feel bound seriously to consider the call which you purpose to make and to give you answer in the shortest possible time."

George told the St Cuthbert's people that Govan Church was prepared to return to the territorial principle and to deal with an area of about a mile long and half a mile broad round about the church, and "for working there they had to offer me one of the most beautiful churches in Glasgow, a large Institute, what corresponds to a parish house in the Institute itself, and a stipend sufficient for securing an adequate staff. They offered, in other words, perhaps the only area in Scotland where there is the problem and the means of dealing with it in one and the same place. Faced (as the Church admits itself to be) with a grave problem in its industrial areas, here was the chance of an experiment offered to one who has constantly referred to the need for such an experiment. It is that call which I could not see my way to refuse, but I cannot think of any other call throughout the length and breadth of the Scottish Church at the present time that would have prevailed on me for a moment.

"Whether the experiment will come off is, of course, another matter, but it should surely be given to the Church to learn something from either its success or its failure."

It is interesting that George MacLeod, at the age of 35, was now fully addressing the question about the Church in industrial areas, which he had first asked Norman Maclean at Park Church in 1913, at the end of his Winchester schooling. And he was addressing it not just with his words, but with his life.

Thus the history and the experiment. What about the guilt? When Govan had first approached George, the same historical and experimental reasons were there – but George had pushed Bruce Nicol into the front line. The platoon commander was a casualty within six months. Aaron was dead. Now it was the turn of captain

Moses himself, bearing the marks of survivor's guilt, to go up the line. Duty, vision, conviction and guilt constituted a formidable driving force. Had the luckless Bruce Nicol not succumbed to tuberculosis, would there have been an island rebuilding and an Iona Community?

St Cuthbert's tried desperately to keep their popular minister. They offered him an increase in stipend, but his mind was made up. The voting: For Rev. G. F. MacLeod, 326, Against, 7. He was inducted on 8th October, 1930, at a packed, all-ticket occasion, with lots of St Cuthbert's people there in support. Many of them must have wondered if he was making the right career move. His mother certainly did: George wrote to her reassuringly that it was still possible for him to reach the Moderator's chair by way of Govan.

He immediately took up residence in the Pearce Institute – a controversial step which some members of the congregation did not like, preferring their minister to live at a better address. He continued to be looked after by Mr and Mrs Fallon. (When asked if he would go to Govan, Fallon replied gruffly that he would go to hell with Mr MacLeod.)

Right from the start there were surprises, as George was to recall later.

"I certainly suffered a personal depression when I found it proper to go to Govan. Edinburgh had not proved distant or reserved in personal relations and I believed I had got its wave length. But the two nations had haunted me. I felt I must concentrate on that other nation that had beckoned me all through. My personal depression was that the wave length was not what I had envisaged in the artisan west. The wave length I expected was "wild Clydeside", political and cultural. In the affairs of the Church I expected a smaller but deeper witness than in the prosperous east. The Church shook me. There were three thousand on the communion roll – of which only three hundred were men. Moreover, in a congregation with more frequent opportunities for the Sacrament than anywhere in Scotland, only 25 per cent of the people had partaken in the previous two years – almost the lowest figure in the land.

"I was wrong about morals too. Clydeside would not countenance a general looseness that had characterized Edinburgh's prosperity. Noel Coward's *Private Lives* – in which everyone goes off with everyone else's wife – was put on one Monday for a week at the local cinema. They had to take it off by Wednesday. Govan would not countenance such rotten stuff. Even at New Year, there were twelve cases of drunkenness at the Police Court. (Twenty years previously it had stood at one hundred.) As for brotherhood: there is more practical Christianity on the common tenement stair than in eight long terraces in Kelvingrove. Someone always carried up the kindling sticks for the lonely widow. The child of the jailed was everyone's child till the man came out again. The down and out was up and in provided only he was honest. The cripple lad was carried pick-a-back to the boys' club along five long streets; and the rota never forgot its order for this chore."[1]

George's personal depression was part of a wider and more corrosive Depression which was afflicting the country. The giant cranes of the shipyards stood silent, and idle men exchanged gossip and smoked Woodbine at Govan's street corners. National unemployment among men was running at 21 per cent (nearly three million men out of work), but in Govan, nearly two thirds of the men were idle. Sixty years previously, Norman MacLeod of the Barony had looked out every morning from his upper window, over to the Clyde, and the sight and sounds had inspired his early morning devotions.

"People talk of early morning in the country with bleating sheep, singing larks and purling brooks," he wrote. "I prefer that roar which greets my ears when a thousand hammers, thundering on boilers of steam vessels which are to bridge the Atlantic or Pacific, usher in a new day – the type of a new era. I feel men are awake with me, doing their work, and that the world is rushing on to fulfil its mighty destinies, and that I must do my work, and fulfil my grand and glorious end."

This Victorian optimism, based on Britain's pre-eminence as the workshop of the world, had collapsed long since. It was an optimism with which Norman's grandson had grown up, and the spirituality which went with it was one which reflected a secure and ordered universe. But what happened when the roar of a thousand hammers was silenced, when no one wanted Clyde-built vessels to bridge the Atlantic or Pacific, when every order book was empty? What of spirituality then? And what of the Church? These were questions which the Church in the twentieth century had failed to address adequately. Faced with the unemployment, poverty and despair of Govan in the thirties, George MacLeod could not turn to the Church at large for help, though the Kirk did at least recognize there was a problem.

"The indignity, misery and despair which unemployment inflicts upon many, the undernourishment of children, the baulking of youthful aspiration, constitute a sheer tragedy," reported the Church and Nation Committee of the united Church of Scotland. "The lowered prestige of our social institutions and the lessened stability of our civilization are a real menace to further progress. The irrationality of world-wide poverty in the midst of plenty raises acute doubts of the ways of God with man. This, therefore, is not only an economic but a moral and religious question of the first importance."

The Committee did find some scapegoats, though. Calling for the Government to stop paying unemployment relief to men not born in the UK or having less than three years' residence, and asking Scottish employers to give preference to Scottish workers, they again attacked the Irish Roman Catholics living in Scotland.

"There is good reason for alarm concerning the type of people coming to us from the Roman Catholic parts of Ireland. It would seem as if Scotland is being used as a dumping ground for the kind of Irish emigrant who would not be accepted in the United States."

Calling for a defence of the Protestant inheritance of Scotland, the Church and Nation Committee went on:

"It is felt that a serious menace has arisen to the integrity of our Protestant tradition, and that too many of our people, employers of labour, legislators, educationalists and journalists, have allowed tolerance to pass into indifference . . . The time has come for a united Church to recognize that by its unique position in the Presbyterian world it has a large share of leadership thrust upon it, and that no other system of Christian Church government than ours has proved so solidly resistant to Roman Catholic attack in the past."

Govan's new minister found that he had to rewrite all his prayers. The St Cuthbert's mode of address to the deity was inappropriate and inadequate. He was back in a war zone.

Face to face with the new situation, George did what he knew how to do best – work. Given the Church of Scotland's floundering, the only models within his own personal history were those of Norman MacLeod's ministry with the Glasgow poor, and an attempt at mission within the Church of England. The great Norman had run services for the poor and organized refreshment rooms, recreational facilities, reading rooms and social activities. The Pearce Institute provided cheap food, recreational and reading facilities, and a meeting place for the unemployed during the day. It was an ideal base for the new minister's work.

One of George's first tasks was to reclaim the church's sovereignty over the P. I. This was fraught with difficulty, as local groups had moved into the vacuum created by the church's negligence. George had done his homework in terms of Lady Pearce's intentions, and he handled the political difficulties with skill and cunning. As wise as a serpent and apparently as innocent as a dove, he played off two rival ward factions, dominated by Communists, against each other and became the indispensible power broker. Having established his authority, he proceeded to reorganize some of the activities in the Institute and brought them much more clearly under church management (including restricting the playing of cards – a fine piece of irony from the demon *vingt-et-un* player of the Western Front).

George quickly made his presence felt in the church as well. Harry Whitley was his student assistant – Govan Old Parish Church had two full-time assistants and a deaconess as well as a student. ("I can take one or two heresies a Sunday," he told Harry after one sermon, "but not seven.") He announced that only those living within the bounds of the parish or who were active members would be entitled to the services of the Govan Old clergy, and he took the consequent criticism in his stride. He prepared plans for a complete renovation of the gloomy church, and set out to raise £1000 to pay for it.

The 1930s saw a great interest in exploring the countryside, and George started an early morning service for hikers and bikers. Like his grandfather before him, he argued against his critics – who complained about the bicycles piled up against the wall of the church – that the Sabbath should be used creatively and that young people should be encouraged to get out and about. The numbers attending worship increased, and new communion vessels had to be purchased. The new minister and his kirk session went through the church roll, removing, after a visit and a warning, the names of those who had not attended for some time. Govan services were broadcast every month to Scotland and sometimes to the Empire, and many came out of curiosity to hear him in the flesh.

The pace increased. George announced a door to door visitation of the whole parish. He increased the number of elders, and visited the church organizations. If he didn't like what he saw, he said so. Three Boys' Brigade officers resigned, as did the Girls' Club leader. It began to dawn on people that a new minister was in town, and some of them did not like it. Nor did some of his parishioners care for his close relationship with the local Roman Catholic priest either. He shared a platform with Father Devine as often as possible, and the two clergymen went swimming together. George organized an ecumenical service in which Episcopal and Roman Catholic clergy processed through the Govan church nave in their white cassocks. The scripture reading, which contained the words from the book of Revelation, "Who are these arrayed in white?" caused some amusement.

The new man's pastoral concern earned him respect in a community which did not give respect easily. One poor family remembered him less because of his sermons than because of his life.

"He was a friend of ours. He knew us and our children well. There was that time when the baby died and we didn't know what to do or where to turn. He came up to the house and he didn't say a great deal, but he did a lot. In his own arms he carried the wee white coffin across the street to the Pearce Institute to the chapel, where family prayers were said, and it remained there till the funeral. In a short time he came back to our house with fish suppers – great big ones that we all shared and, when we'd finished them, he put the children to bed. You can't forget a man like that, even although he's a minister."[2]

Early one morning, word was sent to George that a widow had tried to commit suicide. She had two children, and she kept a dairy. When he got to the room behind the shop where she lived, he found her sitting there gloomy and dejected, so he made some tea. As they talked a lorry drew up at the door of the shop, and soon there was the noise of crates of bottles of milk being dumped in the street. He brought them in and at six o'clock opened the shop. In a little time she came and joined him behind the counter and eventually took over.

One of the local GPs, Dr Alistair McCrone, had a patient who wa dying of cancer. He remembers how George used to visit her at the end of a hard day, taking champagne to help her get to sleep.

What hurt George most was the sheer, grinding poverty. Was it for this that men had died in their thousands in the trenches?

"Once I entered a house where a woman was suffering from puerperal fever," he recalled, "and the family were sitting around silent and dismayed. 'Get hot water bottles,' I cried, 'six of them' – and nobody moved. You see, they hadn't money for one, let alone six hot water bottles. There was no health insurance. Only one doctor could be relied on for midnight calls among ten thousand people, and he, the saint, was a coloured man. I saw a lad of ten crying with the toothache. 'Oh yes', said the mother, 'he can get it pulled. But not till Friday when the dole's paid out.'"

A single man got 12 shillings a week parish relief, and a married couple received 21 shillings. Some children were entitled to free clothing and footwear but many parents refused this since everyone could tell parish clothing by its appearance.

When he visited the local hospital, he would have a word for the staff as well as the patients, and he liked nothing better than to go down to the furnace and have a cup of tea with the men who kept the heating system going.

When George visited the poor of his parish, he found that St Cuthbert's meant nothing to them. He also discovered that some members thought more of old John MacLeod than they did of the younger MacLeod. He used to talk of being greeted by one old lady in a tenement – "Come awa' in, meenister. I've scarcely had a veesit since the Reformation. Dr John MacGloud, aye, that was a man! Jeannie, fetch that picter o' Dr MacGloud, it's under the bed." The picture would be fetched out and presented for inspection.

He admired the good humour of the Govan poor, the people who had learned to survive at the bottom of the heap. Where had he heard that kind of humour before? Yes, in the trenches when the shells were flying. Yet the war in which so many of his friends had died was supposed to safeguard a land fit for heroes, and here he was ministering in rotten slums amid people who were poor, hungry and affected by tuberculosis and rickets without the economic means to ensure adequate medical attention. He had seen poverty and hardship in Edinburgh, but Govan was on a scale which was difficult to comprehend. And where was the Church in all this? It was "no' for the likes o' us" said the Govan poor, echoing their Edinburgh counterparts. Except, that is, as a place of charity. After every daily service, there was a bench full of men and women seeking handouts. George gave lots of his own money away, and kept an account open at the local chemist for those who required medicine but could not pay.

"Unemployment was all about us," he recalled. "Scotland's finest artisans had nought for their fingers to handle. They stood idle in the market place. At night-time, unable to face the prospects of an idle dawn, dozens of them used to walk through the empty streets to achieve a spurious fatigue."

Some went out every day, pretending to go to work. Idle men stood outside the Elder Library, where the burgh coat of arms jeered at them, "Nihil Sine Labore" (Nothing Without Work). It became transmuted in the local patois into "Nae Sign of Work".

He was impressed by the spirit of the unemployed men, and was deeply moved by three men who went to sell their blood at £5 a time. Only one man had the right blood, and he divided the money with the others.

The work of the Church continued unabated. By 1932 the church roll was down to 1900 members, but attendance at worship was vastly improved. He encouraged observance of the Christian Year, believing it to be a more mature Christian approach. Much of the new interest was due to George MacLeod's preaching and visiting. Miss Cathy Walker was Guardian of the Girls' Guildry when Mr MacLeod came as minister. Over fifty years later, when 94 and living in a Govan hospital, she recalled:

"My parents were married by Dr John MacLeod. My father was a member of St Mary's and didn't want to change, but when he went to hear George MacLeod preach, that convinced him. His sermons were an inspiration. Every time you went, you got something to think about. He wasn't only a great orator, but a great visionary. He had a vision for Govan, and as a natural leader he took other people with him. He made enemies, but he usually won them over in the end. He was a man of character who wouldn't give way if he thought he was right.

"We were in awe of ministers at that time, but when Mr MacLeod came he made us laugh. He was very unorthodox. He would come into the house and sit on the table and swing his legs. When he left Govan, my mother cried."

He was a modern and approachable pastor, but not trendy. His view of the matter was uncompromising.

"Let us be under no delusion that in these modern days pastors are expected to dissemble their profession," he wrote. "If they are good at games or can crack a passing joke, that is all well and good. But still what people look for – especially the non-church-goers – are men who are prepared to pray when they visit in their houses: to rebuke men's sins and to ask them back to church. If we hesitate in these primary activities, and labour to conceal the seal of our commission with the fob of modern fashions, not only is our pace slowed down, but folk are frankly mystified as to why we move at all. Grooves can, of course, be graves, but not infrequently they are healthy indications of a well-worn track that at least leads somewhere. Above all things men seek today some definite direction. Let parsons then be parsons unashamed, renouncing not 'the cloth' but labouring lest it appear to men a shroud."[3]

Not a few Govanites still have a photograph of the second MacLeod Pope of Govan above the fireplace. The sight of the Rev George MacLeod, tall and striking in his dark blue double-breasted suit and dog collar, striding through the streets of Govan, was an unforgettable one. He was, as always, in a hurry, and he was determined that he would make the experiment which had drawn him from the comforts of Edinburgh.

The pace of work took its toll, however. In April 1932, he was in a nursing home. The stories went around that the energetic minister had cracked up.

"I need hardly say that the somewhat violent rumours regarding my health, which achieved enough currency to reach my ears," he wrote in the parish magazine, "were quite without foundation. One always feels more important when one has some 'unknown' disease, but I was simply suffering from ordinary 'flu of a rather concentrated nature. I have not come back wrapped up in cotton wool or with secret instructions to go only 'half steam ahead'; but, on the contrary, am better than I have been for some time past."

The truth was that he was driving himself beyond his considerable energies. He did not have the protection and support of a family, and there was a steady stream of visitors to the top flat of the Pearce Institute. He had to give in, and appeal to callers to come at set times, except in emergencies.

Within nine months, he was ill again.

"I am extremely sorry to find myself away for so long," he told his anxious parishioners, "but I apparently belong to the 'get up too soon' variety of mysterious influenza. I have made several attempts to get up and come back to Govan, but the doctor has at last persuaded me that it would only mean that I would be away for even longer, so I am just staying off until I am a hundred per cent fit. I hope to be up soon."

He was not up soon. The reality was that normally ebullient George MacLeod was suffering from severe depression and was at the point of breakdown.

Twice-Born Man

*Any fool can write learned language. The vernacular
is the real test. If you can't turn your faith into it, then
either you don't understand it or you don't believe it.*

C. S. LEWIS

*They are insignificant little people, submissive as dogs,
and they sweat with embarrassment when you talk
with them.*

ADOLF HITLER, ON THE
PROTESTANT CLERGY

It was in Jerusalem, while taking part in a Russian Orthodox
Easter Sunday service, that George MacLeod truly became a twice-
born man. Easter Sunday, 1933, was the time at which the
breakdown became a breakthrough.

What caused such an energetic and confident man to reach the
point of nervous breakdown? One reason was certainly overwork.
There were not enough hours in the day to do all he wanted to do,
and he was giving out all the time. Hugh Douglas, who was one of
George's assistants in Govan, put it down to the stresses and
conflicts of the whirlwind start in Govan.

A further clue can be found in George's own description of this
crisis in his life. He said he had been suffering quite stupidly from
a "feeling of hopeless depression", what a friend called "a bad
attack of world depression".[1] Captain MacLeod was a casualty on
a new and bewildering front. He was losing the war.

He had understood the First World War as a national purgation,
in preparation for a new way of life. It may not have been an
adequate theological explanation, but theology itself was shell-
shocked by the unthinkable horror. The "queen of the sciences"
had been tarted up, but her mascara was running and she had been

106

indecently assaulted by Freud and Marx. The world would never be the same.

The Twenties had been punctuated by a great deal of rhetoric about reconstruction, and there had been some action. Housebuilding had been undertaken on an unprecedented scale, and some social benefits had been improved, but the brittle and elegant decade had not promoted a substantial engagement with reality. Idealism had understandably given way to disillusionment as the old class modes of thinking took new and more subtle root, and the outlines of a land fit for bright young things began to emerge. The Wall Street Crash and the Depression were the terrible morning after a night before which had been redolent with illusion. For some, the hangover proved to be a terminal illness.

What if, whisper it, the First World War had been an enormous mistake? What if all those young men had died in vain? The Twenties' unhealthy silence about the carnage was broken by angry voices articulating repressed, unthinkable thoughts. Works such as *Goodbye to All That* and *All Quiet on the Western Front* shifted public perceptions about the war.

For the Rev. George MacLeod, these questions were like the detonation of time bombs submerged within him. Surely the blood of the courageous men of Flanders had not seeped into the mud around him to no purpose? And surely they had not been sent to aimless slaughter by incompetent leaders? Had they not sacrificed themselves to build a better world?

Like Govan, 1933?

George had agonized over the two nations, privileged and deprived, and had tried to do something about it. His base had been in one nation and he had reached over to the other. Now he lived physically in the midst of the second nation and the evidence of its daily misery was round his door, was in his bones. The world view of his father was no longer adequate, as he had probably suspected. Empire, race and class, laced with genial optimism and buttressed by pliable Christianity, looked more and more like the features of a god that had failed. The National Government of Tories and Liberals, headed by Labour's Ramsay MacDonald, had reduced the dole from 17 shillings to 15/3d, and had instituted the humiliating means test, encouraging neighbour to spy on neighbour. Not much more than a decade after the First World War, three million unemployed were being asked to sacrifice themselves to build a better world . . .

George MacLeod

These questions had come up in George's preaching, and he was defiantly wrestling with them. He pointed out how, for nearly a decade, people had talked of building a new world before they died.

"A new world did seem to lie before us resplendent for our taking – in those glad foolhardy years. But obstacles were larger than even the wisest dreamed. We all know today the measure of the slowing down: the change of gear in the knowledge of an uphill task: till today, it is the hill before us, rather than our rate of progress, that engages men's concern. Many indeed there be who, once content to listen to the prophets of a newer day, have long since fallen back on the prophet's old complaint: 'Who will show us any good?' Old and young then enter a new phase. But let us still carry the weapons of our spiritual warfare. Let us still rebut the question: 'Was it an illusion that out of war some finer thing might come?' Once let us admit that, then indeed these men have died in vain. Let us hold to the truth that they died for things worth while – for truth and goodness and beauty – however rarely they confessed it. Else were these rotten war books the end of the story – and life for many would become that vanity that the preacher claimed."[2]

Sometimes it was hard to tell whether the preacher was simply waving, or actually drowning.

The truth is that the world depression was burning inside George MacLeod's brain. He tried the well-worn MacLeodian solution of work, and more work, but the world declined to change. Worse, his body refused to function. As an intensely private man, whose public persona was that of someone who was in charge of his section of the universe, he found it difficult to relax and be vulnerable with other people. He was known to many of his colleagues and helpers as "The Boss", a title which hardly invited mutual pastoral inquiry. He was friendly and immediate, yet at the same time somewhat distant, keeping strict controls on access to his innermost core, where the puritan carefully policed the passionate. The language of one's own innermost feelings was not in the MacLeod family lexicon – that would be the slippery slope which led away from duty in the direction of self-indulgence – and he had the MacLeod reputation of omnicompetence to protect and uphold. (Though the darker underside of the public MacLeod story was that in addition to Norman of the Barony's melancholy bouts, Pope John of Govan had spent a year in a sanatorium in Switzerland mending his broken mind and body.)

George MacLeod found himself overwhelmed by the idealist's despair in the face of a world that will not change. As he was to put it later so succinctly:

"As you look at the world's distress, how far are we still from achieving even the semblance of a Christian civilization after these two thousand years; how often are we borne down by the thought of how much there is to do and how few there are to do it."[3]

Thus it was that the latest dazzling, wounded, MacLeod found himself on a boat, with his father, heading for the Holy Land in April 1933 as part of a three-month convalescence.

It was an absorbing pilgrimage, which provided one of the deeply formative experiences of George's life. Father and son stayed at the King David Hotel in Jerusalem – "compared with which Gleneagles is a youth hostel". George noted that the communion table in St Andrew's Church, Jerusalem, for which his father had helped to raise funds, was of Iona marble. He preached in the "Scotch church" on Good Friday.

The Easter early morning service of the Russian Orthodox Church moved George deeply in a way that few services had, and he was to refer to it again and again. He had intended to go for a short time, but it so gripped him that he stayed till 3.45 am.

"Only eight priests took part," he noted in his journal, "and a hidden choir, but they were all quite perfect. They have the supreme gift of drama, and all had perfect voices. It was really the same service as at the Sepulchre, but done by perfect artists. When the Patriarch was heard arriving, the gates of the sanctuary were flung open – two young priests, with flowing hair and beards, rushed out to meet him – the choir sang Responses – Actions – they all entered the sanctuary – they all rushed out – *Christ is risen* – Candles! Quick procession – every movement was sprightly. Out of the church we all ran behind them – lighted candles in our hands – round the church three times singing, in the crisp star-laden night. Here was the answer to Modern Criticism! *Of course, Christ had risen!*

"Levitation? . . . Physical? . . . Subjective? . . . Objective? . . . These were all meaningless words. *Christ had risen* was the sheer obvious fact! Back into the church, the two young people sang to the Patriarch. He replied in song and beautiful movements of hand and head – the two priests took the incense and swept through the congregation (not a large one) censing us and telling each one that Christ had risen – back to the centre – whenever a priest finished his part, out rang the Heavenly Choir, while some new 'formation' was taken up by the priests – not one had a book – not one took a 'cue', and yet for three and a half hours it went on without a pause in the centre of the church."

George was enraptured, moved, changed. Easter, 1933, was his resurrection morning.

"For sheer worship I have never seen anything like it – nor shall see again on earth – we can never touch it in the West – not even Rome could do it. It was the devotional presentation of the New Life, beyond 'Acting' and beyond 'Lesson' – simply Worship – It was the earnest that Bolshevism must pass. There was more Reality in the Patriarch's little finger than in Stalin's whole council assembled."

As he made his way to his hotel in the cold clear morning, George told his companions that he had discovered worship for the first time. He said that he found the worship utterly evangelical, producing in people's eyes "such a light as Moody and Sankey might produce after saying 'Jesus Saves' 60 times." He had rediscovered a sense of the Church as the corporate Body of Christ. The combination of action, mystery and theatre had completely overwhelmed this inheritor of the Govan Scoto-Catholic tradition.

For George MacLeod, lukewarm, conventional Presbyterianism finally died in the Holy Land on Easter Sunday, 1933. The old structure of individual devotion and duty had cracked in the crucible that was Govan in the hungry thirties, and he knew in his heart of hearts that it could not be repaired by more work, or even by more faith. He needed, for his healing, a new way of *seeing*, and he found new vision in the midst of overwhelming, mysteriously beautiful worship. It was a vision which was personal, political and cosmic *all at the same time*, and it appealed to the Celt in him. Holiness had become wholeness had become holiness. It was as if the spiritual and the material fused in a never-to-be-forgotten rapturous moment of revelation.

The rest of George MacLeod's life would consist in the acting out of this compelling vision, and Iona Abbey would in time become his theatre for the glory of God.

He summed up his experience, echoing his grandfather's words after his visit to India, by saying prophetically that the West must learn from the worship of the East, and the East must learn from the service of the West. The YMCA in Jerusalem had been opened the day after he left: costing 2 million dollars, it was equipped for a wide range of activities.

"In many ways it is a horror," he wrote in his journal, "but it is fine – they are the only group that care a dottle for the young men of Jerusalem, for all the hundred churches there! They are appealing to the young life, and giving bodily health and fellowship. I am glad it is there – it completes the only conceivable expression of worship that was absent, and it does it as blatantly as its generation! Yet, conversely and clearly, the mere Gospel of Service, of swimming pools and libraries and footballs and cafeterias is 'all that is left' of the Gospel in the West – which has so lost grip on 'All-Life' that we have our present Niagara of Materialism. We too must learn putting first things first – Contemplation – God-consciousness – 'All Out' pilgrimages, in which we are housed utterly in our religion, at least for a time – when the calendar becomes meaningless and Calvary eternal – these we must get again from the East, in exchange for our YMCA."

In a sermon broadcast to the Empire from St Martin's-in-the-Fields, London, later in the year, he revealed how the dirt, materialism and cynicism of Jerusalem had touched him and helped him find renewal of faith.

"The worse appearances are, the more thrilling does the Cross become in its intensity, and Easter, Ascension, Pentecost, Trinity, become doubly thrilling in their power. In the light of our faith, insignificant Bethel becomes charged with the highest meanings: Jordan runs clear for those who have eyes to see: and the very paltriness of Jerusalem reflects an eternal light of hope. The thrill, you see, becomes capable of infinite extension. Why, every insignificant river in England, Scotland and Wales becomes of utmost significance. In actual fact, Christ is seen walking on the waters, not of Gennesareth, but Thames. Our old sluggishness becomes stirred: our faithless mutterings (that it was all very well for God to do great things in the old days, when men were men) become meaningless."

George's old sluggishness had become stirred, and his faithless mutterings had gone. He was ready to face the grime and ordinariness of Govan again, and see it as a place transfigured by the light of Christ. He was determined to create a new kind of disciplined community in Govan.

One of the first things he got was a letter of resignation from

Harry Whitley, who was feeling overwhelmed by feelings of inadequacy. George told him in his reply that Charlotte Square had been a community of zest, Govan so far had been a community of demands, but from now on there was going to be a new page – a community of the will of God.

"I am going quite frankly to *lead* it," he wrote, "and the whole damned staff can leave if they don't like it. I am frankly tired of this Night Club Community of Half Baked Good Fellows: greying at the temples and regretting the inevitable passing of their youth. God alone can keep us young to the end of our days. And if I am irritated with the present ping pong variety of our corporate life, the irritation is no less when I realize it is all my fault.

"That community I am going to make: with or without you: it's not going to be great fun, and it's going to be difficult. It's not going to be a miracle, but it's going to be real. If it helps you to hear more about it, before deciding, then stay over Monday night. But I warn you I shall never again discuss your character: nor am I interested in your theological balances: nor your morbid processes of dropping loyalties and friendships one by one into a meaningless sea. Much of your distress is your own damned fault – quite apart from mine."

Ouch! It was a new George MacLeod who was in town.

Back home, his door at the Pearce Institute was ever open. The destitute poor of Govan made tracks for him, and the list of visitors from different parts of Scotland, seeking advice and inspiration, reads like extracts from a "Who's Who" of later Scottish church life.

David Cairns, who would become an outstanding professor of theology at Aberdeen University, was one of many who found his life turned around by George MacLeod. A brilliant student at Oxford, Aberdeen, and Zurich, he was very uncertain about his future. He was both attracted and repelled by the Oxford Group, and wondered whether this was the vital movement in Christianity everyone was looking for. The Group, which was particularly influential in the universities, stressed absolute moral standards (it eventually became known as Moral Rearmament) and encouraged mutual confession at house parties. They concentrated on winning over people they identified as leaders, and were often accused of brainwashing and manipulation. David Cairns had worked with Frank Buchman, the movement's founder, in Canada and the USA and was thinking about working full-time with the Oxford Group when George asked him to come to Govan to see him.

"I at once felt that in George's circle there was an open-air type of Christianity that tolerated considerable differences," he recalled. "I was seen off at King's Cross station by Frank Buchman, who apparently telephoned to one of his pals who met me at Waverley Station, and I felt that I was being played like a fish. And the man who met me in Edinburgh had the same mannerisms as Frank, and the same tones of voice. George was cut to a different pattern, though there were some 'little Georges' about. He did not speak of his own conversion, though we did know that there had been a time when he was not gripped by the same faith as he now possessed."

George was evidently persuasive: David Cairns joined the Govan staff as a volunteer.

The conversations in George's study were memorable. On his mantelpiece there stood an Italian ivory figure: turn it one way and there was a skull, turn it the other and the visitor was faced with the head of Christ. The conversations usually had a similar evangelical force.

George Reid was invited through to spend the weekend in Govan. Then somewhat timid and introverted, he was overwhelmed by MacLeod.

"In George MacLeod I encountered the most magnificent extrovert and fearless personality. I admired him enormously and was greatly attracted, but his ideas of the place of the Church in society were all strange to my immature mind and experience and made little impact. George inhabited a much larger world than any I had known. I was not fit to be one of his disciples."

When he left the P. I., the somewhat staid divinity student pressed a tip into Fallon's hand and was slightly disconcerted to hear the Irishman's muttered response – "Ach, you bugger!"

Another future Moderator to make the Govan pilgrimage was Rev. David Steel (father of the future Liberal Party leader). He had elected to be further educated by doing a year's survey of nearby Plantation Parish instead of going to Union Theological Seminary in New York. He often took his problems to the Govan minister, and learned a great deal in his company. Yet another future Moderator who made the trip and joined the Govan staff was Hugh Douglas.

What George MacLeod was doing was to assemble a team of the

most able people he could find. The Govan minister's stipend in 1930 was £1000 a year, a very substantial sum in those days. George had a fairly spartan lifestyle, as did the bachelor ministers who formed a little community in the upstairs flat in the Pearce Institute. (For a man of means, he spent very little on himself. His shoes always seemed to be in a perpetual state of disrepair, and he bought little in the way of clothes. His wallet was often open, but it was for others.) With Presbytery grants and endowments, it was possible to employ two full-time ordained assistants, a student assistant, a church sister and two secretaries, as well as having some volunteers. Some of the expenses of the operation came out of George's pocket. Men of the calibre of Duncan MacGillivray, Hugh Douglas, John Symington, Harry Whitley and David Cairns ensured that what happened in Govan would be the talk of the Church. Some ministers with much smaller staffs and lower budgets were understandably jealous of the Govan set-up.

George MacLeod had come to Govan to make an experiment, and by the end of 1933, restored in health and backed by his talented team, he was ready to go. What happened turned out to be one of the most talked-about experiments of the Church in the Thirties.

As with so many things, George got the idea of the mission of friendship from someone else, and put his own distinctive stamp upon it. It became the most influential model of mission in the Church of Scotland and still reappears, often unacknowledged, in various guises today, even though the confident assumptions undergirding the model have long since collapsed.

The prototype was developed just before the first World War by Cyril Garbett, future Archbishop of York, then vicar of Portsea, one of whose curates was a certain P. B. Clayton. George launched his model on unsuspecting Govan in September 1933, when he announced a two year plan of mission. In a pastoral letter to every member of the congregation, the Govan minister said it was useless to pretend that in material things the immediate outlook was much brighter than the previous year, but at least people were thinking more deeply and seriously than before.

"People are beginning to see that a new social order must be born if the majority of men are to share and enjoy the wealth and plenty that even now science has put within their grasp. The problem of coming days is going to be how best to arrive at that Christian Commonwealth which alone can satisfy our legitimate aspirations. In other countries, all kinds of 'short cuts' are being employed: some are flying Blue Eagles to see which way the wind blows; others are fashioning variations of the Cross and producing Swastikas; others again are ever trying to unite the two. But everywhere attempts are made at New Planning, New Discipline, New Ways. Everywhere it is agreed that the Fundamental Problem is Moral.

"It has never been a characteristic of this country to lose its head; or explode; or unitedly to grasp the latest patent medicine for its social ills – and it will not do so now. And yet we feel we should be doing something. No political party seems adequate in itself – it is hard nowadays to find anyone with a passionate faith in any one of them. And that is because we know, in our hearts, that our real problem is moral rather than political. Before we can deal with the details of 'how to share' (Politics) we feel we must capture the 'will to share' (Religion). If that be so, has not the Church of Christ a mighty challenge before it, if its eyes be open in days like these?"

It is hard not to hear echoes in this of the "godly commonwealth" of Thomas Chalmers, mentor of the great Norman. Chalmers had moved energetically into the Tron Kirk in Glasgow in 1815 and immediately surveyed his parish with a view to launching a mission. Appalled by the poverty and misery he found, the great divine held forth the vision of society transformed into a "godly commonwealth of Christian communities". One of his answers was to divide the parish into units and to organize poor relief on the old rural model.

In some ways George MacLeod's mission to the Govan poor was in continuity with that of Chalmers and Norman MacLeod of the Barony, taking its place with their work as among the few outstanding urban missionary endeavours in the Church of Scotland in the last two centuries. All three men had tremendous unquestioned confidence in the Church and its message, and they all believed that if only the Church brought its life and organization into conformity with its gospel, the disaffected poor would come gratefully into the fold. The difference between George MacLeod and the other two was that his message in 1933 had become less individualistic, and more concerned with justice and sharing than with hand-outs either from the Church or the State.

George spelt out his missionary strategy for Govan. Stage one was to be a mission to the congregation itself, Stage two was to be a mission to the parish. A survey showed that following the limitation of parish boundaries after the Union in 1929, there were now 10,000 souls mainly living in tenements in an area round the church which could be covered by foot in 15 minutes. Of 650 Protestant households, only 175 had a church connection (in 1880 the number had been 500), and only 10 of the 175 were connected with Govan Old Parish. The remaining 165 households were connected with 23 churches scattered throughout Glasgow.

In a pamphlet about the mission, published by the Church of Scotland under the deathless title "Are Not the Churchless Million Partly the Church's Fault?" – Ellen Murray, ever keeping her brother's feet on the ground, snorted in response, "Are not the unsold copies partly the author's fault?" – the Govan minister argued that the parish system of the Church of Scotland had now broken down and must be renewed if the Kirk was to remain in any sense a national church. Pointing out that ministers were criss-crossing the city visiting their members resident in distant parishes, MacLeod went on: "There is an element of Confucianism that has strangely gotten hold of many Presbyterians – a resolve to worship at the tomb of their ancestors! They would rather miss four communions than 'lift their lines' from the place where their fathers never dreamt of missing one."

In the first stage, congregational mission was intensified, and members were urged to take part in the many organizations of the Church. The lapsed were invited to renew their commitment, and those with grievances were encouraged to come to the minister and state them. The culmination of the first stage was a witness of loyalty in Holy Week, 1934. Extra chairs had to be brought in on Palm Sunday when 120 new members joined the Church, and as many as 500 attended the evening services during the week. George was able to report that membership had increased by over 300 in six months, that many more were coming to worship, and that some of the church organizations had doubled in membership. His only lament was that not enough men were coming, "largely because they are unshepherded".

Pope John MacLeod himself could not have put it better, even though the assumptions were by now highly questionable. Was it really the case that the men of Govan were not coming to church simply because they were "unshepherded"?

The mission was not merely about people coming to church. Deeply affected by the sight of skilled craftsmen standing at the street corners, George determined to make a simple sign of work.

The area around the war memorial, near the entrance to the church, was very run down, and he decided to make a beautiful garden there. He recruited volunteers from the ranks of the unemployed. Arrangements had to be made with the dole authorities and the trade unions. No pay was given, but gardening equipment was provided. No man on the dole could be expected to be fit for the heavy work unless he were properly fed, and an arrangement was made with the local pub owner, who was an elder of the kirk, for a solid dinner to be provided for the forty or so workers. (Coming out of the pub after one lunch, the Govan minister collided with the worthy president of the Temperance Society. "I never thought to live to see this day," she said to him. "Madam," he replied, "what would you assume if you saw me coming out of the maternity hospital?") 2500 paving slabs were manhandled, 600 tons of earth laid out, and 1000 daffodils planted. The project was opened on October 14, 1934, at a ceremony attended by over 1000 people who sang psalms in the pouring rain.

The second phase of the mission of friendship was in full swing by this time. Every household in the parish was visited twice by two volunteers. Those who claimed allegiance to another church were encouraged to go regularly to their own place of worship. Those who were loosely attached to Govan Old Parish or who went to no church were invited to a number of events and services. Regular teams of volunteers took part in a "chain of prayer" for the visits, and the whole scheme was co-ordinated by George MacLeod, who was like an adjutant at the Pearce Institute, dictating messages to his secretaries who made sure the information got out to the front line.

The visitation came to a climax with a special week of friendship from October 21–28, 1934. Posters were prepared by draughtsmen from the shipyards. The chain of prayer, involving 100 volunteers, continued in the church all day. Every afternoon several streets in the parish were visited and short meetings held. At seven every evening, street preaching went on at different points in the parish, and the robed boys' choir processed from stance to stance to bring the people into the church. From 9 till 10.30 there was a women's meeting in the P. I., and the men attended a "question time" on the social issues of the day. On the final evening the marching crowd went through every street in Govan, singing and giving a message of welcome to the church.

George MacLeod summed up the venture: "Throughout the

week not one single untoward word was heard, nor an unsympathetic gesture seen. The coalman gave us his stance on one occasion: the local fried-fish shop owner came out to proffer us chips and to express a sincere message of friendship; two small side streets, where no preaching had taken place, sent deputations on the third day to ask why they had been left out – were these small things? To some of us they, with a host of other signs, were the utmost rebuke at the extent to which the Church of Scotland has neglected a patient people who are only waiting for the Church seriously to ask for their allegiance."

But were people only waiting expectantly for the Church to ask them?

The results were certainly impressive. Over 200 children joined the Sunday School. Over 100 folk came forward with old church lines. 220 others came forward to join a ten weeks' course of instruction in the meaning of the Christian faith, and of these only 20 fell away. Over 80 came forward for adult baptism.

George MacLeod, full of optimism, pointed the way ahead in familiar military terms. In the parish magazine he quoted Douglas Haig's words to a group of officers at Passchendaele: "Thank you, gentlemen, rest well and quickly. I shall be asking for your services again on this same ridge."

"We have indeed captured the first objective on Friendship Hill," George went on. "Already we see new ground ahead; old defences battered in; half cut wires of prejudice that only individuals can wholly clear; wounded souls crying louder, for they now can see our lights; and craters for our taking quite different in dimension, now we can see them close."

Not everyone was pleased. One worthy Govanite who had witnessed the laying of the foundation stone of Govan Parish Church in 1886 complained that the kirk on Sundays was full of strangers.

"It was for them, too, that the foundation stone was laid," retorted the Govan minister.

In the Church of Scotland pamphlet, George said his primary conviction had been proved to the hilt.

"The Churchless Million are largely the blame of the Church herself and, until we set our house in order, we dare not blame one single soul. If only she would lift up her eyes and look into the fields, she would still find them ripe unto the harvest. If the Church cares even now to take her serious part, the answer to Scotland for Christ is as certain as the dawn."

Really?

But how precisely should the Church set her house in order? George had an answer. He said that many areas were overchurched and many parts of the cities understaffed. He jocularly suggested that a "Minister for Readjustments" should be appointed, with full powers to close down churches, and that he should be given an armoured car as part of the job! He felt the Church should act decisively, risking unpopularity, and redeploy men in teams to staff the city churches. He was particularly concerned about the work of the Church in the new housing schemes which were growing up on the boundaries of the cities.

"Year after year there emerge from our divinity halls a proportion of the very best students asking ever more imperiously whether they cannot serve the Church in teams, with something of the forthright intensity of foreign missionaries, rather than become lost individually in a witness that is single-handed, and less than the best, for all its nobility. Their appeal cannot remain for ever unanswered. Deep shame upon us that we have temporized for so long. Let at least a start be made with newer ways, for newer days, in the vast new housing schemes."

In the Scotland of 1934, George MacLeod was confident that if the city churches were adequately staffed and organized, and if they reached out in missions of friendship, the people would come flocking in. With his team ministry in Govan, and with careful planning and work, he had seen it happen. His confidence was contagious, and helped waverers to believe. At the same time, he did not have confidence that the Church at large would act on his vision of team ministries for the new housing schemes. He would have volunteered to go out in the armoured car himself and take prisoners, but the Church had no commanding officer who could direct such a battle. Perhaps he would have to go out himself with a chosen team into no man's land?

Thus as early as 1934, the germ of the idea of the Iona Community was growing in the mind of this increasingly impatient visionary. The man who had come to Govan to make an experiment would have to leave it to make yet another experiment. In so doing, this conservative gadfly, this most loyal and passionate defender of the Church and of its parish system, would be called a disloyal renegade.

But not yet.

Many Nostrums, Many Saviours

*I would never have written and signed anything
heretical while my beloved father was alive. I would
have been damned for a humbug rather than hurt him.*

DICK SHEPPARD TO LAURENCE HOUSMAN

*Christianity is the most avowedly materialist of all the
great religions.*

WILLIAM TEMPLE

Nineteen thirty-four was a decisive year in George MacLeod's life.
The mission of friendship had demonstrated a new model of
outreach for the Church; a book of his sermons, "Govan Calling"
sold well among the many admirers of his broadcast talks; the
church and the Pearce Institute were bursting with life; an exciting
new outdoors project had been embarked upon; and his father
died.

George was ever loyal to his father. His sense of duty and loyalty
would not have allowed him to utter it to anyone, but his father's
assumptions about the universe must have been more and more
painful to him the longer he was in Govan. The experience of living
amidst the "second nation", and the disillusioning effect of the
collapse of the post-war hopes of national regeneration could not
be denied, and George would either have had to come to new
conclusions or crack up. A completely new stance would have been
hurtful to his father; it would have seemed like an assault on all he
held dear, and it is not without significance that George's more
radical views on war and social justice did not emerge fully until
after his father's death.

Whether by this time he was a "closet" pacifist who only "came
out" after the death of his father, or whether the event released

him and gave him permission to think more unthinkable thoughts is not ascertainable: what is known is that the change in George's thinking became more pronounced as the decade rolled on. Govan radicalized him. George could only tear up part of the dynastic script when there was no MacLeod around who would himself be torn apart in the wrenching.

George had certainly been thinking deeply about the state of the Church of Scotland, and believed that something new was needed. His inborn MacLeodian instincts are shown in the way he turned to the Celtic tradition for answers. In an important speech to a symposium titled "Scotland in search of her Youth", he argued that the collapse of the puritan tradition – with its family worship, long preparation for Holy Communion, observance of the Sabbath, simplicity of worship, austere buildings, and discipline of life – had left the Kirk without direction.

"Merely so to sketch the trend and purpose of the Puritan tradition," he said, "is to reveal the distance that almost unconsciously we have moved in these days from the ground where once we stood. For reasons that would take a book to encompass we have, in recent decades, been engaged in that manoeuvre which in every other warfare spells almost certain defeat – changing position at the dictates of circumstance, without consciously choosing our next alignment. Had the Church of Scotland resolutely maintained her Puritan tradition she might have had a great purpose to perform today: had she alternately planned her line of movement more decisively she might have performed an even greater. Her deepest distresses are due to the fact that she has done neither."

He said that family prayers had largely gone, and the preparation for the sacrament had lost its solemnity. Starved of symbols in their churches, Scotsmen had turned to Freemasonry for ritual. Crosses were erected at war memorials throughout the land, but were not allowed in churches for fear of being thought Roman. A return to Puritanism would not satisfy. Youth was pointing the way forward.

The minister of Govan Old Parish Church, which stood on the site of the ancient Celtic place of worship, argued that some answers could be found "back where Scottish worship first began, in the Celtic church of St Columba."

"If we would be patient we can discover here the link that saves the chain. For it was a return to the simple primitive Catholic Church which was the desire and purpose of the first Reformers.

How many who today invoke the name of John Knox really know the things for which he stood? – frequent communion; read prayers from a liturgy; daily service in the churches; the reciting of the Apostles' Creed in worship; the response of the people to prayers; the offering of praise from the Communion Table; the pronouncing of the Benediction from the Communion Table. How many of these acts today – when they are enacted in a Scottish church – are called 'mere aping of another Church'? And yet they are in reality the things which John Knox practised in his endeavour to recover for Scotland her ancient primitive faith. Perhaps the first reformers are to be vindicated at last, in coming days, by a return to what they sought. If not (at least, if we just drift on), then there is thunder in the air. But it will not be the passing thunder of warring religious sects, but the thunder of materialism, of atheism, and all manner of unloveliness."

The last paragraph was a reference to Communism and to Nazism. In 1930, he had kept his promise to go with a youth group from St Cuthbert's to Oberammergau, and they had stumbled on a Nazi youth rally. George had been horrified by what he saw and heard, and during the Thirties, he kept warning that Britain must find alternatives to the ideas and practices which were beginning to captivate the youth of Germany.

His talk was magnificent, sweeping, polemic, bound to infuriate. And it did. What the latest MacLeod was advocating was the reintroduction of Catholic practices into the worship of the Kirk, arguing that they really were Celtic or Protestant emphases. The crafty Celtic maverick was going behind Roman Catholicism to argue for Catholic practices, and stamping them with the *imprimatur* of no less a venerable Scottish Protestant personage than John Knox.

Did he have a case? To a large extent, yes. A good deal of Protestantism had become post-Victorian post-Puritanism gone to seed, often lashing out at Catholic practices which had been the staple diet of the worship of the Reformers. On the other hand, George's setting off of the Celtic tradition against the Roman Catholic was largely unhistorical. The Celtic tapestry was a richly coloured one, and George was not averse to a little embroidery of his own. After all, wasn't truth more important than the facts? John Knox would also have been a little surprised at the views attributed to him from time to time by George MacLeod.

George was not a historian: he was a man with a profound sense

Above George's grandfather, Norman MacLeod of the Barony

Left George's father, Sir John MacLeod

Right George aged ten at Cargilfield School, Edinburgh

George with his sister Ellen in 1914

George in 1918 wearing the insignia of the
Argyll and Sutherland Highlanders

George (centre) at Coney Island, New York, in 1922 with a group of friends

In the late 1920s while minister at
St Cuthbert's, Edinburgh

Speaking at the opening of the Govan Church Garden, 1934

At work in the library of Iona Abbey, 1943

George and Lorna on their wedding day, 28 August 1948

of history, which is a different thing. It was natural that the Celtic period should hold enormous appeal for a romantic MacLeod. Its poetry, its love of beauty, its sense of nature shot through with spirit, its wholesome earthiness and profound holiness made it an attractive model, all the more so because many of its sources were so imprecise. George could make of it what he willed – and he did, he did.

To actually hear the rhetorical Celtic magician – now you see it, now you don't – sweep through history was to be in danger of being mesmerized. He rummaged through the drawers of ancient history, and left what did not suit his argument lying on the floor. And it was always typical of George MacLeod to buttress his most radical and daring suggestions by appealing to ancient historical precedents, some of which, the ungracious cynic might suspect, were only a day or so old. Yet his instincts were often right, even if his treatment of the details was somewhat cavalier. As Columba himself might have said, or on the other hand might not, in the Beginning was the Story.

What George was trying to do was, in essence, to find a Scottish theological base for his life-changing Russian Orthodox experience. Post-Calvin Calvinism had demystified the faith and turned it into something approaching ordinary duty. Roman Catholicism was too totalitarian for George, especially in its political aspects. The primitive kinship between Celtic and Orthodox theology and worship appealed to a man who was a romantic traditionalist in his heart and a modernist in his mind. Holiness and wholeness became one in the Celtic panorama as painted by Columba and redrawn by MacLeod. The Celts knew what it meant to be "we" as opposed to simply "I", every bit as much as the Orthodox did.

Grimy Govan was no Celtic Eden, but it was buzzing. Cobblers, craftsmen, dramatists and seamstresses enlivened the life of the unemployed at day classes in the P.I. George closed the men's club and reopened it on new lines – "a ruling principle of the new club is to be that there will be no cards issued for play except for whist or bridge drives organized and supervised by the committee". Girls' work was developed through the appointment of Isabel Rutherford, later to be Mrs Hugh Douglas, who formed girls' clubs on the model of the successful YWCA. Eventually there were 300 members and 60 volunteer helpers. The "YW" had pioneered joint youth work, but George MacLeod – ever fearful of the opening of the sexual floodgates – was dubious about it. When the door between the boys' and girls' clubs was eventually unlocked, the feared collapse of the moral universe failed to materialize.

In the church, what was reckoned to be the first Christmas Eve service to be held in a Protestant church in Glasgow in three centuries or so, was held on December 24, 1934. More new furnishings, including 500 kneeling pads, were dedicated. George defended himself against Protestant attack by saying that for over 1300 years out of 1400 in which there had been Christian worship in Scotland, Scotsmen had either stood or knelt for prayer.

"It was only some seventy-five years ago that Scotsmen could not be bothered to stand, and then found that their pews were so constricted that they could not kneel. This is the sole reason for the tradition that Scotsmen sit during divine worship!"

The Govan minister did not get things all his own way. The session minutes record that the elders voted down his proposal that the offering be received by young men who were not elders, resolving that "this deviation from tradition be not followed". When the session decided to cut the organist's salary from £125 to £100, George asked that his dissent against the decision be recorded. It was in small matters like these that traditionalists who were irritated by all the innovations got their own back.

George was wise enough to lose the petty battles in order to win the big ones.

Driving out in the country, three miles above Barrhead, on the edges of Fenwick Moor, he saw a ruined mill. He had been concerned that many people in Govan could not afford a holiday and he had wanted to find a place in the country within easy reach of Glasgow. He had also been impressed by the way unemployed men had responded to the war memorial garden project. The idea came to him: why not rebuild Fingalton Mill and make it a holiday and conference centre for Govan people?

He got the scheme going right away. The mill was gifted, materials were donated, unemployed men volunteered their services. The structure of the mill was retained, but the machinery was taken out and new floors and roof put in. A fireplace was made with the broken grinding stone. Water was piped in from a nearby field.

What was impressive was the spirit of co-operation, as Protestants and Roman Catholics, working together, rediscovered old skills. It wasn't exactly shipbuilding, but idle men found their skills and labour valued. George found that as men cheerfully offered their labour in a worthwhile cause, community began to form quite naturally. Serious issues were discussed in the context of work. The men greatly admired "The Boss", who twisted the arms of local businessmen to produce the wherewithal to make the project work. Men learned to laugh again, and a few to worship.

It was an exhilarating experience for the Govan minister. He persuaded George Adie to give up his job as a driver with a shoe company to come to the mill and take charge of the domestic arrangements.

On June 29, 1935, a gloriously sunny day, Fingalton Mill opened for guests. With pride, the workers showed their families what they had created. The mill could accommodate 30 people and had a swimming pool in its 2½ acre grounds. George described its purpose as to "provide a Govan in the country at the lowest possible charges, where folks can get good air fresher than at the coast." Lying 500 feet above sea level, the mill and its estate provided fresh "lungs" for hard-pressed Govan families. People could stay for weeks or weekends, and day trips were also organized. Women could not stay, but could come for the day. A booking office was established at the Pearce Institute, and an old bus was purchased – George MacLeod was officially registered as a bus operator, despite protests by bus companies – to take people the ten miles from the P. I. to the mill. The cost per night was 3d. It was made clear that the centre was for the whole of Govan, and not just for church members.

George loved the mill, and rejoiced to see families get a break. He enjoyed playing with children, and the project seemed to bring out the child in him. Sometimes he would drive the bus – which he nicknamed "Govan Crawling", parodying the title of his book of sermons – and would wear a driver's cap and exchange banter as he sold the tickets.

George had maintained his concern for youngsters who had got into trouble, and he was a member of the Polmont Reformatory Visiting Committee. He arranged for groups of boys from the Reformatory to spend a week at the mill and he was heartened by the responses of the lads.

Soon, George was able to report "with amazed thanksgiving" that more than 700 adults were now of the church fellowship who were outside two years ago. With young people and children, the figure would be about double that.

By the middle of the decade, backed by a talented team, George was running a church "show" which was the envy of many. He should have been happy – the experiment which he had come to Govan to make was manifestly working. Yet there was a restlessness within him. He knew in his heart that the Church at large was losing the war.

The decade was marked by a battle of ideas, and the Church appeared to be sounding the retreat. The disciples of Sigmund Freud explained much of human behaviour in terms of early training and underlying sex drives. The language of the "unconscious" and of repression permeated the times. Traditional Christian explanations of human behaviour seemed unsophisticated, unscientific and implausible by comparison.

The high moral ground of politics appeared to have been captured by the disciples of Karl Marx, who had provided a "scientific" (important Thirties code word) historical analysis of conflict in the public realm to go along with a passionate and appealing call for justice. Many of the leading thinkers of the day opted for Marxism, at least of the theoretical variety.

The Left Book Club, founded by Victor Gollancz, sent cheap paperbacks throughout the length and breadth of the country to an eager readership. The literary intelligentsia, such as Auden, Day Lewis, Spender and MacNeice saw it as their duty to puncture the complacency and illusion of the Twenties, and their poetic barbs drew Establishment blood. The old authorities lacked power, and what was seen as the Church's complicity with the ruling class in the First World War eroded its position. The exciting moral passion seemed to belong to the political left. When the Republican government in Spain came under attack from nationalist forces, many socialists from Britain joined up in a romantic and heroic crusade which ended in bafflement and defeat.

It was a day of extremes. The Left was opposed by the blackshirted British fascists organized by George MacLeod's old Winchester classmate, Sir Oswald Mosley.

In the 1930s, there were many nostrums, many saviours. Nature therapies were touted. The great outdoors beckoned. Those who wanted none of this could retreat into the world of radio, or that great dreamhouse of darkness, the cinema. "Talkies" had come into their own since 1926, and super cinemas, holding up to 3,000 people, sprang up in different parts of the country. The cinema stars, promoted by the mass circulation newspapers, became household names. For 6d, it was possible to block out the problems of the world, and be caught up in the dramas on the fascinating silver screen.

The mass of British people were neither marching nor crusading. Nostalgia was "in". The Empire was very popular, and the extent of British power and influence was continually overestimated. After all, hadn't Britain won the war? The royal family were idolized. When King George V celebrated his silver jubilee in 1935, the warmth shown to the King and to Queen Mary was remarkable, as the country celebrated with street parties.

Despite the patriotism and the nostalgia, Britain was a deeply divided country. The two nations coexisted uneasily, and the Marxist analysis pointed to a revolutionary situation. Many people who had work were quite well off. The building trade was booming – one third of all houses in Britain were built between the wars – and the new electronic industries were doing well. With the decline in domestic service, labour-saving devices began to appear everywhere. The introduction of plastics and man-made fibres brought a new and exciting range of goods before a public captivated by the presence of Woolworth's stores (everything priced 6d or less) throughout the country.

Although by the middle of the decade the worst effects of the recession had begun to wane, unemployment was still a very serious problem. The decline of heavy industries hit the northern towns very badly, and the poverty and squalor constituted a national disgrace which the National Government, under the direction of the lethargic Baldwin, did not have the energy or the will to alleviate. Hunger marches of men, women and children were publicized – the march from Jarrow, a shipbuilding town in the north of England, won special sympathy on the Clyde – but they produced very little in the way of results.

In 1935, Mussolini marched into Abyssinia. The League of Nations was powerless to prevent it. The following year, Hitler moved into the Rhineland. No one stopped him. Britain was convulsed by the abdication crisis, when King Edward VIII renounced his throne in favour of marrying Mrs Simpson. (George MacLeod was deeply upset by the abdication. When the Prince of Wales had visited Govan and the Pearce Institute, George, who had managed to let the Prince see some unscheduled squalor, had been impressed by Edward and had thought he would make an excellent monarch.)

Where was the Church in all this chaos? The answer is that

although it still wielded symbolic power, and although its rhetoric presupposed business as usual, it no longer occupied central ground. It had been quietly shunted off to a siding marked "religion", a quiet place for those who liked that sort of thing. A long-term casualty of the First World War, which it had uncritically and even jingoistically supported, it now commanded the allegiance of a minority.

The movement of population from the city centres posed problems for the Kirk. The building of new houses on the city peripheries gave working class families in the slums the chance of a new life. After the Union, John White poured his considerable energies into the church extension movement, overcoming the opposition of many of his more cautious contemporaries to raise money for churches in the new schemes. George MacLeod was very enthusiastic about the scheme, and organized collections in Govan.

George's position amidst all this turmoil was fairly clear. He believed the Christian gospel was the answer to the problems of society, and that the main obstacle to belief was the fact that the Church was not living its message in ways which commended it to ordinary people. He had a fundamental confidence in the gospel – though not as a static message – and in the Church, and believed that if only the Church could live out its message and reorganize its life on a missionary pattern, the people would come in. If that happened, the national established Kirk, with its parishes in every part of the land, would reclaim its rightful place at the heart of Scottish life.

Never a man to be a disciple of any human being, George was, however, attracted by the life and thinking of two English churchmen, William Temple and Dick Sheppard, who seemed to him to be addressing the problems of the twentieth century. Both men had been involved in founding the Life and Liberty movement in the Church of England, seeking to reform the Church and to present a living faith to ordinary people.

William Temple was the thoughtful theologian and churchman, Dick Sheppard the enthusiastic activist and irritant. As Archbishop of York, Temple addressed the social and moral issues of the Thirties and placed them firmly on the agenda of an established Church which largely gave the impression of wanting to be engaged elsewhere. In his writings, Temple emphasized the doctrine of the Incarnation, arguing boldly that since God had taken on human flesh in love for the world, all of life was sacred and under the rule of Christ. Unemployment and poverty were therefore offences not just against man, but against God.

George greatly admired Temple and saw him as a source of hope. (The admiration was reciprocated. After Temple became Archbishop of Canterbury, he said he found a regular place in his prayers for the Iona Community, as he regarded it as one of the most significant of contemporary Christian movements, and he wrote to George in 1942, asking him to be on his advisory committee on matters of social justice.) George was to say of the Church of England: "They have been willing to listen to the Temple bells, but not to beat the Temple drums."

Dick Sheppard had characteristics not unlike those of George MacLeod himself. Flamboyant, warm-hearted, impatient, idealistic, melancholy, and provocative, he passionately desired to make Christianity relevant to the common man. He transformed St Martin-in-the-Fields Church, London, into a vibrant centre of mission – a place for activists and down-and-outs. Sheppard was impatient to transform the Church of England, which he saw as obsessed with ecclesiastical trivia and out of touch with the ordinary people.

George's pilgrimage through the Thirties had brought him gradually and inexorably closer to the pacifist position. In 1934, in an address to the Student Christian Movement at Swanwick, he had argued that the Church needed to find a moral equivalent to war, even though he did not rule out the need for force in certain circumstances.

"So long as we cannot yet altogether renounce the sanction of force in civic matters – so long, that is, as we shall require the police – it is useless to envisage a world in which force plays no part at all. There are still 'police' duties to be performed by civilized countries, where their responsibilities under God impinge on uncivilized territories. The 'policing' of civilization's boundaries by the minimum army and navy still seems inevitable, for its alternative would be chaos. But, after experiencing in our own generation the holocaust entailed in wars between civilized peoples, it becomes the instant duty of Christian patriots to plead with their countrymen to explore new approaches altogether. Some of us believe it becomes their instant duty to take, at once, their own uncompromising stand.

"And here we approach the possibility of patriotic pacifism.

'Turning the other cheek' is a positive and not a negative act: it is physically an action and not a motionless acceptance. This principle of positive non-resistance has long been found practicable when dealing with individuals: it is, in fact, present in all acts of patient love that cost anything at all."

George's move towards pacifism was itself part of a national reassessment of the First World War. He was responding to the failure of his own inherited world view. If reconstruction had collapsed in cynicism and disillusionment, if the war drums were being beaten in Europe again, if millions of unemployed men were being asked to go to the wall for the sake of the better off, what had been the purpose of it all? And could the Church support yet another war to end all wars?

The issue had been debated by the General Assembly in 1933 – the year in which the young men of Oxford had declared they would not support king and country again, the year in which Adolf Hitler assumed control of Germany – when a pacifist addendum to the Church and Nation report was proposed. Thanks to the intervention of George MacLeod's theology teacher, Professor W. P. Paterson, during the stormy three-hour debate, the addendum was not accepted, but was referred back for further study. When the report came back the following year, the influential Dr John White argued successfully against the pacifists in the Kirk.

As an all-or-nothing man, George MacLeod pursued his thinking to the extreme. Dick Sheppard had formed a Peace Army (this appealed to George, who thought continually in military terms, and saw life itself as a battleground), which became in turn the Peace Pledge Union. Sheppard asked people to send him postcards saying: "We renounce war and never again, directly or indirectly, will we support or sanction another". More than 100,000 postcards arrived in the post. George MacLeod was impressed: so much so that he spent the rest of his life trying to get people to sign things.

In October 1937 Dick Sheppard stood for the post of Rector of Glasgow University. George headed up his Glasgow campaign, speaking at student meetings along with C. E. M. Joad, Aldous Huxley, Middleton Murry and Rose Macaulay. Sheppard won decisively, defeating Winston Churchill, Professor Macneile Dixon, and Professor J. B. S. Haldane. George sent Sheppard a telegram saying, "Read Psalm 29 and apply for immediate canonization". The new rector replied, asking George to be his assessor at the University court. Within a few days, Dick Sheppard was dead.

George spoke at open-air meetings in Govan in the cause of peace, and encouraged people to join the Peace Pledge Union. Now a member of the Church and Nation's sub-committee on peace and disarmament, he was spelling out a vision of the Christian Church as an international body, transcending nationality, with the potential to shape a new world. He knew a world war was coming again, and he wanted a reconstruction which would be total this time.

On one occasion, he dramatically threw down his war medals from the Govan pulpit to make his point. Although conservative in theology, he was not a fundamentalist in his view of the Bible – except in regard to the teaching of Jesus.

It was ironic that while George was preaching peace from his pulpit and at Govan Cross, more and more Govan men were in employment because of the rearmament programme. The empty Clydeside berths were filling up with warships.

Open-air speaking at Govan Cross was nothing new for George: he had often preached the gospel at the local market place. He had also debated with the local Communists. On one occasion, he advertised a sermon on Communism, followed by a debate in the Pearce Institute. More than 1000 people came along. The Communists were easy to identify at the church service – they were the ones who resolutely kept their "bunnets" firmly on their heads.

George was implacably opposed to Communism, but he had a great respect for people who were so committed to their beliefs. The respect, and indeed affection, were mutual.

"See you, MacLeod," one of the Communist leaders told him. "When the revolution comes, we'll string all you lads up on lampposts. In your case we'll make an exception – we'll come to your funeral!"

The memory of George's open-air preaching is still strong in Govan. One of those brought up on the MacLeod legend was Alex Ferguson, the former Rangers footballer who went on to become manager of Aberdeen, and Manchester United. His father was a Govan shipyard worker, and Alex, who was a member of the local Boys' Brigade, was brought up in a socialist household.

"George MacLeod influenced so many people," he recalled. "It was amazing to have a minister standing on a soapbox at Govan Cross. Govan was a working class community, and everyone respected him because he was fighting for their ambitions and desires. Working class people needed someone like George Mac-Leod, with his kind of moral conviction and leadership. He has been a great man – we could do with more like him."

George admired the Communists' passion for social justice, and wished it would be matched by Christians. His own political views were changing, faced by the distress he saw around him. Charity was no longer enough. He lashed out from the Govan pulpit at captains of industry who built slums and mission halls at the same time. In his views on war and social justice, George MacLeod was going well beyond the Morvern dynastic role. It was as well his father was peaceful in his grave.

Sir John would have been proud of his son, though, in June 1937, when George Fielden MacLeod had the degree of Doctor of Divinity conferred upon him – the fourth of his family in lineal descent to receive an honorary doctorate. Proposing the toast to the honorary graduates after the ceremony, the Principal of the University, Sir Hector Hetherington, turned to George and said that he almost had a hereditary right to his degree. He described the Govan minister as "a preacher, a missioner, a troubler of the conscience of his time and city, and the inspiration of remarkable and beneficent work in the parish of Govan."

George wrote to Petrovitch: "Glasgow University have made the singular mistake of offering me the degree of DD. As Walter Elliot has put me on the Physical Education Board for Scotland, you realize that it stands for Daily Dozen. The boys' choir imagine it stands for Deadly Dull, and if I go on you will regard me as Definitely Drunk. More seriously, I am glad – if it had to come – that it has come from Glasgow . . . somehow Glasgow represents Honest to Goodness Life more than Edinburgh."

All Govan rejoiced for him. At a meeting in South Govan Town Hall, he was presented with his DD robes and hood, a set of pulpit books and a bookcase, subscribed to by over 1000 families in the district. Govan Old Parish Church were proud of their minister.

Little did they know that he was soon to leave them, at the height of his powers, while running one of the most successful and talked-about parish ventures in the country. He must make an experiment.

In March 1938, Hitler marched into Austria. Neville Chamberlain, the British prime minister, flew out to meet the German dictator and came back announcing "Peace in our time".

In April 1938, George MacLeod resigned as minister of Govan

Old Parish Church. The Kirk Session minutes recorded that "his regret at leaving Govan was acute and, after several members of the Session had expressed their sorrow and wishes for their minister's prosperity and success in his great venture, it was unanimously resolved that the Kirk Session put no obstacle in the way of the Presbytery granting Dr MacLeod his petition to demit his office." The Very Rev. Dr White was appointed interim Moderator *pro tempore*.

"What does George want?" inquired the Moderator of the General Assembly of a friend. "He's had St Cuthbert's, he's had Gowan, what more does he want?"

George knew what he wanted. He was leaving, he said, because he was haunted by a Govan man called Archie Gray.

PART FOUR

*

THE NEW COMMUNITY

10

Tell Me the Old, Old Story

It is not given to man to begin; that privilege is God's alone. But it is given to man to begin again – and he does so every time he chooses to defy death and side with the living.

ELIE WIESEL

It is only the unimaginative who ever invents. The true artist is known by the use of what he annexes, and he annexes everything.

OSCAR WILDE

There is a Gaelic term, *Seanachaidh* (pronounced Shenachay), which fits George MacLeod. It means a story teller, a Celtic bard who tells tales and hands on the oral tradition. These folk tales are not just for interest, though they are truly interesting; they are told over and over, and the retelling helps bind the community together.

Jesus of Nazareth was, on one level, a *Seanachaidh*. He told vivid stories and parables which gripped the imagination. The tales had punchlines and stayed in the minds of his disciples, and are still retailed two thousand years on. The Sermon on the Mount was a composition of oft-repeated sayings and word-pictures which haunt the imagination. Vividness, concreteness, and atmosphere are essential to such stories and sayings, which can be much more easily passed down the generations than can a thesis. St Columba of Iona was a *Seanachaidh*, his poems and word pictures luminous in the Celtic mist.

George MacLeod was aware of the power of the story. In his lectures to Church of England ordinands in 1936 (he also gave the Warrack lectures on preaching at Edinburgh and St Andrews Universities the same year) he advocated what he called "modern parabolic" preaching – the use of powerful stories and images to engage the imagination. He practised what he preached, repeating and repeating and repeating until his stories became a community litany.

How did the Iona Community really begin? The *Seanachaidh* tells it himself.

"I remember preaching individual salvation in the street in Govan one day – yes to 500 men on a weekday at 4 o'clock. What else was there for them to do in the market place but listen to curate or Communist? An outspoken man in question time, speaking almost as God spoke to Isaiah, asked: 'Do you think all this religious stuff will save?' Very down at heel he was, but very clear of eye. Suddenly, as he was speaking, I realised he was preaching the gospel and not I. I asked him to come up on the platform, but he refused and left the meeting.

"Some weeks later I received a message asking me to go to hospital and see a man called Archie Gray. I had never heard the name before, but when I reached the hospital I found it was my questioner from the meeting and he was dying of starvation. The man was single, in a whole household of unemployed, which he had left because he felt he was eating too much of the rations. Out of 21 shillings a week he was sending 7/6d a week to a ne'er-do-well brother in Australia. He said he was bitter about the Church, not because it was preaching falsehoods, but because it was speaking the truth and did not mean what it said.

"Archie Gray was the true founder of the Iona Community."

Typically, there are several versions of this story with variations and embellishments, all told by George at different times. The facts are now beyond recall: the truth lives on. At the heart of the myth there is the reality of a street encounter between an unemployed man and a privileged upper class preacher, in which the minister suddenly finds himself addressed by God in a moment which changes his life. To hear George retell the story with all the oratorical gifts at his command is first to be drawn into the Govan street crowd, and then to be addressed directly. Thus in the riveting modern parabolic preaching of the theatrical Govan *Seanachaidh*, a raw Glasgow street encounter becomes living story becomes contemporary Word-event becomes life-changing moment.

The story, and the repetitions of it, provides the main clue to the understanding of George MacLeod as he moves towards the founding of the Iona Community. It points to the burning heart of his conviction: that the Church has the message which the world needs to hear and it must not be apologetic about it in the face of other ideologies – but the message is being denied by the life and practice of the messenger. The story tells us more about George MacLeod than it does about the shadowy figure of Archie Gray. George despairs of the Church precisely because he loves it, and because he believes the Church to be the one body which can point the way forward for the world. The point is made in his lectures on preaching.

"One of our local Clydeside brilliants, a quasi Communist who has smoked more of my cigarettes than any other man alive, suddenly burst into my room unexpectedly to proclaim, 'You folk have got it: if only you knew that you had it, and if only you knew how to begin to say it.' It was his certainty that rebuked me; his implied need that moved me. What in effect he said was, 'You know you could save me and you know you aren't doing it.'[1]

In leaving Govan, then, George MacLeod was seeking to make an experiment which would help the Church be true to its own message and, in a deep sense, to find its message. In particular, he was concerned about the work of the Church in the new housing schemes. He felt that teams of young men were needed for the work, and he also believed that the training provided by the divinity halls was inadequate.

There is a sense in which George had been seeking a new kind of fellowship ever since the cessation of hostilities. The divinity college, Toc H, youth work in Edinburgh, 8 Charlotte Square, the top flat of the Pearce Institute and Fingalton Mill were all attempts at the recovery of a lost comradeship and the establishment of a new community. He thought continually in military terms, and admired military discipline and fellowship. On one level, the creation of the Iona Community was Captain George MacLeod's latest attempt to establish a new, disciplined regiment trained and equipped for a new fight. It was a reconstructed Toc H, this time with the satisfaction of being his own commanding officer. If he could not find an existing regiment, he would create his own.

George was impressed by doers of the Word rather than speakers, and imaginative experiments appealed to him. He was attracted to the Cotswold Bruderhof, a pacifist Moravian Brethren group which established a community farm in the Cotswolds in 1936 and attempted to live a simple life based on the Sermon on the Mount. He referred to that example on a number of occasions and it clearly made a deep impression on him. In the 1930s the brilliant young

German theologian Dietrich Bonhoeffer established a community for young seminarians in the Confessing Church – the group which opposed Hitler's "Germanizing" of the Church – and though George does not refer to it directly, it is likely that he would have been aware of it. These were all signs of a move within certain parts of the European churches to find more communal expressions of the Christian faith. What was required, George MacLeod believed deeply, was not more pamphlets, but a living experiment in community which at least matched the Communist cells which he admired so much.

"I think I shall go mad if the Student Christian Movement produces another book on *Christianity and Communism, Christ or Chaos, Deliverance or Doom,*" he wrote. "Everything that can, need, or ever will be said has now been said, a hundred times over, about the superiority of Christianity in theory. We have enough theories to last a generation. The modern world knows quite well what our theory is, what they are interested in is whether we are prepared to show the vaguest signs of putting it into practice."[2]

The living experiment would happen on the island of Iona.

The way he tells it now, one could be forgiven for imagining that the whole thing was suggested by others – George himself has "blamed" it on different people at different times, the front runners being his sister Ellen, Harry Whitley and Hugh Douglas – and that he was forced into it, kicking and screaming, in 1938. The reality is a little different.

If George had had his way in 1929, it might not even have been Iona. At that time, he took some friends, including Bill Rogan, in a boat to the island of Incholm, off the coast of Fife. The attraction was the ruined Abbey of Incholm, which the young St Cuthbert's minister thought should be rebuilt as a retreat and renewal centre. Had Bruce Nicol not died in Govan in 1930, there might well have been in the Kirk a relatively conventional Incholm Community rather than a group of turbulent Iona *agents provocateurs*.

Why, then, Iona?

For someone with such a romantic sense of history as George MacLeod, Iona was a special gift from God. Ever since Columba's great voyage from Ireland in 563 AD, the small Hebridean island off the west coast of Mull had been renowned as a place of spirituality, community and mission. Columba's "island soldiers" evangelized – and in some cases re-evangelized, after the work of St Ninian of Whithorn in the fourth century – many parts of

Scotland, and the Columban monks also preached their way through Europe. Columba, a prince with a legitimate claim on the Irish throne, was imperious, impatient, poetic, awesome, driven. He ran the community and directed the mission, stamping his formidable personality on the whole enterprise. His voice could be heard over in Mull, shouting at his disciples, who revered him even when they found him a hard taskmaster. Just before his death on 9 June, 597 he uttered the famous prophecy about Iona:

> Unto this place, small and mean though it be, great homage shall yet be paid, not only by the kings and people of the Scots, but by the rulers of foreign and barbarous nations and their subjects. In great veneration, too, shall it be held by holy men of other churches.

By the time of the saint's death, Iona had a special role in the formation of European Christianity. The orthodox theology of the Irish-Scottish Celtic Church differed from Roman theology in ethos and style, but the churches, although they differed in organization and priorities, had no difficulty in recognizing each other as fellow Catholic Christians. The Celtic Church was based largely around the monasteries and the abbot was therefore the important figure: the Roman system centred on the cities, where the bishops had their seats.

The Celtic style was distinctive. The pursuit of holiness was at its heart, and prayer, penitence, corporate worship, the eucharist, pilgrimage and martyrdom were important elements of the Celtic Christian journey. Gaelic theologians followed the druids in seeing all things as impregnated with spirit; they both accepted and transformed this tendency by using the framework of the Trinity. Celtic theology was poetic and imaginative rather than speculative, linking deep spirituality to a reverence for the earth. The redemption it preached was cosmic; a redemption for the whole created order. In personal terms, it saw life as a conflict, and emphasized Christ's victory over the powers of darkness. Beauty, redemption and care for the outcast were inextricably linked, as were the lovely intertwining symbols of eternity which decorated the Celtic crosses of Iona. The religious poetry was gentle and evocative.

At the Synod of Whitby in 664, the Celtic Church came formally under Roman jurisdiction after a great deal of struggle. By the twelfth century the flickering Celtic flame was out. The Benedictines came to Iona in 1203, forming a vital new Iona community, and began to build the present Abbey on the Columban site. Fine scholarship, regular prayer, hospitality and ordered worship provided the foundations of a stable structure, symbolized by the strong, stone walls of the Abbey. Iona represented holy ground – the burial place of many Scottish and Norwegian kings including, it is believed, Macbeth and Duncan. The island and its Abbey became a pawn in the game of West Highland politics and ecclesiastical manoeuvres until the Reformation, when the Abbey -- by then the Cathedral of St Mary – was allowed to fall into disrepair.

In the latter part of the eighteenth and into the nineteenth century, during the romantic revival of interest in Highland affairs, visitors came to walk through the ruins and invoke ancient memories. Dr Johnson said of the holy island: "That man is little to be envied whose patriotism would not gain force upon the plain of Marathon, or whose piety would not grow warmer among the ruins of Iona."

Sir Walter Scott, Keats, Wordsworth (who described Iona Abbey as "this Glory of the West"), Mendelsson, Prince Albert, Earl Grey, Robert Louis Stevenson all made the pilgrimage; as did the Rev. Norman MacLeod, *Caraid nan Gaidheal*, who visited the island in 1828 and wrote after his visit:

"For many years this famous isle, where dwelt so many holy men and noble divines, and which shared the light of the Gospel with other countries and nations, was itself left without church or settled preacher or public worship. It was a sad change which came over Iona and shameful to relate, but a better time is coming. It is said that shortly before his death Columba uttered these words:

> Iona of my heart, Iona of my love,
> Instead of monks' voices there shall be lowing of cattle:
> But ere the world comes to an end
> Iona shall be as it was.

"The first part of the prophecy has come to pass, but whether the island will ever be as honoured as it once was is difficult to say. Amid the many changes of the changing world, who can say what may happen?"[3]

Who indeed? *Caraid nan Gaidheal* would have been astonished, unless he had the Gaelic second sight, to have been told then that his own great-grandson would be the one who would help to make the second part of the prophecy of St Columba come true.

Church pilgrimages were made from time to time. Pope John MacLeod of Govan and his brother, the Very Rev. Dr Norman MacLeod of Inverness, took part in an ecumenical pilgrimage to the island on the occasion of the 13th centenary of the death of St Columba in June 1897. Two years later, the Duke of Argyll, who had tried to keep the ruins of the Cathedral in reasonable repair, handed them over to a public trust "in connection with the established Church of Scotland." In the Trust Deed of 1899, the Duke expressed his wish that members of other Christian churches should be allowed to hold services in the Abbey.

The Duke of Argyll's ecumenical generosity had already brought rebukes and vitriolic correspondence from the island parish minister, and in the title deed the Duke expressly forbade the parish minister and kirk session of Iona from having any part in the management or worship of the Cathedral "except in so far as the use thereof may be allowed to them for the purpose of worship by the Trustees."

The Iona Cathedral Trustees, who included the Principals of Aberdeen, Glasgow, and Edinburgh Universities, the Principal of St Mary's College, St Andrews, the ministers of St Giles' and Glasgow Cathedrals, and the Moderator and Procurator of the General Assembly of the Church of Scotland, set about raising the necessary £20,000 to reroof and restore the Abbey church. John MacLeod, MP, was appointed honorary treasurer of the West of Scotland branch of the appeal committee.

The MacLeod family at that time regularly holidayed at Tavool at Loch Scridain in Mull. George MacLeod still delights to narrate his first memory of Iona.

"When I was a boy of nine we went over to Iona. My father said, 'I want you to talk to Mrs McCormack – she's 85 years old, and I think you should shake hands with her.' So I shook hands with Mrs McCormack, a little embarrassed. My father said, 'Now I'll tell you why. When she was nine years old she shook hands with a Mrs Campbell who was then 85 years of age, and Mrs Campbell, when she was nine years of age, stood at exactly this point on the jetty and watched the boat going down the Sound of Iona taking Bonnie Prince Charlie back to France.' Now that was wonderful education – two handshakes away from Bonnie Prince Charlie!"

The cattle were certainly lowing in the ruins, but they were moved out of the choir as the rebuilding proceeded. By 1910, the Abbey church had been beautifully restored. A communion table of genuine Iona marble was placed in the sanctuary. The island continued to attract pilgrims, and students came for retreat. The first principal of St Colm's College, Annie Hunter Small, dearly loved Iona and brought students to the island at least as early as 1913. George was to say later that Miss Small turned his attention to Iona. The Reports of the Schemes of the Church of Scotland for 1921 refers to a retreat held by divinity students the previous year.

The retreats had been started and funded in 1920 by Dr David Russell, who had enlisted the enthusiastic help of George MacLeod from the beginning. George was a popular lecturer at the annual Iona events. The potential of Iona for retreat, renewal and ministerial formation was obvious to him. The history of Iona and its special atmosphere – he described it as a "thin place – only a tissue paper separating earth from heaven" – greatly appealed to him.

In 1929 the Iona Fellowship was formed. It consisted of those who had been on retreat at Iona. Members of the fellowship agreed to set apart a period between 7 am and 8 am each day for private devotions, and they drew strength from the knowledge that others in the fellowship were praying at the same time: thus was the ground laid for the Rule of the future Iona Community.

The relationship between David Russell, an Iona lover who had visited the island regularly since 1898, and George MacLeod, was the crucial element in the move towards the restoration of the living quarters of Iona Abbey. Dr Russell, a man of social conscience who owned a paper mill in Markinch, was impressed by the younger man's enthusiasm and organizational ability. Dr Russell talked about possible restoration schemes with George, and in 1931, with the permission of the Cathedral Trustees, he had plans prepared by Dr Reginald Fairlie, who had restored St Salvator's Chapel, St Andrews. He put these plans, which included the restoration of the cloisters, before the Cathedral Trustees in April 1933. The Trustees were interested, but decided that the height of a Depression was not the time to launch an appeal to fund the restoration of the living quarters of Iona Abbey.

Dr Russell was not the only one with ideas about the restoration of the rest of the Iona Abbey buildings, however. As early as 1926, a group of Highland émigrés in the United States, calling themselves the American Iona Society, had mooted the idea of forming a Celtic College in Scotland. Their romantic idea was that of restoring the living quarters of Iona Abbey as a new seat of Celtic studies. One of the society's influential backers was no less than the Rev. Norman Maclean, senior minister of St Cuthbert's Church. George MacLeod could not have been unaware of these discussions in the late 1920s.

After much to-ing and fro-ing across the Atlantic, American romanticism was tempered by Scottish realism. It was eventually agreed that the college should be sited on the Scottish mainland.

The Americans did not, however, relinquish their Iona dream altogether. They came up with a compromise: that the college would be on the mainland, and the Abbey would be restored as a spiritual and educational centre. On October 1, 1935, they wrote to the Iona Cathedral Trustees with their proposals, and saying that the Society would bear all the costs of the restoration, as well as maintaining buildings through an endowment fund.

The Trustees were suspicious of the "educational subjects" proposed by the society, and wondered how theologically orthodox the whole thing would be. A holding letter was sent, asking the Americans how much money they actually had.

When the day of decision, November 20, 1935, arrived, things were fairly tense – there were actually two proposals for rebuilding on the table. The second was more tentative and had no promise of funds. It came from the Rev. George MacLeod, minister of Govan Old Parish Church. What had prompted his proposal?

While in Govan, George used to have a month's holiday in Iona every August. Quite often his assistants would go with him, and the ruined Iona Abbey was a frequent subject of conversation. In George's official version, repeated over many years, the success of Fingalton Mill gave him (or one of his assistants, or sister Ellen) the idea of rebuilding on Iona. But given George's interest in rebuilding Incholm Abbey in 1929, given the ideas in circulation since 1926 about the possibility of an American rebuilding on Iona, and given David Russell's plans in the early 1930s when George was regularly on the island, it is distinctly possible that Fingalton Mill – an outstanding idea in its own right – was, in fact, a dress rehearsal for a more serious project being enacted in the theatre of the fertile MacLeod mind. He put the matter in an interesting way in an interview.

"I had the same kind of 'nudge' I had when I decided to become a minister and when I decided to go to Govan. I didn't want to do it, but every time I passed that ruin on Iona it seemed to be talking to me, just simply saying, 'Why doesn't somebody rebuild me?' I can almost remember turning my head away because I didn't want to be disturbed by this idea."

The longer he looked at the restored sanctuary and the ruined living quarters, the more he saw it as a parable of the situation in Govan and in the world – a beautifully tended sanctuary surrounded by a community in ruins.

"Very faint at first, these beckoning walls, as I walked past the Abbey," he said, "like a simmering kettle when it first begins to whisper . . . but by 1937 the very lid of that kettle was rattling. I know I was rattled. Why escape to an island when involvement was the need? 'Get thee to a monastery' seemed the reverse of what our world was needing. Why do you shout so loud at me, you most uncomfortable ruins?"[4]

Gradually, the issue clarified into an idea of a purposeful rebuilding.

A strange incident made a deep impression when he was on holiday on Iona.

One night when he was passing down the road in the dark, he saw a tiny light shining from the Abbey. Almost apprehensively he crept in: and heard music. A single candle stood on the small harmonium in the south aisle. Round it crouched a group of five adults and three children. They were singing the 23rd Psalm to the tune "Wiltshire". It was pathetic in its inadequacy; moving in its simplicity. What a wonderful place, he thought, not just for a single family but for the family of God.

The most likely historical scenario is that the idea of rebuilding the living quarters of Iona Abbey had been around for years, particularly in the mind of David Russell, and that George MacLeod had always been interested. George's genius lay in making it all happen, but more than that – brilliantly wedding the notion of restoration to a bold experiment in training ministers for a new kind of Church. It gradually took shape in his mind with the power of a call which could not ultimately be denied, and came to a point of decision and now-or-never commitment when it became clear that the Americans were serious about their proposal.

His private and confidential document for the Trustees, dated November 15, 1935, showed that the Govan minister had done his political homework. The man who would become notorious for his leftward and Catholic tendencies played on fears of Communism and Roman Catholicism.

"If Christianity is the only answer to Communism, Christianity must become more concerned with its Corporate Witness (or shall we say its Collective Witness), and if the Church of Rome is not to be allowed to be the only purveyor of this Witness, the Protestant Churches must play their part in developing this emphasis within their own field: or else we deserve to perish by default."

George MacLeod said in his paper that the Church of Scotland was facing the greatest challenge ever made to its reputation as a national Church by reason of the great movements of people to areas where there were no churches. "One man" ministries could not cope with the situation: teams of ministers were required. Specialist non-parochial ministries were also needed to deal with young people and people with psychological problems.

What was required, he wrote, was a brotherhood within the Church of Scotland into which men could come for the first two or three years of their ministry. The first six months after leaving college would be spent in such community life as would help them rediscover the technique of living together – something which the divinity halls failed to teach. They would then be ready to be drafted out to the congested areas and the housing schemes, where they would put their training into practice. Others again would be seconded to extra-parochial specialist ministries. After two or three years in the brotherhood, they would leave it and serve the Church through its more usual channels.

The monastic buildings of Iona would be ideal for such a centre: it would be the modern counterpart of St Columba's original intention: the new light of Protestantism would be lit to meet the new day, as his lamp had met his. But how would the buildings be restored?

"If Columba built his settlement by the labour of his own hands; if during the Roman period, men were found of sufficient consecration to build the present Abbey; is Protestantism so bereft that it must leave such rebuilding to a contractor and hired labourers at enhanced wages? The matter cannot be gone into in this paper, but I believe that there is still a wealth of idealism latent in many of our young craftsmen today. There are skilled masons, carpenters and plumbers, loyal members of the Church of Scotland and as proud of her as ever were the monks of their Mother Church: men who never have worked just for a wage: who would be glad of the opportunity to express their craftsmanship to the glory of God. Is it not conceivable that a community might start work – housed in log huts – composed both of such craftsmen and of the first group of young ministers: the craftsmen to restore the Cathedral, while the first group prepared themselves for their work as outlined above. Each would learn from the other of a Church that was setting its sails to a new pattern, albeit to catch the same breezes that first brought Iona's Message to the Mainland. A Cathedral so restored would itself be a sermon of the modern vitality of our Church life, instead of a mere recapitulation of an age that everyone knows is past."

In his memorandum, George said that these ideas had been under discussion before the American Iona Society had approached the Trustees. He had talked his proposals over with Mr Angus Robertson, a former president of *An Comunn Gaidhealach*, and a supporter of the American scheme. Mr Robertson had agreed that the new proposals would meet his aspirations.

"I would add one more word," he said in a crafty postscript. "I understand that the late Duke of Argyll refused over £100,000 for the island of Iona from representatives of the Roman Church. What they would have made of the island had they obtained it, we all know well. As in fact the Church of Scotland holds it, is there not a duty upon us to make more use of it – or at least to attempt to make more use of it – than so far we as a Church have contrived to do?"

So: far from being dragged reluctantly by others into rebuilding the monastic buildings of Iona in 1938, George MacLeod, who had thought of rebuilding Incholm Abbey in 1929, and had been involved in discussions about such a project on Iona for several years, was competing against another Iona restoration proposal as early as 1935; and was doing so with all the persuasive skills at his command. Having got wind of the firm American proposals, he had got together again with Dr Russell – who recognized in MacLeod a man with the drive to make his restoration dream come true – to present again the plans for the complex which had been drawn up four years previously. Not only that, he had managed to convince the main Scottish protagonist of the American scheme that this new idea would fulfil their purpose!

The Govan minister's intervention had the desired effect of putting the American bid on ice. George MacLeod's alternative had the merit of being a Church of Scotland proposal which went so far as to invoke the sacred memory of St Columba the Blessed Protestant! George's paper was a persuasive mixture of high visionary idealism and low political cunning.

It is ironic, in the light of the subsequent development of George MacLeod's views and reputation – causing headaches at various times for the Cathedral Trustees – that in 1935 his was seen as the more conservative, safer, less problematical option. After all, in 1935 the Trustees were dealing with a Morvern MacLeod, one of the Kirk's most admired men, who would one day become Moderator and therefore an Iona Cathedral Trustee himself.

Faced with the two proposals, the Trustees officially hedged their bets, but agreed unanimously to the principle of "restoring the old buildings adjoining the Cathedral as near as possible to their original form and adapting them as a retreat for worship, meditation, study and instruction." They decided to approach the American Iona Society with a view to creating an Iona Trust which would make grants towards the restoration, and would found scholarships for the study of the Celtic language.

In other words, although they did not state it in these terms, they preferred George MacLeod's scheme but wanted the Americans' money, an outcome which delighted the Govan man. The Americans were less delighted. Division in Scotland over their plans further lessened their enthusiasm, and eventually, in May 1937, they wrote to the Cathedral Trustees to say they could expect nothing from the Society. The way was open for the Govan minister.

By March 1938 he was ready.

He produced the restoration plans first prepared in 1931 – Dr Russell and Dr Fairlie said he could use them provided Ian Lindsay, one of Dr Fairlie's staff who had surveyed the Cathedral for the earlier plans, could be persuaded to take charge – along with an extended version of the paper he had written in 1935. In the preamble, he said that in the course of the decade in which they were living, nearly a quarter of the population of Scotland had moved into new areas. Only ministers trained to live in community could cope with the problems and opportunities which would emerge. It was essential for people to work co-operatively if the world were to survive.

"It is this need that makes the Fellowship witness of the Church its most pressing concern. Her deepest hope resides in the fact that she possesses the only key that will ultimately open the way . . . It cannot, however, be claimed that the Church's key is presently ready for insertion. It appears to fit; but – its body is bent by an undue individual emphasis in Victorian days: its incisiveness rusted by our divisions: its pointer blunted by our uncertainties – it somehow sticks. Nor can it be claimed, within our national problem, that the Divinity Halls adequately train men in the supremely important technique of fellowship."

George went on to argue that with the collapse of the Puritan ideal, Presbyterianism needed to work out a new structure. In this quest it was helpful to look back to Celtic and Roman times on Iona – these periods preserved things which were essential to a modern Presbyterian witness.

As usual, the Govan minister was arguing that in order to go forward the Church must first go backwards, to ransack the drawers of its own past and find garments which would fit for today and tomorrow. From the Celtic Church he drew a sense of the totality of all life infused by the Spirit, from the Roman Catholic Church a sense of universality, from the Reformers the doctrine of the priesthood of all believers.

George MacLeod was seeking to annexe the whole Christian past as a living resource for the new Presbyterian future. He was willing to dream this new future and even, by imaginative leaps of his creative historical imagination, to make up the past to suit his future purposes.

He proposed that the new Iona brotherhood be formed immediately, with licentiate divinity students acting as labourers to the artisans. The young ministers would also study the problems of housing scheme and specialist ministries, before going out in teams to "start their ministry in difficult places".

Who would have responsibility for the experiment? George suggested that a group of sponsors from the Church of Scotland be formed to oversee the direction of the project. He produced a master stroke – he informed the Trustees that he had persuaded the Kirk's father figure, The Very Rev. Dr John White, to be a sponsor of the new experiment. If Dr White was for it, who could be against it?

While the sponsors would have general oversight, one person would need to be in charge of the day-to-day arrangements on the island, the recruitment of volunteers, and the raising of funds for the rebuilding. In a leap of faith, George Fielden MacLeod made an offer which translated the proposal from paper to flesh and blood reality. He was prepared to put his body where his mind was.

"For the purpose of its inception, I would myself be prepared to leave my present work at any time now and would undertake to stand by the experiment full time, resisting any conceivable inducements, for a term of five years. For such time during that period as I remained unmarried I would offer my services without reward, but would ask for the payment of my essential expenses when travelling in the name of the Brotherhood."

The spotlight now shifted on the Iona Cathedral Trustees. They were faced with a rebuilding proposal without funding attached, but the main protagonist was prepared to put himself on the line. The Trustees unanimously agreed in principle that the use of the buildings suggested by Dr MacLeod was the right use, and granted permission to erect a wooden hut on the site – "it being understood that no financial burden would fall on the Trustees." They agreed to the creation of a water supply on the hill to the west of the Abbey and stated that they agreed to the principle that "while it would be desirable that such restoration should be in harmony with their original outline, the restoration should also express the spirit of the present age." The work should be done in stages, and approval would only be given to each stage when the money for it was guaranteed.

George MacLeod, at the age of 42, was taking a tremendous risk in leaving the security of an outstanding parish ministry. In later years, he was to look back and write to a friend, "I don't know why I went to Iona. God wanted it, and it was such a hell of a gamble that He could only find George MacLeod, who lost £40 one night at poker when he was waiting to be demobbed from the Agile and Suffering Highlanders."

So it was that the Govan gambler staked everything on a shoot-out with American rivals over the future of Iona Abbey.

And that, in essence, is how the "Glory of the West" was won.

11

The Boss

*If you board the wrong train, it's no use running along
the corridor in the opposite direction.*

DIETRICH BONHOEFFER

*Renounce religiosity and all its works. But do please,
brother, keep the Faith.*

GEORGE F. MACLEOD TO HARRY WHITLEY

When the Iona Cathedral Trustees said Yes, George MacLeod
immediately wrote a letter to every member of Govan Old Parish
Church. Rumours had been circulating in Govan that he was about
to go to a church in London (Govan people were getting used to
offers being made to their star minister. He had been invited to be
Principal of McGill University in Montreal, headmaster of Mer-
chiston School, Edinburgh, minister of Glasgow Cathedral, and
senior minister of St Cuthbert's – "I refused them all to the
annoyance of my congregation and to the relief of the offerers in
each instance", he told Petrovitch). He told his congregation that
when he first thought of the Iona scheme it had looked like a
dream, but now the main obstacles had been removed.

"Could I have said No?" he wrote to his disappointed congregation. "Could I have said 'I am safe and happy in Govan and I am
not going to take any risks whether half of Scotland goes pagan or
not?' Or again, could I have gone on getting into Govan pulpit and
saying to our young people 'Christianity is an adventure; you must
have faith; you must be prepared to take risks for Christ' and
things like that (which I so often say), if in my heart I had known
– and you had not known – that all these 'pointers' had once come
to me and I had skirted round them and just stayed on in a much
safer billet than the one I am going to?"

The Boss

On 22nd May, 1938, Govan Old Parish Church was packed for the 50th anniversary of the dedication of the church. It was fitting that it should be John MacLeod's great-nephew's last public service at Govan. The Kirk session minutes record that one of the elders, John Brown, said that Dr MacLeod had done great things inside and outside the church. His going away was one of the most courageous things he had done, and he felt the new venture would succeed because of "his personality, his magnetism and the social atmosphere he could create."

With that, George MacLeod left Govan and stepped out into the unknown.

But was he also stepping outside the official ministry of the Church?

He certainly did not feel this to be the case: yet he was leaving the parish ministry to set up an organization which was not recognized by the Church. It was quite different from becoming padre of Toc H. Then the appointment had been approved by the Kirk, and he had been ordained by the Presbytery to that office. He had not taken his plans for the Iona brotherhood to the General Assembly, primarily because he did not relish the prospect of his beloved idea making its way slowly through church committees, and being picked over by unimaginative and disapproving minds. Nor did he want such people having oversight of his experiment – he feared that his baby might be strangled at birth.

But what would be the relationship of the Iona Community to the Church of Scotland? In his memorandum to the Iona Cathedral Trustees, George compared the Community to brotherhoods attached to the Church of England: in those cases the bishop appointed an official Visitor. Perhaps some similar arrangement could be made with the Presbytery of Mull?

"If it seems to give me a free hand," he said, "it also places me in the not altogether enviable position of being personally and entirely responsible in the event of its failure. In the last resort therefore I ask the Trustees and the Sponsors to trust me personally that my purposes are utterly loyal to the Church of my fathers and my supreme concern is the preservation of Presbyterianism."

It was doubts about the preservation of Presbyterianism which lay behind the rumblings which went on in the Kirk about the project. Many ministers were suspicious of this charming, charismatic, Scoto-Catholic, with his dynastic pedigree, privileged upbringing and Winchester accent redolent of the English ruling classes. His allegedly Anglican and Roman Catholic ways, along with his pacifist and socialistic tendencies, made him a confusing and suspect as well as fascinating figure. Not a few ministers were simply jealous of this dynamic preacher and broadcaster who was popular with the masses.

Bluntly, George wanted the support and recognition of the Kirk, but not its dead hand. (Rev. Dr A. A. Morrison recalls a conversation he had with George on Iona in April 1937, during one of the regular student retreats. George talked enthusiastically about his plans for a new community, and when the student commented that his biggest difficulty might be with the General Assembly of the Church of Scotland, George replied that he wouldn't ask the Assembly – he would simply go ahead and do it and present the Assembly with a *fait accompli*.) If there was one thing he had learned in the war, it was that incompetent direction from above could stifle all initiative. He was determined to be his own commanding officer: he knew that he could do it better than anyone else. If the project failed, it would at least be because of his own mistakes and not because of someone else's infuriating incompetence.

Was this a case of Morvern dynastic and Winchester born-to-rule arrogance, or simply strong self-belief based on hard-won experience? Whatever the case, the Church of Scotland woke up to find that there was an exciting and bewildering new show in town – revamped Presbyterianism in Celtic drag, with Catholic song and dance routines – and it was going to run and run, whether they liked it or not.

By persuading senior churchmen of the stamp of John White, David S. Cairns, Charles Warr, John Baillie, Donald Baillie, James S. Stewart and Sir D. Y. Cameron to be official Sponsors of the experiment, George had solved the immediate problem by creating a sufficiently strong credit balance of support to get his new project off the ground. Such measures were insufficient for the long term, however, and whenever there was a run on the ecclesiastical credit bank, the Sponsors became understandably nervous. The signs were there at the General Assembly in May, 1938, when some commissioners expressed annoyance about the fact that they had first learned of the scheme through the newspapers.

The Rev. Arthur H. Dunnett, joint secretary of the Home Board, charged that not even the Home Mission Committee of the Kirk had been consulted, and nor was the General Assembly now being given an opportunity of declaring their approval or otherwise of the scheme.

"All I have seen of the scheme," he complained to the Assembly, "suggests that Dr MacLeod fears the hand of a constitutional body within the Church."

He was right, he was right. But he went on to add generously, "If it is within the power of any man to carry through such an experiment it is Dr MacLeod, who has been able to make a world-wide public by means of the wireless, and who has an extraordinary appeal to young people." He hoped that the General Assembly would welcome the splendid adventure, even though Dr Mac-Leod's method of setting out on it was not what some members might have wished. He was supported by Dr John White.

The Assembly concurred with Dr White, as it usually did, and it set up a committee to monitor the new venture and to report to the next Assembly.

George MacLeod's high risk strategy of presenting the Assembly with a *fait accompli* had worked. His experiment had the backing of the Kirk – in the meantime. It also had the enthusiastic support of many divinity students and young ministers who were looking for a lead, and admired the daring of the man who had, at considerable personal cost, opted out of the safety of the ecclesiast-ical career structure and set up an imaginative venture without first getting the approval of the Kirk's ruling authorities. There was glee in the college common rooms and mumbling in the gentle-men's clubs.

Thus far, the Establishment's most controversial and increas-ingly suspect darling was protected by the old boys, but as MacLeod and controversy became inextricably linked, the Iona experiment was to produce volatile and extreme emotions on the floor of the Assembly.

In the Spring of 1938, George MacLeod needed much more than ecclesiastical accreditation. He badly needed a financial credit balance. He did not want to get money from the Church, because that would have involved accepting ecclesiastical direction. Let the *Seanachaidh* himself tell how the first donation came. The litany could be recited off by heart by any Iona Community member.

"I wrote to the richest man I knew. He replied, 'There's a good psychiatrist at 214 Bath Street – perhaps you should see him for the good of your health and for the good of the Church of Scotland.' Then I wrote to the second richest man I knew, but he hasn't replied yet: and as that was fifty years ago I don't suppose he will now. Then I wrote to Sir James Lithgow. I asked him for £5000. He invited me to spend the night. This surprised me because we were not very close: he was building battleships and I was already a pacifist. Before I left, he asked, 'If I give you £5000, will you give up your pacifism?' 'Not on your life!' I replied. Then he said, 'Then I will give you £5000'."

Thus was the Iona Community's frail coracle launched by a battleship-building capitalist whose part in the war preparations in the Clyde was putting far more Govan men back to work than George MacLeod could have dreamed of.

The Govan minister had encountered Sir James Lithgow before, when the shipbuilder had asked him to bless a battleship in his yard. He recalled:

"I replied that as they had not had a service of blessing at the launching of the Queen Mary, which had been built to advance harmony between nations, it seemed a bit odd, at this point in history, to ask God's blessing on a battleship: and pointed out that I was a pacifist. But I added that if ever he was to launch a tradeship, however small, I would come and ask God's blessing, even if there were no champagne lunch or any of the trimmings.

"He sent me a very brief letter on a very large bit of paper. It read, 'Dear Dr MacLeod, I respect your opinions. Yours sincerely . . .' Not long afterwards I was surprised to get a letter asking me to go and bless a tradeship though there were no trimmings and no champagne. I met him for five minutes at that little launch and he chipped me for giving him such a red face before his fellow directors, refusing to bless a battleship."

Sir James used to sail to the Hebridean Islands in his yacht, and not long before George wrote to him, he had wondered aloud why no one had rebuilt the remaining ruins of Iona Abbey. Lady Lithgow had asked how it might be done, and Sir James had placed chocolate sweets around a drawing of the Abbey, to show where the workmen's huts might be placed. George MacLeod had arrived at his house with a similar diagram.

"If you call that a coincidence," George was wont to say, "then I wish you a very dull life."

Sir James, as Dr David Russell had done before him, realized that he was talking to a man with the boldness and drive to make his dream possible. George MacLeod, the well known pacifist, was prepared to take the warshipbuilder's money. The minister with the Victorian standards of morality saw it as neither a coincidence nor a contradiction. ("Give me tainted money and I'll untaint it," he used to say.)

With money to pay for the first summer, George recruited students from the theological colleges, and ordered the wooden hutments. A special service was held in the Abbey in May 1938. A young divinity student from New Zealand, Jack Somerville (now the Very Rev. Dr J. S. Somerville) was present with two young compatriots, and was so moved by the sermon and so stirred by the hopes expressed that he enrolled on the spot as a supporter, with a donation of ten shillings. George saw the possibilities in such enrolment: thus began the Friends of the Iona Community. An article in *The Glasgow Herald*, giving the first public account of the new proposals, produced more than a thousand letters in response, most of the writers giving a strong and encouraging Amen. George MacLeod was touching a nerve in the Church, particularly among the disaffected who wanted imaginative and costly action.

Advance parties went up in June 1938, to begin erecting the huts close to the ruined walls. Adjutant MacLeod wrote memos to his new regimental recruits, telling them what clothes to buy (navy double-breasted suit for Sundays, navy fishermen's jersey, navy trousers, and heavy boots for work. Each man got a postal order for 31/6d to buy a pair of working boots with plain soles – tackets to be added later, if necessary – and one pair of black walking shoes. Each man would get £1 a week, plus keep). George was thoroughly enjoying himself. He knew, though, that there was a long, long way to go and there would be many setbacks. He did not have to wait for long.

The Duke of Argyll, who did not like the new scheme and regarded Dr MacLeod as something of an impertinent upstart, withdrew permission to pipe in water from a source outside the Abbey grounds, and said that no stone could be taken from the Mull quarry. The Duke owned all of the island outside the Abbey grounds, and he informed George that since he could hardly build without water and stone, he might as well pack it in. The worry reached dramatic proportions when the Ministry of Works, peeved at first reading news of the Iona rebuilding in the press, announced that they were planning to schedule the Iona Cathedral ruins, and work could not go ahead. The Cathedral Trustees immediately panicked and withdrew permission for the summer programme!

George used his charm to persuade the Ministry of Works to lift the ban which they had placed on the hutments (which were at that time being erected anyway) and agreed with them that the rebuilding itself would not start for a further year, giving the officials time to go over all the plans in detail. The day had been saved, and precious time had been bought. The problems had in many ways been caused by George's impatience: slow diplomacy and patient groundwork were never his strong suit. Once he got a glimpse of a corner of the kingdom of God, he went after it by the shortest possible route, relying on his charm and persuasiveness to get him out of trouble.

It was an excited group which gathered in Glasgow for high tea before setting sail on the MV *Dunara Castle*. Those on board were Bob Allan, ex-policeman; Jimmy Dalgleish, insurance clerk; Jack Doyle, slater; Bob Mackie, electrician; Johnny Macmillan, handyman; David Scott, shipyard worker; Hamish MacIntyre, Uist Macdonald and Robbie Fulton, probationer ministers; George Johnston, Roland Mackay and Bobby Ross, final year divinity students; Milorad Petrovitch, doctor; and George MacLeod, Leader. Crauford Dunlop, secretary, and Alastair MacQueen, architect, were already on the island, putting up the huts.

Robbie Fulton counted himself fortunate to be on the trip. After being licensed as a minister he had been uncertain what to do, until, that is, he read Dr MacLeod's article in *The Glasgow Herald*. His response was typical of many young men who came in contact with the ideas or person of the Govan minister.

"I read it, went into my father's study, said 'this is just the thing for me', caught the next bus to Glasgow, went to Govan, and found that George was on Iona! He was with the annual group of selected final year students from the four colleges. I went home and wrote a seven-page letter saying this new idea rang all the bells and could I join? George wrote a note to say there was no room, and I – very sadly – set about looking for an assistantship. After some weeks I got the promise of one, and agreed to go to Irvine. Then, early in June, word came that someone had dropped out – I never learned who – and would I still like to come? I ditched Irvine very cavalierly – as I see now – got measured for the navy blue outfits that we all wore, and joined the others on the *Dunara*. Neither then, nor ever since, have I regretted doing so for a moment."

The historic sail from Lancefield Quay, Govan, to Iona was not a smooth one. The seas were choppy, and some of the heroic adventurers spent the day and night leaning over the rails being sick, making spiritual contemplation of the historic moment extremely difficult. None of the men had bunks, and simply stretched out on the saloon benches. Finding it too stuffy, Bob Allan, Robbie Fulton, Dr Petrovitch and George MacLeod went on deck and took refuge in a small shelter built against the funnel, where they slept fitfully. At 6 am a steward banged on the door, saying that two women passengers were feeling seedy, and would they get out? Petrovitch emitted some horrible-sounding Serbo-Croatian words and the steward blanched, but they did get out and leaned on the rail till the boat put in at Islay. Columba's journey from Ireland in the coracle was probably more comfortable.

The first thing the men learned when they came ashore to a meal prepared by the Fallons was that water had just been found! Water diviners from the mainland had searched the Abbey grounds for a water source, but they had found nothing. On the day they were due to leave the island, the steamer was delayed. To pass the time, they dug around the round tower foundations outside the west door of the Abbey church, in the hope of finding old coins. What they found was a dried up well. It eventually gushed forth 400 gallons a day.

George MacLeod remembered the Iona Community's first day with particular vividness.

"It was a slightly dazed company – truth to tell – who sat down for their first meal together out in the open, beneath the old Abbey and beside the solitary log cabin that was to be their dormitory, sitting-and-dining room for the next three months! Few knew more than two of the others previously, the majority were sitting in a community of complete strangers. Had we been too hurried? Would we all get on together? As we looked at the size of the hut, some must have wondered. But as we looked at the Abbey we were reminded that what it stood for 'still worked'. Evening worship on that first night in the half light of a dying day was our first confirmation that the thing would go on. Some folk from the island, visitors and residents, came and by their presence there symbolized, from its very inception, the truth that this was no 'community apart' but an experiment within the world community as it is."

With the purpose consecrated and the hutment blessed, the men lay down to sleep on the site where the Benedictine monks and Columba's Celtic pioneers had lain before them. George MacLeod did not sleep. The years rolled back twenty years for him: the steady breathing of the men in the tidy barracks reminded him of the front, and the whine of a distant shell would not have been unfitting to his thought. Would this experiment lead some day to the shaping of the moral equivalent of war? How many times had he not heard regretted, by how many soldier friends, that the spirit of the war years seemed incapable of recapture in days of peace? Would co-operation work at last? These were the thoughts which kept going through his brain as the waves of the Sound of Iona maintained their steady rhythm through the sleepless night. Some of the questions began to find an answer in the days that lay ahead.

"Only the Spirit – we all agreed – could so quickly have welded us into a fellowship. Never had more diverse characters, with more diverse backgrounds, been brought into such close proximity for so shadowy a purpose. Yet the old throb was there, that thousands had known so well in Flanders, and hundreds in mission fields or outpost expeditions. True, there was a tendency for us parsons to ape the artisan, and occasionally a tendency by the artisan to ape the parson. But friendships fused and split regardless of former differences. Groups inevitably formed but never assumed the danger of cliques. Opposites met.

"The man most near to Communism in his philosophy of life was perhaps most often seen in the company of the artisan who had come amongst us because of his passionate advocacy of individual salvation. High Church and Low Church seemed absurdly trivial subjects now to excite much conversation from the parsons. The questions of the artisans were of a more fundamental thrust and some of us – who thought we were old hands – were reminded for the hundredth time what nonsense most of our sermons must sound. The parson who was heard in the first week attempting to clarify an argument with the actual words, 'your premises having fallen, your conclusion is false' (which so clarified the argument that it stopped altogether) was the centre of an argument in autumn that evaded such atrocities and was clarified by simplicity.

"And time and time again we were reminded that artisans are better men than parsons – not just at their jobs but at piercing through by instinct to those real issues which mental acrobatics so utterly confuse."[1]

This romanticization of the working classes notwithstanding, the first summer was clearly a profoundly moving experience for the initiator of the Iona venture. Having launched out into the deep, there is a sense in which, for him, the experiment simply had to work.

Living in community was not easy. The things which caused offence were not differences in theology or ecclesiastical practice, but matters such as snoring and eating habits.

"We were a splendid community," said George "except at meal times! We parsons behaved as if we were craftsmen. Attempting high-hearted happiness, we lapsed into high-handed heartiness. We knew nothing about manual work. The craftsmen were worse. Thinking they were embarked on a religious work, they tried to discard their humanity. You see, you can try to look holy for half an hour or so on a Sunday morning, but you can't look holy eight hours a day.

"Then an almighty row broke out between two of us. Someone suggested a special prayer meeting about it. When I pointed out that we already had worship in the Abbey each morning and evening, someone said, 'Oh yes, that's just ordinary divine worship', implying that no one expected much to happen in ordinary divine worship.

"Thus in no time, we knew that we were the reflection of the Church which we condemned. We'd forgotten it was a carpenter who became the Eternal High Priest. And that the atonement at least means at-one-ment between work and worship. We had forgotten that nothing is nearer divinity than honest humanity. We'd almost forgotten the point of public worship, which is reconciliation."[2]

The Community found that confession and forgiveness were not just words, but living necessities. The daily office, adapted from the high Govan liturgy, contained mutual forgiveness for the congregation and leader of worship.

One visitor that summer was James Maitland, a divinity student, who remembers George MacLeod's directness of speech. He, like many others, was deeply influenced by meeting the man himself on Iona.

"I remember at the end of our Abbey walkabout sitting on a pile of rubble listening to George making the Columban mission 1300 odd years ago take life and meaning for Scotland's new housing areas. All of a sudden he stopped, stood up, and with that warm, prophetic ring in his voice that only he could produce, said, 'James Maitland: you are going into the ministry of the Church of Scotland. What have you learned and what do you know about the fellowship that is in Christ?' Because I had no answer then and because at the end of college and a year's working in a parish I was still without any real answer, I joined the Iona Community in 1941."

To be addressed thus personally on Columba's holy isle by George MacLeod was often to experience a deep call. Countless ministers in the Church of Scotland and other denominations owe their vocations to just such a meeting.

The men worked around the site, constructing the huts. They found that the boundary wall of the Abbey precincts was made up of weathered stone which had come from the ruin itself – far more sympathetic material than newly hewn stone from any quarry. Thus was the obstructionism of the Duke of Argyll defeated, as the God of George MacLeod made the wrath of man to please him.

The Community also had to fight against the obstructionism of MacBraynes, the Highland carriers with a monopoly of cargo and passenger trade, who seemed to contrive to make the supply and landing of materials as difficult as possible. The Iona men used to sing as they worked:

> The Earth belongs unto the Lord
> And all that it contains
> Except West Highland ports and piers
> For they are all MacBraynes'.

Worship was held twice daily in the Abbey, conducted by the leader. ("What shall we call you, Doctor MacLeod?" his men asked. "Call me the Boss", came the reply.)

"Being a natural leader, his personality left us free to develop in our own way and yet together," Robbie Fulton remembered, "and so we became a band of brothers. We lived rough – in the one hut – sleeping on low truckle beds, each with a suitcase for a wardrobe. George was up at the far end, and shared the lot. Sometimes we shaved in the burn and bathed in the sea, rubbing off the dirt with handfuls of sand, until some local people took pity and we had occasional hot baths."

George ran the show like a commanding officer. Discipline was important. The men went to the village dances, but had to come back before the last dance. Hamish MacIntyre and Jimmy Dalgleish got permission to go down in their lunch hour to see off their girl friends on the King George V steamer. They went aboard ship with them as it sat for an hour in the Sound, and they were so intent on their goodbyes that they were still on board when the boat left. Next stop was the island of Staffa, where they sat all afternoon until they could flag down a motor boat. Meanwhile, George MacLeod was nursing his wrath to keep it warm at Iona Abbey, and, like Columba of old, his voice might well have been heard on Mull as he rebuked his disciples and confined them to barracks for a week. The new island soldiers were being trained for battle, and such frivolous indiscipline would not do.

So the fledgling Iona Community's first summer passed. The almost continuous rain had made things difficult, particularly for the divinity students who were unused to labouring in bad weather. The close living conditions – Uist Macdonald likened it to living on board ship – caused strains from time to time but they had survived the experience and in the process had learned things about real, as opposed to ideal, community. Out of it had emerged real, as opposed to ideal, worship.

George MacLeod was well satisfied, but was worried about the following summer. Where, in a time of impending war, would it be possible to get skilled masons?

One day a stranger walked around the ruins. He was on a walking holiday, and had just climbed Ben More on Mull. He had heard about the interesting experiment on Iona and wanted to know more about it. George explained the problem about masons.

"I am a master mason," said Bill Amos.

Bill Amos's work was to become a cornerstone of the restored living quarters of Iona Abbey. A pacifist with a strong social conscience, he was known to spend a couple of days putting up scaffolding to point a wall, and take it down because he had discovered a bird's nest halfway up the wall. A great Shakespearian and a man of faith, he was a model of the craftsman George MacLeod was looking for.

The interest in the Iona experiment was extraordinary. It was as if many people, not just in Scotland, had been waiting for such a committed venture and were willing it to succeed. So many letters came in, seeking further information, that George decided to start a magazine called *Coracle*, named after the type of leather-skinned boat which brought St Columba from Ireland to Iona in 563. In the first issue in October 1938 he explained for the benefit of a wider public the reason for the experiment.

The Iona leader said that the world was going collective, and the great challenge ahead was to find a form of society which would have both collectiveness and individual freedom. Christianity was best placed to do this, but unless Christian democracy made a more forthright experiment than Fascism or Communism, youth would not be interested. The Iona Community would be no more than a laboratory of co-operative living. Because it was not a permanent group sharing life together the whole year round, it could not claim to be the new social order in action – "because we frankly admit that we do not know what that Social Order is going to be in terms of Christianity (and humbly submit that nobody else really knows). It is a Laboratory working under the sign of all good laboratories – which is a Question Mark."[3]

After the summer, George went back to live part of the time at a Govan off-shoot called Plantation House, and the rest of the time at 4 Park Circus Place with his increasingly disabled mother. Ever a proud Fielden who had never properly accepted Glasgow, Lady MacLeod would sit in her chair facing the door, back to the window, moving her foot backwards and forwards to ease the pain, wearing a patch in the carpet.

A famous man of letters enjoyed working the lift installed for Lady MacLeod, reciting, "This way for hosiery, toesiery, slumber-wear and underwear. Next floor theology!" The poor man had come a cropper and years later, when Elizabeth Whitley laughed at some daft Iona scheme – what George MacLeod himself would call a SOKOP, Sounds OK on Paper – the man was suddenly serious and said, "I could never criticize anything of George's. He took me in when no one else would touch me." There were many like him. In the midst of all his visionary ideas and struggles with the Church, George MacLeod's concern for individuals, especially life's walking wounded, remained paramount. For all that he could be autocratic and sometimes domineering, when confronted by individual human need his heart melted. He often took alcoholics and people with other troubles to Iona, where no alcohol was available, and this was not always to the liking of the islanders and resident visitors.

By the autumn, George found himself exhausted and depressed by all the difficulties he had experienced. Harry Whitley was worried about his state of mind. George wrote immediately to assure his friend that he was not too low.

"I am not spending the day choosing a high rock from which to dash myself, nor even a convenient vase in which to be sick. The whole thing is in the hands of God. I was right to come here."

Reflecting on his days of depression, George went on, "For twelve years I have existed on the dope of 'getting ready for the next meeting'. Then on June 1, the Divine Doctor stopped the dope. How foolish to have expected an immediate transformation to a steadier life! True, my brain has ceased to function: my heart is sore: my feet are leaden: but are these things incompatible with the recorded experiences of Christian pilgrimage? Is not the Church's real malaise the fact that so few hearts are heavy and so few feet leaden?

"Had gaiety and breeze been the first immediate experience of this strange new beginning, what else would we have builded than a holiday home for clerics? Then indeed it might have been said that we had sold our Govan birthright for a mess of potage."

Telling Harry "by all means go on lighting candles, but not so many that they topple over and burn the dog," George went on to face the possibility of failure.

"Eclipse may be the portion God is carving out for me, temporary or final," he wrote. "The failure of Iona might well be His deep-laid scheme to shock the Church to newer action: a tiny Pentecost even because of a tiny cross. All signs, however, point to a kindlier Hand above us, spreading enough dust around us to give us GRIT, but strewing the path around us already with brighter flowers than faithless hearts deserve."

In November 1938 he went to India to fulfil an engagement made prior to the formation of the Iona Community. He was a Church of Scotland representative at the World International Missionary Conference at Tambaram, Madras.

The conference invigorated him and confirmed him in his direction. 470 delegates from 70 nations discussed the future of the Church against a background of impending European breakdown.

George enjoyed the global dimension of the gathering, and it made him reflect on the international impact which Iona could make. He was very impressed by the gentle Japanese theologian, Kagawa, who pointed out that Western ways of thinking were not essential to the doing of theology. Tambaram, more than any other event, lifted George MacLeod's horizons from Govan and Scotland to the whole world.

The dynamic Scottish minister was one of the star preachers of the international conference. The delegates were moved to hear contemporary Scottish Presbyterian preaching at its oratorical best.

"What has gone wrong?" he cried. "Why the recurrent defeatism in some of our hearts? Edinburgh Castle, high up on its rock, used symbolically to hold the fire that burned at the heart of Scotland. In recent years we have not been so sure that that spiritual fire was as bright as once it used to be. So we have floodlit the Castle to kid ourselves that all is still bright and alight. Similarly what is wrong with some of us is that we are floodlighting our doctrines instead of being burned up by them. We have the answer, but are we prepared to carry it in jeopardy of our lives?"

Back home, he flirted with the notion of returning to Govan Parish Church, which, by November, still did not have a minister. Despite the success of the Iona summer, part of him was still in Govan, and, encouraged by some members of his old church, he thought about seeking to return to Govan in order to implement the Iona ideals in a mainland parish. His plan was to appoint an assistant to look after the parish while he was on Iona business.

When some Govan members suggested this to the vacancy committee, which had been established to search for a new minister, they were immediately rebuffed. After all, Dr MacLeod had written clearly in his letter announcing his resignation that he had played with the possibility of not leaving Govan while still embarking on the Iona experiment, and turned the idea down.

His view had now changed, or at least was wavering. George's backers circulated the congregation with a petition seeking his recall, and it was signed by an impressive 1817 members out of a total of 2500. They had not wanted their minister to go in the first place, and they wanted him back, even though he would be less often seen in the parish. They sent the petition to Dr MacLeod, imploring him to return. He said he would return to Govan if called by the congregation, unless the Presbytery thought it was against the best interests of the Church.

The vacancy committee threw the petition out, saying it was unconstitutional. The petition's sponsors argued that it was the only way in which the wishes of the congregation could be made known, and they organized a packed meeting in Govan Town Hall. The meeting was a tempestuous one, with accusation and counter-accusation being tossed around. The matter was referred to the business committee of Glasgow Presbytery, who decided on 1st December, 1938 that it was "unconstitutional and contrary to the fundamental laws of the Church for a vacancy committee to submit as nominee the name of any minister who has other interests involving annual continued absences from his parish and also further frequent absences from his pastoral and pulpit duties." The matter decided, the vacancy committee continued their business, and the Rev. T. B. Stewart Thomson was nominated to fill the vacancy in March 1939.

The matter caused deep division in Govan. George MacLeod was once again at the centre of a church controversy, arousing, not for the first time, strong passions for and against him. From this distance in time, it is hard to resist the conclusion that he showed poor judgment in allowing his name to go forward for the vacancy, so soon after leaving Govan.

Little did people know at the time that the Govan controversy was a dress rehearsal for a much more damaging stand-off in 1948, with George MacLeod in public conflict with no less a figure than the redoubtable Dr John White.

The Iona Community leader was making a name for himself. That name was trouble.

12

MacLeod's Folly?

We shall build on: we shall build on –
On through the critic's scorning,
On through the coward's warning,
On through the cheat's suborning,
We shall build on.

G. A. STUDDERT-KENNEDY

The Christians who do not realize that they must take
part unreservedly in this war must have slept over their
Bibles as well as over their newspapers.

KARL BARTH

Summer, 1939. Europe is about to be laid waste again. On a small island on the edge of Europe, a strange little rebuilding is beginning. But not without controversy.

This time it is over the huts in the Abbey ruins. The newspapers are full of complaints. The huts are spoiling the sight of the ruins, and it is a disgrace having a motor lorry on the sacred island. A man signing himself "Spectator" writes to *The Bulletin* in a fury, suggesting that the islanders of Iona draw up a petition against "Dr George MacLeod's strange new stunt", and attacking the "self-appointed successor to St Columba". In the same issue, a number of young people resident on Iona have a letter defending the rebuilding, saying they are "glad to see this sign of life and adventure in our Church, and welcome it as a relief from a great deal of drabness elsewhere."

One outraged visitor to Iona wrote to *The Bulletin* to complain about the men's washing flapping on the line near the Abbey – and on a Sunday at that! It brought a response from another reader, who sent George MacLeod a cheque for £5000, saying that cleanliness was next to Godliness.

MacLeod's Folly?

"We hung out our washing every Sunday after that," said the Iona leader, who had an answer for those who complained about the signs of human life among the ruins.

"Folk must make up their minds about a prior question. If what they are looking for in Iona is a dream of the past; some place apart where, amidst mouldering stones and wild grasses, they may let their minds wander back to days 'when Christianity once was great'; a setting in which to indulge a suitable melancholy – if that is what they seek, then, of course, the wooden house will irritate. But we dare to suggest that, were that Iona's destiny, it would have been far better not to have re-roofed the Abbey (as was done some years ago) so that the whole scene might have responded to an atmosphere of ruined glory. Now that it is re-roofed and a potential centre for most enthralling worship, the whole environment cries out for life again . . . Do men want Iona as a memory of the past, or as an inspiration for days of difficulty ahead?"[1]

Angus Robertson publicly pledged £7000 to pay for the restoration of the refectory, describing George MacLeod as the spiritual leader of young men in Scotland. This support from a prominent Gael was especially welcome in view of the attacks on the Iona project by the Free Kirk and some Highland Church of Scotland ministers.

The critics were disappointed that the Iona experiment had gone into its second year, and they went on to the attack. It was a Presbyterian sell-out, they said. The Community was "half-way towards Rome, and half-way towards Moscow." It was an enclave of pacifism and sedition. The Iona men were playing at monks.

The dormitory huts became known as "The Rome Express". The origin of the nickname was a popular film of the same name, in which people had to keep squeezing past each other to go along the corridor of the Rome express train – just like the passageway in the hut. The name stuck, but with different connotations.

George MacLeod answered his critics in the summer issue of *Coracle*. The Iona Community was not a return to Rome, he said, but was precisely the opposite. Nor was it a pacifist community.

"We hope that men of strong views will join it from time to time and not be ashamed to hold them – whether for or against that solution; but a further reference to the names of the Sponsors should prove – beyond a peradventure – that its emphasis is neither pacifist nor otherwise.

"It is not a visionary movement – seeking helplessly to play at being Franciscans! (May we occasionally, with due acknowledgment, be delivered from our too enthusiastic friends, lest in the ultimate they be disapppointed!) It is on the contrary an exceedingly calculated movement within the normal purpose of the Church. Poverty is not our aim, far less is the principle of celibacy involved. Those who come here will claim no 'sacrifice'; we only claim a privilege to make perhaps the sacrifice of those who work in really difficult places a little less acute. Please drop the grand absurdity of 'banishment to a lonely desert island'!"

Describing Iona Abbey as "the envy of every denomination in Western Christendom", Dr MacLeod said it was the perfect setting in which a thrust toward the future could be made. It was a place in which the Reformed doctrine of the priesthood of all believers could be enacted, where the mason and the labourer and the clergyman could discover together their shared ministry.

With an eye on the continent, the Iona leader again pointed to Christianity as the only way forward – if it were seen to work.

"In the face of Fascism, we believe that man has an ultimate loyalty finer than the State; in the face of Communism, we believe that man was made to worship God and not just to glorify himself. And we are right. But have we finer things to show for the Faith that is in us, than just 'more words'?"

At the May 1939 General Assembly, the committee appointed the previous year had presented its report. Lord Wark, the convener, had a hard time dealing with searching questions on the floor of the Assembly, but in the end the Assembly approved of the scheme, with the amendment that the Home Board be instructed to watch over the development of the scheme and report. George MacLeod had got what he wanted from the Kirk – recognition without control. He had also got what he wanted from the Ministry of Works – approval for the first stage of the rebuilding. So the work began.

Cameron Wallace, who had just finished his theological training, and who would become one of Scotland's pioneering industrial chaplains, remembered the power of George MacLeod.

"When I was a divinity student at New College in the late 1930s, things were in a confused state theologically and politically. George MacLeod came to give a talk on his plans for the Iona Community. We were very much taken by his zeal and vision, and the new hope he brought. He had a new conception of the Church, and a new incarnational theology. He gave us hope and direction. I know that

I would not have stayed within the ministry of the institutional Church had it not been for George MacLeod."

The first commissioning service for the Iona Community was held in June 1939. A few months beforehand, George had told his men to get measured for dark navy blue suits and send the measurements in. When they got together before the service, they found that the suits were all the wrong sizes, and they had to change them around to be in some kind of order for the service.

"It was an autocratic kind of government by George in the early days," said Cameron Wallace. "He was much older than we were. He was a true aristocrat with his sense of leadership, his training in war, his commanding appearance and his sense of authority. Having been brought up in a mining community, I had a chip on my shoulder about people of another class. We sometimes had sharp words, but never did I lose my tremendous regard for this man. If ever there was a true successor to Saint Columba, George MacLeod is the man."

It was heavy and exhausting work during the glorious summer of 1939. The day, organized with military precision, began with reveille at 6.45 am, and a swim in the freezing sea. George MacLeod would throw off his tattered MacLeod kilt and lead the charge into the water, throwing himself naked into the waves. He insisted that the Celtic monks bathed in the sea every day of the year – "stink or swim" became the Community's motto – and resisted the arguments of faint-hearted ordinands who failed to see why they should slavishly follow masochistic Celtic customs.

Breakfast at 7.30 am was followed by worship in the Abbey church. After worship, the artisans went out to work on the buildings, following the detailed plans prepared by Ian Lindsay, while the ministers cleaned out the Rome Express and did what other chores were needed. (Barracks were inspected every Saturday by C. O. MacLeod.) At 9.30 am there was half an hour of meditation, followed by the lecture of the day.

In the afternoon, the young ministers, assisted by a lazy donkey which was supposed to haul the buggy, had to recover Abbey stones from walls, and to dig them out of the ground. As the ministers worked as labourers for the craftsmen, the walls of the erstwhile derelict chapter house began to grow. The craftsmen liked to cut the theologians down to size, but they also taught them a great deal about workmanship. They pushed their labourers very hard on matters such as the hours ministers worked. The craftsmen suggested that when the ministers went back to the mainland, they take rigorous note of the hours they actually did work, and report back. Out of these discussions on the walls of the ruined medieval chapter house of Iona Abbey grew an important part of the Rule of the Iona Community – the planning of time.

After another swim and evening meal, there would be choir practice, or discussions, or football matches with the locals – bloody battles in which Mull and Iona crofters and young ministers kicked lumps out of each other. There was understandable suspicion of this strange rebuilding experiment, and on Monday evenings the Community members would don their dark blue suits – George made it a rule that the men should wear their suits whenever they went down to the village – and visit the island houses to explain what was happening. Public worship in the Abbey was at 10 pm, and the men were expected to be in their beds by 10.30 pm. They were usually exhausted.

The weekend regime was more relaxed. Concerts – led by George who would sing and play the piano – and dances were highlights. Like the Abbey services, these were public events, attracting islanders and guests holidaying on Iona.

Out of this 1939 summer season, in the calm before the storm, a community was formed around the growing chapter house walls. George MacLeod's new regiment was taking shape, ready for the battle. Some of the advance party, the class of '38, were already on the mainland, in parishes.

The experiment attracted visitors and attention from reporters, curious to know what was going on. The controversy increased. The Iona leader was comforted by a letter which Tubby Clayton sent to "my dear old George".

"Prophets are always wrong to their near neighbours, and heroes never heroes when next door, but when the prophet or the hero dies, his critics change their tune and build his shrine, and welcome pilgrims to his place of piety, provided they will buy sham souvenirs. I am glad you have left Govan, though the wrench must have been just terrific on both sides. Had you gone on in the Pearce Institute you would have been worn out in a few years, whereas Iona will enable you to be mature without growing old.

"You are a churchman of profound devotion. I wish I could say this of myself. You and your men are probing a problem which the more normal ways of parish life have failed to meet. Their failure is acknowledged and acute. Mere lamentations are no remedy. A

series of endeavours must be made to test the working power of
supplemental bodies such as yourselves, and these must be
accepted by the Church, welcomed, supported, blessed and understood. Jordan must overflow its sabbath banks if it would irrigate
the pagan world."

George always acknowledged his deep personal debt to Tubby
Clayton. In later years he would say that he had known ministers
who were good with their congregations, but Tubby was the first
to focus his attention on those who were "outside the wall".

On September 3, 1939 it was not the pagan world but Christian
Europe which erupted. Britain was at war with Hitler's Germany.

There had been so much talk about the damage caused by
bombing raids, that many people expected almost instant annihila-
tion. Even Winston Churchill, still in the political wilderness,
feared immediate ruin and carnage. Official sources had predicted
that 100,000 tons of bombs would rain on London in the first two
weeks. Hospitals were cleared, millions of cardboard coffins were
made, and lime-pits were organized to dispose of the expected high
number of corpses. 38 million gas masks had been issued in 1938
in anticipation of German gas warfare. Black-outs were enforced,
and three and a half million people were evacuated to the
countryside.

And another British Expeditionary Force was on its way to
mainland Europe twenty years after the war to end all wars.

The press announced that the Iona experiment had closed down.
The announcement represented wishful thinking on the part of the
Cathedral Trustees and some of the Sponsors. George MacLeod,
who knew what British Expeditionary Forces were all about, was
angry. He announced that the experiment would continue because
the need for community workers in the housing schemes would be
intensified by the incidence of war, experiments in new community
were more urgent than ever, and "there is surely justified symbol
in persisting in restoring a ruin, while so many ruins are incipient
on the mainland of Europe; justified symbol in a missionary centre
going on being built towards the New Day.

"WHEREFORE BE IT KNOWN," he added defiantly in
capitals, "that building is actually going on at the present date: that
we are laying plans to continue to build next summer."

So there!

George had learned from bitter experience that it was useless to
concentrate all energy on the war effort, and leave all talk about

reconstruction until after the hostilities. Nothing would deflect him.

"If man's extremity be God's opportunity," he insisted, "it is clear that a time of war should call forth from such spiritual ventures as the Iona Community not a battening of the hatches but rather a crowding on of more canvas. There is not a purpose for which it stands the need of whose prosecution is not made more insistent by the probabilities before us. Should the war be shortened all the problems referred to will emerge again with gathered potency; should the war be long the problems with which almost delicately we were dealing will be found to challenge us as stark imperatives. The problem is not whether the Community should continue but into what new channels it should regulate its forces."[2]

In spite of his defiance, George had to face the fact that his experiment might have to fold up under the pressure of events.

"If this place is to be known as MacLeod's Folly," he wrote from Iona to Harry Whitley, "I would like to finish the chapter house, if only to remind a coming generation that we can build as well as ever in our own day, and rattle someone to finish the job.

"I am oddly unperturbed about the crack-up at this end of things. Before I launched away, I faced with myself the issue that a war might ditch it. And now that it has – for we can't expect money to give top dressing to ministers and build ruins – well, there are such interesting things to be found in the ditch. I am quite sure we were meant to come to Iona and am sleeping excellently."

In the same letter, he advised Harry as to what to say when his parishioners prayed for the safety of their own sons in the war.

"What does our God offer? Safety from death? Not in the New Testament. Safety from sin – that is what is offered. Cold comfort? No, it is everlasting life now; his happiness if he returns; his happiness if he dies. Then the other world breaks through as a reality at last, and prayer, and true theology. God ceases to be the one who may hold the scimitar and becomes the God of love now. His love is not dependent on the casualty lists."

The Iona experiment could not simply carry on as before. George said that since it did not seem likely that young ordinands worth their salt would apply to spend three summer months on Iona, he felt that while the rebuilding should continue, the nature of the summer activities on Iona should change. Weekly courses should be run in the summer for ministers and lay people, who would live in the "Rome Express" and attend lectures on themes which were close to the heart of the Iona Community. The experiment in common living and training for new ministers should be transferred to the mainland. Members would be given a soldier's pay, and would offer their services to the Church particularly in the housing schemes, the army huts, and country charges where evacuees had flooded in.

These wartime decisions were to have a profound unforeseen effect on the future of the Iona Community. Iona became a Christian educational academy for ministers and lay people from different parts of the world, rather than simply a place for training ministers from the Church of Scotland. Once embarked on this road, there was no way back to the original simplicities of the Iona Community. The signposts to Iona became a pilgrim route for many seekers who were yearning for a new style of church. It was as if George MacLeod had swung on a bellrope at Iona Abbey, and the sound had been heard in distant parts of the world. That strange, vulnerable rebuilding on a remote Scottish island was an inspiration for many Christians while another European mass slaughter ran its bloody course.

George MacLeod's pacifism brought him bitter hostility. He defended himself and his community in *Coracle*.

"If anything that is formed is to continue to be known as the Iona Community it cannot stand for anything essentially different to that for which it was formed. And the Community has always been broad-based as regards applications of the Faith. It has already had within its membership men who were destined for the army both as soldiers and as chaplains, and also pacifists. The Community is neither pacifist nor non-pacifist – which is a reflection of the actual situation in the Church today. Anything we form on the mainland must have its doors open to all – as any Church has anyway. But just as our soldier members would be untrue to themselves if they now resigned from the army, I must also record that I feel I would also be untrue to myself if I now renounced the views I hold.

"The one supreme conviction that I cannot get away from and – without any dramatics – am quite willing to die for, is that only the spiritual can mould any future worth having for the world."

At a time when Britain was bracing itself for invasion, such views were popular neither in the Church nor in the country at large. The BBC decided that George MacLeod, MC, the war hero who had come close to death for his country on several occasions, should not be heard on the airwaves. Scotland's best known radio preacher, whose voice was known to listeners throughout the Empire, was banned from the radio, silenced. He was in good company, along with the likes of Charles Raven, Donald Soper and Archie Craig.

The decision to ban conscientious objectors from the airwaves was part of a long and bitterly fought battle at the BBC over controversial broadcasts of all kinds. George, who had told a Fellowship of Reconciliation meeting in 1939 that pacifists should enlist for the most dangerous jobs possible, consistent with their principles, was a problem for the BBC and the government in that he was acknowledged to be one of the most brilliant religious broadcasters in the country. George told the BBC that he did not wish to preach as a well-known pacifist – "I do not think pacifism is the Gospel from which all else springs: the Gospel is that from which, for me at any rate, pacifism springs" – but simply as a minister of the gospel. The argument raged on within the BBC and government circles, and the ban was eventually lifted in 1941.

George MacLeod's broadcast sermons from Iona Abbey had been very popular. (People thought it miraculous that seagulls always seemed to be around the Abbey while the service was going on, giving a true island atmosphere to the worship. There was nothing miraculous at all: the Celtic showman had simply arranged for fish to be strewn around the church while the service was in progress.)

It was around this time that George had a strange, mystical experience on Iona. He told no one at the time, but he communicated it to Petrovitch.

"We had twelve men going to the Foreign Field in retreat with us last week, and a most wonderful Communion Service on Thursday night at ten thirty. It was half light and stormy and – as I broke the bread – I am informed that a sweep of birds sailed past the window as if trying to get in. I only know that when I was praying the intercession prayer with my eyes closed I heard steps coming towards the Table and opened my eyes in case someone was coming. There was no one there, but a wind rushed round me so real that I felt myself pressed backwards. It was a strange experience that I have communicated to no one here. Afterwards I remembered the old story that late at night monks walk down the centre of the Church and can be seen walking right through the Communion Table. I saw nothing at all. But it is an experience I shall always remember whenever I administer the sacrament. It is the more remarkable as I was not feeling in the least eerie and certainly not anticipating any such experience. I like to take it as an omen that the thing is meant."

It was not to be the only such experience on Iona. George MacLeod was not a mystic in the sense that he spent hours in prayer, waiting for visions: yet for all his sophistication and whirlwind energy, there was an intuitive, child-like quality about his faith which was open to direct experience. He would see extraordinary occurrences as signs laden with meaning. There were times when, quite simply, he felt that God was addressing him directly and specifically.

Just after the outbreak of war, George's brother Norman died of tuberculosis at the age of 48. The adored elder brother and favourite son had never quite fulfilled the expectations held of him.

George was deeply saddened by his brother's death. He had always enjoyed Norman's humorous company, and used to save up stories and incidents which he knew his brother would savour.

The baronetcy passed to Norman's son, Ian Francis Norman MacLeod. Taught at first by governesses, Ian had then gone to Winchester. He would spend Christmas in Rome or Switzerland with his parents and his Italian family, and his summers in Scotland: he loved both families, and was aware of the tensions as each tried to bridge both cultures.

When Norman died, George felt a special responsibility for Sir Ian. He was very fond of him, and became like a father to him. He took him up to Iona just before he was due to go overseas with the diplomatic service in Rome.

In the winter of 1939–40, as Britain relaxed a bit more after the expected German onslaught had failed to materialize, the Iona Community dug into its mainland base. The Rev. Ronald Selby Wright, minister of the Canongate Kirk, had gone off to be a chaplain in the Forces (he would become well known as the "radio padre") and he had offered his manse as a wartime base for the Community. Acheson House had a large meeting room, refectory and chapel. New members came for short, intensive courses, and for practical training worked in the Canongate parish.

George went to live in Acheson House and made it his working base: his two secretaries, Miss Dalgleish and Miss MacKenzie, went in each day to deal with the masses of correspondence from enquirers. Ever the adjutant, George MacLeod adopted the habit of answering letters the day they came in. Dictating in a machine-gunfire staccato, he would send a stream of letters and memos out to different parts of the globe. He loved to plan activities like military operations, organizing things down to the last detail. (He had a Filofax at that time: the firm whose name is now synonymous with the upwardly mobile culture began as a small organization helping clergymen to organize their time.)

The Community was accused of pacifism and left-wing politics, but not all of its sympathizers shared these views. Peter MacEwan, a divinity student, was a Tory who had been captivated by George's broadcasts.

He had first met George at Acheson House – "George was at the height of his fame and popularity," he remembered. "His name was on everybody's lips. Of course, he was utterly charming, and I was hooked.

"George fished for students for his Community as other men fished for trout. I was assistant to Dr P. C. Millar in West St Nicholas, Aberdeen and was very happy in that job. Alas, George came up to Aberdeen a-preaching and also after my scalp. He had me into his hotel room and tried to persuade me to join up. He spoke to me like a dutch uncle. He could be horribly kind and understanding and persuasive all at once. George never wore a cloth cap and muffler but he often wore an old school tie.

"He was Winchester and I was Glenalmond, and he was very old school tie that night. Anyway, he hooked his fish and I agreed to join. Silly ass. From that moment I had a love-hate relationship with the whole caboodle and to this day I can never make up my mind whether it was the best or the worst thing I ever did."

George's pursuit of Peter MacEwan was typical. He identified the brightest of each year's crop of divinity students and would arrange an individual meeting. The style was seductive: he would bow and call the student "sir", and would give him his full attention. It was very flattering to be courted by such a charming and charismatic and famous figure: furthermore, the vision he laid before them was a captivating and exciting one. Students who agreed to join the Community were often puzzled to find George a more distant and autocratic personality during the joining programme: it was as if he had to become more remote in order to exercise what he saw as necessary discipline. For all his engaging attractiveness, there was a thus-far-and-no-further aspect to his personality, protecting an inner, private core.

George was greatly encouraged by an offer from an anonymous donor (later to be revealed as Sir James Lithgow) to pay for four teams of two ministers to go to four needy places each year for the next six years. Some of the Community men were already in tough parishes, and George went to help them organize parish missions on the lines of the Govan friendship mission. He needed whatever encouragement he could get, especially when the phoney war ended in May, 1940. With the collapse of the French Government and the increasing menace of Hitler's forces, the British Expeditionary Force had to make an ignominious retreat from Dunkirk. Winston Churchill had been called from the political wilderness to replace Neville Chamberlain as prime minister, and the country braced itself for the worst.

With the country in defiant mood, preparing for slaughter, it was not a good time to be a pacifist. (George always said that he enjoyed the First World War and was miserable during the Second.) As with the First World War, people who had lost loved ones resented those who refused to fight. No one could pin the label "coward" on George MacLeod, but there were plenty of other titles to hand.

He felt isolated from the main body of the Church of Scotland. The Church and Nation Committee affirmed in May 1940 its conviction that "Britain and France were justified in entering on the present war in which the adversary is not merely an enemy state but demonic forces of evil which have captured the soul of a people."

George MacLeod felt lonely and weary. He had heard it all before. Yet despite the criticism (John White warned him of rumours that he was hiding pacifists on Iona), he held to his conviction that the Iona Community was needed even more.

"Our Church seems incapable of firm decision in any direction," he wrote to an unidentified friend. "As a result, I oscillate between joining the Communist party and entering the Roman Church, and shall undoubtedly do neither, which seems to prove that I am also a typical member of the Church of Scotland as by law embellished.

"What I feel is that we are coming to the end of an age (short pause to allow you to get over the originality of this thrust) and that the Church of Scotland is well and truly laid in that age, as no doubt befits a national church. The Iona Community is rather like a blind scout with one arm in a sling, and a gammy leg; it has unwittingly got over the hedge with its right leg and still has its gammy leg stuck in the old order of things. The only justification of this precarious attitude is that we can see over to its most entrancing prospect (not the John White 'end-of-all-things fear'), and we are sufficiently near to the main bourgeois body to say 'hey, fellows, come on – our right foot is bogged down but it is bogged in damned good earth; not in the soil erosion muck of so many sowings that you are getting bogged in'. So far, admittedly, the main body have replied, 'but my dear fellow, you haven't any philosophy or theology or known ecclesiology'. To which my reply is, 'but plenty of johnnies have; they are away up in aeroplanes chucking pamphlets at each other.'"

During the summer of 1940, the courses on Iona were very well subscribed. Unlike the previous year when there were visitors from Ireland, France, America, Rumania and Czechoslovakia, the guests were mainly from Britain. 240 Church of Scotland ministers and as many lay people came for a week's study. The number of Friends of the Iona Community rose to near the 3000 mark. George was delighted with the response. On the building side, the chapter house had been finished and the walls of the refectory raised up.

Yet there were problems. The Rev. Donald MacCuish, the Iona parish minister who had been well disposed to George MacLeod and the Community, had left. He had been replaced by the Rev. Murdo Macrae, who wrote to the Cathedral Trustees to complain about what he regarded as the unPresbyterian nature of the worship being conducted in the Abbey church (responses, use of candles – there was no electricity – and frequent communion). The Trustees stalled, but refused George permission to use candlesticks.

There were problems with the national Church, too. As the nation braced itself for the blitz which was to kill so many people and destroy so much property, George found some of his supporters distancing themselves from him. John White wanted to call a meeting of the Sponsors of the Iona Community, saying that he considered the Community with its pacifist sympathies to be a dangerous and disruptive influence on the life of the nation at that most critical hour. The meeting never took place, but two of the Sponsors resigned.

George defended himself by saying that out of 16 Sponsors, only one was a pacifist, and out of 35 members of the Iona Community, only five were pacifist.

Despite eloquent defences of his position, George failed to address adequately the question of precisely how Hitler and Mussolini should have been opposed. Decency and diplomacy had had no effect, as it had become clear that the European dictators were about to impose their will on smaller nations. George said that when war eventually came in 1939 the only thing Britain could do was to enter the war: indeed, at the 1937 General Assembly he had said that Britain had a clear choice before her – either recall Winston Churchill or go pacifist. His critics were entitled to ask whether the pacifist movement had not encouraged the dictators to be bold. Had the pacifist groundswell not been partly responsible for Britain's lack of preparedness to meet the Fascist attack? George's answers to these questions were less than convincing.

To be associated with George MacLeod, MC, had once been a good thing. As the war fever increased, so it became more common to name him as an enemy rather than a friend. The darling of the Establishment had found the limits of the establishment's tolerance.

Rumours of the Community's harbouring of pacifists and revolutionaries continued, and some vicious things were said about George MacLeod's supposed indifference to the war. The reality was that the Iona Community had offered itself as a unit to the Church of Scotland to use as it wished, and that George had gone to London to make a similar offer to the YMCA and to the Dutch Refugee Service. Such facts did not matter. The truth, as his most severe critics saw it, was that MacLeod and his Community were betraying Britain and undermining Presbyterianism. To be called a pacifist, a Communist and a Roman Catholic in Scotland in the dark days of 1940 was not to be in receipt of compliments.

George wondered sometimes what he had done. He became depressed, exhausted, pale, and thin, and some of his friends feared he was heading for another breakdown. "I sometimes wonder whether the first spasm of heaven will not be to sleep peacefully for the first thousand years," he wrote to Harry Whitley.

While he was sitting on a hillock on Iona, contemplating his misfortune, a complete stranger clambered up to greet him. George didn't welcome the intruder.

"Self-pity hates to be interrupted. 'Are you being successful yet?' he said. 'Well,' I said, 'it depends on what you mean by success.' He said, 'Do you not know what success is? Success is hearing the voice of God no louder than thunder in distant hills on a summer day.' And he went down, and I never saw him again."[3]

Such strange events he read as direct encouragement from God.

"I would have gone stark staring mad in these last few months," he wrote to his friend Petrovitch, "if I had not had the framework of a Faith that was real and full of content. I am such an indolent brute really that I suppose God knows it requires crises to keep me faithful at all."

A sharp reminder of the war came to Iona, when the body of an unknown sailor was washed up on the island's shore. George wrote a poem about it, which was published in *The Scotsman*.

> Out of the mist and seawrack
> Washed by a myriad foam,
> Borne on a hundred currents
> The nameless man came home.
> Safe in the Relig Oran
> With King and Priest and Chief,
> For mourners, shepherd, crofter,
> For pall, the falling leaf.
>
> South in the ancient city
> Set in the chiselled nave
> Hard by the Stone of Destiny
> The Unknown Soldier's grave.
> Here in the grand mosaic
> Of earth and sea and sky
> Destiny brought the sailor
> With older kings to lie.
>
> Duncan, MacBeth, King Louis,
> Whose last rites swayed a crowd,
> Tell him his port of landing,
> Unloose his nameless shroud.
> Lest he forget the story,
> Whisper the Christ's true claim –
> No man in earth is nameless
> Who bears the Sacred Name.
>
> Dear God, Who guides each tiderace,
> Whose spirit flecks each foam,

MacLeod's Folly?

From Thee no man can wander,
Smite us and bring us home.
Swayed by a hundred currents,
Wearied of fortune's slings,
Give us the name that is deathless
Make us priests and kings.

The seas were to deliver up other gifts. In September 1940, when the incendiary bombs were raining on London, it looked as if the rebuilding might have to be stopped because of lack of timber. Then the deck cargo of a Swedish ship, carrying wood from Canada, had to be jettisoned. The timber floated all the way to Mull, directly opposite Iona – all the right length.

"Whenever I pray", said the beleaguered Dr MacLeod, "I find that the coincidences multiply."

13

Courage, Brother!

Faith can see in the dark, where nothing whatever is visible.

MARTIN LUTHER

I am plagued with doubts. What if everything is an illusion and nothing exists? In that case I definitely overpaid for the carpet. If only God would give me some clear sign: like making a large deposit in my name in a Swiss bank.

WOODY ALLEN

The nervous Cathedral Trustees inquired delicately of Dr MacLeod "if the authorities had sanctioned the retention of the timber which had been cast up on the shore of Iona?" The reply was that he had twice offered the timber to the government but had received no reply.

One can sympathize with any official body trying to deal with a miracle, especially with the fiery figure of George MacLeod in the foreground. The officials must have felt like Roman bureaucrats asking, with a polite cough, whether Jesus had a catering permit for the feeding of the five thousand.

The timber was put in store to dry: then George got volunteers to take it out to become weathered: then it was taken in to dry again . . . and so on. He did it because he knew that, as a picture was worth a thousand words, so the privilege of actually seeing and handling the famous timbers would stay in men's minds all their lives and would encourage them during their own times of lack of faith.

Another story which has stayed on in people's minds is that of how the celebrated silver-plated Celtic cross which now stands behind the communion table in Iona Abbey came to be there.

184

Courage, Brother!

David Russell had invited George to go with him to Hampstead, where there was an exhibition and sale of silver work of the late Omar Ramsden, so that George could choose a piece suitable for Iona. He saw the wonderful cross in the midst, but did not like to ask for the most important thing in the show, so he pretended to be looking at chalices.

"You're really looking at the cross, aren't you, George?" observed Dr Russell. When they asked about it, Ramsden's widow told them it was not for sale because her husband, who considered it his finest work – it had been displayed at the Empire Exhibition in Glasgow in 1938 – had intended that it would stand in Iona Abbey one day . . .

. . . Over the Rev. Murdo Macrae's dead body, of course. The Trustees elected not to take the side of the pacifist MacLeod in a war to the death with Iona's protector of embattled Presbyterianism: and so the offensive object was not allowed to be displayed in the Abbey. Once the dusts of controversy had settled, the cross was placed behind the marble communion table of the church, in front of the great east window. So far, there have been no recorded cases of Presbyterians being struck dead while looking upon it.

There was growing aggravation between the Cathedral Trustees and George MacLeod, and it had more to do with pacifism and personalities than with miracles. The Trustees were being questioned as to why they were allowing a bunch of revolutionaries and conscientious objectors to find a base in one of Scotland's most hallowed sanctuaries. They were having to deal with some of the ferocious criticism directed at the Community and its leader – criticism which continued through the war and well beyond it. As one of the Trustees, the Rev. Charles Warr, minister of St Giles' Cathedral, put the matter:

"For years the extremists of all ecclesiastical parties were united in one thing. The High Churchmen might dislike the Evangelical, and both might dislike what they regarded as the latitudinarianism of Broad Churchmen. But they were all at one in their hostility to the Iona Community! The most fantastic stories went about. No canard could be too fanciful or absurd. The Community was Romish. The Community was Communist. The Community had been founded to indoctrinate the Church with a heretical theology. The Community was a menace because it had no theology at all. The most amazing ongoings were reported as taking place on Iona, and it was even rumoured that the members of the Community believed themselves able to raise people from the dead and had been trying to do so!"[1]

Some of the most hostile behind-the-scenes criticism of George came from people who were offended and bewildered by this Wykehamist who wore his old school tie and his Military Cross with pride, yet talked in impeccable accents about pacifism and the need for more equitable social arrangements. They felt let down: he had betrayed his class. For some, this was the equivalent of the sin against the Holy Ghost. It was infuriating and disconcerting to be complaining in these terms to a Trustee over a drink in an Edinburgh club, only to find the man himself bursting through the door. George MacLeod was in a position not unlike his grandfather, Norman, on the sabbath issue: not quite hissed at in the streets, but certainly whispered against in the clubs. And like Norman, he relished a fight against the odds. Courage, Brother, do not stumble!

As well as a barrage of national criticism, the Trustees had to face sniper fire from the Iona parish minister, who wrote complaining about the Community advertising their Communion services in the village, arguing that it was an encroachment upon his pastoral rights and duties.

There were times when the Iona Cathedral Trustees must have yearned for the American rebuilding option which they had rejected in 1935, and must have been dismayed by the sight of that troublesome priest, George MacLeod, striding purposefully towards them with a look of battle in his eye. To think that in 1935 MacLeod's proposal had seemed the safer of the two! As they held their position by virtue of their office rather than through overwhelming personal interest, some of the Trustees were indecisive in the face of terrible conviction. They mumbled on the mainland but hid on the island when confronted by Iona's High Priest in full flight. George was a belligerent pacifist who liked a good fight, and he was determined to see his project through.

"I have led a ramstam life for weeks," he wrote to Petrovitch. "I still build an Abbey: still fight the Trustees: still wonder what we are doing and am still amazed that two hundred folk in the week since Coracle went out have buzzed in their subs and begged us to go on."

He also informed "Petro" that his successor at Govan, now a chaplain in the army, had wired offering to resign – "but I am not considering the merits till it happens and till (and if) I am asked what I feel about it. It would be a difficult decision as the divinity students are drying up in numbers. From one point of view it would be a release to apply I.C. to a parish of my own. But from another it would probably mean getting lost in details again. To return would probably keep me in the Church. Not to, I sometimes think, will put me out of it before I am finished."

Mercifully and wisely, the Presbytery declined to accept the Govan minister's offer to resign. The big confrontation over Govan would have to wait for another day.

He received an invitation to do parish work from another troublesome priest, the Rev. Mervyn Stockwood, a Church of England ordinand with whom he had shared a platform on several occasions. Stockwood had a good rapport with the Scot, and both could hold student audiences spellbound. In January 1941, Stockwood wrote to George, saying that the Bishop of Bristol had asked him to become vicar of a local parish.

"If I do accept it, is there any chance of you coming in on it? You are a practically free man for part of the year, and I think that possibly we might be able to do something about Christian unity. I know that this is a completely mad scheme – but after all we've talked about reunion for 30 years and we've done practically nothing; it may however come when folk of different denominations share the same burning passion."

The restless Scot was tempted, but resisted the temptation. History was thus spared the sight of Mervyn Stockwood (later to be a radical and unconventional Bishop of Southwark) and George MacLeod working in tandem – a prospect liable to keep any sensitive bishop awake at night, trembling.

Instead, George threw himself into mission work, conferences, fund-raising, university work, preaching, recruiting and writing. Hawick, London, Edinburgh, Largs, Winchester, Cambridge, Stepney, Nottingham, Dundee all received whirlwind visits. He was invited to Bermondsey to talk to social workers who were emotionally shell-shocked by the blitz.

When Hitler turned his attention to Clydebank in March 1941, there was only one place to go. The tall tenements around the shipyards took a pounding: only seven houses out of 12,000 escaped damage. 528 people were killed, and 35,000 were made homeless. Before the blitz there were 16 Reformed churches in the town: two days later, nine were still standing.

The churches could not minister as before. Denominational differences seemed irrelevant amid the ruins, and George MacLeod and the Iona Community helped make hurried plans for a united witness – one of the first such ecumenical ventures in Britain. His experience with the Govan mission of friendship was invaluable.

Iona Community men were seconded to Clydebank to help with the devastation and its follow-up. Thousands of homes were visited, and special services were held. Churchmen from different denominations spoke at crowded open-air meetings outside the shipyard gates. George MacLeod persuaded Dr John White and Archbishop William Temple to come to Clydebank to address the crowds.

Adjutant MacLeod, who loved helping with the blitz work, offered the Abbey restoration team, now depleted by call-ups, for mainland building. In fact, the government gave permission to carry on at Iona, and, with local help, the stonework in the refectory was completed.

The problem was where the money for the next phase would come from. True to form, a ministering angel appeared, right on time, this time in the form of a little old lady who wanted to make a "little gift" for the rebuilding.

George suggested that a candle sconce might be appropriate. She said she could give a little more, and agreed to foot the bill for the expenses of bringing some of the lecturers to the island.

"That night the telephone rang: the same diffident voice. She had meant to give more. Could I make a more responsible suggestion? I promised to write – and wasted no time. Would she, I asked, care to give the east range? It would cost £10,000. But, said I, if we are to move into that sort of realm, should we not gather our lawyers too? After all, I knew nothing of her, nor she of me.

"Before eleven that morning, the telephone again. Yes, she would give the east range and as she always liked to do things quickly, could I and our lawyers come to lunch in her house THE NEXT DAY. To luncheon we all went: she had no maid, and at once suggested we should get our business done, the better to enjoy our luncheon. Her lawyer began to protest. 'These things take time to execute,' he demurred, with a dry cough. 'Nor have I with me a large enough piece of paper.' 'I have plenty of large paper,' she countered, and opened an empty drawer. Extracting from it the large sheet of glossy paper that is the base of every drawer in a well-ordered house, she carted this mass of white, more like a well-ironed cotton sheet than a missive, and dropped it in the lap of the hesitant lawyer. All he could think of writing, when it came to the point, occupied a tiny corner of it. All was duly signed. And we sat down to a simple carefree lunch. Thus in forty-eight hours we had moved from a candle sconce to a range holding 18 rooms: from £5 to £10,000.

"Later, I came to know well this little lady who walked in out of the blue. I asked her what had prompted this series of actions. Her answer was disarming. She had hardly heard of the Iona Community, save in name. But she had read in the press a violent attack by a correspondent. She had made enquiry, found the criticism nonsense: and decided to back us to give us heart. Perhaps you will understand me when I say I have hopefully welcomed all further press criticism ever since! Soon afterwards I met the violent press critic and sincerely thanked him for his unwitting assistance. He roared with laughter, undertook a serious investigation of what we were really trying to do and became a co-operator in our work. There is perhaps another moral. Criticism is good for a movement. More often than not the criticism can teach you things, and also rallies invariably more friends than foes."[2]

The mainland mission work continued to develop, with Iona teams in difficult parishes. It also continued to be hampered by George MacLeod's pacifism. Even so, the Community continued to be a lifeline for many people, such as the Rev. W. A. Smellie, the influential minister of St John's, Perth.

"What I am grateful for," he wrote to George, "is the absolute confirmation that the Community is the most important thing that is happening in the life of the Church of Scotland just now. In my morbid moments, which are more frequent than yours (and properly enough so) I say 'the only important thing'. If it weren't there I think I would hand in my own checks."

The Iona Community was exciting, but was it also heretical? George MacLeod's pacifism was already regarded as deviancy, but fresh accusations of heresy came when his flirtation with the ideas of Rudolf Steiner, an Austrian philosopher who founded a school of thought known as Anthroposophy, became public knowledge.

Steiner felt that religion had become separated from life and from science, and he sought an integration. Anthroposophy developed highly elaborated doctrines of the origin of the world and the various epochs of mankind.

Steiner's ideas appealed to the Celtic mystic in George MacLeod, as part of his wider quest for a theology to match his experience in

Jerusalem, 1933. He felt that it was not enough to reform the Church: the post-war world needed a theology big enough and deep enough to address the problems of modern scientific man. He believed that post-First World War religion had inhabited ghettos, and had therefore been unable to help man find bearings in the bewildering new age. As the scientific world view had taken over, religion had retreated to a private area marked the "soul". Only a religion which treated the material order seriously, but saw it infused with the spiritual, could claim the attention of modern man.

What George saw as necessary was a total gospel, what he called "whole salvation rather than soul salvation" – a gospel which held Christ as the centre of the whole created order, and therefore Lord of science and matter as well as of the individual human soul. His was a Christ-mysticism, seeing, as with the Celtic poets, the spirit of Christ in all things. And it was a spirituality which had to be expressed in material action.

George was also attracted by the mystical theology of Nicolas Berdyaev, a Russian philosopher of Marxist leanings who had been exiled by Lenin, and whose spiritual journey brought him back to the Orthodox Church. Berdyaev proclaimed a modern "spiritual Christianity", a vision of the material shot through with the spiritual. He was much more directly Christian than Steiner, but he did not care for tight doctrinal definitions, and he was sometimes accused of unorthodoxy. His combination of slightly anarchic spiritual discernment and social analysis appealed to George, who nevertheless picked ideas and themes from the Russian without engaging rigorously with his thinking.

The Iona Leader's intuitions were supported during his regular discussions on Iona with Professor Charles Raven, the noted Cambridge naturalist, historian and theologian. A liberal and a pacifist, Raven was attempting to forge a synthesis of science and religion which would make sense to contemporary man. George saw Steiner and Berdyaev as providing a helpful philosophical undergirding for a new, integrated approach, and he became a committee member of the Fellowship of Ministers for the study of Steiner's work. Their aim was to study the implications of Steiner's teaching for Christian life and thought, and to work out solutions for the new age that was believed to be coming.

There were two problems. George MacLeod was not a systematic theologian, and Steiner's work did not sit easily with Christian orthodoxy. George simply did not have the patience or the mental discipline to work at the intellectual issues involved. He was an intuitive thinker, a poet, and a man of action who had an uncanny ability to see important issues long before others did. George's genius lay not in the originality of his own thinking, but in his prophetic ability to "see" the heart of things ahead of his time and to express old and new ideas in brilliant language wedded to imaginative action.

The problem centred in the Christian doctrines of the transcendence and the immanence of God: that is to say, the belief that God is both *outside* all things, and *within* all things. Orthodox Christian theology had done a balancing act in asserting that God was separate from the world and stood over the world: at the same time he was active in and through the world. The doctrine of the Incarnation – that in Christ, God took human flesh – was a daring assertion that God was both judge and lover of the world. Mystics tended to emphasize the doctrine of the immanence of God, the "withinness" of God in the world, and stress God's uniting of all things within himself.

Steiner had no place in his system for an external God: or for an internal one, for that matter. Man's spiritual nature was what mattered. It was one thing to see Anthroposophy as a legitimate protest against a lifeless Christian traditionalism which inhabited an ecclesiastical ghetto: quite another to claim that it could provide the scaffolding for a new Christian edifice.

George MacLeod was attracted to the Steiner community not just because of its theories, but because of its work with handicapped children, and its care for the environment. He felt the Christian Church exhibited little or no concern for the earth, and his insistence in the early 1940s on an ecological dimension to theology and practice was truly prophetic. He became friendly with Dr Karl König, who established a school for handicapped children at Camphill, Aberdeen.

"Our talk and everything connected with it made a deep impression upon me and I felt again the strong connection between us," Dr König wrote to George. "What especially struck me was the different ways through which we are both working to come to the same point – to reach the same goal – to establish Christ in the age of today. I felt most deeply what I am lacking and missing, and what you have got; the absolute piety and faith inside you. But on the other hand, I am trying to see Christ working in the kingdoms of nature around us – and this I feel is lacking in you. If both these streams could join up and become one river it would be real integration."

George felt the rebuke was justified.

When he invited Dr König to write a series of articles for *Coracle*, a furious debate opened up. The leading European theologian of the day, Karl Barth, stressed the transcendence, the "otherness" of God, and the sinfulness of man. Man, he said, could not find God through natural religion, he could only know Him through His gracious revelation in Jesus Christ. "Merely to talk about man in a loud voice is not to talk about God," Barth insisted.

George was unimpressed by the Barthian separation of God from natural human life, muttering that "Barth is easier to pronounce than to apply". Two of Barth's most brilliant Scottish disciples were Thomas F. Torrance and J. K. S. Reid (who would both become prominent professors of theology) and both wrote to George in uncompromising terms, pointing out the error of his ways.

"You have a tremendous influence over youth," warned J. K. S. Reid. "Many of the young people in my own congregation follow what you say and your movements and your lead with the greatest eagerness. This constitutes the greatest of responsibilities for you, and I have no doubt you have often seen the situation in this light. It is all the more imperative that the lead you give should be in the right direction. I am convinced that at this point you are doing nothing but lead those who follow you, both lay and clerical, astray into most pernicious untruth."

George MacLeod's reply was equally uncompromising.

"To me, Christian orthodoxy is essentially a belief in a Person who always has many things to tell us but we cannot hear them now. He has given us the Spirit of Truth that shall guide us into all the truth: a sentence that implies that we must keep moving. I really don't know what heresy is in these terms: though I can see how heresy can be defined if once orthodoxy is admitted as an intellectual set of formulae. If I wanted that I would go to Rome. I do not go there because the Roman Church seems to me the logical result of trying to 'pin down' orthodoxy. Short of Rome there is this mixty maxty business of many opinions: with your school trying to pin us down to 'one opinion' again and calling out all the others as the devil's agents. I am glad your school keeps hammering at 'one opinion': keeps chucking in the spice which Barth said had been left out of the pudding too long. What makes me sad is the insistence that the entire pudding should be made of this spice: this calling out of all the others as the devil's agents."

George MacLeod was both a cosmic mystic and an out-and-out evangelical, who believed in his heart that he had been set free by Jesus Christ. He also believed that the essential freedom of the gospel was obscured, not enhanced, by rigid theological systems like Calvinism. He spelt it out in a letter to Duncan Finlayson, who had asked him some questions about the nature of divine forgiveness.

"What you and I are really whoring after, you know, is satisfaction about our relationship with God . . . You and I come of fine Calvinistic stock: and Calvinism was probably a justified protest against the raging romantic subjectivism of the Celtic character, with its warlocks, witches and whimsy. Now that warlocks belong to lore, and witches to psychopathology, and whimsy died with J. M. Barrie, Calvinism itself is now a concept of the mind, but its virus still lurks in the marrow of our psyche. And we are but Jews with Christian knobs on. Now there is no satisfaction for us in our relationship with God.

"We are in the ditch; soundly, deservedly, and for good. But a ditch is no more than a continuing coffin with the ends knocked off. At any given point in the ditch, coterminous with your length, you are coffined and that is the end: barring a final coffining that took place behind a certain Stone. We are in fact buried with Christ, that with Christ we may rise. Our unrighteousnesses are caught up by Him (this we admit and accept), but the inevitable pride attendant on our righteousness is also caught up and annulled. (This we admit with our mind, but find it almost impossible to accept.)

"When, spasmodically, we grasp that we are accepted, well, Calvin goes over the pavilion for a six – right out of the field. As for me – and here we may part company – my problem at this point is what I really conceive of as God. The overlay of youthful picture books leaves an indelible picture of an Old Testament prophet God. And the picture then is of One who patronizes me and lets me go without a hiding. But this is unsatisfactory, leaving Calvin not quite over the pavilion but sitting on one of its chimney pots ready to return to the pitch: where the damned old bowling starts again, and my arm is already so tired.

"When I can, spasmodically, accept that no man has seen God at any time, and that Christ has declared him as SPIRIT – God is a Spirit and they that pray to Him must pray to Him in Spirit and in Truth – then I am delivered by the sheer reality of the situation. Christ above, beside, within, beneath me, creates a sort of atomic field of relationship. I am free for fun – in the ditch."

George certainly believed deeply in a God who was both "out there" and "in here". He dealt with the contradictions by incorporating them or ignoring them. He certainly did not lie awake at night wondering how all the philosophical insights could be reconciled. All he knew was that the central scientific territory had to be reclaimed for Christ.

"We make the dangerous claim that generations yet to come will look on the recent discoveries of 'scientific man' as veritably pentecostal," he said in a sermon preached in Iona Abbey in 1942, "hidden as yet from men but only adequately described in dynamic terms. No longer has 'matter' its old dead meaning: the whole universe vibrates in terms that men can only glimpse, saying that all creation is 'light energy'. The Psalmist who declared 'the mountains skip like rams, the little hills like young sheep' may have stumbled on more than poetry. Science, once blatant and confident in materialism, now stands mystified and reverent. The Holy Spirit is first openly revealed in nature, in this our age."

Again, the beleaguered George MacLeod was being truly prophetic in the early 1940s as he turned his attention away from Scotland, Presbyterianism and the European war to the cosmic dimensions of faith in a scientific age. He has sometimes been accused of being anti-intellectual, but this is far too simplistic a view. He enjoyed intellectual debate and ideas, but they had to be rooted in or followed up by action. He liked provoking intellectuals by defining an academic as "someone who can hold a vital issue at arm's length for a lifetime", and he also enjoyed telling the story of a Border farmer who told him, "We're no verra intellectual here, which means we just have to use oor brains."

George's sweeping statements about history rightly annoyed academics, who would find that their questions about details were brushed aside: yet his protests against compartmentalizing and fragmenting of knowledge were legitimate. George MacLeod attempted to bring together the theological, the philosophical and the practical in his Iona experiment.

"The nature of a New Order will be revealed not by the searchlight of high-powered brains but in response to the obedience of convinced

Courage, Brother!

Believers. (If the high powered brains accept the obedience and bring their searchlights with them, so much the better.)

"For Christ is a Person to be trusted, not a principle to be tested. The Church is a Movement, not a meeting house. The Faith is an Experience, not an exposition. Christians are Explorers, not map makers. And the New Social Order is not a blueprint which someone must find quickly. It is a present Experience made possible at Bethlehem, offered on Calvary, and communicated at Pentecost."[3]

The building programme continued slowly, hampered by lack of craftsmen and materials. The summer of 1942 was marred by news of the death of Jimmy Dalgleish, the first full member of the Iona Community to die on active service.

George was saddened by that death, as he was by the death of his mother at 4 Park Circus Place three months later. "Our generation will not face the limitations of old age as did theirs," he wrote to Petrovitch. "Salute the Victorians. Her fortitude will be my constant inspiration. I am sure if I live to eighty-four, 200 folk won't write about me."

The development of the growing Iona Community was furthered by the appointment of the Rev. Lex Miller, a New Zealander, as deputy leader in September 1942. An acute theologian of the Barthian school and a sharp political analyst, he helped the Community arrive at an Economic Discipline as part of its Rule: members agreed to try to live on the national average wage, and account to each other as to how they coped. Lex Miller's focus on economics, and his concern to identify with the dispossessed of society pushed the Iona Community and its leader further in a radical direction. He was able to stand up to George intellectually, and would ask him awkward questions about matters such as his membership of the Western Club.

George sometimes wondered aloud whether the whole Iona Community show had been too much of a compromise all along.

"When I decided in Iona in 1938 not to go all out," he mused to Petrovitch, who had criticized him for not being radical enough, "the implications were enormous. They are to deal with the majority and do them a little good: to go slightly faster than the slowest soldier: to be more moronic than vitriolic. The other way we should have lost the Abbey: the Church connection: we would have been a Pacifist show, probably living in huts in Perthshire (if not in Barlinnie prison) with 50 per cent pure gems and 50 per cent cranks. As I am not blood brother to Our Lord but only a distant cousin, I would also have had a nervous breakdown.

"I don't think I would have done anyone much good. So I am dull, but not so dull as not to be fluttering the Church; with jammed Bren gun, but not so jammed as not to hit with one bullet out of five: I will take a hiding from you when I hear YOU have burned your boats. My real me is ecclesiastic after all."

George had days of depression when he thought about his position. He was criticized for being disloyal to the Church and for being too loyal: for being not radical enough and for being too radical: for being too orthodox, and for being heretical. He worried about the craftsmen, and where the next cheque and supply of materials would come from. "It was said that we decided to build on faith: it would be truer to say that we felt the Abbey should be rebuilt, and just failed to consider how the money would come in," he would say. Yet he knew he had to appear confident, despite the criticism and days of despairing self-doubt.

George was told by his doctor to "lie low" for a while, otherwise he would be in "a frightful bad temper" all summer. At one of his lowest moments of unfaith he stood, filled with self-pity, in the chancel of Iona Abbey.

"The red granite walls reflected the overpowering iridescence of light," he recalled. "The whole place seemed almost ablaze with a reddish hue. And there I stood, disconsolate, a thankless brute in all God's brightness. And it was another stranger to my mood who must have read my thoughts. 'Cheer up, George,' he said, 'the Church is never lovelier than when it is bleeding.'"

What in the end kept him going was his personal faith, and the encouragement he received from people who insisted that the Iona Community kept them in the Church. The number of minister Associates grew, and young people in increasing numbers wanted to be identified with the movement. They headed for Iona, knowing that something significant was happening. Soon the Community had to organize youth camps on the island. A Christian Workers' League was started in Edinburgh.

Women wished to be associated with what had been an all-male preserve, and it was eventually agreed that a branch of Women Associates should be formed. George had argued that the Community represented an experiment to reach industrial men, and that the facilities on what was effectively a building site were not appropriate for women. Behind that lay a more rigidly masculine way of thinking: a public school, regimental model. Wives of new members joining the Community were not able to be with their husbands, and this naturally caused tension and resentment. Iona was sometimes bitterly described as "the other woman".

It was not that George did not appreciate the work women did: he greatly admired the women's work in Govan, for instance. In the presence of the opposite sex he was charming and exceedingly gallant and courteous – but also a bit remote, and sometimes awkward. As a very eligible and handsome bachelor he was much admired and, indeed, yearned after, but he was always on his guard so far as women were concerned: thus far, and no further. There was a war to be won – both in the world and in his own soul. Close involvement might open the floodgates. All his energy went into rebuilding an Abbey and leading the shock troops in God's front line. (When asked once by Harry Whitley what to say about sex to a young couple in his church youth group, George's reply was illuminating. "The fellow who goes with his girl is fundamentally showing his desire to become creative in the highest sense of the word, and quite right, too! But until he is in a position to do this – that is, marry her – he is much better with his creative power employed elsewhere, where it can obtain full outlet." All of which raises the intriguing question: was the eventual restoration of Iona Abbey, that "Glory of the West", the direct derivative of powerful creative energy being employed where it could obtain full outlet?)

Through the war the building went on, slowly, as the Iona Community searched for a new vocabulary of work and worship. As he saw it grow, George dreamed of the future.

"It is our hope that the Abbey will be completed as a Laboratory School of Christian Living where large numbers will come to pray and confer. It is our instinct that the essentials for which we seek, with many others, to stand will soon become the subjects round which the whole Church will be forced to confer. It is our prayer that, increasingly, in such conferring we will have gatherings in Iona drawn from many denominations and will together glimpse the day when, as in St Columba's time, Christ's Church shall be One in every land."[4]

In the summer of 1943, announcement was made of an astonishing gift, which further altered the direction of the Iona Community and of its leader. Anonymous donors (later to be revealed as Sir James and Lady Lithgow) promised £20,000 a year for seven years to further the work of the Church of Scotland among young people, "in accordance with the principles of the Iona Community".

An Iona Youth Trust was formed consisting of representatives of the Church of Scotland Youth Committee, the Iona Community, and the donors. It was agreed to use the considerable amount of money to finance youth camps on Iona, to set up three youth centres in congested areas, to establish a residence for men coming home from the war who were contemplating training for Christian work, and to set up a youth house in Glasgow.

A building was purchased at 214 Clyde Street, Glasgow, situated on the banks of the River Clyde. Equipped with restaurant, chapel, library and meeting rooms, it was to be the Iona Community's west of Scotland base for thirty years, and was to be the starting point for many new ventures.

The status of the Iona Community was obviously changing.

So was the rank of its leader. And all because of the death of a British spy behind enemy lines.

14

The Reluctant Baronet

*The task before us now, if we would not perish . . . is
to shake off our ancient prejudices and rebuild the
earth.*

TEILHARD DE CHARDIN

*Is my gloom, after all,
Shade of His hand,
Outstretched caressingly?*

FRANCIS THOMPSON

When Mussolini brought Italy into the war, scenting the spoils of
victory, Captain Sir Ian Francis Norman MacLeod was an obvious
man to do espionage work in Rome.

Having spent half his life in Italy, he was fluent in the language,
and understanding of its culture. He had gone to Egypt with the
Intelligence Corps in 1940, received his captaincy before his 21st
birthday, and served throughout the advance of the Eighth Army
in Africa. As gregarious and witty as his father had been, he was a
very able spy, operating as organizer of a tough and adventurous
espionage unit under the noses of the Germans. On one such
mission in April 1944, he was involved in a motor cycle accident
near Naples.

"I only hope and pray that I may heal fairly quickly so as to
enjoy a few months of happiness, as I have been dreaming of for
years," he wrote to his uncle George from what turned out to be
his deathbed. He was 23 years of age.

George was deeply upset by his nephew's death. "I was down at
Winchester the other day," he wrote to Harry Whitley soon
afterwards, "and was actually sick at memories of our Ian. There
is a sense in which his death ended my life. But another in which

perhaps his death began it. I no longer care a damn about futures at all."

Until the press rang him, it had not entered his head that he would, of course, inherit the baronetcy. He decided not to call himself Sir George. The Court Circular of May 1944 said simply that the new Baronet "desires it to be known that, while he has no desire to renounce his succession to the honour accorded to his father by his Majesty the King, he wishes in all practical matters of address, Church document and public engagement, to retain without addition the sufficient title of Reverend."

The statement symbolized the contradictions at the heart of George MacLeod which puzzled some and infuriated others. It showed a loyalty to his family and upbringing, alongside a refusal to be bound by his dynastic history. It represented a genuine appreciation and enjoyment of his own past, and a willingness to use his old school tie network of privilege to further his anti-establishment causes. It satisfied neither royalist conservatives, who were dismayed by his refusal to use the title, nor democratic radicals, who felt that a full renunciation would have been a help in the post-war dismantling of the British "class show". It satisfied only Rev. (Sir) George F. MacLeod, loyalist, royalist, churchman, iconoclast, radical, maddening gadfly and, above all, his own man.

To meet an almost insatiable demand for information about his Iona experiment, George (who, the year before, had become the first non-Anglican to be Select Preacher at Cambridge), wrote *We Shall Rebuild*. Produced by the Iona Community's own publishing department in 1944, the book fairly soon sold 20,000 copies – a remarkable sale for a wartime book printed on government-issue paper.

The book presented a masterly summing up of the themes of the Iona Community since its inception – the failure of the Church's worship and practice to meet the new day, the need to draw on the best of the past in order to provide resources for a new future, the necessity of finding forms of faith and life which held together the individual and the corporate, and the need to train new shock troops for battles in the toughest areas. Above all, there was the necessity for pioneering ventures which would test new routes for the Church.

The Iona leader insisted, over against both traditional conservative and out-and-out radical critics, thus offending both, that the

Iona experiment was on behalf of the mainstream, historic, visible Church.

"All who find themselves impelled into the ranks of reformers, in any sphere, have times of temptation 'to scrap the lot'. What we – in our very small witness – are convinced about is that it is a *temptation*, and as such to be avoided at every cost. Nothing is more certain than the obligation on a Christian to practise the Faith in fellowship. No one can be a Christian by himself. And we sometimes wonder whether those who 'fall out', to make coteries of their own, grasp that what they are doing is to form new denominations. We wonder because almost invariably in the fore-front of their criticism of the traditional Church is the accusation that it has too many denominations already!

"Thus we are pledged to our Branch of the Church as it is. Nor, let us hasten to add, is that said with a single trace of condescension, but rather with immeasurable pride and gratitude. Nothing is more easy than to criticize the traditional Church. The further you get 'under the thatch', the larger are likely to be the points of criticism that you can muster – if you are in that mood. But the more you get 'under the thatch' of the many 'movements for international brotherhood' or 'social betterment' of this or that community, of that or this new fellowship for human causes, the more you find precisely the same points for criticism – with a few usually added besides!"[1]

By the summer of 1944, the focus in the Church of Scotland and in the Iona Community was on the future of Europe after the end of hostilities. The Kirk had established a heavyweight "Commission for the Interpretation of God's Will in the Present Crisis" under the convenorship of Professor John Baillie, and it reported each year of the war. George MacLeod had been made convenor of the subcommission on social and industrial life. The Baillie Commission, which showed evidence of the impact of the thinking of the Iona Community on social problems, noted with approval "the returning spirit of community after the long reign of individualism."

The mood of the Church was changing. The Church and Nation Committee said that "the economics of *laissez faire* are dead; and for the disastrous economics of national self-sufficiency, with their inevitably militaristic basis, there has to be substituted a planned world economy." The Committee also said of the Beveridge Report, which would form the basis of the post-war Welfare State, that it "deserves to take its place as the foremost social document of the century".[2]

The wayward "communist" Iona Community could hardly have put it better. Were things beginning to go its way?

Attracted though he was by the radical commitment of Marxism and its burning passion for social justice, George MacLeod did not feel that Communism would last the pace. He told his left-wing, agnostic friend Petrovitch:

"Man is so b – d that I don't think Russia will prove 'ideal' enough and lift man from his self centre. That is not to say organized religion will. Indeed the final totalitarianism is likely to be Rome; the while, the individual is finding his feet and a new and interior authority will gradually bring men back to sanity. Before then, however, much blood will flow and Pacifism will rid itself of its errors (through suffering) and Man achieve his next stage. But if you and I live till 90 we shall not see it. Yet, in the other sense, we see it already the moment we see it. I know you agree with this. The odd thing is that it was what St Paul was trying to say."

As the war drew to a close, the Iona experiment attracted more and more European and American ecclesiastical attention, as well as coverage in the national press. *The Manchester Guardian, The Listener, The Times, The Picture Post* all carried major articles, and the European and North American church press featured George MacLeod and his lively community.

Young people made tracks for Iona in ever increasing numbers, and Johnny MacMillan, a former Toc H worker, was appointed to organize youth camps. The young people, male and female, from many different denominations and backgrounds made an enormous impact on the life of the Iona Community – as had the ministers and lay people who had attended the wartime courses. The Iona Community was becoming a bigger organization with a much wider base and task than its leader had ever envisaged. From being a small project for the training of Scottish Presbyterian ministers, it was developing into an inspiring educational catalyst for the World Church.

For many young people, the Iona youth camps were formative experiences, producing a harvest of new vocations, ordained and lay. A weekly "Act of Belief" service was introduced at the Abbey, enabling people to move out of their seats and make or renew a personal commitment to Christ in front of the Iona marble communion table, kneeling where thousands had knelt before them down through the centuries.

A healing service, with prayers for the sick and the laying on of hands, also became part of the weekly liturgy of the Iona Community. Many people made their way to Iona, seeking peace or healing or both. One such person was Ian Cowie, who arrived on Iona in 1945 during the first full week on the subject of the healing ministry. Ian, who would later develop a full-time healing ministry in Edinburgh, had made his way to the island at the end of the war, feeling passionately that peace should now be waged as sacrificially as war had been, and "knowing I'd a call to the ministry, but not being really a member of the Church, and never having met a minister who impressed me. Utterly bewildered by the call to the ministry, I found in Iona George MacLeod and other ministers concerned with peace and healing, two things I felt I needed, and the call began to make sense."

To cope with the increasing numbers of young people, George rented a salmon fishing station at Camas on Mull, a bay opposite Iona. A group of boys from Rugby School got the buildings into shape. Dormitory accommodation was organized, and a small Chapel of the Nets established as a place of worship. University students and schoolboys came to Camas to engage in building work and fishing. George MacLeod, who had been a licensed bus operator in Govan, became a licensed fishmonger in order to sell the Camas salmon – strange but touching activities for a preacher of international renown.

George, who had continued to care for delinquent youngsters – "the only difference between them and us is that they have been found out," he would say – brought groups of Borstal boys to Camas and Iona, as he had done at Fingalton Mill. He was chairman of the Polmont Borstal Visiting Committee for many years, and he was touched by the impact of youth camps at Camas and Iona on individual youngsters.

He was delighted when boys came back to see him, and he told the story of one lad who revisited the island. George had sensed that the boy had problems, and suggested to him that he might write down any burden he had on a piece of paper and seal it in an envelope, before receiving the laying on of hands.

"Laying on of hands is a strange experience: sometimes it is a little more vibrant than perhaps an act of confirmation. But sometimes there is a vibrancy that can be felt, as if something was really coming out of a person. Well, I can only say that with John that night there was a terrific vibrancy.

"When the short service was over, I said to him, 'You know, John, I am not making it up to impress you and I don't say it to everyone, but something really happened then.' 'My God, it did,' said John, stroking the back of his neck. As the light shone forth on the grass, three white doves fluttered up into the air. 'God Almighty!' said John. 'I beg your pardon,' said I. 'Well, ye ken,' he said, 'the night I first went to Borstal it was winter and it was late and I saw the Governor, who sent me to my house across the square. The officer took me down the passage, and as I went down I said a wee prayer to myself that Borstal would do me good and not harm. And would you believe it, when the officer opened the door to cross the grass to the house, three white doves fluttered up into the air.'

"God Almighty indeed. The tension at that moment was so intense that I cleared my throat and said: 'Don't you know that we have three white doves that constantly commute between Polmont and Iona?'

"'Ach,' said John, 'ye're an awful blether.'"[3]

George's commitment to delinquent youngsters was intense. One Borstal boy, Tom, who had been at Camas, got into trouble while in the army, and George, who had been aware that the lad's father had died when he was eleven, went to visit him in prison.

"We knew from his history what he wanted. We knew, too, from psychology, that it is no good telling him what he wanted. He must say it himself. So we spent weary interviews in playing the father, listening to eternal chatter about books, and Rangers, jive, and, occasionally, girls. And the moment came.

"Suddenly he said, 'What I really want is a father.'

"'Someone to look after you, whatever happens?'

"'Yep.'

"'What about God the Father?'

"'For God's sake, cut out that ridiculous stuff.'

"'Sorry,' we said. 'What about my becoming your father, then, for the next ten years. I will always come wherever you are arrested, in Cardiff or in Wick, twice a year for 10 years if you wish – or at any rate, someone will come, not to get you off but to assure the court there is a father waiting for you when you get out.'

"'No,' said Tom, now deathly white. 'I won't accept it.' 'Why?' we asked. 'Because,' after a pause, 'I would have to give up crime.'

"'But isn't that what you want to do?'

"'Yep.'

"'Then is it a bet?'

"'Yep.'

"So he became our son. And, so far, the rest of his story is encouraging. From Singapore, he asks now to be put in touch with the Church. 'Dear Pop,' he actually writes, 'do you know a good parson in these parts?'"[4]

Tom's name might have been MacLegion: there have been many such names in George MacLeod's life. He would leave Iona on the early ferry to plead for a boy in court, and return the next day. He used to contrast his own privileged upbringing with those of youngsters in trouble, and he would defend young people from deprived areas and backgrounds with passionate advocacy. At the heart of his concern was the burning compassion of a man with an evangelical understanding of the gospel – that Christ died for sinners, and that God is a prodigal father who lavishes his love on his undeserving ones.

At a time when George was becoming known as a social crusader, and was being derided by educated men in city clubs for his pacifism and socialism, he was ministering to delinquent youngsters and down-and-outs with an open heart. At a time when he was taking no salary for his work and was sharing dormitory accommodation on an island hut, he was ministering to the needy with prayer and an open wallet.

Despite his generosity, his pastoral work was not sentimental. He asked sharp questions, and did not let people off any moral hooks. He talked directly and simply about sin and repentance and forgiveness. His pastoral work brought him to the conclusion that Protestantism needed something akin to the confessional – a conclusion that reinforced his critics' suspicions that he was hell-bent on leading the Church of Scotland to Rome. He defended himself vigorously in a sermon from the pulpit of Iona Abbey.

"No human being need necessarily stand between man and his Maker. No sin so black, but if a man confess it truly in the secret place of his heart he can obtain forgiveness. I do not doubt the doctrine. What worries me is whether men who proudly so protest in fact confess their sins in the secret places of their hearts. Because it is very hard, very taxing. Our Reformed doctrine is the highest of them all. But do we in fact employ it? Do we in fact confess our sins in the secret places of our hearts in any regular way? If we do not, believe me, in our restless, burdened age, we may preserve our doctrine, but ever larger crowds will gather on the lists of the Marriage Clinics, and in the waiting rooms of the psychotherapists."[5]

His concern for individuals also developed his interest in the ministry of healing. Weeks on the subject of healing were held on Iona. George MacLeod saw healing as part of the total gospel, individual and corporate. Individual people needed healing in their lives, as did communities. He argued passionately that it was not enough to pray for a child dying of tuberculosis: it was essential to campaign for the removal of the conditions which bred the disease. It was not enough to pray with Borstal boys; it was necessary to clear the slums and build new houses and schools. Prayer, confession, forgiveness, the laying on of hands and political action were all part of the total Christian mission according to MacLeod.

No wonder people found George MacLeod maddeningly difficult to categorize. He was an evangelist, with a simple, almost child-like faith in God. He believed in conversion, in the direct intervention of God, and in miracles. He also believed in a cosmic God who was in and through all things, yet had revealed his nature as being that of suffering Love for individual persons. George was a Protestant who believed in such "Romish" things as candles, responses, weekly sacraments, and confession. And as well as being a loyal churchman intent on rebellion, he was a crusader with a political fire in his belly: a man of privilege calling for a radically new social order. His socialism was not of an ideological nature: it was a gut reaction springing directly from his concern for individuals. Much as he admired Marx's social passion and believed him to be a prophet raised up by God to rebuke his Church, he was opposed to the Communist ideology: and his socialism was primarily a deep concern for justice for all God's children, rather than a theoretical adherence to a political creed.

As an exhausted Europe moved towards the end of its second total war of the century during the summer of 1945, George MacLeod's eye was, as always, on the future. At the age of fifty, he was entitled to look back on considerable achievement. It seemed miraculous that the rebuilding of Iona Abbey had continued, albeit slowly, in the midst of war. The chapter house, the library and the reredorter had been completely restored: the great east range dormitory was being rebuilt: the refectory walls had been restored: money had been provided for the abbot's house and the Michael chapel.

The Cathedral Trustees were still nervous, and a title deed was drawn up, attesting that occupation of the Cathedral buildings by the Iona Community could be terminated at any time and that "all restoration work carried out upon the old monastic buildings shall belong in property to the Trustees, irrespective of who carried out the work and paid for same."

That is to say: although George MacLeod had raised almost all the money single-handedly, and the restoration had been carried out by the Iona Community, the Community could be ejected from the buildings at any time by the Trustees without a single penny of compensation.

When George had been given permission to carry out the restoration, it had been agreed that he would bear responsibility for the costs, and that permission would be given a stage at a time when the money had been given or pledged. When George had wanted to proceed with work on the refectory before all the funds were promised, he had to sign a legal undertaking that he or his executors would be personally responsible for all debts, thus freeing the Trustees of any liability.

The Iona parish minister did not see the Abbey rebuilding as heroic: it was for him a Romanist affront in his own backyard. The Rev. Murdo Macrae fired off letters to the Trustees complaining about the Community holding daily worship in the Abbey church, and asking that the collections taken at Iona Community services should be counted as part of the givings of the local parish church. The Trustees managed to keep cool, though exasperation breathes through the Trust minutes of the time. They told the local minister that he had no right to interfere in the administration of the Trust, that the Community's services were not being held at the same time as his own, and that no, he could not count the Community's service collections as part of the parish church's liberality.

Such conflict might have been avoided if George MacLeod had been less impatient and more of a diplomat, though that is doubtful. It was understandable that a small, island parish should see the growing Abbey and burgeoning community as a threat. The fact that the experiment was attracting people from different denominations, different cultures and different parts of the world only made the threat worse. The Abbey's attraction for delinquent youngsters and mentally unstable people seeking healing stretched the tolerance of islanders, and the sight of Dr MacLeod striding around the island like a Highland laird was a further irritant. The posse of newspapermen and the BBC radio technicians around the Abbey, and the consequent publicity, left the parish church feeling out in the cold. And the Iona parish minister was not a man burdened by a vision of the world-wide task of the Church.

George MacLeod was intent on remaking the Church and the world – an agenda not lacking in ambition. His concentrated purposefulness meant that many people in his peripheral vision were ignored. Nitpickers protecting their tiny Presbyterian empires remained marginalized blurs. The immense compassion poured out on Borstal boys and down-and-outs failed to reach as far as irritating church legalists and petty officials of a failed ecclesiastical empire. There was so much to do, and so little time in which to do it.

Yet there was a cost. Like Winston Churchill (whose style was not so unlike his, and for whom he had a sneaking admiration), he was pursued from time to time by the "black dog" of depression. There would be days of self-doubt and questioning, wondering what he was doing. With so many people depending on him, looking to him for inspiration, the strain was enormous, especially when he did not know where the next gift was coming from. The extrovert man of utter self belief and apparently boundless energy had a shadow side of introspective doubt and despair. The ebullient actor who enjoyed being centre stage and relished the theatre of controversy, wondered sometimes whether it was only an act. The compassionate pastor with a burning concern for the underprivileged was plagued by fears that he was manipulating people into a life drama which was rooted only in his own messianic needs. He of all people needed confession and forgiveness and healing. His soul was an arena of fierce conflict, a no-man's-land in a war of attrition in which God and the devil seemed to struggle to gain a few yards of territory. There were days when George MacLeod was convinced he was losing the war.

★

August 6th, 1945, the Feast of the Transfiguration. A light brighter
than a thousand suns illuminated the Japanese city of Hiroshima.
When the shadows fell, 140,000 men, women and children lay
dead. George did not appreciate the full significance at the time,
but the event and his interpretation of it were to play a formative
role in the rest of his life.

"Suppose the material order, as we have argued, is indeed the
garment of Christ, the temple of the Holy Ghost? Suppose the
bread and wine, symbols of all creation, is indeed capable of
redemption awaiting its Christification? Then what is the atom but
the emergent body of Christ?

"The Feast of the Transfiguration is 6th August. That is the day
we 'happened' to drop the bomb on Hiroshima. We took His body
and we took His Blood and we enacted a Cosmic Golgotha. We
took the key to Love and we used it for bloody hell.

"Nobody noticed. I am not being cheap about other people. I
did not notice it myself. I was celebrating the Feast of the
Transfiguration in a gown and cassock, a hood, a stole, white
bands, saying with the whole Christian ministry, 'This is my body,
this is my blood'. The while our 'Christian civilization', without
Church protest, made its assertion of the complete divorce between
Spirit and Matter."[6]

To hear that sermon preached with enormous passion and
oratory on Iona, where spirit and matter seemed to be interfused,
was to be addressed at the deepest level of one's being. The logic
of his cosmic Christ-mysticism led George MacLeod to see the
atom as part of the Body of Christ himself, and the universe as a
sacrament. ("Atoms help us to adore Him!" he used to cry,
parodying the line of the hymn, "Angels help us to adore Him".)
It therefore became the utmost blasphemy to rend the Body of
Christ in order to create hell on earth. He believed that this spirit-
matter dualism was responsible for the split between religion and
life, Sunday and weekday, Church and world – precisely the split
that the Incarnation was meant to mend.

In 1945 Lex Miller left to work in Canada and New Zealand. In
some ways his sharp and piercing theological questions had been a
thorn in George's side. The uncomfortable nature of the questions
was not eased by the fact that Lex was doing what Dr MacLeod
was good at – earthing heavenly talk. When Lex left there was

genuine gratitude on George's part for his contribution to the life of the Iona Community, mingled with a sense of relief. ("Karl Marx through the week and Karl Barth on Sundays", was one of George's pithy comments about Lex, who in turn said that George's social analysis was about thirty years out of date. His view was that George's really creative contribution had been in the area of worship – "One of the greatest half-dozen liturgists in the history of the Church" was his verdict.)

Community House in Glasgow was beginning to make its presence felt under the joint wardenship of the Rev. Ralph Morton and his wife Jenny. They had served as missionaries in Manchuria for ten years, before Ralph became minister of St Columba's Church, Cambridge. The Mortons' first visitor at Cambridge in 1938 had been George MacLeod, whom Ralph had known as a fellow student. He had shared with Ralph and Jenny his vision for a new community on Iona, and had insisted that they come up to Iona that summer to witness the beginning of the experiment. It was the start of a long and fruitful partnership.

Ralph Morton was a shrewd and canny man, and a fine theologian. He turned out to be a good foil for the more impetuous MacLeod, and he was to have a crucial role in the growth and development of the Iona Community. Jenny was an able and articulate intellectual, conducting radio debates with humanists, formulating new versions of the Iona Community's Economic Witness, and organizing dinner parties noted for choice food and stimulating conversation. Under their leadership, Community House was well placed in the immediate postwar era to host discussions on the future direction of Scottish society.

The new Labour government's commitment to health, welfare and housing improvements had the support of many people in the country. There was a determination to avoid the rhetoric and consequent disillusionment which followed the First World War: at the same time, there was a sense of new possibilities. A country which had united against Hitler's threat could surely this time work together to build a land fit for ordinary heroes. How should it be done? The search for radical ways forward and the quest for knowledge meant that places like Community House had no difficulty in attracting people for classes on religious and political themes. There was a resurgence of interest in the Church, and a rise in the number of mature men studying for the ministry.

Early in 1947 George MacLeod was joined by Dr Archie Craig,

pioneering secretary of the British Council of Churches, as deputy leader of the Iona Community. A Biblical scholar and a pacifist, Dr Craig was highly regarded by the Church. (He had first got to know George when he was at St Cuthbert's, when he was attracted to the "sparkle of the man, his eloquence, diction, poetry – the feel of poetry in his personality", and he talked of "a powerful new religious force unleashed in Scotland, channelled through a man of genius".) With MacLeod, Morton and Craig in the leadership, it was not surprising that the Iona Community was attracting some of the most able of the men from the divinity halls. The Iona Community was where much of the forward thinking and the action was. And its leader was sounding the post-war trumpet with no uncertain sound.

George MacLeod's theological strategy was not to concentrate on the narrowly "religious" – the private areas left over after Darwin, Freud and Marx had had their say – but to go right to the centre and to claim it for Christ.

"Christ is the key to every mortal thing," he wrote. "The key! That is the one thing these ecstatic 'one dimension' modern materialists have not got. The baker simply knows that wholemeal bread is 'better'. The farmer simply knows that organic agriculture is 'healthier'. The psychologist simply knows that man is a 'unity': the scientist, that this unity is represented in all nature. And the atomic power expert, that the ultimate constituent of matter – of the atom, or of the world – is a construction he calls Light/Energy.

"In the meantime, the rest of us 'simply know' that they are all in hopelessly divided compartments without a common purpose or direction. Indeed, the rest of us have an uncomfortable feeling that if matter is left much longer simply in the hands of the material politician and the material scientist they will succeed in blowing us all up."[7]

This excerpt is so contemporary in its feel that it is hard to believe that it was written in 1947 by a very busy man who had little time to read books. "I don't know how it is with George," said Archie Craig, "he reads little – he hasn't the time to – but he seems to breathe important ideas out of the air." His feel for the issues that really mattered repeatedly put him ahead of his time. Again, his genius is seen not in the originality of his thought, but in the originality of his synthesis and his brilliant expression. As a pillager of thoughts which were the province of the specialist, he was without peer. He seemed to have an uncanny sixth sense which told him what was important even when he himself did not completely understand the matter and had neither the time nor the inclination to pursue it (he would have been hard put to answer any questions on scientific theory). Above all, like the German theologian Dietrich Bonhoeffer who was executed in a prisoner of war camp for his part in a plot to kill Hitler, he understood that Christianity had to address the centre of life rather than the "religious" margins.

In February, 1947, Dr MacLeod refreshed himself by going on a five weeks' speaking tour of America and Canada. He gave 70 addresses in 35 days, raised 30,000 dollars, enlisted 2228 Friends of the Iona Community, and influenced not a few men in the direction of the ministry. He broadcast to 4 million people in New York for half an hour without a script, and conducted a day retreat at Union Seminary. He enjoyed being back at his old seminary and talking with Reinhold Niebuhr, H. E. Fosdick, Paul Tillich and E. F. Scott. He visited Kirkridge, a community of clergy and lay people founded by his friend John Oliver Nelson and modelled directly on the Iona Community.

He returned to Iona elated rather than exhausted. The New World had given him a buzz, a renewed sense of the possibilities of life. He felt ready to take on the Church of Scotland, the Cathedral Trustees, the Iona Parish minister and anyone else who wanted to argue with him.

The summer of 1947 saw big numbers of visitors come to Iona to participate in the courses. They came from New Zealand, Canada, America, France, Holland, Poland, Czechoslovakia, India, Africa, China, Ceylon, Cyprus and Egypt, bringing with them the insights from many church traditions.

Archie Craig left after a year to take up an appointment as a lecturer at Glasgow University. The two men parted amicably and remained the greatest of friends – Archie continued to do work for the Community and remained one of its most enthusiastic advocates – but there is a distinct impression that it was not easy for the two men, both giants in the Kirk, to work together in such close harness. George could not easily dominate his very able deputy, who was a star turn in his own right. Iona was too small for two contemporary Columbas.

That summer saw another amazing phenomenon – a ship on the horizon bearing timbers from Norway. The gift arose out of a conversation on Iona four years earlier between the Rev. Alf

Wathney, a chaplain with the Norwegian forces, and Dr MacLeod. As they looked at the big refectory, the conversation went like this.

"You will have to have an awful big storm, George, to get enough timber to cover this one."

"Well, you as a Norwegian are a direct descendant of the Vikings. The Vikings destroyed this place three times in the ninth century. The least you can do is to make reparation. Send us some of your fine Norwegian timbers as soon as the war is over."

Thus came the reparations, bobbing once again on the Iona sea – beautiful Norwegian timbers, a gift from Church and industry, which now roof the ancient refectory on Iona.

George MacLeod was rightly satisfied with the way things were going. Even the Church of Scotland seemed to be coming his way. Its report on Evangelism, "Into All the World", contained much that was in line with the Iona Community's thinking. Was the tide turning?

1948 was to provide stunning news, and an enormous trial of strength.

15

Making Smooth Places Rough

There are two tragedies in life. One is not to get your heart's desire. The other is to get it.

GEORGE BERNARD SHAW

I look at the Church, again and yet again
And think of those who house together in hell,
Cooped by ingenious theological men
Expert to track the sour and musty smell
Of sins they know too well.

EDWIN MUIR

George MacLeod had been in a foul temper on Iona for nearly a week.

One night he wrecked a perfectly normal ceilidh in Shuna – one of the houses on the island owned by the Iona Community – by storming in at 11 pm and sweeping everyone back to the Abbey, saying it was much too late. Then he disappeared for a few days.

It is now Monday 2nd August, 1948. History is in the making.

Hector Ross, one of the new men joining the Community, calls his colleagues into his room in the Rome Express, and asks them if they can hear anything moving. They listen sagely, but hear nothing.

"It's St Columba," says Hector. "That's what it is. The saint is moving, heaving in his grave, whirling in his tomb."

"Why?"

"Because *THE BOSS IS ENGAGED!*"

The news that the Iona leader had become engaged to be married at the age of 53 caused immediate shock waves. George had invited people to a party in Shuna, not indicating what it was about, and when he announced that he was to marry Miss Lorna Macleod, one of his many female admirers fainted on the spot.

214

Making Smooth Places Rough

"He has no business getting married, no business at all," groused Johnny MacMillan to the rest of the crew on a boat trip from Camas. "He's married to the Iona Community."

As a handsome, eligible bachelor, George had been much sought after, but had kept his devotees at arms' length. He had also kept his courtship of Lorna Macleod very quiet.

Who was she, and what was her pedigree? To answer that, it is necessary to go back to that manse of Fuinary . . .

Lorna's grandfather was the Rev. Dr Donald MacLeod, brother of Norman of the Barony, and himself chaplain to Queen Victoria and Moderator of the General Assembly of the Church of Scotland in the year when his grand-nephew, George MacLeod, was born. Her father, also the Rev. Donald Macleod (he used the lower case "l"), was senior minister of the Old High Church in Inverness.

Lorna was born into the large manse family in 1921. Educated at Heatherley School for Girls, Inverness, she was delighted when, at the age of 18, a rich uncle offered to send her to finishing school in Switzerland, even though the Munich crisis was looming. So it was that the shy Scots girl spent a formative year sharing her classroom with refugees and aristocrats right in the eye of the storm, and it was a changed young woman who returned to Inverness. Soon she was in uniform as a telephonist in the regional commissioner's office at Inverness. She later joined the WRENS, in which she served till the end of the war. Her infectious *joie-de-vivre* earned her the nickname "Sunshine".

The war over, she wrote to her second cousin, George MacLeod, asking to be involved in the Iona movement. He approached Roy Sanderson and asked if she could help at the Barony kirkhouse, one of the youth projects established by the Iona Youth Trust. (The youth club was held in the adapted MacLeod Church, known as the "Moleskin Church" – the building in which the great Norman had held his services for the Glasgow poor.)

A subtle courtship ensued – so subtle that it was invisible to the naked eye of keen observers of such matters. George wrote to Jean McGregor, who ran youth camps for girls on Iona, saying that "a broth of a girl" who was related to him, was coming to help, and warned that she had red hair! Jean recognized that Lorna was very fond of George, and said to her, "You're the only person George can marry!"

Thus it was that George announced to a stunned audience in Shuna that he was marrying his second cousin, who was 26 years

215

his junior. The news caused consternation among the various members of the Clan MacLeod as well. Lorna's father wrote to her with an account of being interviewed by one of George's formidable aunts.

"She remembered George as 'the dearest little boy about this size', and she measured a foot and a half with her hands. 'He would insist on walking on the dining room table, and kept me in a state of terror by nearly falling off it.'

"I thought this an excellent parable of his present career. She then asked Torquil, 'Is she witty?' T. said she was. Turning to me, she asked, 'Is she pretty?' I replied non-committedly that I understood many considered her pretty. She said she was glad to know it. I expect she really expected that George, being such a brilliant member of the MacLeod family, would marry a princess."

They were married, less than a month later, in Crown Court Church, London, on Saturday 28th August 1948. The bride's father officiated, assisted by Rev. Allan Murray, the groom's brother-in-law. The bride was attended by her sister, Ursula, and Jean McGregor. The best man was Rev. Douglas Trotter, a member of the Iona Community. The ghost of the bride and groom's great grandfather, Rev. Norman MacLeod, *Caraid nan Gaidheal*, no doubt hovered over the proceedings.

Why London? The reason was that George was committed to leave on the Monday for a speaking tour of Australia and New Zealand. Thus it was a working honeymoon for Dr George and Lady MacLeod, the trip beginning with George disconsolately unloading books from their too heavy baggage at the airport. It wasn't like this when he was a bachelor!

His bride's adoption of the title showed her to be her own woman. Warm, witty and vivacious and certainly neither socialist nor pacifist, Lorna MacLeod was in many ways to humanize the intense husband she adored, and to help bring a different feel to the all-male ethos of the Iona Community.

The Iona leader's visit was at the invitation of the Presbyterian Church of Victoria. The honeymoon journey, which took eight days, was memorable – at each point they landed there was political trouble of some sort.

Opposite the MacLeods on the plane sat a little old lady from Balham. Britain personified, she played patience, read the *Christian World*, and hoped that at each place she landed she would get a "nice strong cup of tea", oblivious of the political vortex at each point of the journey. For George MacLeod, typically, it was a parable filled with meaning.

"I mention her," he wrote in *Coracle*, "in order to confess that the essential tension of my own ministry is whether we should concentrate on the Vortex or on Balham! Should we 'bless her or warn?' If warn, where do you begin: perhaps with the tea, its cheapness to us, and the 'cost' of its cheapness which is in fact the Vortex! I tried that, but out came the Patience and the *Christian World*. Better perhaps that the Church confine itself to morality in Balham: easier certainly. But then – the Vortex!

"How well I knew that this tension was the essential reason why the Presbyterian Church of Victoria had asked me out – to discuss how 'parish missions' might make the Faith relevant to modern life. As harmless as that: and, if really to be answered, as dangerous."[1]

After addressing the General Assembly of the Australian Presbyterian Church in Sydney, Dr MacLeod spoke at 140 meetings in ten weeks, packed or unpacked 84 times, and travelled 4000 miles. He loved the hospitality and the food – far from rationing in Britain with its post-war austerities – saying that Australia was good for the body.

"But – till you realize what is happening – it is dangerous for the soul. The churches are crowded for you: in most towns a civic reception greets you: the pipe band is out, the town hall is filled: a Chevrolet carries you four thousand miles, with a tour manager, a secretary and a chauffeur. You almost imagine you are a remarkable fellow – till you realize what is happening. It is simply that you are a Scot. They do much the same with similar results for all Scots preachers."[2]

The good Doctor MacLeod was being more than a little modest. His preaching tour was an outstanding success, bringing a sharp understanding of mission and producing the usual harvest of vocations.

One 17-year-old Australian law student, John O'Neill, was deeply impressed.

"What struck me is that he was never ingratiating," he recalled. "There may have been jokes at the start, but the stuff itself was in earnest. He looked like somebody under orders. He could think, he could argue, and he expected me to think with him. And he thought in pictures, matter-of-fact and vivid. His God was not the endlessly loving and other-worldly God of pulpit piety. God was the God of judgment as well as mercy. God expected justice in this world. George MacLeod mightily helped me to see I had to change from law to history, and to prepare myself to be a minister."

John O'Neill is now Professor of New Testament Studies at Edinburgh University.

Perhaps the secret of George's success was that he refused to play the "Scottish preacher" game. He knew well the temptation, while speaking to the Caledonian Society or the clan gathering, of conjuring up the mists of the Highland glens to which none of the emigrants, with their growing standards of living, would ever dream of returning – except perhaps on Hogmanay with five whiskies inside them.

George MacLeod made such a profound impact because he was a man on fire with the love of God and was concerned to bring the Christian message to bear on a world in turmoil. He told the Australian churches in uncompromising terms that they must cease seeing themselves as Balham transported, as centres for nice cups of tea, and must address the vortex of change in the name of the One who was at its centre. Why was Australia pioneering in things secular, but not in things ecclesiastical? Why were their homes modern but their churches Gothic? The message was inspiring and uncomfortable and sometimes even painful.

"I still believe you asked me out," he wrote later to his pained Australian friends, "because you knew I was not satisfied with a nice cup of tea. Why did I not help you more? Partly because I did not want to hurt you. More, I suppose, because I did not want to hurt myself: none of us likes to be unpopular. But most because we none of us yet know the technique or the answer."[2]

If George was ever tempted to become pompous, Lorna's sense of the absurd kept his feet on the ground. When a local herald announced, "Sir George Fielden MacLeod and Lady MacLeod" at a ceremonial ball, Lorna hummed out loud a dee-ti-dee tune as they marched to their place. "Incredible and outrageous," was George's comment, "but exactly appropriate."

He wrote to Harry Whitley about married life.

"Quite first class – with quite minor qualifications, such as having to brush my hair, and pare my nails and trim my moustache, and not leave the hotel when I am ready but when she is. I fear her list of qualifications would be longer and more serious, and all justified: but I am learning to behave, being, as you know, of a patient and long suffering disposition."

Making Smooth Places Rough

The purpose of the New Zealand trip was to raise the timber to cover the dormitory block of Iona Abbey. Interviewed on his arrival at Dunedin Airport, he said he had been inspired by the story of Norman MacLeod, who in the eighteenth century, took his congregation from Scotland to Auckland in boats of their own building. As one MacLeod had taken wood from Scotland, another MacLeod might take wood back there! "Iona is the mother of us all," he told the press conference.

Eighteen days and 2000 miles later, the task was accomplished. Wellington Town Hall, with the acting prime minister and the leader of the opposition present, was filled with a bigger crowd than for the visit of De Valera, prime minister of Eire, a year previously. By the end of the trip, more than 1400 New Zealanders had signed on as Friends of the Iona Community. Much of the organization was done by the Rev. Jack Somerville, the first ever Friend of the Iona Community who had asked to sign on after hearing George preach in Iona in 1938. Jack Somerville remembers the 1948 visit.

"George was at his rampant best when he was cadging for the restoration of the buildings on Iona. He sold his story to big businessmen and also to the rank and file with no holds barred. It was fighting stuff. Nothing got in the way of his single purpose.

"He had a way with all sorts of people. I remember him quipping to a reporter who came to see him in my study and before even the poor fellow could get a word in, 'Are you a Christian?' Attack rather than defence was his style."

George created a whirlwind wherever he went, and thoroughly enjoyed being the centre of attention. Jack Somerville saw him close up – "It was on that visit, though I had worshipped as it were from a distance, that I came to see something of the foibles of the great. Wherever George MacLeod goes, somehow the world centres around him."

It was hard not to be swept along by the charm of such a big man with a big vision and a big soul and a big ego, and a sure sense of theatre.

And, of course, there was the usual timber miracle.

A sympathetic contractor was required to assemble the beautiful Heart Rimu New Zealand timbers. After various dead ends, George learned that Sir James Fletcher, a timber merchant, was flying back to New Zealand from a visit to his native Scotland and arriving the day before the Iona leader was due to leave. Yes, he would do it free of charge. It just so happened that at the turn of the century his brother had had to choose between a job as a carpenter on the restoration of Iona Abbey, and the chance to seek his fortune in New Zealand. He had chosen the more distant shore, and had established with James, who was earning 36 shillings a week as a joiner, Fletcher Holdings Ltd. So wasn't it good that now there was a chance to do something for Iona, nearly fifty years on?

Well, wasn't it?

The wood was shipped to Ireland. A Belfast company transported it free to Iona, because hadn't Saint Columba sailed from Ireland to Iona?

Well, hadn't he?

As usual, George returned from the gruelling trip abroad fired up and ready to fight.

And what a fight was waiting for him.

The seeds had been sown in February 1948, when the Rev. T. B. Stewart Thomson had left Govan Old Parish to go to Bridge of Earn. The vacancy committee had a list of seven names before them, and George MacLeod's was among them. He was still hankering after Govan.

Why? Because he felt that after ten years of the Iona venture, it was time to make a proper mainland parish experiment. When he had begun the project, he had not intended being involved so long on a full-time basis. He was still a parish minister at heart, and had only left the parish ministry temporarily in order to do something which would help parish mission develop in a much wider way: and Govan was in his blood. Yet nostalgia was never his thing. His intention was not simply to repeat what he had done in the thirties. He had learned new things since then: especially at the Peckham Health Centre in London, which he had visited earlier in the year. The experimental centre's work was based on a positive understanding of health, as opposed to a narrow focusing on symptoms and disease. Its far-seeing philosophy stressed wholeness, community and integration.

The experiment was regarded with great suspicion, because of its break with orthodox medicine. In the course of a lecture, George had expressed admiration, but had also said it was not spiritual enough. Dr Scott Williamson, the founder of Peckham, wrote to George asking him to come and see for himself.

One man who never forgot the visit was Douglas Trotter, one of the Community's bright young men, whom George had invited to accompany him.

"I was witness to an amazing evening with these two giants," he said. "They went on for four or five hours, arguing and discussing. Scott Williamson said to George: 'The trouble with you, MacLeod, is that you're too materialistic!'"

Materialistic or not, George was impressed. He persuaded the Iona Community to pay for Douglas Trotter to observe Peckham for three months – he ended up on the staff for nearly three years.

As well as wanting to make a new experiment in Govan, incorporating the new Peckham insights, George still bore scars from the last Govan-Glasgow Presbytery campaign and the pugnacious Iona pacifist relished nothing better than a new fight to the death. The adrenalin was flowing.

He wrote to the vacancy committee outlining his plan, but it was voted down. The interim moderator was instructed to write to two other candidates on the list.

George MacLeod was not so easily shrugged off. From what his Govan allies had told him, he gathered that his proposal had been misrepresented. He wrote a full memorandum about his ideas, and sent a copy to the clerk of Glasgow Presbytery so that it would be available to the Presbytery if Govan decided to call him while he was in Australia.

In his memorandum, George said that he would be prepared to accept a call to Govan on condition that he retained his connection with the Iona Community. He said that the Community was now financially stable, that it had a master of works on the island and two secretaries on the mainland, and that he himself had a full-time deputy. Since he did not look upon his leadership of the Community as an official Church appointment, there could be no objection to his holding the two posts at the same time. He would, from his Govan stipend, pay for a full-time ordained colleague, and he himself would be away from Govan for no more than three months in the year. This, he argued, was no less than the time some ministers were away from their parishes.

George met with the convener of the Govan vacancy committee and went over the proposals with him. When Dr MacLeod's name was brought up at the next meeting of the Committee, there was an overwhelming majority in his favour. The replies from the other two ministers were not positive, so it was decided to pursue his nomination. Thus began the notorious "Govan Case", which took nearly two years of bitter debate, hard work, and political manoeuvring to resolve.

The matter went to Glasgow Presbytery's Advisory Committee on Vacancies, whose view was that the list of duties of Leader of the Iona Community was such that they could not recommend that such a man be called to a busy church with 2,000 members.

The Govan Old Parish church vacancy committee rejected this advice, and proceeded with George's nomination.

The Presbytery's business committee, which contained one or two of George's most bitter opponents, went into action. It reaffirmed the decision made in 1938 that it was unconstitutional and contrary to the fundamental laws of the Church for a vacancy committee to submit the name of any minister "who had other interests involving annual continued absences from his pastoral and pulpit duties." They sent a cable to Dr MacLeod in Australia telling him of their view.

This was the stage in the argument at which George had backed down last time. Not this time.

"I hereby accept the call," he wrote back immediately. "I have used no undue influence, either by myself or through others, to receive the call. As I am a member of the Presbytery of Glasgow, you already hold my Presbyterial certificate and my certificate of status."

The Iona leader was throwing down the gauntlet to Europe's biggest Presbytery. In a follow-up letter from Australia, he said that his full-time colleague on Iona would take on much of the work, and he would make "an entire re-adjustment that would be in favour of an efficient ministry in Govan, and the change would not endanger the Community."

The Presbytery Clerk told the Govan vacancy committee that the nomination of Dr MacLeod was not valid in terms of the General Assembly Act, which stated that a man might hold a second appointment if it were under the jurisdiction of the Church, or if it were voluntary, but not if it were not under the jurisdiction of the Church and was paid.

The vacancy committee decided to carry on. George MacLeod preached on 2nd December, 1948 and was elected by a vote of 503 to 26. He announced his acceptance of the call.

The Presbytery formed a special committee to investigate the matter, and there was more than a suspicion of political intrigue behind the scenes. There was a definite feeling among some powerful opponents that the time had come to nail this big-headed upstart to the Presbyterian floor. MacLeod had had it coming for years, and now was the moment. Roy Sanderson, who was known to be an admirer of George's, had accepted nomination to the investigating committee, but his name was mysteriously dropped and it was too late to rectify the matter. It meant that Arthur Gray, minister of St Francis-in-the-East, was left alone to support the view that a way should be found to allow George to return to Govan.

John White was persuaded, somewhat against his will, to be convener of the committee. By then 81 years of age, the Kirk's patriarch was perhaps unwise to get mixed up in what was to prove to be a nasty battle. If anyone could "fix" a difficult situation it was Dr White, but this one was to prove beyond even his powers of persuasion and wily ecclesiastical joinery. At the end of the day some of the blood on the floor was his.

Dr White was fond of George, even though he found him exasperating. He had worked closely with his father, and admired George's missionary zeal, his preaching ability and his deep concern for the Church Extension areas. What raised the patriarch's blood pressure was young MacLeod's pacifism and socialism, and his infuriating tendency to act as a law unto himself. Dr White, ardent supporter of the British military efforts in the First and Second World Wars, scourge of Glasgow's Irish Catholics, liked peace in the Church: Dr MacLeod, pacifist and internationalist, really rather enjoyed a good war. Dr White appreciated a judicious compromise, with, perhaps, a little whiff of intrigue thrown in: Dr MacLeod preferred things clear cut, with the battle lines drawn up.

Dr MacLeod admired Dr White even though he did not entirely trust him – and, indeed, had used him. The Barony minister had conveniently provided ecclesiastical credibility for the infant Iona Community: the attacks had to be muted a little as long as the great man was a Sponsor of the experiment. Dr White had provided the artillery cover under which the pacifist MacLeod worked. The impetuous younger man pushed him to the limits of his patience, but, at the end of the day, the authority of the ecclesiastical statesman was needed to enable the radical experiment to function under the overall umbrella of the Church. Dr White, whose way with ambiguous words annoyed the absolutist crusader, was needed by Dr MacLeod if he were to remain the churchman he deeply felt himself to be.

The Govan Case was one which could, and should, have been resolved by way of compromise. It should have been possible to find a formula which would have allowed the Iona leader to go to Govan and mount a new and exciting experiment on behalf of the Church: and John White was the kind of man who could provoke three such formulae before breakfast every day.

Why did it not happen? After a close scrutiny of all the evidence and reminiscences, it is hard to escape the conclusion that it did not happen because of the venom of George's opponents – cloaked as it was in procedural language; and because of George MacLeod's intractable thrawnness and desire for total victory – cloaked as it was in the language of high moral principle. This is not to say that procedures and principles were not at stake: it is to say that they became idols in a battle in which there were heavy casualties.

George took his stance on the ground that he was not actually covered by the Assembly's Act, since he was not technically employed by the Iona Community and had never been paid a salary. The act required that a minister resign employment which was not under the jurisdiction of the Church, but since he was not "employed", he had nothing to resign from. The special committee were not impressed. After obtaining legal advice, they said that Dr MacLeod could not be inducted to Govan until he resigned his leadership of the Iona Community.

Giving his report to the Presbytery, Dr White said that the Presbytery was not called upon to pass any judgment upon the work at Iona – "may God prosper it and its chosen leader" – but to consider whether that same leader should be called to a busy and demanding parish.

"The responsibility rests upon Dr MacLeod. He must make up his mind whether he is prepared to accept the call to Govan – if the Presbytery places the call in his hands – or to continue his leadership at Iona . . . Our high regard for Dr MacLeod must not bias our judgment, nor must any critical attitude to the Iona Community affect our decision."[3]

Replying, George said that the Iona Community could hardly be considered to be outside the jurisdiction of the Church. The Community had been started with the sole purpose of training Church of Scotland ministers for work in the Home Mission field. It was *de facto* within the Church of Scotland.

It was the classic "prophet versus priest" argument. The roots of the discord lay in the fact that George MacLeod had quite intentionally started his Iona experiment without going through the ecclesiastical procedures, while at the same time wishing to be part of the Church. He wanted the blessing but not the control of the Church, and the price to be paid was a constitutional mess. The mess would not have been so bad if George had not been so stubborn: but had he not been so stubborn, Iona Abbey might still be in ruins while churchmen argued in committees.

The argument was confused by the fact that George was trying to have it both ways. One minute he was arguing that the Community was under the jurisdiction of the Church, the next that his job was not under the same jurisdiction. It was further confused by the fact that a lawyer consulted by Arthur Gray had come to the conclusion that the Act did not apply to George MacLeod's case.

Amidst great public controversy, it was agreed that the matter should be referred to the General Assembly of the Church of Scotland. The decision to refer the matter was a shrewd piece of political footwork. Had the Presbytery decided against George and he had appealed, the Presbytery would have come before the bar of the Assembly, and none of its members would be allowed to speak or vote.

The case was heard at a packed General Assembly on 27th May, 1949. Counsel for the special committee and for Dr MacLeod spoke at the Bar of the Assembly, and outlined the cases. Professor James Pitt-Watson, a superb orator who had in the past eloquently opposed Dr MacLeod's pacifism, argued that the Iona Community was outwith the jurisdiction of the Church of Scotland, and that the Act certainly therefore applied to its leader.

The Assembly supported Professor Pitt-Watson's view by a large majority: Dr MacLeod could not go to Govan and still be leader of the Iona Community.

George had prepared a speech to be given if the Assembly had decided otherwise, and had gone on to debate the desirability of the Iona leader's going to Govan. He had intended to address the fears that had been raised that as leader of the Iona Community as well as parish minister of Govan he would not be under the jurisdiction of the Presbytery.

"Let us assume that as leader of the Iona Community, I decided to celebrate High Mass in Govan," ran his intended text, "or put a hammer and sickle above the pulpit (and there are a few people who can never make up their mind which we are likely to do first: though there is no conceivable chance of us doing either). Let us assume that as leader of the Iona Community I did something outwith the principles or practice of the Church of Scotland. Would the Presbytery of Glasgow be in the slightest degree embarrassed in their oversight of me? Would they wring their hands and say we ought to take action, but because he is leader of the Iona Community we can take no action? Not at all. They would proceed against me at once and quite rightly."

Some good did come out of the debate. John White moved, and it was accepted, that a special committee be appointed to bring in a detailed scheme whereby the Iona Community could be brought within the organization and jurisdiction of the Church, and integrated with the life of the Church. Dr White wearily agreed to be convener of the committee. He felt that for the peace of the Kirk, it was time for the status of the Iona Community to be resolved, once and for all.

The issue of whether George MacLeod would return to Govan was not yet dead, however. George wondered whether some agreement could be worked out whereby he would resign as leader of the Community, thus fulfilling the terms of the Act, but have the title of "consultant". John White, still wishing to find a face-saving formula, was interested, but when George was pressed as to what would be involved in his consultancy, he said that he would retain a number of the important duties he had fulfilled as leader. He said he intended to "maintain some contact with the divinity halls, speak in furtherance of the work of the Community, and attend the more important phases of the summer training on the island, as well as continue in advisory oversight of the abbey building." He insisted that this list of duties be agreed and published, to save further controversy in the future.

Professor J. G. Riddell, convener of the Assembly's Committee Anent the Iona Community, and Moderator of Glasgow Presbytery, said that Dr MacLeod was apparently yielding everything, then taking it all back by an ambiguous interpretation. It looked to him like an attempt to get round the judgment of the Assembly.

Uist Macdonald wrote to George expressing anger about the bias he felt Professor Riddell was showing in a report to the General Assembly. George replied that he agreed, but felt there was no point in taking the matter up.

"Two things are now quite clear to me," he wrote. "The one is that Riddell, for whatever reason, is not interpreting his remit as I am sure the Assembly meant him to do. The other thing I'm even more clear about is that God is in His heaven, and not even Riddell can engineer any removal in that quarter."

George refused to budge from what he called "the essentials", saying he was not putting them forward as conditions, but merely clarifying what he would do if he went to Govan. At the next Presbytery meeting, Dr White said they had still been prepared to consider Dr MacLeod, in view of the kirk session's stated preference, but Dr MacLeod had laid down some "essential" conditions that the committee must accept before it nominated him.

"I am more than sorry that, after our patient efforts to make the rough places smooth," he told the Presbytery, "Dr MacLeod has proceeded to make the smooth places rough. The Committee can do no more. We have done everything we could do constitutionally. The decision rests with Dr MacLeod.

"I am confident that if Dr MacLeod, in accepting nomination to Govan Old as any other minister would be asked to accept it, should require an occasional short leave for work in Iona, or in connection therewith, the Presbytery would grant it with a benediction. But that is very different from laying down conditions . . ."

George replied that the committee's view was an invasion of the liberties of his private time, and was a blow at a fundamental principle of Presbyterianism. These questions, he said, had never been asked of any other ministers in relation to their private interests, his own interest being in a purely private society.

Professor Pitt-Watson said that the committee did not feel Dr MacLeod had given an unconditional reply, and since he had been offered the Govan charge on condition that his acceptance of the nomination be unconditional, they could not proceed. Rev. W. Roy Sanderson moved that as Dr MacLeod's reply was, in essentials, an unqualified one, the Presbytery should proceed with the nomination. He argued that there was only a small area of difference of opinion between Dr MacLeod and the Church, and it was not big enough to justify saying no.

By 252 votes to 45, Glasgow Presbytery decided that the reply was not an unconditional one, and therefore they could not proceed with the nomination. George MacLeod intimated his intention to appeal, but later withdrew, on the grounds that it would prolong the Govan vacancy.

The Govan elders were angry. The minute of the kirk session's meeting of 15th November, 1949 expressed the session's "sense of dismay and frustration and, in large measure, its indignation at the ultimate resolution of the present problem. The Session are disquieted to realize that the inexorable application of Church Law and Procedure has thwarted, and for the present stultified, the spiritual life of the congregation. It is the considered judgment of the Session that the problem could, and should, have been resolved in a spirit of charity and understanding, worthy of the highest traditions of the Church – at a level far removed from mere legal quibble and argument."

If George MacLeod had been prepared to come and go a bit earlier on, would he have been minister of Govan, able to do the things he wanted to do? The opposition would still have been strong, and sometimes vicious, but John White's authority would probably have carried the day. George refused John White's lifelines. Dr White's verdict, at the end of the day, was as follows:

"We were impartial and sympathetic. But we could not change the constitution of the Church to suit the Govan-Iona ultimatum. We tried every road before we finally set aside the nomination of Dr MacLeod."

George had underestimated the power of the forces against him, and by his obstinacy and inflexibility, had played into his opponents' hands. The proud MacLeod had felt that all he had to do was to stand his ground and claim victory: the reality was that too many knives had been sharpening for him since before he began the Iona Community. His pacifism, his socialism, and his perceived Catholic tendencies, combined with his almost arrogant disregard of due Presbyterian process in 1938, had alienated different sections of the Kirk: and there was the plain jealousy of lesser men. As an international church celebrity, he was vulnerable to the kind of holy venom in which disappointed Christians specialize, not to mention the ferocious Scottish delight in bringing national heroes – especially those who have gathered international recognition – crashing to the ground.

The Presbyterian system is at its strongest, and sometimes its worst, on legal matters: to take on the Glasgow Establishment on a legal case was to risk death by a thousand quibbles. All done in the name of Christ. Cool and righteous legal talk is an excellent ecclesiastical cover for an underlying and unacceptable unholy vendetta: and to give even an appearance of putting oneself above the law is the unforgivable sin against the Presbyterian holy ghost.

Professor Riddell, for instance, was able to oppose George on procedural grounds: the unstated reality was that the Professor, who used to do all he could to dissuade students from joining the Iona Community, did not like the Iona man, and was infuriated by what he saw as his playing fast and loose with the Presbyterian system. He was by no means alone.

The tragedy of the Govan Case was that George MacLeod's tactics allowed his opponents to make the running, and prevented his many admirers, or even neutrals, from working out a common-sense solution which would have allowed another imaginative experiment to go ahead with the blessing of more than fifty per cent of the Kirk.

The Govan Case was never simply a legal and procedural dispute: it was a Presbyterian bloodletting, in which the protagonist, consciously or unconsciously, helped his prosecutors to cut his throat.

In February 1950, the Rev. John Symington was inducted as minister of Govan Old Parish Church. Leonard Small had previously been sounded out by John White and J. G. Riddell, but had refused.

The long-running Govan Case was over, and its victim-martyr lay bleeding on the Presbyterian floor.

16

Glory to God in the High St

Everything begins in mysticism and ends in politics.

CHARLES PEGUY

*In truth, the Church was framed for the express
purpose of interfering (or as irreligious men would say)
meddling with the world.*

JOHN HENRY NEWMAN

The deep wounds did not heal until 1957. Till that time, George
MacLeod felt rejected by the Church he loved. For a man who saw
everything he did as being for and on behalf of the Church, it was
a painful experience.

"It is terrible to see the life go out of this child!" George told
Elizabeth Whitley in despair after the Assembly's verdict. He felt
that somehow John White had outwitted him. He still admired the
great man ("Georrrge, Georrrge," Dr White had said to him at one
stage in the debate, looking at the younger man through his steely
eyes, "is what you propose in the best interests of the Churrrch?"),
but could not trust him utterly.

George's fascination with John White was such that he hoped to
write his biography. (Dr White had himself said that he wanted
George to write his obituary, as he knew the younger man would
be fair and not too fulsome.) When Hodder & Stoughton phoned
him, he thought it was to offer him the job: in fact it was to ask
what he thought of Augustus Muir as possible biographer! When
Muir's book was published, Alastair Hetherington, editor of *The
Manchester Guardian*, asked George to review the book, which
contained a fairly sanitized version of the Govan Case. His reply
shows how the matter still rankled.

"I have not seen the John White book. But those of my friends who have read the forty pages on the Govan Case have not only climbed up the walls, but are apparently permanently congealed to the cornice: positions in which their wives are finding it more and more difficult to feed them. Others, of course, whose myopia is so extensive that they do not like me, are opening bottles of champagne in the middle of their rooms, causing a temporary crisis among the wine merchants of Glasgow."

For some people, the pre-Govan Case Iona Community represents the golden age, the Hebridean Eden before the Fall.

On this reckoning, the Iona experiment was a radical attempt to change the missionary strategy of the Church of Scotland by means of an innovative training scheme for ministers – a project which would have been further earthed and developed in Govan: after 1949 it lost its direction and became an international ecumenical discussion group. The merit of this view is its simplicity: but it does not do justice either to George MacLeod's early sense of the need for international change or to the Community's continuing commitment to ministry in Scotland. However, it does draw attention to the fact that the Govan Case decision accelerated the existing trend in the Iona Community towards diversification – a trend which had come in the first place because people from different denominations, from different parts of the world, lay as well as ordained, had come to Iona seeking answers to their urgent questions.

Bob Craig had been deputy leader of the Community during George's absence in Australia, and during the Govan Case. (After his spell at Perth, George had asked him if he was a pacifist. When he said no, George told him he should be in the forces. He did, in fact, join up in 1942.) He enjoyed working with George, but found that he had to stand up for himself.

"He was authoritative, but not authoritarian," he recalled. "He respected you if you stood up to him. There has always been a tolerance in George. He was always an eternal optimist about people. He felt there was hope for everybody, even when people let him down."

More and more people wanted to join the Community, and a new camp under canvas at the north end of Iona was started to cope with the numbers of young people. The classes at the Abbey were well subscribed, and eminent guests were often surprised to find themselves expected to share in the chores, as well as providing profound thoughts.

"Why do we waste our time doing this when there is so much we could be discussing?" asked one minister of George as he kneeled beside him to clean out the lavatory.

"To prevent you doing what I did for eight years in Govan – talking about the dignity of labour," the Iona leader retorted.

It was the combination of worship and work which was the essential genius of Iona. George had learned at Fingalton Mill that the best discussions often went on over a shared physical task. The symbolism of an Abbey being restored by craftsmen and ministers was very potent.

"I was born a symbolist and not an expositor," George had written to Professor Pitt-Watson at the height of the Govan crisis. "And such a message as I get across requires pictures. Iona is one: and I think it has caught the imagination because it is a sign which folk understand, without being able to describe."

The broadcast services from Iona Abbey were widely appreciated. The distinctive male singing was unusual at a time when women greatly outnumbered men in congregational life. Reginald Barrett-Ayres, the director of music at the Abbey, would gather the Community and the visitors – most of whom had never sung in a choir before – who had arrived for the week, and teach them four-part harmony. When the service was broadcast the next day, there would be a strong, virile, harmonizing sound. The prayers and sermon were equally inspiring.

"His prayers united, searched deeply and inspired the listeners," recalled Ronald Falconer, who produced most of the programmes. "His preaching frequently divided, for his word was often upsetting, with its pacifist and socialist undertones, striking at comfortable personal belief unless it pointed towards the caring for the world of men.

"BBC London more than once told me he ought not to say this or that in his scripts. I was duty-bound to make these points to him, but I can't remember his ever accepting them; he believed he knew best. This seemed arrogance to some; a matter of principle to others. His more radical statements frequently drew blood and there would be a flood of protest letters addressed to the Director-General downwards. But I held to the fundamental freedom of the air for anyone, Plymouth Brother or George MacLeod, who believed God had laid something upon him to say. Many a time I sweated it out on Iona, knowing the storm would break on my return to the mainland. It was worth it!"[1]

His ability to communicate in exciting ways with all kinds of people was evidenced again in a visit to Cambridge.

"His humanity, his commitment and his vision quite over-whelmed me," recalled a theological student of that time, "and I thought, 'this is the best stuff I've heard.' George MacLeod influenced me then, and I've tried to keep in touch with the Iona Community and its works. I've seen George from time to time and I've encouraged him with the thought of that day, since we haven't always agreed about everything."

The student's name was Robert Runcie.

When much later he was Archbishop of Canterbury, he was rebuked by the Iona man for his support of the British Falklands expedition, then praised by him for his preaching about reconciliation afterwards.

"George was a man who wasn't afraid to be adventurous when there was too much timidity," said the Archbishop. "He was not afraid to be generous when there was a lot of sourness about in religious debate. He had a kind of humility at a time when the churches had a bit of a conceit about themselves."[2]

Another man influenced by George MacLeod around this time was Robin Barbour, who had won the Military Cross in the Second World War. He would become Professor of Biblical Criticism at Aberdeen University, and Moderator of the General Assembly of the Church of Scotland.

"I've known him, I suppose, ever since he came to Cargilfield School somewhere about 1932 and preached a stirring sermon and then came and threw pillows at us in the dormitory, which stirred us even more and made the matron furious," he recalled. "It was in the years just after the war, around 1948–50, that I think he had most influence on me, when I was trying to decide what to do with myself and felt very fed up with most of what I saw of the Church – but not with him and not with the great bunch of boys around him on Iona. Since then I've known and loved him, as countless others have done, as a very great man."

The great Dr MacLeod was not appreciated by everyone. Calum McCorquodale, late minister at Callander, used to tell the story of his sister, who was no great fan of George, making her first transatlantic flight. The pilot indicated that they were flying at 30,000 feet, and the little speck on the port side was the holy island of Iona.

"That reduces that man MacLeod to his proper proportions!"

was her sotto voce comment that went the whole length of the plane.

George was often accused of acting like a bishop – one of the worst sins in the Presbyterian book. No one was more aware of the instinct of clerics to seek power than George MacLeod, who had encountered more than a few such Protestant closet prelates in his life.

"All this bishopric temptation is a very real thing," he wrote to Harry Whitley. "We cannot defeat it by discipline or kicking it out of ourselves. The genius of Jesus is to OFFER THE BISHOPRIC, not deny it, TO EVERY TIKE IN THE GORBALS."

Despite his sometimes authoritarian manner and his recognition of the need for accountable, rather than covert, power structures George was at heart an Evangelical with a childlike faith in the undeserved grace of God. The same letter to Harry, who often agonized over his own sins and temperament, went on: "It is not really first the Thorns and then the Crown. It is 'here is the Crown in order that you can say to hell with the Thorns'. He wore the Thorns that we need not wear them. But we are such damned masochists that we buy more. The ultimate pride is to try to save God's world for Him – which is as silly as me going around collecting money for Community House when the darned place has already been bought."

In the 1950s, George moved much more overtly into political issues. At the beginning of the decade, he stood as Labour candidate in the Rectorial Election at Glasgow University, losing to John MacCormick, the Scottish Nationalist. One of his campaign managers was John Lang, later to be a Moderator of Glasgow Presbytery. He was surprised to find that, despite his utterances, George wasn't actually a member of the Labour Party. Faced with a decision, he joined the Co-operative Party, which was affiliated to the Labour Party. The truth was that George was too much of an individualist to toe any party line or to be subject to the discipline of any political group.

In February, 1950 he appeared on a public platform in support of the Labour candidate for Hillhead, George Thomson, one of the "Forward" group of young socialist thinkers who based themselves at Community House in Glasgow.

In his speech in what was at that time a Conservative stronghold,

Dr MacLeod said he thought the Labour Party was the best instrument for what particularly concerned him – bringing more love into the world. The real issue was whether people were going to be planned in the name of God or materialism. He was on the side of the Labour Party in the cause of love and because he did not like the Communists.

"I do not hate the Communists because of their ultimate programme, which is indistinguishable from the Christian one," he said provocatively, "but I do not like their methods."[3]

George Thomson, later Lord Thomson of Monifieth, remembers the occasion well.

"It was a very rowdy election, before the television age, when election meetings attracted big crowds. In those days the candidate did several election meetings each night, and the Hillhead Town Hall meeting was the climax of that evening. I was due to arrive while George MacLeod was speaking, and then make the winding-up speech. My two earlier meetings were noisy and full of violent heckling.

"When I reached the Town Hall I felt something must have gone wrong with the arrangments, because it was silent as the tomb. When I slipped inside I found George MacLeod addressing an absolutely packed meeting from a lectern that had been provided for him. The audience was totally silent and hanging on his every word. I believe it would have felt as blasphemous for anyone to interrupt his address as it would have been if he had been delivering a sermon in church. The moment, however, that I had to take over the uproar began again and we were back in the normal atmosphere of the hustings. I always remember it as a wonderful example of the dominating presence of the man as a great preacher."

When reports of the controversial speech appeared in the press the next day, there was a furious reaction. The correspondence columns of the papers were filled with letters attacking the Iona Community leader, and the Rev. Alan Boyd Robson, minister of the parish church in the Hillhead constituency, issued a rebuke from the pulpit and passed it on to the press.

"If a minister is going to speak as a minister in the name of the Church or Christianity from a political or any other platform he should watch his words and be sure he does not make statements which are contrary to Christian truth and doctrine," Mr Robson told his congregation."[4]

The relationship between Christianity and Communism had

concerned George MacLeod since the 1930s, but it became a constant theme against the background of the world political turmoil of the 1950s. As the Capitalist West struggled with the Marxist surge in different parts of the world, the issue perplexed the churches.

Although George was accused of being Communist from time to time – and he gave his opponents weapons with his deliberately provocative remarks – he was totally opposed to the Communist philosophy and practice. His essential position was that excessive individualism had failed: that for justice to prevail, there must be some kind of planning: that if Christians opted out of politics they simply left Communists to do their kind of planning.

At the 1950 General Assembly, George said he agreed with the Kirk's Commission on Communism's view that the Church was theoretically a not less formidable opponent than Communism of exploitation, poverty, big business and other social evils, but regrettably he had to say that in practice it was not.

"Is the Church of Scotland prepared to be the opponent of the status quo which produced the rise of Communism?" he thundered at the fathers and brethren. "It is not a pleasant question, but it is the question that folk ask when, in a passion for social justice, they choose between the Church in practice and Communism in practice. The awful thing is that when they choose Communism they choose a lie for lack of any alternative practice in the name of truth."[5]

George was fired on from all sides. Political socialists felt he was too religious, and religious conservatives felt he was far too political. He had to fight hard against the view that religion was a private matter for the individual soul, and should not concern itself with the body politic.

George MacLeod and his Community were often held in great suspicion in the Church of Scotland, and in the heat of the cold war between Capitalism and Communism, the emotional temperature was raised further amid accusation and counter-accusation. The Iona Community was seen by some as a Jesuitical conspiracy marching the Kirk simultaneously towards Rome and Moscow. Iona Community members found the doors of many parishes in Scotland closed to them: they were seen as dangerous men.

Divinity students contemplating joining the Community were warned about their career prospects.

"How I wish some of my real church friends would see the nature of the crisis," sighed Dr MacLeod. "How I wish some of them, who say that the situation is getting so raw that we are better to keep our hands out of it and concentrate on what they call 'the spiritual', how I wish they could see that it is they who are playing right into the hands of the Communists. Why? Because the Communists have no objection at all to a religion which simply deals with a 'side extra' called the soul."[6]

In the MacLeod view, his opponents were guilty of abandoning large areas of Christ's rightful domain, crowding into beautiful but lifeless private chapels on the fringes of the main battlefield. He wanted to claim the central ground for Christ: he was for life rather than religion.

The battleground can best be illustrated in the correspondence between George MacLeod and Brigadier Bernard Fergusson, one of the leading conservative figures in the Kirk. Brigadier Fergusson berated the Iona leader for his political involvement. George's reply was warm – calling Bernard "dear heart" – and pointed. (He managed to remain good friends with people with whom he disagreed violently, and liked nothing better than a ferocious debate with an old school tie man with a war record.)

"Well, sir," he wrote to his old adversary, "John Knox took part in politics, the Covenanters lifted their eyes to the hills as eagerly to see what had happened in the East Aberdeen by-election, so to say, as to see the angelic cohorts coming to their more spiritual rescue. In the nineteenth century the Free Kirk clergy were Liberal to a man, and the Auld Kirk Conservative to the last manse. Nay, sir, enter the Conservative Club in Princes Street of this very day and you will see round the fire at Assembly the relics of the cohorts of John White dastardly plotting the next Moderator . . . If churchmen are not politically involved, you soon get the spectacle of RCs and Communists dominating our trade unions – as now they do. I have my most horrible suspicion that had I been associated with *Conservative* politics, I would have been a 'good outspoken fellow, what?'

"As to a Labour choice, it is not a bad thing to induce the Faith into Labour policies, which, left to secularists, could indeed veer into Communism . . . What matters even more is the continuance of democracy as a living cause in our midst and not the Labour, or any other party, in permanent ascendancy. But to achieve this, Christians must be involved. As to the clergy taking part, since when have the clergy in Scotland been a caste apart? True, we must keep it subordinate but then, bless you, I have spoken on ten party political platforms in my *LIFE* and addressed ten religious meetings last *WEEK*."

The heart of MacLeodian theology can, typically, best be exemplified in a story which the *Seanachaidh* told over and over and over again.

"A boy threw a stone at a stained glass window of the Incarnation. It nicked out the 'E' in the word HIGHEST in the text GLORY TO GOD IN THE HIGHEST. Thus, till unfortunately it was mended, it read GLORY TO GOD IN THE HIGH ST.

"At least the mended E might have been contrived on a swivel so that in a high wind it would have been impossible to see which way it read. Such is the genius, and the offence, of the Christian revelation. Holiness, salvation, glory are all come down to earth in Jesus Christ our Lord. Truth is found in the constant interaction of the claim that the apex of the Divine Majesty is declared in Christ's humanity. The Word of God cannot be dissociated from the Action of God. As the blood courses through the body, so the spiritual is alone kept healthy in its interaction in the High Street."

George MacLeod's politics sprang from a theology of the glory of God, a glory which could be traced in the heavens and in the High Street, at the heart of the city.

Glory in Glasgow? That is what Community House stood for. Under the shrewd and intellectually vigorous leadership of Ralph and Jenny Morton, Community House had become one of the most exciting centres of debate and action in the West of Scotland. In these days before television, classes on the meaning of Christianity drew many young people, and debates on Christian topics were often packed. Classes on Christianity and Communism, or Christianity and Industry, conducted by Penry Jones, the full-time industrial and political secretary based at Community House, attracted up to 200 each evening. A mock parliament was organized in the House, and young politicians such as George Thomson, Bruce Millan, Gregor McKenzie and Dickson Mabon, all of them future MPs, cut their political teeth in these debates. Crowds packed into the building to hear big names like Stafford Cripps, Trevor Huddleston and Sybil Thorndyke.

In more modern times, when the live political meeting has all but died – save for set-piece rallies with television in mind – it is hard to appreciate the excitement of those days of passionate political debate and interesting social experiment. It is also hard to imagine the Church being at the centre of such excitement. The fifties represent the last era in which the Church of Scotland engaged with the central realities of Scottish political, social and cultural life on anything like an equal footing, and Community House in Glasgow was a pre-eminent centre of such engagement. What thrilled the young people who went to Community House was that the Iona Community talked unapologetically about religion, and tried to relate it to the central concerns of human life rather than keep it to the safe periphery.

Serious politicians expected Christians to have thought-out things to say on the burning issues of the day, and the Iona Community won the respect of some hardened campaigners for its disciplined thinking and action. The Church of Scotland as a whole may have been suspicious of the blue-suited Christian commandos, but it was often the children of the severest critics who were in the front rows at Community House or involved in the drama productions under the guidance of Oliver Wilkinson, the full-time drama director.

The first full-scale production by the Iona Youth Theatre, as it was called, was a dramatized version of George MacLeod's *We Shall Rebuild*. Street theatre was used extensively: crowds would gather on bomb sites and the play would be staged when the square was packed and the tenement windows full of watching heads. After it was finished, George MacLeod would mount the soapbox and preach, while the actors gathered their props on to the lorry and moved on to the next site.

The Iona Youth Theatre gave many young people acting skills, and even led some to a career in the theatre. One shy and rather withdrawn boy gradually became involved: John Grieve is now a well known Scottish actor and entertainer. Another young man, John Gibson, worked as a scene designer with Oliver Wilkinson, and went on to work with Tyrone Guthrie and Samuel Beckett as a distinguished radio and television producer with the BBC.

The drama work focused theological and political questions for many people, and some became Christians in the process. Debate was a two-way process, however, with no guaranteed outcomes. One Church of England vicar, the Rev. Alan Ecclestone, became a

Communist – and remains so, while still a vicar and author of one of the most profound contemporary books on spirituality.

As a born actor and showman who enjoyed an audience, George loved the theatre. His own sense of drama and impeccable timing made him identify with the acting profession. Had he stayed with his earlier choice of law, he would have made an outstanding courtroom advocate, holding the jury spellbound as he pleaded for the life of the unfortunate accused. His distinguished, imposing bearing meant that whenever he entered a room, people were immediately aware of his being there. He had the actor's sense of "presence".

Drama was regarded with suspicion by many churchmen, but, as a man who thought in pictures, George saw drama, and film – Community House was the headquarters of the Scottish Religious Film Society – as a vehicle for imaginative truth. As the best known radio preacher in the country, who was earning excellent reviews for his "People's Service" broadcasts, he knew full well the value of dramatic communication.

George's theatrical gifts represented a temptation with which he had to struggle – and he sometimes found himself losing the war. He had a horror of misusing these gifts. For him, they came from God and must be used to glorify God. He used to tell the story of a dinner party at a country house, at which an actor and an old parson were among the guests. At one stage of the evening, the actor recited the 23rd Psalm, The Lord is my Shepherd, with great beauty, and was applauded by the guests. The parson repeated it, and moved people in a different way.

"The difference is that I know the Psalm," said the actor, "but you know the Shepherd."

Iona Abbey was George MacLeod's theatre, in the best sense of the word. He knew both the Psalm and the Shepherd. George was internationally known as a social crusader and political prophet, but in many ways he was at his best as a priest, as one drawing others into the presence of God.

Iona Abbey, with its simplicity of line, its strong evocation of historical pilgrimage redolent of Celtic poetry and Benedictine chant, the pink of its stone in the sunlight, and its sense for so many of being "home", was the perfect liturgical theatre in which to enact the mysteries of a holy yet accessible God. Round about: the ever-changing beauty of the island, the sparkling colours of the sea, the kings sleeping in the nearby graveyard. Everywhere, every thing, whispering of God. In the Abbey, George Fielden MacLeod, a modern Columba, lifting heavenward the broken loaf and the chalice with the blood-red wine, his magnificent voice declaiming "This is my body . . . this is my blood": awesome, dramatic silence: time shot through with eternity: pure, holy, theatre, moving and profound and converting.

For God's theatre, there could never be enough preparation and practice. The roots of this holy rehearsal lay deep in Fuinary. Up the river near the Morvern manse there is a ledge called "Mac-Leod's pulpit", where Norman and John practised their sermons, over a period of a hundred years, the eloquent words drowned in the torrent. The latest MacLeod went over and over his sermons – wearing out the carpet in Dunsmeorach, a family house near the Abbey owned by the Community. Every phrase, every pause, every gesture was rehearsed, leading to the moment of worship when the held-back emotion and torrent of well-chosen phrases poured out in a Celtic kaleidoscope of words and images. Each MacLeod sermon was a Word-event, a happening, an experience which could both raise wild goosepimples and change lives.

Nothing but the best could be offered in God's theatre, which is why George MacLeod abhorred shoddy worship, ill-prepared prayers, and casual address to the Almighty. ("The most beautiful churches and the most beautiful, colourful and ordered worship are an expression of God's worth-ship (worship)" he wrote. "God is worth it, and we should express that worth.") His objection was not to contemporary language, which he used himself to good effect, but to mumbled mateyness. His language in public worship sprang from deep personal experience linked to his ancestral Highland "feyness". He believed in demons and in angels as participants in the warfare of life, and he saw Iona Abbey as part of that battleground.

In the early days of the Iona Community, George used to go into the Abbey church early and alone to pray. One morning he had a profoundly disturbing experience: all he would say of it was that some strange force rose up and compelled him to leave the church. He never went back to the Abbey church early and alone.

For George MacLeod, Iona itself spoke to him of God.

"What, fundamentally, does Iona conjure up for me? Oddly enough – one must be honest – not its history, though, of course, that stirs me.

George MacLeod

"Nor even its Abbey. Too fickle is that Abbey; at one moment massive as the Cairngorms, at another – somehow – quite diminutive: almost a Gothic dwarf. At one moment again, that Abbey seems to be an easy place in which to be convinced of the living Communion of Saints: positively caparisoned with angels. At another it seems to need all its granite strength to hold it to the ground against the battery and assault of demons. Nor is it caparisoned with angels when the sun is shining: and standing ground against demons when a storm is on. I have known it in the sunshine to be battling with demons: and, in a storm, serene in victory. I must be honest. Too fickle is that Abbey."

Saying that it was the island itself which got through to him, the Iona leader went on to talk of a simple experience.

"It was late in Spring. Once in my life I have actually seen a crop agrowing and heard the deep rustle of its growth. And, though it was Spring, some foretaste of that lush magic was in the air. Cool and inexpressibly still: yet I felt the whole earth burgeoning to life. And there, before me, silhouetted against a pink sky, was a lamb without blemish on iridescent green: motionless. All the breath went from me. I was waiting to see a flag held in its forefoot and upright across its flank: sealed for St John. It was not there, of course: the flag. It was just a lamb, upright: yet motionless as if it had been slain. 'All in the April evening, I thought on the Lamb of God.'

"I do not think I will see the Abbey when I come to cross the final bourne. But I think I will remember that eternal moment. It was nature, just nature, preaching the Gospel to a man."

George incorporated the moods and colours of the island in his beautifully worked prayers, which are profound examples of a modern Celtic poet meditating upon the creativity of God. In his prayers above all, he articulated his vision of cosmic and personal integration: holiness become wholeness become holiness. Only the language of poetry could begin to convey his meaning.

A five-minute prayer would take him five hours to prepare – five hours carved out of a week of turbulent activity: but what beauty and soul-stirring inspiration came from that five hours.

Almighty God, Creator:
The morning is Yours, rising into fullness,
The summer is Yours, dipping into Autumn,
Eternity is Yours, dipping into time.

Glory to God in the High St

The vibrant grasses, the scent of flowers, the lichen on the
    rocks, the tang of seaweed,
All are Yours.
Gladly we live in this garden of Your creating.

But creation is not enough.
Always in the beauty, the foreshadowing of decay.
The lambs frolicking careless: so soon to be led off to
    slaughter.
Nature red and scarred as well as lush and green.
In the garden also:
always the thorn.
Creation is not enough.

Almighty God, Redeemer:
the sap of life in our bones and being is Yours,
lifting us to ecstasy.
But always in the beauty, the tang of sin, in our consciences.
The dry lichen of sins long dead, but seared upon our minds.
In the garden that is each of us, always the thorn.

Yet all are Yours, as we yield them again to You.
Not only our lives that You have given are Yours:
but also our sins that You have taken.
Even our livid rebellions and putrid sins:
You have taken them all away and nailed them to the Cross!
Our redemption is enough, and we are free.

Holy Spirit, Enlivener:
breathe on us, fill us with life anew.
In Your new creation, already upon us, breaking through,
    groaning and travailing,
but already breaking through,
breathe on us.
Till that day when night and autumn vanish:
and lambs grown sheep are no more slaughtered:
and even the thorn shall fade
and the whole earth shall cry Glory at the marriage feast of
    the Lamb.
In this new creation, already upon us, fill us with life anew.

You are admitting us now into a wonderful communion,
the foretaste of that final feast.
Help us to put on the wedding garment of rejoicing
which is none of our fashioning
but Your gift to us alone.
By the glories of Your creation,
which we did not devise:
by the assurance of Your freeing us,
which we would not accomplish:
by the wind of Your spirit,
eddying down the centuries through these walls renewed:
whispering through our recaptured oneness,
fanning our faith to flame,
help us to put on the wedding garment.
So shall we go out into the world,
new created, new redeemed, and new enchained together:
to fight for Your kingdom
in our fallen world.[7]

Iona was indeed a 'thin' place: never thinner than when the great
Iona High Priest was leading public prayer in his beloved Abbey.

PART FIVE

*

WINNING
AND LOSING

17

The Whirlwind

The man who says that Christian pacifism is a super-human and an unnatural ideal is expressing the truth with theological exactitude.

DICK SHEPPARD

It is improper for a man to long for the transcendent when he is in the arms of his wife.

DIETRICH BONHOEFFER

The 1950s saw the Iona Community expand rapidly, and its leader reach the zenith of his powers.

Professor J. G. Mackenzie, the well known Christian psychologist who lectured regularly on Iona, had observed shrewdly that as a result of his marriage, George MacLeod's powers would develop and increase. There is a sense in which the single-minded man was a married bachelor all his life; nevertheless, the delightfully warm and witty Lorna provided her husband with the emotional security which he needed. He was no less busy – indeed more so – but he became more relaxed.

Lady MacLeod did not hold at all with her husband's socialism and pacifism, and she deflated him in his more pompous flights of fancy with affectionate but no less barbed wit. She found the sycophants and bores who took up a good deal of George's time somewhat exasperating, and she delighted in finding ways to outwit them. She regarded with amused understanding the women who gazed into her husband's steely blue eyes as they talked of spiritual things. In the process, she helped to change the feel of things on Iona. The all-male bastion had been subtly infiltrated by the irreverent and hospitable Queen of Dunsmeorach.

A daughter, Mary, was born in 1950. "Every night I shall pray for both of you," George had written to Lorna while he was travelling, late in the pregnancy. "I know that when your time comes you will rise to it, though why you have all this suffering I don't know. But I do know that the joys of a wee one will far outweigh the duties, and you know it, too. I am a very bad husband and you are a very good wife. But for you, I would have gone mad in these last months."

When Mary was a few hours old, George wrote a letter to his new-born daughter.

"Our life and design are from God, so you are really all the garment of God, cut out from the garment of God that is your mummy and daddy . . . so I think you should know about us, with whom you are going to spend your life on earth. There is a Lady who feeds you with her whole being. It looks like milk, and so it is, but it is more than milk, it is all of Lorna, and from her you will learn, because you imbibe, a wonderful purity of spirit and a great wealth of love. You will find her grand to romp with. She is most effacing and has only one blind spot – she continues to believe I am worth loving. But I am really self-centred, nervy and not worth it. I can only suppose that God sent her to love me, so that I can know more of God whose great glory is that He really loves impossible people, as Lorna loves me.

"Then again, you will have to grow up into a hard world, so God has arranged that you should have early experience of it in this little community of us three. If you can learn to put up with me, then you will be well trained to cope with a hard world. And, underneath the hard world, there is a core of love – even in me. And you will find it peeping through, just as you will find it radiating out from your mummy."

There is a tender wistfulness in the letter which is touching. His feelings of inadequacy as a husband and as a father were with him for the rest of his life: yet his love for his family was deep, even at the points at which he knew he was neglecting them. He would write short love letters to Lorna, as he travelled – sometimes brief notes simply saying, "All I want to say is that I love you."

George had always delighted in other people's children and, indeed, they had drawn out the child in him. Parents would sometimes dread a visit from "Uncle George", in that he would get their children into such a state of excitement that it would take days to get things back to normal.

"What day is it? Friday? That's the day we don't use cutlery!"

he would exclaim to the delighted children, hauling off the table cloth, causing the knives and forks to clatter to the floor. Then the inside of a box of matches would be blown out, showering the contents everywhere. Plates would disappear and reappear, hand-kerchiefs would turn into mice, and all kinds of conjuring tricks would be performed. He would dandle mystified children on his knee, pacifying them by reading excerpts from the Westminster Confession or singing daft songs to them.

In 1950, George made history when he became the first non-Anglican to preach in St Paul's Cathedral. He had been invited at the suggestion of Canon L. John Collins, chairman of the Christian Action Movement, who told the press that the Iona leader was being asked to preach because he was "a modern prophet, perhaps the only real prophet we have today." George preached a fairly innocuous sermon, but when he was invited back the following year, he was more controversial.

"Increasingly I am told that Christians should not involve themselves too closely with materialistic constructions and should fly a hundred miles from having conference with a Communist. The reason given, in effect, is that Communists will flatten out our witness and 'then make circles round us'. It sounds plausible, but it is really a polite way of saying an ugly thing – that Stalin and not Jesus Christ is the ruler of our world: now at this present time! Anyone who fears that Communists can make circles round him simply does not believe that Jesus Christ is King of kings and Lord of lords (or – to make the title sound a little more like what first it sounded – King of Truman and Lord of Stalin).

"But once again if you really stand by working with everyone who is seeking peace – whatever his label or profession – there is persecution waiting for you, ready-made: not only in political parties, but in Church circles if not indeed in Church courts."

Spoken with feeling. Heard with feeling, too: one member of the congregation stood up, shouted a protest and stomped out of the Cathedral.

It is interesting that in the same sermon, George seemed to take a step back from pacifism.

"My only qualification to speak is that at least I represent confu-sion. In the First World War I was a serving soldier in a Highland regiment of the line: in the Second World War I was a pacifist in the doldrums. At the present time, if I face my Christian responsibilities, I am not, without qualification, prepared to be either."[1]

Despite his reputation as a totally convinced pacifist, the truth is that George wavered from time to time.

"The trouble is, I can't stand pacifists!" he would sometimes cry: and he was certainly more at home with military men than with convinced pacifists. He always described himself as a "reluctant pacifist", and he was at pains to distance himself from people he called "passive-ists", quietists who felt that the correct Christian response was non-involvement in the affairs of the world.

"What kind of a pacifist are you, George?" Alec Vidler, the Cambridge theologian, asked him as the two men sat with Ronald Selby Wright in the University Club in Edinburgh.

"Fifty-one per cent," was the reply.

In 1951, a major issue was resolved when the Iona Community was finally brought under the jurisdiction of the Church of Scotland. John White had worked hard to produce a formula which would satisfy all parties. It was agreed to set up an Iona Community Board, with a majority of nominees from the Iona Community, which would report to the General Assembly each year. The Community would have freedom to make its own policies, though these could be called into question on the floor of the Assembly, and would continue to raise all its own finances. George MacLeod, designated as Founder of the Iona Community, would be convener of the new Board, which would replace the Sponsors.

"It has been a difficult task," said a weary Dr White, "but I think we have succeeded in squaring the circle. The report is unanimous, and I can say that Dr MacLeod concurs with the recommendations."

Thus ended a 13-year wrangle. Though the Iona Community reports continued to raise much steam in the General Assembly, its status was at last resolved: it was now officially part, albeit a wayward part, of the Kirk. It was like having a pet which bit its master every three weeks: but at least it had now been decided to live with it and license it rather than try unsuccessfully to have it put down or let it roam the streets without a collar, causing untold mischief. And there were even times when it was possible to show off the wretchedly unpredictable beast with nervous pride.

It is also true to say that the Iona Community, though still very controversial, was no longer simply an *enfant terrible* saying outrageous things in front of the guests. Thirteen years on from its foundation, it had a very impressive track record in terms of directing able and committed men into frontline situations of parish ministry and industrial chaplaincy in Scotland. However unorthodox its views, it was hard to argue with its commitment to the wider work of the Church.

Nor was the Community a voice crying in the wilderness. The Church of Scotland's stances on mission, worship and social policy were not now so far away from the Iona Community's, as evidenced by various reports. The growth of the evangelical academies and the Kirchentag – a huge gathering for Christian education and inspiration – in Germany, the Worker Priest movement in France, the development of industrial mission in England, and the launching of the "Tell Scotland" movement at home all spoke of new and deep concern for mission. In the early 1950s, there was a renewed spirit of commitment to evangelism and to social action in the churches, along with a conviction that mission was the responsibility of the whole people of God, lay as well as ordained. It seemed as if the liberal evangelicals who had dominated the Kirk since the First World War, the social gospellers and the dialectical theologians (the disciples of Barth and Brunner, whose starting point was biblical revelation rather than the situation in the world) had come together in a coalition, however shaky, based on the need and opportunity for mission in a Scotland which showed a renewed interest in the old faith. There was also a spirit of ecumenical cooperation in the air. In this atmosphere, the Iona Community did not seem so strange, and Iona itself was the perfect training centre for such a renewed Church.

The Iona Community itself was also changing. Like its leader, it was still radical, energetic and sometimes outrageous, but it had also learned to appreciate domestic delights. The original intention had been for members to leave the Community after their initial two year training, but they had insisted on staying! They wanted support for their new work. The consequence was that the Community became bigger than intended, and more clergy-oriented. Also, when minister members moved to their second parish, which might not be a housing scheme or inner city area, they brought new concerns to the life of the Community. By this time they had learned that radical revolution was not just around the corner, and that the pace of change might have to be slower. And the Iona Community itself was becoming institutionalized. It was also learning to speak the more settled language of the institutional Church.

George busied himself with missions of friendship, which were known in the Kirk as "Iona missions". He also visited the parishes of Community members to bring them encouragement and cheer, even while delightfully disrupting the lives of their children. A typical such member was Bob Henderson who, inspired by George MacLeod, had gone to work in a huge Glasgow housing scheme. George came to speak to the sixty-strong "bad boys' club", which was open to boys with approved school or equivalent background, and their girl friends.

"He sat with a group of six or more, knowing only their first names," Bob Henderson recalled. "He assessed them almost by instinct and spoke to the needs of each, picking out the lad who couldn't keep a job, the lad with the homosexual tendencies, the lad with the razor in his pocket, the lad with the drink problem. That evening was magic for them, and for me listening in the wings."

Television was just beginning to make an impact, and George saw its potential for communicating the gospel. In 1952 he preached at the second normal church service televised from Scotland. He said afterwards that the TV camera resembled nothing so much as a four-barrelled trench mortar. He was to become very familiar with it.

George's life was a whirlwind of activity. In January 1952, he made a trip to Eastern Africa, Northern and Southern Rhodesia, and South Africa. His itinerary was, as usual, breathless. He addressed 130 meetings in 82 days in Nairobi, Luanshya, Kitwe, Bulawayo, Gwelo, Que Que, Salisbury, Johannesburg, Dundee, Durban, King William's Town, Sulenkama, Alice, Lovedale, Fort Hare, Grahamstown, East London, Port Elizabeth, George, Cape Town and Stellenbosch.

In Nairobi, he visited David Steel shortly after the dedication of the new St Andrew's Church. When he spoke at a packed meeting in the evening, one of the audience spontaneously suggested that a collection for the Iona rebuilding should be taken there and then. George protested, knowing they had a huge debt on the new church, and only agreed on condition that the collection be divided – "half to one of the finest of the oldest churches in Christendom, and half to one of the finest of the newest."

The visit to South Africa was eventful and exciting. While at Natal University, where Bob Craig was by now Professor of Theology, George received the news of the birth of his son and heir. (At the time of the pregnancy, the Iona Community used to hold Christian Socialist meetings at Community House. Lorna, Peter MacEwan and Margaret Henderson, wife of one of the members, felt it was a challenge they could not refuse, and began a Christian Tory group. When Lorna and Margaret both became pregnant within the year, Lorna commented, "That's a sign we were winning. It's the only way they could stop us!")

"My own most darling one," George wrote to Lorna from Durban, "I was sitting at the breakfast table ten minutes ago, when the waiter brought me the telegram. I went up in the lift without opening the envelope and knelt down at my bedside to know. A SON – AND BOTH VERY WELL. I don't know which gave me the most pleasure. But I was glad I was on my knees, both because it was the right place and because I had less distance to fall. Thus I gave you and Max and Mary and myself to God in love and thanksgiving and joy. When I got up from my knees I went on to the balcony and there were just lots of little ships in the bay."

George MacLeod and Bob Craig (also later to become a Moderator of the General Assembly of the Kirk) celebrated the far-away event in Scotland in ways which assuaged their thirst in the heat and dust, and substantially reduced their ability to string coherent theological sentences together.

As the guest of the Presbyterian Church of South Africa, George travelled to Rotary Clubs, civic receptions, parliamentary luncheons, and Caledonian gatherings, as well as to the tiny manses of African pastors.

He did not always tell people what they wanted to hear. The *Eastern Province Herald* reported in surprised tones that Dr Mac-Leod had told the members of the Johannesburg Rotary Club that Britain's National Health scheme was the greatest legislation that had reached a statute book anywhere.

George was shocked by the workings of what he called "the fantasy of apartheid" in a land with ten million blacks and coloureds, and two million whites, and was appalled by the pass laws, the prohibitions on skilled labour being performed by Africans, and the affronts to dignity in separated shops and counters. In Cape Town he watched a two-hour cavalcade of history, celebrating the arrival of the Dutch settlers, and was horrified to see that only one African was represented – and her part was played by a European with her face charcoaled.

What distressed him most was that the Dutch Reformed Church actively supported the system, highlighted by a conversation he had with a Dutch Reformed Christian just before he was due to address a meeting in Durban.

"Give them the gospel red hot!" urged the white South African. "Only the gospel red hot is any good for our day."

"I agree," replied Dr MacLeod. "That is why my subject is the social implications of the gospel."

"What do you mean?" he asked.

"Well, I take it that the gospel at least implies that all men are made in the image of God and entitled to an equal dignity."

"Yes," he replied.

"What, then, do you intend to do with the Africans and Indians here in distressful Durban?"

"For my part," came the reply, "I wish the whole damned lot were sunk in the harbour."

George uncompromisingly hammered out his theme that by abandoning the political sphere, Christians handed over the initiative to the materialists. The Dutch Reformed Church had a high level of attendance at worship and a generous support for missionary work: at the heart of their heresy was the divorce between whole salvation and soul salvation – "The closest sons of Calvin none the less denying the central insistence of their spiritual father! The most perfervid evangelists none the less the instigators of the most reactionary civic policies in Western culture!"

He asked whether the dichotomy between faith and politics could be transmuted into the total concern which was the unique mark of the gospel.

"If not, then the churches will more and more assume the outline of the church in Russia: confined to the eternal 'verities' while history pursues its headlong course to mutual destruction. In the meantime, the transmutation, either here or there, remains unpopular. Nearly all who attempt its incarnation in any realist way are labelled Communists or fellow travellers. Thus Stalin, ironically, gets the credit for every forthright progressive programme."

Not all of his sermons were political. He spoke about the Cross under the oaks at Lovedale, and the reporter from the *South African Outlook* told of the hush which descended over everyone at the end of the sermon.

"Many who were present will never forget that service under the oaks lit with the sun," he wrote, "and will ever thank God that He sent a man with a message so living and powerful on a too-short visit to our land."[2]

Despite the controversies, George brought back £3000 towards the restoration of the Michael Chapel on Iona, and enrolled 840 new Friends of the Iona Community.

As usual, he returned reinvigorated from the gruelling trip, and enthusiastically told the congregation of Canongate Kirk of the lessons he had learned in South Africa. The following week, his old friend Dr Selby Wright, with whom he disagreed fundamentally on so many issues, began his sermon: "Last week we were privileged to hear the stirring comments on South Africa by one of the most distinguished prophets of our Church. Today I wish to tell you the truth!"

George MacLeod's visit to Africa gave impetus to the campaign against the proposed Central African Federation – a campaign in which the Iona Community played a prominent role. A British commission set up to bring forward proposals to settle the future of about six million Africans and 180,000 Europeans in Nyasaland and Northern and Southern Rhodesia had proposed the establishment of a federation of the Central African territories. Their plan was for a Federal parliament dominated by Europeans. Church of Scotland missionaries, including Iona Community members, working in the territories, vigorously opposed the proposals, which they felt did not take seriously the aspirations of the African population, and would create another white South Africa, led by Southern Rhodesia, north of the Limpopo.

The Kirk could hardly escape being involved, since its missionaries had persuaded the Nyasaland chiefs to accept the British protectorate 61 years previously. From the days of David Livingstone, the Scots missions had provided leaders for the people.

With the Conservative government committed to the Federation – it was established in 1953 – protest meetings throughout Scotland were organized by the Iona Community. Tape-recorded interviews with African leaders were smuggled out by Iona Community members, and were played in many MPs' houses. Dr Hastings Banda, representative in Britain of the Nyasaland African Congress, spoke at a packed meeting in Community House, at which a motion was passed demanding that no scheme for closer association of the Rhodesias and Nyasaland should be imposed without the free consent of the African peoples.

The General Assembly of the Church of Scotland supported the protests, and its role was widely acknowledged to be a highly influential part in the campaign which led to the eventual break up of the Federation. The Church of Scotland view became a constituency party resolution to the Labour party conference and, with the help of George Thomson, was adopted as Labour party policy.

George was one of the dominant figures in the General Assemblies of the Kirk in the fifties, even more so than in the 1940s. There was a buzz of excitement whenever he strode to the rostrum, and his oratory held the fathers and brethren spellbound. Debates with Professor Pitt-Watson and some of the other greats of the time were riveting, soul-searching affairs, thrilling the packed spectator gallery as well as the main body of the Assembly. Serious matters were debated and, as with the Central African issue, the voice of the Kirk could not be easily ignored by the government of the day.

The man seemed to be everywhere. Ireland: invited by Queen's University, Belfast, in February 1953 to give a series of lectures on the topic, "What has the Iona Community to do with Ulster?" The blurb in the programme said that MacLeod was already a legend, and that his name was now better known in connection with Iona than St Columba himself.

More than a thousand people crammed into the University hall to hear the Iona leader explain the philosophy of his Community.

"If there has been a more stimulating lecture at Queen's of late than Dr George F. MacLeod's *tour de force* of Tuesday evening, then this writer has not heard of it," wrote the University correspondent of the *Belfast Telegraph*.

Protestant demonstrators had gathered outside the main door, and George was advised to go out by the side door. He refused. The most vocal of the demonstrators was a young, relatively unknown, preacher by the name of Ian Paisley. George was ready. He loved to tell his version of what happened next.

"Do you believe in the Bible?" he asked Mr Paisley, who couldn't but agree that he did.

"Does it say in the Bible, 'Love your enemies'?"

Agreed.

"And I am your enemy?"

Agreed.

George took an old envelope out of his pocket, wrote on it, "I love George MacLeod", and asked Mr Paisley to sign it – and even gave the Irishman a pen with which to do so!

The Whirlwind

As Ian Paisley's reputation grew, George used to describe him as the most dangerous man in Europe, playing with matches around a powder keg.

George MacLeod was hated by the extreme Protestants, who saw him as, well . . . the most dangerous man in Europe. The Rev. Alan Hasson, Grand Master of the Orange Order in Scotland, a publicity-seeking Church of Scotland minister who flamboyantly led parades on a white horse, used to bait him. A public debate between the two attracted a huge crowd. After Hasson fell from grace in the Orange movement and left the ministry under a cloud, George used to visit him.

Further controversy broke about George's head when he wrote an article attacking the Lord's Day Observance Society for their views on the Sabbath. It made front page news in the national press.

"The real convictions of that association are difficult to determine," wrote the latter-day Norman MacLeod. "At times they show signs of perceiving the real issue at stake: at others their apparent pronouncements are reminiscent of letters written by Mrs Grundy from a separate room in Bedlam. They cannot very much longer have it both ways.

"If the Lord's Day Observance Society is officially opposed to young people in our slums kicking a football about in a park on Sunday afternoons, then the association must share some of the responsibility for some of these young people kicking other people about on a Sunday."

No wonder the mere mention of the name MacLeod could raise blood pressure in church homes up and down the country.

In the summer of 1953, over seventy men sat down to eat in the refectory of Iona Abbey – under a beautiful roof of Norwegian timbers, a masterpiece of exact construction – for the first time in over 400 years. (The next week, the new arrivals were told by the great Iona stage manager himself, "You can claim to be the first people to eat in the refectory for the first time since the Reformation . . . with the windows in." Thus it went on, week after week, so that hundreds of people could claim to be the first . . . they usually forgot the qualification in the retelling! It meant that the numbers of those who had eaten in the refectory for the first time – like those who had handled the famous jettisoned timbers – ran into a cast of thousands.)

The money for the rebuilding was assured, but the finances on the mainland were in a different position. The Lithgow covenants were running out, and the Community required to find renewed covenants for the next seven years to the tune of £4,000 a year, simply to keep Community House operational: all this was in addition to the monies required for the general work of the Community. The Community would have to do its own fund-raising among its 6000 Friends if it wished to keep the work going.

One way not to do fund-raising was to preach pacifism, but that is what George did. May 1954, saw probably the greatest of the set-piece debates on the subject involving two of the Kirk's outstanding orators, James Pitt-Watson and George Fielden MacLeod. The packed General Assembly was hushed as Dr MacLeod argued that it was meaningless to ban the hydrogen bomb and justify the atomic bomb. It was meaningless to ban all the instruments of warfare, conventional and unconventional, and then justify bacteriological warfare. Someone had to call a halt, but once one got on the slippery slope it was found there was no halting place until one went down to stark pacifism.

"You go down into that dark, seemingly grave-like valley that is called pacifism, a valley largely untrodden since the first three centuries of Christianity. When you first find yourself there, phantom serpents seem to be hissing at you, 'cowardice!' and imaginary beasts seem to be breathing in your face the word 'treason!' All the centuries-old traditions of Scotland and our fathers whisper around you and half of your best friends, if only by their silent eyes, seem to be saying, 'Mad! Mad! Mad!' and yet there is no halting place of sanity higher up.

"The time is past when men can speak of war as an instrument of policy. Surely in such a plight the only people left who can give the releasing word are the people of God? For only they know the secret and significance of the grave. They alone know the paradoxical possibilities of resurrection. Only the Church of Jesus Christ can now release our world."

There was silence in the Assembly as Dr MacLeod paused, then said: "I for one cannot press that button. Can you?"

Opposing the pacifist motion, Professor Pitt-Watson commented: "I do not think anyone in this Assembly could be otherwise than deeply moved, not only by the eloquence, but by the deep passionate sincerity of Dr MacLeod," before going on to argue that the pacifists had not been the true peacemakers in the

The Whirlwind

1930s when Hitler rose to power: the true custodians of peace were those whose counsel was dismissed as alarmist by the ignorant and indifferent, and as sinful and warmongering by the sincere and conscientious pacifist.[3]

Feelings ran so high that for the first time for many years, the Moderator led the Assembly in prayer before the members voted. The result: a crushing defeat for Dr MacLeod.

His sadness at the defeat was nothing compared to the news that Lorna's brother, Norman, had committed suicide. He had written George a long letter just before taking the overdose. George immediately took charge of the situation, and went down to London to make all the necessary arrangements. He spent some time in prayer beside his dead brother-in-law, then he wrote to Lorna's mother:

"I found no difficulty in praying for him, and became profoundly aware that he was neither in torment nor, to be honest, in sincerity, did I feel him serene. The profound awareness was that he was asleep: in the reallest sleep since he was a boy perhaps, and that he would just sleep for a long, long time.

"Later in the day I went looking for a church, and was led into what men call Rome: which is both fiercest in its doctrine and richest in its provision for praying for departed souls. Also, there are always others praying, which gives the feeling you are in a workshop of natural activity and not an ecclesiastical furniture store. I found myself beside a crib, and remembered how children loved him, but again I found no urge to pray for him, in any sense of plea. He was still deeply asleep. And I felt strongly that vital prayer was needed for you all, as the restless ones."

George was a true pastor to his mother-in-law.

"Norman had been ill for a long time," he wrote, "and, in an odd way, I do believe he acted for the best. The only thing that matters in life is intention: and I think – in an 'ill' sort of way – he intended by this to do the right thing by you. And God knows men's hearts.

"You must be happy now that you never dropped him. He would have gone to the wall if you had, with almost certainly the same conclusion. Then you would have been in a far worse 'pother' – wondering if your broken relationship had caused it. You cannot blame yourself for failure. And no one must ever blame themselves for their effort to express love – which you did so costingly through the years.

"Ah yes! You may have harmed him by helping so much. But 'to them that love much, much will be forgiven'. That is, we are all to blame every way. But the least blame is in loving to the end. You could have done no less and no more. So when, in the night watches, you say to yourself, 'Was it I?' say to yourself at once, 'Now, Eva, don't get morbid,' and go to sleep: else you might disturb *his* sleep."

Nothing did more to bind George and Lorna together than his pastoral care for his mother-in-law in the time of her deepest distress.

It was at the level of personal encounter with individuals that George was often at his best. At the youth camp on Iona, he would sit at the table, take a fork, spin it, and ask the person to whom it pointed whether he or she was a Christian by conviction or by convention. Or he would startle an unsuspecting soul by demanding, "Are you a Christian or a Presbyterian?" On one visit he said grace, then asked the young student sitting next to him if he had closed his eyes. When Douglas Alexander replied no, he had been too busy praying, George asked him what he was planning to do with his life. Douglas wasn't sure, but was thinking about the possibility of the ministry.

'Come down to the Abbey tonight, I'm giving a series of lectures this week," George invited. "By the end of it, you'll want to be a minister."

Douglas did attend the lectures in the Rome Express.

"I'd never heard anything like it,' he remembered. "And I did want to be a minister by the end of it."

The lectures the young student was hearing formed the basis of the Cunningham Lectures, delivered at New College, Edinburgh and published by the Iona Community under the title, *Only One Way Left*. The book, which bore the inscription "Dedicated to my wife, who is always Right", was an immediate success, running into three editions.

It was brilliant polemic, taking up the favourite MacLeodian themes of the previous decade. It was much less parish and kirk based than *We Shall Rebuild*, reflecting the global issues which took up George's attention: hunger, justice, politics, the Bomb, the environment, the interrelatedness of all things, the individual and the corporate, the cosmic Christ. Passionately rhetorical, *Only*

The Whirlwind

One Way Left was a classic full-flood MacLeodian plea for a Total Gospel, with Christ as Lord of the whole created order as well as of the individual soul.

The argument may be summed up in what has become one of the most oft-quoted passages in modern spiritual writing:

"I am not pleading political concern to the exclusion of the multifarious interests and obligations of men. I am not really arguing that the mother of five should leave them with a neighbour to address envelopes at Labour headquarters, or that the doctor should scamp his patients' lists to attend the Conservative convention, or that the artist should leave his studio to paint posters for the Economic League. I simply argue that the Cross be raised again at the centre of the market-place as well as on the steeple of the church. I am recovering the claim that Jesus was not crucified in a cathedral between two candles, but on a cross between two thieves; on the town garbage-heap; at a crossroad so cosmopolitan that they had to write his title in Hebrew and in Latin and in Greek (or shall we say in English, in Bantu and in Afrikaans?); at the kind of place where cynics talk smut, and thieves curse, and soldiers gamble. Because that is where churchmen should be and what churchmanship should be about."[4]

The sales of the book at home and abroad confirmed George MacLeod's position as a leading figure in the world church scene.

In September 1954 he was off to America again, this time for an eight-month spell as the first Fosdick Lecturer at Union Theological Seminary, New York.

It was to prove to be an exciting visit, interrupted by the most traumatic episode in George MacLeod's life – the trial of a man accused of the bloody murder in a Govan flat of the former secretary of the Iona Youth Trust.

The tormented young man in the dock, facing the death sentence, had kept in touch with his guardian, the one man who had spoken up for him on many occasions in his troubled life.

The name of that guardian was George Fielden MacLeod.

18

Making a Grave with the Wicked

America is the only country in the world where failing to promote yourself is regarded as being arrogant.

GARRY TRUDEAU

Only the preacher proceeds still upon the idea that folk come to church desperately anxious to discover what happened to the Jebusites.

HARRY EMERSON FOSDICK

Yes, George loves abroad: this time with wife and children in tow: back at one of his favourite places on earth.

To be invited to be the first Harry Emerson Fosdick Visiting Professor at Union Theological Seminary was honour indeed. Beyond the pale he might be for many Scottish churchmen, but the man's standing in the international church scene was not in dispute. When the Moderator of the General Assembly, Dr Hutchison Cockburn, had been asked in America if it would be safe to invite Dr MacLeod, he had replied, "Every campus will be electrified as it has not been for a generation."

Professor MacLeod's lectures and sermons were received with tremendous enthusiasm. When he protested to Dr Fosdick – probably America's most outstanding preacher in the first half of the twentieth century – about the unanimity of praise even when he knew he had done badly, the great man replied sagely, "It's all right, George, so long as you don't inhale!"

Union was a ferment of ideas. With theological giants like Paul Tillich and Reinhold Niebuhr on the staff, the Seminary attracted some of the brightest and best of the divinity students in the country. George MacLeod did not have the intellectual clout of these greats, but his ability to communicate exciting ideas, and to talk from a base of hard experience in Govan and Iona, made him a star in the New York theological firmament. He also spoke to students and congregations with evangelical simplicity and directness, and not a few young Americans decided for the ministry after hearing him speak. His visit led many American churchmen to visit Iona over the following two decades.

He rarely turned down an invitation to speak.

"When he was asked to do something, he'd look at his diary, and if there was a blank space at the time requested, he'd say yes and scribble a note," recalled Professor Robert Handy. "We younger members of the faculty at that time wondered how he ever found the time to prepare, but he seemed always ready, always scintillating, very forthright, well liked even by those quite opposed to one or another of his views."

At a time when sixty per cent of the American people went to church – a figure rising by the decade – mainstream American religion was in a comparatively healthy and vigorous state. In these heady days before the dominance of the tele-evangelists and the fragmentation of the religious tradition into individualism, the mainline American churches were still in the business of creating a public theology, a theology by which the nation might be guided. The churches concerned themselves not only with the living rooms and bedrooms of the nation, but with the civic rooms where public policy was discussed. The views of men like Niebuhr and Tillich were eagerly sought when public issues were being dicussed. Sure, there were other voices, other trends: Billy Graham was a very popular figure, Norman Vincent Peale was attracting enormous attention with his Power of Positive Thinking, and the rabid anti-Communist wing was very vocal; nevertheless, there was something of a mainstream consensus about the public nature of theology, even though many people might in practice pursue more individualistic and private versions of the American dream.

George went to see several projects which claimed inspiration from his Iona experiment. They included the Kirkridge Centre, which had been founded by his old friend John Oliver Nelson, the Church of the Saviour in Washington – a remarkable group of committed people with a determination to deal with the racial problem – and East Harlem Protestant Parish in downtown New York.

While in Harlem, George also went to visit a remarkable project run by a curious 80-year-old priest, Father Divine, who had established hostels for people, black and white, in dismal inner-city areas. He held huge "heavenly banquets" for poor people. George and Lorna went one Sunday night.

"I had addressed the previous Thursday the St Andrew's Society at their Waldorf Astoria Banquet: but the napery there was not as clean as at Harlem, nor the silver brighter, nor the soup warmer, nor the turkey and vegetables and cranberry sauce and stuffing and coffee more enticing, nor the ice and fruit salad colder. While the meal progressed, constant choruses rose from a heavenly choir and intermittent witness was made from here and there in the hall . . . Occasionally a negress rose and went into one of those trances, well short of delirium and well within decorum, and with eyes closed spoke with tongues such as St Paul recognized as genuine if somewhat perplexing. The immediate neighbours were not put out and saw that she got the cranberry she might have missed, when she came to. After all, she had come in from a highway or byway and the heavenly entry is not primarily dependent on conduct (Praise the Lord). But in the main a superbly excellent time was had by all, compared with which the third table at my previous St Andrew's night dinner at the Waldorf Astoria, at least as seen from the platform table, though it was not teetotal, resembled a group of undertakers in a town where nobody had died. I have simply to confess that the experience was overpowering."

George reported that when he got to bed that night he could not get to sleep for hours.

"What are you thinking about?" asked Lorna, around 3 a.m.

"A man."

"Not Father Divine, still?"

"No, John Calvin."

"She was probably right," George commented, "to tell me to go to sleep at once. Or was she?"[1]

Doctor Calvin certainly could not help Doctor MacLeod interpret all his experiences in America.

Although George still had what he called "the virus of Calvinism" lurking within him, he now knew for sure that the good Doctor of Geneva's theological system was not broad or adaptable enough to cope with the undeniable experiential evidence of his own life, ranging from Govan to Jerusalem, from Iona to Cape Town, from Edinburgh to East Harlem. While he still recognized the granite-like strengths of the Scottish Presbyterianism in which he had been nurtured, and which he still loved and passionately defended against all comers, he knew that its range of illumination was limited.

After the three month spell at what the Scottish professor called "the most remarkable divinity hall in the world," it was time to hit the trail across America. Twenty states in eight weeks. By Christmas, 1955, he had given 134 addresses, excluding the Union lectures.

Across the Mason-Dixon line, Alabama, the Carolinas, Tennessee, some towns seemingly composed of Macdonalds and Mac-Leods. Quiet speech and old courtesies. Invitations to relax in huge mansions – "admittedly, if you go, eight strangers have also been invited to assist in the relaxation, four of whom want to go to Iona, three of whom were there in 1947, and one of whom thinks it is an island off Athens."

Texas. The Peyton Lectures: four addresses to a thousand ministers. Santa Fe. Prayers for the Iona Community in a small adobe chapel bearing the gateway date of 1640. California.

Ah, California in February, peach and apple blossoms breaking out. 190 major addresses have been given, only fifty to go.

But how did the Christian faith measure up to the plight of the wretched John Gordon, standing in the dock in the High Court in Glasgow?

George had worried about the situation constantly. The week before leaving for America had been spent getting an advocate to defend Gordon for nothing. He had succeeded, but the advocate withdrew from the case when Gordon put up an absurd defence. George wrote from Canada, asking Harry Whitley to visit Gordon and urge him to tell the truth.

"I personally believe Gordon had a blackout, his whole frustration bubbled up at last in violence, and that he had deluded himself into believing the cock and bull story which he claims in his defence. Had he come out with the truth, however appalling, I would have flown back (if so advised) to plead compassion in the light of his years.

"One is thrown back on the gospel. Far more of us should be 'making our grave with the wicked' and realize it is really a grave: for it is only we who know that the grave is empty. Even if it transpires that it ends in a real grave, the gospel still stands. Jesus knows what to do with folk who are crucified with Him. All good be with you and yours, and thank God for having, and having had, a good home."

George, who had kept in touch with the trial daily, had to make the most difficult decision of his life. He had rung from the States to ask if the counsel for the defence could be sounded out on the advisability of his appearing to give evidence. On learning counsel's view that it would indeed be beneficial, he decided to fly back immediately. He explained the importance of the matter to his Californian hosts, promising to be back in a day or two to complete the remaining engagements.

When he arrived back at Prestwick, he came off the plane in a very distressed state. James Maitland accompanied him back on the bus from Prestwick Airport. When James remarked on how marvellous it was that he should walk out on all these high-powered conferences to return home for such a sordid business, George commented simply that a man's life was at stake, and nothing else in the States or in Scotland could weigh against that. And then, he added, half to himself, the biblical reference to Christ, "He made His grave with the wicked", and quietly repeated it two or three times.

George was going to the aid of the 24-year-old man in the dock to try to prevent him hanging. He had first come across the accused when the lad was five years old, living with his mother in a campsite near Fingalton Mill. The boy was very inquisitive, running across to the workers restoring the mill, full of questions. George had kept in touch with the family, and was dismayed when the boy was in court at the age of 10, then had spells in reformatories, Borstals and in prison. He had run away from home and changed his name from Robert Weir to John Gordon, calling himself after the editor of the Sunday Express, whose column he read obsessively. He had joined up with the Royal Army Medical Corps and was later transferred to the Welch Regiment, but was discharged with ignominy. George MacLeod had kept an interest in him, speaking up for him in many courts, and had become his official guardian.

After the body of George McNeill had been found in his Govan flat in July 1954, Gordon was picked up in Spain, having fled to the Foreign Legion. George had asked Duncan Finlayson at Community House to pray for the McNeill family, while he prayed for Gordon. He had then knelt down and prayed in sorrow for "that fugitive soul".

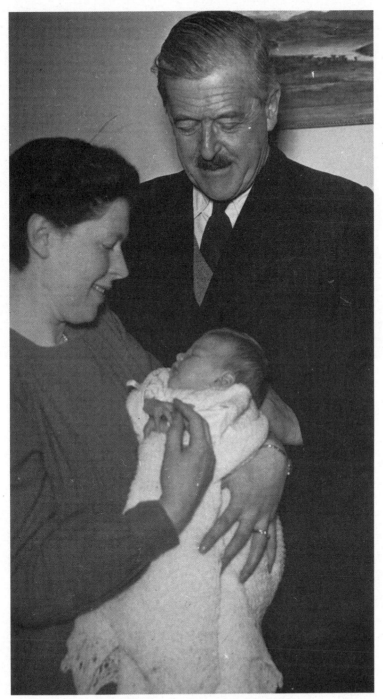

Mary MacLeod's christening, May 1950

The Kirk's Moderator on a tour of the Borders, 1957

Outside Iona Abbey with the Queen Mother, 1967

In Rome with Pope Paul VI, 1967

George, Mary his daughter and his son Neil with the Duke of Edinburgh after receiving the
Templeton Award at Buckingham Palace, May 1989

With Leah Tutu, wife of Archbishop Desmond Tutu, at the dedication of the MacLeod Centre on Iona, August 1988

Outside the Abbey on Iona, 1986

Making a Grave with the Wicked

Over 160 witnesses were cited for the trial, at which Gordon was accused of murdering 47-year-old George McNeill by striking him on the head with an axe or other instrument. The court heard that McNeill had been recruited by George MacLeod to work as secretary of the Iona Youth Trust in 1943. After some years he had resigned to become director of the Pearce Institute in Govan, and after a year or two had joined Fairfields Shipyards as personnel officer.

"I had a long talk with Sir John Cameron (counsel for the defence) tonight," George wrote to Lorna, who was still in America. "He is more and more convinced that John Gordon, though a pathological liar, did not do it. He is terribly glad I came home, as there is a vague nastiness about everywhere – not about me but about Community House."

George MacLeod took the stand on March 1st, 1955, near the end of the case, as sole witness for the defence other than those already cited by the Crown. He told the court that he was chairman of the After Care Council, a member of the Scottish Advisory Council for the Rehabilitation of Convicts, and vice chairman of the Visiting Committee at Polmont Institution. In evidence, he said that he had known Gordon had been unbalanced since he was 12, and had known him as a "demented man" for eight years. He had known the accused as a person of great potentiality and had appeared at courts in England, Wales and Scotland on his behalf. He had visited him in prison in Inverness, and the young man seemed sincerely determined to have done with the past and start off properly.

"I told him that if he was sincere he might be able to help people who had been in the same kind of difficulty as himself," he told Sir John Cameron, QC. "I thought someone who was going straight might be able to help more than we could because of our senior age and difference of background. I suggested that same day that 'Convicts Anonymous' might be formed parallel to 'Alcoholics Anonymous'".

Then came a dramatic piece of evidence which astonished the packed courthouse.

Sir John Cameron: "I must ask you this. Do you know whether in George McNeill's past there had been any personal tensions of a homosexual kind?"

"There had."

"That he had homosexual tendencies and temptations?"

"Yes. George McNeill was one of the ablest workers in youth that I have ever known. For years he ran a club in Dalry, and scores of boys are grateful for his interest and concern, in the best possible meaning. He and I have run camps for Borstal Boys at which three or four hundred have attended.

"In connection with that work, McNeill has been a mainstay all the time, being quixotically generous with the most desperate cases from the highest kind of motives. Large numbers of boys are profoundly grateful for what he has done.

"At the time of the crime, John Gordon was in an excitable state towards good. He was desperate to do good. I felt I had led him too quickly into trying to help other people, by asking him to help criminals."

Dr MacLeod said that when it came to his knowledge that there had been a case of homosexual tendency in McNeill, he had gone to see him.

"It was the most painful interview of my life. He showed a tremendous guilt complex and tremendous frustration at being reminded of what had happened some years previously. I got him to promise to see a psychotherapist."

He did not consider McNeill to be a man likely to corrupt the morals of young people. When some terrible thing like that happened, one must try to keep the person in circulation, he said, or he might become a menace to society.

Sir John Cameron: "Is it still your belief that there is good in Gordon?"

"Yes."[2]

Two days later, John Gordon was found guilty of murder by a majority verdict. He showed no emotion as he was ordered to be hung at Barlinnie Prison, Glasgow, on March 24th, 1955.

Petitions for Gordon's reprieve were immediately circulated, with the Rev. Nelson Gray, minister of Parkhead Congregational Church, doing much of the organization. 14,000 signatures were collected, and the petition sent to the Secretary of State for Scotland.

The day before he was due to hang, John Gordon was reprieved. The sentence was commuted to life imprisonment. The news was conveyed to him by the Lord Provost of Glasgow.

George's evidence brought obloquy upon him. The homosexual issue had not been mentioned in the trial until his evidence, and McNeill's mother said she knew nothing of her son's tendencies.

She and the other members of the family were furious, believing that McNeill's name had been blackened.

What was even worse was that the homosexual label was put on George MacLeod himself. When the Iona Community was founded, homosexual smears had been made, along with the Communist and Catholic labels. It was an easy accusation to insinuate subtly over cocktails: after all, the Community was all-male, and its leader was an attractive bachelor. What were they doing away up there, anyway, on that strange island? As well as leading the Kirk to Rome and Moscow, and trying to raise the dead, were they not up to other unsavoury things as well? It was an accusation without a shred of foundation, and not a semblance of evidence was ever adduced to back it up, but the rumour, once off and running, was impossible to refute.

As a strict, Victorian puritan in all matters sexual, George was hurt and horrified by these whispered allegations. (When a family friend once alleged that someone was a homosexual, George asked for proof and, when none was forthcoming, he strongly rebuked the friend, saying that he knew the pain of such false stories.) He knew full well that by giving evidence at the trial he would be making himself very vulnerable to the homosexual smear, but he believed that the truth had to be told. He felt the murder was a much more complicated story than had been allowed, and he could not have lived at peace with himself if he had not testified. He may also have felt guilty about his knowledge of McNeill's tendencies, as well as about what he considered to be his premature encouragement of Gordon's activities in helping others.

George's compassion for youngsters who had been deprived of love in their own background was overwhelming, and he simply could not be silent while there was a possibility that Gordon would hang. There was no need for him to give evidence – Gordon requested him not to do so – and being on a lecture tour of the States was reason enough for not even being within a thousand miles of the trial.

Amidst all the many public achievements of an astonishingly active life, George Fielden MacLeod's courageous decision to fly home to testify on behalf of John Gordon was his finest hour. As one of the reporters present at the murder trial put it: "George MacLeod's evidence in court seemed to judge us all." The Moderator of the General Assembly, the Rev. Dr E. D. Jarvis, wrote a note to Ralph Morton to say "with what sympathy and admiration

I have regarded the Iona Community in the sad trial occasioned by the recent case in the courts. I expect Dr MacLeod has returned to the USA by now. Perhaps you would let him know how proud we in this house – and we represent many – were of the way he acted and spoke."

George returned to complete his engagements in America and Canada before his next confrontation with American religion – in Britain.

The "Tell Scotland" group had decided to invite Billy Graham to lead an evangelistic crusade in Scotland in 1955. It was a crucial decision, since it provoked opposition and criticism, and was one of the key factors in the eventual break up of the shaky coalition of groups seeking a more missionary approach within the Church in Scotland.

One of the key figures in the "Tell Scotland" movement pushing for the Graham invitation was the Rev. Tom Allan, who was field organizer of the movement. A charismatic protégé of that craggy doyen of Scottish evangelists, D. P. Thomson (Church people often divided themselves into Thomson men or MacLeod men), he had, after his student days, been unable to decide whether to be a minister or a Labour MP. He had gone to seek George MacLeod's advice, and the older man had said without hesitation, "Be a minister". He had an outstanding ministry at North Kelvinside, reinvigorating his parish by missionary work which had been influenced by the Iona mission of friendship model.

Tom had been sympathetic to the Iona Community, but had not joined. He and fellow divinity student John Sim had been invited to meet George at Community House to talk about the matter, but the interview did not go well.

"George harangued us as if we were a public meeting," John Sim recalled, "marching up and down his long study, scarcely giving us a chance to get a word in edgeways. He seemed to be trying to bombast us into membership of the Iona Community. I was not impressed, and rather resented the strong-arm tactics. In fact, I was put off by this close contact with the man, George MacLeod.

"Yet I knew how much I was indebted for the integrating of my own faith to George MacLeod, the prophet, the visionary, the dynamic soldier of Christ. Reluctantly I decided that I must join the Community. I often wonder what difference it would have made in the Church of Scotland if Tom had."

It was sad that George MacLeod and Tom Allan, both passionate Christian communicators, came to be seen as symbols of two divergent and mutually exclusive methods of mission. Ian Cowie persuaded Tom to have another meeting with George, to see if the gap could be bridged.

"I knew that Tom, too, had fire in his belly about peace and justice," he remembered, "and I knew, too, that many had been converted under George. I felt deeply that the two had more in common than most people thought. So I sat back and watched and prayed as the two joined battle. Both agreed on the socio-political implications of the faith, and Tom was as left-wing as George, having come from a poor working class home. But Tom insisted that in order to work out the political implications of the faith, one must first be a Christian. To spell out the implications to the unconverted was a waste of time. George insisted that unless one took the 'one way' he had outlined, one could not become a real Christian. So the two parted."

As, in effect, the national leader of the "Tell Scotland" campaign, Tom Allan was very influential. Up till 1954 it had been a broad-based liberal evangelical ecumenical movement, under the chairmanship of Bill Smellie of Perth, with excellent teaching and evangelistic sessions on radio and television – indeed it was out of BBC broadcasting under Ronnie Falconer that the movement had sprung in the first place. The group agonized over whether to invite Billy Graham.

George MacLeod was in no doubt; he was utterly opposed to mass evangelism, which he saw as a tempting, glamorous short-cut which would turn out to be a divisive diversion from the genuine congregational missionary task. "Have nothing to do with this theology," he said. "Graham will set back evangelism by a score of years!" Tom Allan went south to hear the American evangelist, and felt convinced that Graham should come to Scotland under the auspices of the Tell Scotland movement.

There is no doubt that George MacLeod was disappointed in what he saw as the individualistic direction taken by Tom Allan, whose zeal for Christ he admired. He mused aloud wrily as to whether he had given him the right advice in directing him to the ministry. He once asked the young evangelist his views on an important social matter: Tom had replied that he had to rush to catch a train to Wick. Thereafter George used to castigate conservative evangelicals as men who always had to catch a train to Wick when controversial public issues were on the agenda.

The main burden of George MacLeod's case against Billy Graham was that he, too, was always setting off for Wick, or Ohio, when the social issues of the day came up for discussion. In his criticism of Graham, George was being utterly consistent. He had fought all his ministry against notions of religion which restricted it to the private sphere – and here it was, in mass form, on live television! The Iona man often used to preach against what he called "extractionist salvation" – the notion that as individuals people are caught in a swamp and have to be levered out, one by one. (At this stage in the argument he would make great squelching and sucking noises, to make sure no one missed the point.)

The whole matter was particularly painful for George because he liked Tom Allan and Billy Graham. He invited the American evangelist to Community House, and greatly enjoyed his company. He also sat beside him at a luncheon for clergy, and was impressed by his sanity and his humour. As one who knew the trials of constant travels, luncheons and speech-making, George admired Billy's constant courtesy, and said that his unaffected manner despite all the publicity, "marks out beyond peradventure a man of consecration." Yet the Iona leader felt compelled to stand out against mass-individual evangelism. In so doing, he had to ask himself seriously whether he was not motivated by jealousy of another great communicator.

"Some of us feel we must oppose the present content of his mission," he wrote in *Ariel*, the Winchester College magazine. "Even this is a responsible decision. It is seemingly to ally oneself with cynics and materialists. It holds the danger of splitting the unity of the Church's message, when unity is our need. It arouses the unmanning question in one's secret soul whether our opposition is more than a rationalization of our envy and jealousy: those ugly sisters whose wardrobe of disguises is so varied. Yet we must speak. The present conspiracy of the popular press, and even the BBC, to refuse responsible criticism while he is in our midst is not ultimately good for any cause."

George argued forcibly that Billy Graham's fundamentalist attitude to the Bible was simply not adequate for the modern mind: in his view, it encouraged escapism from modern problems and was a seductively false solution which would set the Church back for years.

"The leaders of our churches who, by backing Graham, imply that 'all this doesn't matter' incur a grave responsibility. For vast numbers – not of Graham's section – to stop at such conceptions is not so much a form of Faith as a 'fear to launch away'. His ecclesiastical backers should not forget the sadness of the nineteenth century when multitudes of honest minds were driven regretfully from the Church through its continuance of such claims. Nor is it any comfort to the Church that many of their grandchildren have landed in an arid wilderness called 'Science' that can no more save us than a literalist adherence to Scripture. Just at the moment when 'Science' is becoming conscious that it only has husks to feed on, and when the mutual labour of decades is making possible a new synthesis between Faith and psychology, Faith and sociology, it may well accumulate to the proportions of a new tragedy if youth have to face again a false dichotomy of choice."

George went on to attack Graham's comment on the horrifying McCarthyist anti-Communist witch-hunt in America – "I have no views on that, my message is spiritual", the evangelist was reported as saying.

"He is entitled to his reply. But, in this regard at least, he is not entitled to his constant chant that 'this is what the Bible says'. The Bible, with terrifying repetition, claims that God makes His Judgments plain through the historic process. Throughout the social prophets, knowledge of God is constantly clarified by reference to the various McCarthys of their contemporary experience. If by 'spiritual' he refers to some ethereal controversy between man and his Maker which somehow continues independent of the historic process, then Graham may well have an interesting religious theory to present to men, but it is not the religion of Abraham, Isaac and Jacob. The same argument goes for his constant avoidance of any significant comment on the H-Bomb."

George was not at all impressed by the argument that Dr Graham's one job was to convict men of Christ – and after that they would be in a position to face their social responsibilities. After all, he said, Dr Graham himself had made his "decision for Christ" years before, yet he still refused to comment on the burning social issues of the day. If he, as a mature Christian, could not come off the fence, how could his followers be expected to do so?

Arguing that Graham was not dealing in Bible conversion but in a reversion to nineteenth century individualist salvation, George MacLeod concluded: "If he is really the significant prophet of our time, then he is the first Christian prophet whom no one has wanted to persecute. To dare such a criticism immediately demands that we make like confession for the vast majority of us in the Christian Church today. The real criticism of the modern Church is that no one wants to persecute us. There is really nothing to persecute us about."

The argument is worth quoting at some length, not simply because it went to the heart of Scottish church life of the 1950s, but because it is a recurrent issue more than thirty years on. George MacLeod was by no means the only churchman saying such things, of course, but in Scotland he became a symbol of articulate opposition. He was accused of rocking the boat, and of causing disunity, particularly when Scotland became caught up on the glamorous Graham publicity as the "All-Scotland Crusade" band-wagon began to roll. Not all of the Iona Community agreed with their leader, and some Community members trained as Crusade counsellors: they argued that while they disagreed with Graham's literalistic view of the Bible, he nevertheless preached Christ in a way which brought people to personal commitment. George's point was that it was not a question of first one thing, then the other. He believed that the old cry of "get self right first" ignored the fact that it was only in the "we" that the true self could be found.

With big audiences at the Kelvin Hall in Glasgow, and crusade meetings being beamed live, the newspapers gave generous and almost uncritical coverage. Was it not churlish to complain, when religion was again causing such public interest? Some over-excited churchmen talked about a revival which was sweeping through Scotland. It was wishful thinking.

In the course of the six-week crusade, 20,000 people out of the 830,000 attending went forward to make "decisions for Christ": of these, 62 per cent were already regular church attenders. Indeed, the bulk of the largely middle class audiences each evening consisted of regular churchgoers.

For those who did make personal commitments, the crusade was obviously very important. Some date their call to the ministry from that time, and it might be argued that this in itself justified the effort. However, the debit column was heavy. In surveys following the crusade, most ministers of the Church of Scotland reported "little or no effect" from the 1954–6 evangelization effort. Once the cameras and the hype-merchants had gone, Scotland's problems looked pretty much the same. The cruel reality was that the decision to invite Billy Graham, and all the energy that had gone into the venture, had destroyed the unity of the "Tell Scotland" coalition, and those who had gone along with the decision against their better judgment felt they had let themselves down.

It was to prove to be the last major missionary effort of the old religious Scotland. From the peaks of the mid 1950s, when 1.3 million people identified themselves with the national Church in Scotland, the church rolls began their inexorable and apparently unstoppable decline. Other, more corrosive, influences were eating away at the religious foundations of a nation which would be more and more hard put to describe itself as a Christian country in any cohesive way. The Emperor's threadbare clothes were flying away in the wind, and not all the religious prose in Scotland – not even the brilliant rhetoric of a George MacLeod – would be able to change the situation.

America would remain religiously vital, but in increasingly individualistic ways. The Billy Graham message therefore continued to have appeal, but disillusionment was to come to this fundamentally decent man as he heard the Watergate tapes roll, and discovered that he had been mute court chaplain to a cynical and manipulative administration in Washington. Individualistic conversion and biblical literalism, even when tricked out in new and dazzling clothes, were simply not up to the job.

Never mind. In the midst of change, some things remained the same. More wood was on its way to Iona: this time, from Canada.

The names in the story of how wood was negotiated in Vancouver, after the murder case, vary a bit in the different versions, but the outline of the story is roughly the same. Let the *Seanachaidh* tell it like it probably wasn't.

"I went to some Presbyterian ministers and said I would be back in three months, but only for three days. Could they gather some Scottish timber merchants for a luncheon, when I could plead the cause? Splendid idea, they said. Leave it to us. Well I sent them some appeal leaflets and left it to them. When I duly appeared for my three days, I went to the Presbyterian minister to whom I had sent the appeal literature. There it was, unpacked on the table . . . He had meant to let me know . . . he was sorry . . . and that was that.

"Disconsolate, I walked up the street and met an Anglican priest

I had not seen for three years. 'You look glum,' he said. 'Come and have a coffee,' I said, and told him all. 'But this will never do,' he said. 'I know a Yorkshireman, a devout Anglican, he owns the biggest store in Vancouver.' I protested we only had three days. 'Come right now,' he said. Well, our dear friend had come from Yorkshire 20 years ago and his accent had not changed one whit. 'Eh, lad, what can I do for you?' he asked. I explained, 'Well,' he said, 'there's Bill Mackay.' So he rang him up.

"To my horror, my would-be benefactor spoke thus over the phone. 'Say, Bill, there is a man MacLoid here, he comes from Ionia where Columbia built an abbey in the 14th century.' The responsive noise from Bill on the muffled phone was obvious. 'He ain't going to help,' said our Yorkshire friend, 'we will try Tom Maclagan'. Once again . . . MacLoid . . . Ionia . . . Columbia . . . 14th century. Once more menacing muffles from Maclagan. 'He ain't going to help,' said Yorkshire. 'I know Alec Niven,' and he rang him up. The while I prayed. I did not kneel, I did not shut my eyes, but I said, 'Dear Lord, this is the kindest man in Vancouver and at the moment he is doing more harm to the cause of Iona than any man in town. Please tell me how to leave politely, because he is rather a dear, but . . . but . . .', on which the Yorkshireman put his hand over the mouthpiece of the phone and said, 'Were you praying then?' Embarrassed, I admitted it. 'All right, friend,' he said, 'we have got your roof.'

"Well, in the subsequent conversation it turned out that Alec Niven had years ago been an apprentice in my father's office in Glasgow, where my father was a CA. Not for Iona's sake, not for my sake, not for Columba's sake, but because of my father, Alec Niven fixed up a luncheon in thirty-six hours . . . of the biggest timber merchants in Vancouver. We raised four thousand dollars before they finished coffee. If you think that was a coincidence, I hope you have a very dull life."

Anyone who believes every detail of the story deserves a very dull life too. But though the facts are perhaps a little fickle, the truth is constant, especially the way the sparkling Celtic hypnotist tells it.

And that, give or take a fact or two, is the truth of how Vancouver timbers today cover the cloisters of the restored Iona Abbey, this Glory of the West.

19

In From the Cold

*I'm a bit puzzled. Here you have been rampaging
unpatriotically against war and breaking most of the
Thirty-Nine Articles of our modern social belief, and
the King goes and makes you one of his chaplains. Is
he a stealthy pacifist, or is it only his Charlie Chaplin
he intends you to be?*

LAURENCE HOUSMAN TO DICK SHEPPARD

*Flying is like war: days of unsupportable boredom
enlivened by moments of acute fear.*

GEORGE FIELDEN MACLEOD

It was in 1956 that the pedigree of Scotland's most notorious
ecclesiastical wild beast was rediscovered with acclaim. The
prophet was brought in from the cold.

In March 1956, it was announced that the Rev. Sir George
Fielden MacLeod, Bt, had been made a chaplain to Her Majesty
the Queen.

The great Norman would have been proud of his grandson, as
would all of the royal MacLeods. It was as if he had been born to
the ecclesiastical purple, but his rightful inheritance had been
delayed because of some youthful indiscretions which had best be
forgotten. George MacLeod, socialist and pacifist and thorn in the
establishment's side, was delighted by the royal patronage. Such
delight confused both friends and opponents.

George MacLeod the revolutionary was also George MacLeod
the loyalist and traditionalist. The socialist and pacifist never at
any time renounced his own past, nor did he break completely with
the Establishment. That is what made him such a maddening

277

figure, a risk to the blood pressure of high Tories and radical socialists alike. As someone impossible to categorize, he raised ire in people who looked for complete consistency. For George, there was no inconsistency. He was a conservative, a traditionalist, a socialist, a pacifist and an iconoclast, and he consistently held to all of these positions. What could be more consistent than that?

One thing he was clear about, though: his ultimate loyalty was not to any earthly sovereign, but to Jesus Christ. When, soon after the war, a member of the Iona Community suggested to George on the island that since the King was due to broadcast at 9 pm, it would be a good idea to change the time of the Abbey evening worship, he received short shrift.

"We will worship the King of kings at nine o'clock!" was the brusque response.

Queen Elizabeth herself visited Iona, with Prince Philip and Princess Margaret, on August 12th, 1956. Over 1,000 people were there to welcome her to the island, and the royal party walked to the Abbey for Sunday morning worship. The Community members were gathered in the Abbey church, dressed in their blue double-breasted suits, blue shirts and blue ties. "Who are these sinister men in the dark suits?" whispered Princess Margaret.

During the singing of the last praise, the clergy and the elders moved to the north transept of the Abbey where Dr Charles Warr dedicated an oak screen which had been gifted by the Queen when, as Princess Elizabeth, she had been married to Philip. This unprompted gift, at a time when the Iona Community was undergoing considerable criticism, had been welcomed by Dr MacLeod as a sign of great encouragement.

George took great satisfaction from the royal visit, which he saw as some kind of vindication of his purposes. There were mutterings among the more radical sections of the Community about royal patronage – not all of the membership agreed with their leader's view that the monarchy was somehow outside of the political process and class structure. They were more embarrassed than excited by royal approval, and they felt let down by the man who had taught them to look at politics from a radical perspective. They did not fully understand that their leader's roots were so deeply embedded in established Auld Kirk soil, and that Fuinary, and even Balmoral, were important parts of his life script. George simply shrugged their views aside. He did not want a separation between Church and state and monarchy and parish as part of a socialist revolution: he wanted an established Church, supported by the state and the monarchy, with national responsibility for every parish in the land, *but he wanted all of them to be shaped and reshaped by the gospel of Christ*. This was the nature of his radicalism.

The summer of 1956, even without the royal visit, was memorable in the history of the Iona Community. The east range dormitory block was dedicated: in a moving ceremony the members of the Community left Sunday worship in the Abbey by way of the new staircase which linked the Abbey church to the completed range. Thus was established the important practical and theological link between the sanctuary and the place of the common life. The place of worship, the place of eating, the place of discussion and the place of sleeping were now symbolically under one roof, in an architectural unity. It was a beautiful parable of MacLeod's purpose, a true sermon in stone.

The completion of the main phase of the building also meant that the Community could move out of the famous Rome Express huts and into the Abbey itself. The Community was no longer camping out, but now lived within the security of the ancient Hebridean sanctuary. The Iona Community, like its leader, was coming in out of the cold.

But what was the restored building to be *for*? It had been built as a sign of the integration of worship and work, and as a place of training for young ministers. Beyond that, what purpose would it serve? For eighteen years, increasing numbers had used the "Prayer of the Iona Community" which had been composed by Ronald Selby Wright:

O God our Father, who didst give unto Thy servant, Columba, the gifts of courage, faith and cheerfulness and didst send men forth from Iona to carry the Word of Thine Evangel to every creature; grant, we beseech Thee, a like spirit to Thy Church in Scotland, even at this present time. Further in all things the purpose of the New Community, that hidden things may be revealed to them and new ways found to touch the hearts of men. May they preserve with each other sincere charity and peace and, if it be Thy holy will, grant that a place of Thine Abiding be established once again to be a Sanctuary and a Light. Through Jesus Christ our Lord, amen.

The place of abiding had now been established. What had not been established was the purpose of the new abiding. "Pray for more light, and follow the light that you see," was an early motto of the Community: more light was urgently needed. In 1956, with the restoration nearing completion, the simple truth is that the Iona Community did not know what it wanted the new building for. George MacLeod pointed out that work on the cloisters would take another two years, and the west range would be rebuilt if a further £15,000 could be raised.

In November 1956 came the news that George had wanted to hear. He had been selected as the next Moderator of the General Assembly of the Church of Scotland.

"About Time Too!" was the headline in one of the daily newspapers, and it summed up the feeling of a good number in the Kirk. George MacLeod could be passed over no longer.

George received the news with unfeigned delight. He said in a later interview that it was the greatest moment in his public life "after being labelled as a Communist, a Roman Catholic, an Anglican, a monk and an escapist."

Why did he not show a more becoming Christian reticence? Because it was not in his nature to dissemble. He was an ambitious man who loved his Kirk deeply. He felt he could do the job as well as any, and better than most. The adjutant had always felt he could do a better job than his commanding officer and, like his Moderator grandfather before him, he wanted to be at the head of everything.

It was not simply a matter of personal ambition and dynastic expectation, however. George exulted in the news because he had been so badly wounded by the Govan Case verdict. He had experienced it as a rejection of his ministry and, for a MacLeod, that was an intolerable blow. The Moderatorial nomination felt like a reversal, a vindication.

It was also, he felt, vindication of his grown-up baby, the Iona Community. His wayward offspring had been declared legitimate in 1951, but there were still those who considered it to be an ill-conceived and ill-mannered adolescent brute. The Moderatorial nomination was perceived by Dr MacLeod to be a celebration of the child's coming of age.

Were they now part of the establishment's toothless menagerie? And had the good Doctor MacLeod been co-opted as tame chaplain-in-residence to the highest royal and ecclesiastical courts in the land?

By the end of December 1956, George and Lorna were on their way to New Zealand. Invited to address the Ecumenical Conference of Youth in New Zealand, he took the opportunity of visiting Community members in America, Australia, India and Italy.

George addressed over 1,000 young people at the Ecumenical Conference, and was encouraged by "that buoyant, quite unchurchy, battalion of roaring but never ribald Christian youth."

Next stop was Dunedin, to stay for a week at the manse of the Rev. James G. Matheson, who was himself to return to Scotland and become an outstanding Moderator of the General Assembly. George was also met at the airport by the New Zealand press, who avidly reported his comments about the Suez intervention (which caused great division among the churches) and his observation that church people were the dullest people in the world because they took no interest in political and international affairs.

The comments were reproduced in the British press, as was news of the controversy caused by George's attack on the New Zealand press for what he saw as right-wing bias. Leader writers denounced his comments, and also his view that New Zealand's immigration policy needed examination.

James Matheson found him "elated and excited" about his nomination as Moderator, and he was in high and hilarious spirits during his stay. James had asked the Dean of the Anglican Cathedral, an Irishman, if George could preach in the Cathedral. He agreed immediately.

"Are you sure it will be all right with the bishop?" inquired the Scots minister, nervously.

"Is George MacLeod not in direct succession from St Columba?" was the immediate answer.

The sermon was a spellbinder, enthralling the Anglican congregation.

Apart from the well-attended public meetings, George insisted on meeting as many Iona Community supporters as possible. He was determined to see one man, whose address he did not have, and not a day passed without him asking his host if he had tracked him down. As on all his trips abroad, George had a list of people to see on behalf of others, and when he got home he would always report back immediately on what he had learned.

As usual, he had particular rapport with young people.

"On the Sunday evening, after two huge church services and many interviews, we had the usual crowd of students and other young people in Knox Manse," James Matheson remembered. "About forty of them sat around our sitting room, George sitting on the floor among them, and he held them in his spell as in answer to their hungry questions he gave them his vision of Church and world, war and peace, Christ and humanity."

Lorna never forgot George's sermon on the seven words from the Cross, which he preached in Bombay. The church was like an oven, and the fans made an almost hypnotic sound as he preached. The sermon became more and more passionate as it moved towards its climax, at which point George raised both hands in the air and shouted, "And the curtain of the temple was rent!" There was a profound silence in the church. The fans had stopped, and it was almost as if hearts had stopped as well.

Australia, Fiji, Calcutta, Karachi, Baghdad, and Rome were all on the itinerary of the seven week trip. George took the opportunity to look up Iona Community members, Associates and Friends, and give them first-hand news of what was happening in Scotland.

When the Almost Right Reverend George Fielden MacLeod, MC, DD stood, with uncharacteristic nervousness, outside the door of the General Assembly of the Church of Scotland on 22nd May, 1957, waiting to be acclaimed as Moderator, his dress incorporated the lace ruffles worn by his great grandfather and the silver buckles of his great uncle; and on the Moderatorial chair was the 140-year-old rug which had belonged to the great Norman. He might well have echoed the words of his grandfather, as he prepared to go to the General Assembly as Moderator, on 18th May, 1869: "I record my gratitude to God for the quiet and comparatively unbroken fortnight I have had, and the measure of good health also given me, and the peace of mind to prepare my long address for the Assembly. I go tomorrow to reach the highest point in my public life . . . Oh, may this be a talent used lovingly, humbly and unselfishly for His glory! Such is my earnest desire."

The approval of the name of the Moderator-Elect was usually a formality: but this was George MacLeod.

In From the Cold

Introducing the new incumbent, the retiring Moderator, Dr R. F. V. Scott, said that when Dr MacLeod left Govan to found the Iona Community, there were many who doubted the wisdom of his choice; there were none then, and there were none now, who doubted his sincerity and courage.

"I think that the Church today would say that Dr MacLeod's choice then has been abundantly blessed. The Iona Community has aroused very great interest throughout the world and has drawn into its membership men and women of many races and many denominations, and I think we all agree it has made a vigorous and telling impact upon the life of the Church of Scotland.

"Dr MacLeod has had a long time to wait before that movement of his was integrated within the framework of the Church itself; he bore that time of solitude very bravely and very courageously, and I am sure the whole of the Church rejoices today that the man we are about to call to be Moderator of the General Assembly has his movement right back in the heart and framework of the Church, and he is himself a real son of the Church of Scotland."

The whole of the Church did not rejoice.

When the officials were invited to call Dr MacLeod in to the Assembly Hall, one of the commissioners, the Rev. J. S. Malloch, a missionary from Ghana, rose to ask that his dissent be recorded.

"Dr Whitley, in his sermon to the Town Council a week ago, was quoted as saying that he felt elections nowadays were not democratic enough," said Mr Malloch. "I agree with him entirely, since with the gentleman at the door and robed for the office, there is no real choice open to any of us, nor any liberty. I regard the nomination as untimely and unfortunate, and I rather think that in view of Dr MacLeod's Episcopal emphasis . . ."

"Are you going to record a dissent?" interrupted the Moderator. "Would you kindly just do so without further remarks."

Enter MacLeod on right to a tremendous ovation.

It was the first time in the history of the united Church that an objection to the incoming Moderator had been raised, and it stunned the Assembly. George MacLeod, used to controversy, took it in his stride.

The background to the objection was that a report was due to be presented to the Assembly by the Inter-Church Relations Committee, under the convenership of Dr Archie Craig, calling on the Church of Scotland to consider taking on board the notion of bishops-in-Presbytery in order to make union with the Church of

England possible. The merest mention of the word "bishop" was a provocation for many sections of the Kirk, and Mr Malloch objected to the fact that the incoming Moderator was on public record as a supporter of the scheme. The proposals had caused enormous controversy, with the *Daily Express* running a vigorous campaign against them. Dr MacLeod was one of the *Express*'s main targets. (A few years earlier, George had been involved with a curious organization called "The Panel of Advocates of the Church of Britain", which sought ecumenical change. Sending a verbose report of its activities to Archie Craig, George had written, "Nothing is more confusing than a long verbal report of what has occurred, but I think if you read the enclosed once, then put a wet towel round your head and read it again, then soak the towel in whisky and suck the edge of it while reading a third time, we will start fairly level when we meet together.")

The Queen's Lord High Commissioner at the Assembly, the Conservative MP the Rt Hon. Walter Elliot, said it was proof of the vitality and vigour of the Church of Scotland that the Church should possess, and the Assembly should have called to its highest place, one of the most challenging personalities among the churchmen of the day.

"It may be said that some men are born Moderators, some achieve Moderatorship, and some have Moderation thrust upon them," he told Dr MacLeod amidst laughter. "After a long struggle against your destiny, it is here fulfilled."

In his reply to the Queen's representative, Dr MacLeod said that his kind references to his ancestors did not embarrass him – "after all, I am in no way responsible for them. Seriously, I believe I owe to them and to God my very fate, and certainly I am persuaded I owe to them my position in this chair today."

Even George's severest critics admitted that he chaired the Assembly with impartiality, grace, generosity and humour. He was in his element in the Moderatorial chair. He would interrupt the proceedings to say: "Now I want the next two contributions to come from elders."

The presentation of the so-called "Bishops Report" was a personal triumph for Archie Craig. The report had its origins in conversations in the 1930s between the Church of Scotland and the Church of England. The World Council of Churches third world conference on Faith and Order at Lund in 1952 had encouraged the churches to work together on the things which they held in common, and only to do separately the things which in conscience they felt they had to do alone. The Lund conference was the symbol of a new, determinedly optimistic ecumenical mood, in which dreams of a united Church were common. The General Assembly of the Kirk had asked for study of "the kind of modification in the two church systems which, in the context of the hoped-for integration of Christendom, might be regarded in the long run to be requisite."

These were heady ecumenical days, in which all things seemed possible. But when the Inter-Church Relations Committee proposals became known – asking the Kirk to take a measure of episcopacy into its system, and the Church of England to incorporate some form of eldership – the reaction in Scotland was furious. By the time the matter came to the Assembly, it was clear that a salvage operation was in order. In a magnificent three-hour performance at the rostrum, Dr Craig persuaded the Assembly to keep the proposals alive, and to send them down to the Presbyteries for further study.

A similar decision was made by the Convocation of Canterbury, and the Archbishop of Canterbury, Dr Geoffrey Fisher, wrote to George: "We all feel the report to have opened a door which, whether we pass through or not, can never again be closed. The open door leads to a strange country by a difficult road. I think all of us felt a special sympathy with our brethren in the Church of Scotland since, from the nature of the report, the country must seem to them more strange and the road more difficult than to ourselves."

Probably nothing was appreciated more than the Moderator's prayers at the beginning of each day. Those who had encountered him only in his more robust and controversial moods were moved by the depth of his spirituality as he lifted the Assembly up to God.

He made sure during the days of the Assembly that he had time for individuals. He restarted the Moderator's reception, and arranged for a busload of people from Community House to come through. He took great delight in introducing young folk and political activists and dropouts to the Lord High Commissioner, bishops and assorted Government officials. Harold Macmillan, the prime minister, seeing George laughing with and entertaining the company on one occasion, remarked to Robin Barbour, George's junior chaplain, with heartfelt sincerity: "He's a really great man, your Moderator."

In his closing address to the Assembly, George delivered a classic *tour de force*. Later published as a pamphlet entitled "Bombs and Bishops", the Moderator set aside neutral chairmanship with relief, and returned to his natural role of passionate advocate. The 1500 commissioners were treated to unforgettable, vintage MacLeod at his searing and soaring best.

Saying he wanted to talk about the two burning issues of the Assembly – what he called "Fusion and Fission", or Unity and the Bomb – Dr MacLeod said the two issues were bound up together. On his recent trip to Asia, he had found that the East was not going to go Christian unless the West moved quicker about Church union and about nuclear weapons.

There was absolute silence in the packed Assembly Hall as he went on: "What I want to confine myself to doing is to ask for two objectives in the coming year: for *patience about Bishops and impatience about Bombs*. And I ask for both in the name of the Lord Jesus Christ."

To describe the quality of bishop-in-Presbytery he wanted to see, Dr MacLeod had, as usual, a story to illustrate what he meant, and to break the tension building up in the hall.

"A general during the war was sitting in a first-class carriage which was quite full, save for one seat. His moustaches could be heard bristling behind a *Daily Telegraph*. Enter a Leading Aircraftman, uncommissioned but dead tired. He swung his webbing on the rack and slumped into the vacant seat. Enter from the corridor a young and whippersnapper Captain. 'Give me that seat, young man,' he said to the aircraftman. 'It's an order'. The order was obeyed: the aircraftman withdrew into the corridor. Then, from behind the *Daily Telegraph*, the steady bristling of the moustache assumed almost the crackle of a forest fire. 'Give that man back his seat,' he said with immense authority. The whippersnapper demurred. 'It's an order,' roared the General. The order was obeyed. The whippersnapper withdrew into the corridor. And out into the corridor came the General. 'Now,' he said to the whippersnapper, 'you take my seat and I'll stand out here.' The crestfallen Captain demurred. 'It's an order,' said the General, and stood outside the rest of the journey.

"That is what is meant by spiritual authority."

To the accusation that not all bishops were like that, he replied that nor were all Presbyters. Just as bishops sometimes got into huddles to fix things, so did people in Presbyteries and committees.

"You see, in this we are not discussing offices at all: but sinning man, be he Presbyter or bishop. What these negotiations are about is something richer than any of us have got – the recovery of the full being of the Church.

"Finally, in our impatience about Bishops, I plead with you, be not led away with the solemnities that these negotiations are untrue to the spirit of the Reformation. The spirit of the Reformers was constantly to be judged, constantly to be changed, by the living Spirit in our midst, urging us for ever to approximate nearer to our Lord."

Turning from bishops to bombs, George argued that the arms race was now out of control, and that nuclear testing was killing babies. He went on: "Let us take the blame. Let me repeat I am not covertly hinting that pacifism is the answer. I am openly demanding that at such a climactic time Churchmen everywhere should know what their answer is and, if it be not pacifism, what is their answer in Christ? The Jews protest, the Japanese protest, German scientists protest and atheist philosophers protest. That is, in all the ambiguities, they choose.

"Too many churchmen neither burke nor back the tests. I have no quarrel with the robust non-pacifist. My quarrel, from this Chair, is with the vast oblong blur of Christian indecision in this, the eleventh worsening year of the Atomic age."

The full-blooded speech was not for the faint-hearted. It was no diplomatic chairman's summing up of the current ecclesiastical consensus, sending the faithful out with good cheer into the warm glow of an Edinburgh evening, but the dividing word of the passionate, obsessive prophet who was convinced that the word welling up inside him and spilling out of the boundaries of human flesh was nothing other than a word from the Lord.

The Rt Rev. George F. MacLeod's year of office was, as expected, a whirlwind of activity and controversy. He preached in many places, including Govan, Balmoral, Polmont Borstal, Winchester, Cargilfield School, Canterbury Cathedral and Liverpool Cathedral. He held a series of youth pilgrimages in different parts of Scotland – an innovation based on the weekly pilgrimage round Iona.

Although George wore the traditional Moderatorial costume with pride because of its family associations, he found it an embarrassment as he went around the country.

"A high proportion of industrial Scotland has long ago decided the Church is 'period piece,'" he commented, "a harmless, even graceful, antique in the midst of streamlined furniture. Large solemn books are being written about communication. Their burden is that we are out of touch with modern man. Is is very wise, in such a setting, to direct the representative of the Church to move about like a ghost from the 18th century, with heavy laces at his cuffs – originally symbols of the class that need not use their lily-white hands?"[1]

At one stage he was going downstairs in Community House, dressed in full Moderatorial regalia, while coming up was a very eccentric lady dressed in complete pre-war Chinese costume (such sights were not unusual in Community House).

"I can't really say anything, can I?" muttered George.

On his visits to five Scottish Presbyteries – Garioch, Deeside, Inverness, Dumbarton and Peebles – Dr MacLeod was harried by the popular Press on his attitude to bishops. The *Daily Express* which distributed 83,000 copies of a pamphlet attacking the notion of bishops in the Kirk, saw the Iona leader as one of the evil forces to be resisted – "The Menace from Iona" he was called. He regularly complained of being misquoted deliberately by the popular press.

He wrote to Lord Beaverbrook, complaining of what he saw as harrassment by the *Express*.

"Are the purposes of our Reforming Fathers really furthered by a constant drip of disapproval falling on the head of the present Moderator temporarily and on the head of the Archbishop of Canterbury perennially?" he asked the Canadian newspaper owner. "By what process of thought is the Moderator's reputation belittled and that of the RC Archbishop of Glasgow never belittled?"

Beaverbrook's reply conceded nothing.

"Of course I am opposed to the scheme for bishops in the Church. It must be recognized that from the Scottish Establishment our Church in Canada derives authority. Therefore, any decision taken at the General Assembly must be of tremendous moment to the Church in New Brunswick."

The row between the Moderator and the popular press erupted when, on a visit to the district of Garioch, in the north of Scotland, he indicated that if the press were present, he would confine his remarks to generalities because of his experience of being repeatedly misquoted. This was interpreted as a ban on the press, and he was attacked in several newspapers.

His exasperation overflowed in a two-column letter to *The Scotsman* entitled "Can No One Do Anything About the Press?" He instanced examples of what he experienced as harrassment and misrepresentation, and said it was useless either to hand out a summary beforehand, or to go over the material with reporters. On matters such as Bishops or the H-Bomb he was misquoted no matter what he said.

The Moderator received a warm private letter of personal support from the Archbishop of Canterbury.

"I applaud your courage," wrote Dr Fisher. "I have suffered at the hands of the *Daily* and *Sunday Express* for a long time. This press has specialized in malice against the Church of England, the Archbishop of Canterbury and anybody who thinks divorce is a bad thing; and all these hates they combine in denigrating remarks about the Royal Family.

"I have refrained from direct attacks upon them, since in a conflict with an enemy which respects no rules of courtesy or truth, one can hardly expect to bring them to apology – but your way may be the better: at any rate I applaud your courage."

Now that the dusts of the controversy have settled, one can only come to the judgment that while George was undoubtedly the victim of a somewhat hysterical campaign – once the troublesome priest had been fingered by Lord Beaverbrook, he was in for the same treatment as others who had the effrontery to raise the press lord's ire – he was oversensitive to the genuine questions arising from the ecumenical proposals. Many people did fear that there was about to be a take-over in the Kirk, and an alien form of church government imposed upon them. The fears were exacerbated by the public hysteria – and the raising of the emotional temperature to ridiculous levels set Christian brother against Christian brother – but that did not mean that the fears were not genuine. Mr Malloch may have been a somewhat cantankerous objector, but the concerns and suspicions of ordinary Church of Scotland members were justified. They feared that their Presbyterian heritage was about to be sold out, and the equivocal statements of some of the leaders of the ecumenical movement in Scotland did nothing to allay those fears. To question the grand ecumenical design was sometimes portrayed as resisting the Holy Spirit, an attribution which provoked rightful indignation.

What is certain is that with MacLeod as Moderator, the Church was seldom off the pages of the newspapers.

Even when he went abroad – to Malta, to address the armed forces, and to Rome, to attend a meeting of the Presbytery of Southern Europe – he was asked about bishops. The same was true in Africa, where he had arrived in February to tour Nyasaland, Northern Rhodesia and Ghana.

In Ghana, he paid a visit to Dr Kwame Nkrumah, the prime minister, in his offices at Christiansborg Castle. There was some talk about church life and church divisions, which set George off on one of his favourite stories about a shipwrecked Scottish seaman alone on a desert island. When he was rescued, the seaman showed his rescuers the little church he had built, then took them round to another part of the island where he had erected another church. Why was it there? "That is the church I don't go to!" said the man.

The story was followed by gales of laughter, until it was noticed that the prime minister was not amused. He had taken it as a barb directed at his own non church-going.

When he went to a mission station in Ghana, the Moderator was presented with a gift of thanksgiving for the ministry of the man who had recently left – the Rev. J. S. Malloch.

George went to Odumase, and preached at a service in the church for the boys of the Presbyterian secondary school in the town, and for the women students on the hilltop above the town. He exuberantly got the boys and the girls competing against each other, singing Ghanaian songs, and they responded well to his extrovert style, swarming around him for photographs. He then had lunch with the fathers of the Church, hilarity mingling with silent, open-eyed wonder at the continuous flow of wit.

Next evening George spoke at a public meeting to which many people travelled great distances. Netta Forman was Principal of the Presbyterian Women's Teacher Training College in Krobo-Adumase at the time, and she has never forgotten the aftermath.

"After this most impressive address," she said, "when the meeting scaled I went into the courtyard alone to wait. And there, sitting on a low surrounding wall, was George MacLeod, by himself, looking the picture of exhaustion and dejection. I withdrew, and have ever since been grateful for the glimpse into the cost of a stimulating address. That picture, complementing the exuberance on the hill-top, I have held since in my prayers for George MacLeod."

To bear the hopes of so many people was a costly, and sometimes lonely business.

On 20th May, 1958 he handed over the Moderatorial reins to Dr John Fraser, thus becoming the Very Reverend George Fielden MacLeod. In his closing speech, he entertained the commissioners by telling them of an incident in an Edinburgh club.

"I passed along the main room and there were two men sitting – I did not know their names – one, I think, was a Major and the other a Colonel, one from Inverness and the other from the Borders. I think that they had resigned their commissions after the Boer War – and I feel it is my duty to record the conversation I happened to hear. One of them said to the other, 'Who is the fellow in the dog collar?' The other answered, 'That is the Moderator.' The first one said, 'The Moderator? I thought he was a Communist,' and the other one replied, 'No, you have got him wrong, he is a Roman Catholic!'

"That simply gives you a clear idea of how I conducted myself during my term of office, and which just goes to show how responsible a journalistic press we have in some of its sections."

On a more serious note, Dr MacLeod drew attention to the fact that the Church of Scotland still had 1.3 million members in a country of just over 5 million people.

"There is certainly no political party or commercial affiliation or trade union congress, no cultural grouping which can numerically touch that or which meets as frequently as does our society – and Christ must know. With such potential to the leaderless nature of our world, what wait we for?"

What indeed. The reality is that the spirit of the age was changing, and that the day when news about the Kirk and the doings of Moderators would occupy columns in the newspapers was about to disappear. The membership of the Church of Scotland was already spiralling into decline. With improved transport, greatly increased leisure facilities and the impact of television, not even the churches in small towns could hold their own.

The modern wind of change which Harold Macmillan detected blowing across Africa was blowing in Britain, too, and the Kirk was ill-prepared for its blasts.

The wind was causing a sea-change, too, in the Iona Community. And its leader didn't like it, didn't like it at all.

20

Winds of Change

When the lives of others are at stake, the prophet does not say, "Thy will be done!" but rather "Thy will be changed".

ABRAHAM HESCHEL

Spontaneous remarks are not worth the paper they're written on.

WINSTON S. CHURCHILL

George MacLeod has a favourite story about an Englishman who owned an estate on Mull. The Sassenach used to be driven crazy by his ghillie's Highland courtesy; he would never contradict anything that was said, no matter the evidence to the contrary. Exasperated, he decided to put the Mull man to the test. The wind was howling, causing white horses on the loch.

"There's not much wind today, Lachie," said the Englishman.

"No," agreed Lachie, "but what little there is is fairly boisterous!"

What little wind there was on Iona was certainly fairly boisterous. The Iona Community was changing.

In its inception, decisions were largely made by the Community's leader, who carried the burden of raising the funds for the project knowing that if he failed, he or his executors would be held liable. The Community had never consisted of 'yes men', but by the nature of things, the man who had risked so much in getting the experiment going had stamped his sometimes overpowering personality upon the whole venture. Moreover, it was not merely some academic or theological decision which had led men to join the Community; for many, a personal encounter with George MacLeod had helped them see more clearly the face of Christ. They would not easily shout down someone who was a living part of their salvation story. Shout him down they sometimes did, though, but it did not come easily.

By the late 1950s, the situation was different – quite different from that envisaged by George when he left Govan twenty years previously. The main phase of the Abbey rebuilding had been completed: the Community had grown to 140 full members, 575 Associates and 5,200 Friends: many minister members were now on their second or third parish, bringing widely differing concerns: the denominational spread of the Community was widening by the year: more and more laymen were joining: women were knocking more loudly on the door: the Community was recognized abroad as a catalyst for change in the Church: at home, many of its concerns were part of the mainstream Church agenda: the Community was old enough to have a history, and big enough to be an institution.

And the natives were getting restless.

The first member to leave the Community had told George that he spelt it wrong: it should be "I own a Community", he said. George's somewhat autocratic, military style fitted very uncomfortably with the increasingly democratic spirit of the age. George MacLeod was never a consensus man; his understanding of leadership was to spell out the vision and lead the men out of the trenches.

But what if they refused to go?

When Jack Kellet joined as a late-entrant minister, he was upset by what he saw as George's arrogance, and told him that he should entitle his next book, "Democratic communities and how to run them". George fixed him with a gaze and said, "I knew I was going to have trouble with you." (Conversely, though, George always admired people who stood up to him: what he disliked was what he conceived to be wishy-washy dithering and confusion.) The stories of the Community deciding one thing and George doing another are legion: of the Community exerting its authority over its leader by voting for a green carpet, and George staying up all night to nail down his favoured red one: of a Community committee making a decision not to appoint someone to a post, then hearing with horror that George had actually told the man he could have the job.

When the adolescent grew up to be a man and challenged his father, feelings were inevitably mixed. George became irritated when a member of the Community telephoned him to ask his permission to send a letter on a political matter to the press – "When will they ever grow up?" was his exasperated comment. He felt burdened by the Community's dependence on him: but that did not mean that he wanted to let the burden go.

Ralph Morton, who had become deputy leader, understood and sympathized with the growing mood much more than George ever did. He was canny, gentle and thorough, yet his slow, unflamboyant simplicity was deceptive. He had a good mind, and indeed was a much better-read theologian than his senior colleague. With roots in the United Free Church tradition rather than the Auld Kirk, he was less clerically minded than George. His concern was to shape a theology for lay people, and to train ministers to work much more co-operatively with the laity. Where George was impatient with detail, Ralph explored issues with great thoroughness. George was brilliant with the big speeches and not so good on questions – which he basically brushed aside, or used as a launching pad for another statement: the gentle Ralph was not a charismatic or exciting speaker, but he had formidable things to say in his quiet, undemonstrative manner. George talked a great deal in visionary terms about politics, but it was Ralph who was interested in the nuts and bolts and unglamorous routine of political action at ward and constituency level.

Ralph was recognized as being a virtuoso of the second string, but this did not mean that such a role was an easy one: in fact it could be maddening. It says a great deal for Ralph's graciousness that he worked with George for more than twenty years. He was the only deputy leader who could possibly have lasted anything like that length of time. He did it because he admired George and his unique gifts, and felt the Community to be well worth devoting his life to. He was supported in this view by the intellectually formidable Jenny, whose devotion to George did not in any way prevent her from striking out in original directions and making a distinctive mark in an essentially male world.

George was sometimes a bit dismissive of Ralph and did not always consult him when he should. He was irritated by his deputy's insistence on seeing all sides of the question. (George used to parody books published by the SCM on "The Problem of . . ." He felt that Ralph belonged in that kind of ambience.)

In many ways Ralph represented the underdeveloped side of George's nature, which is probably why his senior colleague sometimes got so mad at him. It could be hard for a volatile, extrovert, energetic, passionate man-in-a-hurry, who liked to see things in black and white, to work with a phlegmatic, more introverted colleague who questioned certainties and kept advancing alternative lines of thought. George continued to work with Ralph because he respected the man's qualities – and because he needed him. It would be true to say that the two men needed each other in order to get the best out of themselves. Indeed, Ralph in many ways helped to spell out George's vision of what it meant to be "we", and spelt it out in more inclusive terms than George had. MacLeod sketched out the future in glorious poetry: Morton filled it out in practical prose.

Despite the strains in the relationship over the years, it was the members of the Iona Community who were the beneficiaries of this creative leadership team. To this day there are members of the Community who regard themselves as George-men or Ralph-men, but on the whole the Community appreciated the combination of talents and personalities.

What is true is that in the late fifties and early sixties, Ralph was more in touch with and in sympathy with contemporary trends. He was also minding the shop during George's many absences abroad – "Just carry on as if I were dead," he had told his deputy before going off to America – or on official church duty. Consequently, he had much more contact with the new men joining the Community. With the main phase of the Abbey rebuilding complete, George was restless, seeking new fields to conquer. He was happy to entrust to Ralph the running of the Community while he was abroad, or travelling the length and breadth of the country. (Once, when he was asked what he did as deputy leader, Ralph said quietly that he saw what was not being done and did it.)

George MacLeod had plenty to concern him, as his role as a leading figure in the Kirk increased. At the 1958 Assembly, he had successfully persuaded the General Assembly to appoint a special committee to consider Central African interests and report annually until 1962. He said, based on his recent experience, that the Africans were looking to the Kirk to help them.

The Church was increasingly anxious about the Central African Federation, especially as its missionaries reported how little consultation there had been with Africans, and how the Federal parliament was strongly weighted in favour of the whites. When Federation had come into being, the General Assembly had resolved to give it a fair trial, while keeping a watching brief, but their fears had been realized.

"When Federation became law we were implored to give it a fair trial," George MacLeod had told the 1956 Assembly, "so we packed in the organization of protest, and I am still uncertain whether when we packed up we were activated by commendable goodwill or merely throttled by our old school ties."

George was appointed convener of the Special Committee Anent Central Africa. It was to prove to be an exciting convenership. Backed and briefed by Kenneth Mackenzie, the Kirk's foremost authority on African affairs, he did the job with conviction and style.

He also agreed to take on another major convenership – that of the Church Extension Committee. Since the inception of National Church Extension, 140 new churches or hall-churches had been built in Scotland's new housing schemes. The work was very close to the heart of the Iona Community, which had 26 minister members engaged in the work of church extension, and indeed it was largely for that work that the Community had been founded. The Committee had a debt of a quarter of a million pounds to clear off, and it was with that in mind that the successful fund-raiser from Iona had been asked to take the chair which had once been occupied by John White.

As he flew off to the States to represent the General Assembly and preach at the union of the Presbyterian Church of the USA and the United Presbyterian Church of North America, George MacLeod pondered how things had changed. From being the Kirk's wayward son to being Moderator and convener of two key committees was a major shift: while he could hardly be described again as the darling of the Establishment, he seemed to be a man the Establishment could hardly do without.

The period of calm could not, of course, go on. It was shattered by another Iona controversy which was to release tremendous passions, and rally opponents who were deeply upset by the influence of the Iona Community and its leader in the Church.

Just about the most provocative thing George MacLeod could have done in Presbyterian Scotland was to set a statue of the Virgin Mary in the centre of the restored monastic buildings on Iona.

Which is what he did.

The offensive article – the work of the Jewish sculptor Jacob Lipchitz – arrived on Scottish soil on Christmas Day, 1958, and was installed right in the middle of the newly completed cloisters. The heavy bronze statue represented the Virgin Mary emerging from a vast heart formed by a canopy made of three parts of the sky, and held up in the beak of a dove. The back of the canopy carried the legend: "Jacob Lipchitz, faithful to the religion of his ancestors, has made this Virgin for the better understanding of men on earth that the Spirit may reign."

Mrs Jane Owen, from Texas, a descendent of the Scottish socialist and industrial pioneer, Robert Owen, had commissioned Lipchitz to create three identical statues called "The Descent of the Spirit." She had hoped that one would stand in the cloisters of Iona Abbey, if it could be presented by a Scot.

After telling her that the Iona Community were no more than agents for the Trustees of the Abbey, and that any such gift would have to be acceptable and accepted by them, George MacLeod asked her the price. When she said it was £7000, and that she felt sure a Scotsman would give that sum for the Trustees to possess it, George said that if he knew of a Scotsman who would give £7000 to any cause, he would be seeking it for the work of the Iona Community.

"She went sadly away," George recalled, "but returned the next morning to say that if I could find a donor of this statue for the Trustees, she would give £7000 for the ongoing work of the Iona Community. Being human, I became even more interested in her proposition. But being sane, and ignorant in these things, I inquired more widely in the ensuing weeks into the intrinsic worth of the piece of sculpture. It was finally sufficient for me that Sir Kenneth Clark, a lover of Iona, a devoted son of Ardnamurchan and probably the greatest British authority on modern sculpture, commended the artist as quite outstanding and the statue as of lasting significance."

The Trustes accepted the gift in principle, and Sir John and Lady MacTaggart, Presbyterians and art lovers, agreed to put up the money.

Letters of protest poured into the newspapers and to the Cathedral Trustees.

The Rev. J. S. Malloch followed up his Assembly protest with a letter to the Trustees saying that this would lead to violence and worse.

"When Dr MacLeod talks about unity, I find it a glaring hypocrisy," he wrote. "He knows full well that his Roman dreams are confounding the peace and the unity of the Church of Scotland. Over the last twenty years he has talked about unity and made chaos. Nobody known to me has contributed more to disunity by arrogant, selfish ambition. During more than ten years I spent in Glasgow Presbytery he was the troublemaker, determined by every device to plant a Romish pattern on the Church against the will of the vast majority."

Thus were the prevailing winds of controversy fanned.

It was more than the spirit which was descending from the fan. The Iona Virgin became the symbol of what was seen as a Romish plot to take over the Church of Scotland. George MacLeod, already identified along with Archie Craig, his former deputy, with the "bishops plot", was regarded as the Vatican's evil genius. The irony was that George MacLeod, though wanting to recover the truly Catholic aspects of the Faith – and he believed that in this he had the Reformers on his side – was very suspicious of Roman Catholicism, and regarded what he saw as its exclusivist nature with abhorrence. He was described in the Assembly as "the driver of the Rome express", but the notion that George MacLeod was pro-Roman Catholic is part of the mythology, or the Protestant demonology, of the era. He saw the recovery of the Catholic aspects of the faith as a way to outflank Rome, not join it. Many Protestants in Scotland – whom George regarded as having betrayed the Reformers and settled for nineteenth century individualism rather than true Reformed doctrine – saw their position being steadily eroded, and identified George MacLeod as the key culprit. Their protests were made at several Assemblies, and the Iona Virgin was an opportune symbol.

The Rev. Ian Carmichael viewed the Iona Community not just as a Romanist conspiracy but as a Communist plot as well.

"The Iona Community, right since the beginning, before it was an association of this Church – and it is a great pity it was ever brought in – gatecrashed in to the parish of Iona and the Presbytery of Mull without ever referring the matter to the Presbytery or the kirk session," he told the Assembly, "and they have carried on in this independent way; they would prefer to be independent, to use the Church; they use the cover of the Church and of this Assembly to work out their own purposes, and they are trying to control the policy of our Church. They have their representatives in every Presbytery. They work in accordance with the plans of another association which we all know, which is working throughout the world, and instead of being called the Iona Community, some people call it the 'Iona Commune' . . .

". . . I think the time has come when we should bring an end to this association because it is an insidious movement working for its own purposes . . . they are a conceited and arrogant lot . . . and they are continually infiltrating into this committee and that committee, working to a definite policy. They are organized, there is no doubt about it, and they are a danger to the Church."

George MacLeod, enjoying the battle in the way some people enjoy bad health, said that if the Community were guilty of unorthodoxy in any way, it was up to his critics to produce evidence. Replying to allegations by Lord Ferrier of political bias, George said that his Lordship was welcome to come to Community House and join the Christian Conservative Group, of which Lady MacLeod was a member!

The 1959 General Assembly of the Church of Scotland was something of a personal triumph for George. As convener of the Church Extension Committee, he announced plans to attack the debt, breaking the target down to realistic figures for each member. Over a thirty year period, nearly half of the population of Scotland would have moved, and the Kirk had spent more than £3 million on new buildings to cope with the need.

In his speech as convener of the Committee Anent Central Africa, George said that Lord Malvern, editor of the *Central African Examiner*, had accused the Church of Scotland of destabilizing the situation in Nyasaland. The reality was that the events leading up to the state of emergency had been caused by the flaws inherent in the original Federation plans, as the General Assembly had warned.

Proposing a motion that "The General Assembly, recognizing that the time has come for a radical revision of the territorial constitution for Nyasaland, earnestly recommend to Her Majesty's Government that effective power be given to the African community in this land", Dr MacLeod called for the release of prisoners detained without trial.

In one of the most unforgettably eloquent orations ever heard in the Assembly Hall, Dr MacLeod told the packed and expectant house and public gallery that it was no good "lightly crying 'peace, peace' where there is no peace. What we say for the time being is someone must speak for the African. We do not say it to be difficult, we say it because it is the only realistic way to reconciliation.

"Europeans have done marvels for the country, Europeans are essential to the country – all responsible Africans know that perfectly well – but it seems to us that Europeans have plenty to speak for them. We believe that for the time being someone must speak for the Africans.

"Moderator, the ship of State that is the Federation is dangerously keeling over to starboard, and a heavy list is occasioned by the weight of the detainees battened down beneath the hatches of the starboard side. They must be brought up into the fresh air, they must be brought up into the centre of the deck and be divided off either for trial or for hope; only so will the ship of state find a more even keel for the days that lie ahead in 1960.

"At that point, and for the time being, someone must speak for the Africans, and that someone will be the General Assembly of the Church of Scotland."

It was passionate, magnificent, ringing oratory on behalf of the Africans of Nyasaland, and it represented one of the General Assembly's finest hours. Government officials were there for the tense and heated debate. There was an expectant sense of history in the making.

The General Assembly voted in favour of George MacLeod and his committee's radical deliverance. The shock news was headlined everywhere – it had been expected that a more "balanced" compromise would be reached.

The views of the Kirk added to the political pressure on the government. An advisory commission on the review of the constitution of Rhodesia and Nyasaland was established under Lord Monckton.

At the same Assembly, the ill-fated "bishops report" met its end. The Presbyteries had voted overwhelmingly against, and the Assembly decided that "the proposals are clearly unacceptable in that they imply a denial of the Catholicity of the Church of Scotland, and of the validity and regularity of its ministry within the Church Catholic". Archie Craig resigned as convener, feeling that he no longer had a mandate.

In the summer of 1959, the Iona Community celebrated its coming of age with a televised broadcast of the official opening of the restored cloisters, bringing to a completion the original undertaking – free of debt – at a total cost of more than £100,000. The old

Winds of Change

"Rome Express" huts were moved to a site over the road from the Abbey, to begin a new life as a youth camp. An appeal was launched by a new body, the Iona Appeal Trust, consisting of representatives of the Cathedral Trustees and the Iona Community, along with other individual trustees. The chairman of the Trust, the Duke of Hamilton, said that the three-year appeal would be to raise funds to endow the buildings, and to endow some of the island work of the Iona Community.

It had been a decade of incredible activity and achievement, though not without cost. There were times when George experienced the loneliness of a man carrying enormous burdens, and he relied on the emotional support of Lorna, who stood by him in all his troubles. He always appeared confident, and people were rarely allowed to see his more vulnerable side. On one occasion, when Douglas Alexander had driven him up to Fionnphort on Mull, opposite Iona, George, looking across at the Abbey, said that every time he arrived there and looked across, his stomach felt exactly as it did when he was going back to the trenches – though once he was there, there was nowhere in the world he would rather be.

For most people, Iona was a place of calm. For George MacLeod, it was often a place of conflict, of the tightening knot in the stomach. He would often go alone to one of his favourite places – the restored shrine of St Columba – and lift up his troubles to the God he knew to be near, even when He seemed temporarily absent.

Dunsmeorach – the family home across the road from the Abbey – was a great place of comfort and happiness for him, though it was often after midnight before he got over from the Abbey. People wanted to talk with him after the evening service, and he would often finish the day praying with someone in St Columba's Shrine. He made sure that guests and staff were invited over to the house for a drink during the course of the week, and when he unwound in the evening after a hard day, he was hilarious company.

Lorna was a warm and hospitable hostess, though sometimes a little unorthodox. She would miraculously produce supplies – including the odd grouse sent from Balmoral – for unexpected guests, though there was more than one occasion when she crawled under the table on hands and knees to tell her husband to return his bowl of soup as she had run out.

Many distinguished guests and lecturers stayed, or were entertained at Dunsmeorach in the fifties and sixties – Michael Ramsay,

George MacLeod

David Sheppard, Martin Niemöller, F. W. Dillistone, John Wren-Lewis, R. D. Laing, Ernest Southcott, H. H. Farmer, Frank Lake, Sir Richard Acland, Hugh Montefiore, John Collins, F. C. Happold, Ronald Gregor Smith, J. A. T. Robinson, Klaus von Bismarck to name but few. The Dunsmeorach visitors' book reveals the drawing power of the Iona experiment and its renowned leader. Iona, not the easiest of places to get to, drew the great and the humble like a magnet. And when church leaders stayed there, they found themselves sharing in the everyday tasks of the island community with Borstal boys.

Life on Iona in the fifties, when so many people came around and there was no permanent group running the Abbey, was exciting and exhausting. George would often be up late at night writing his sermon – the only time he could snatch in the course of a busy day – under the light provided from batteries charged by a windmill and generator at the back of the house. (Sometimes the hall committee wanted the batteries to light the evening dance in the village, and a compromise had to be worked out.) Then, in the early morning, visitors would have to be seen off at the jetty – "Goodbye, God bless you. There is no joy like unto that of speeding the parting guest!" George was heard to mutter on more than one occasion.

The other early morning activity, of course, was swimming. Frequently he would go across to the Abbey at 7 am and invite people to join him, particularly if he had had a fight with them. He would rap on the door of someone with whom he had had an argument, and shout: "George MacLeod here. To show that I've forgiven you, I've decided to invite you to come swimming with me before breakfast!" Sound of muffled expletives: then George, with guest, would march down to the beach past the fence to the north of the Abbey. He would lumber into the water, throw himself on his back, gasping with the cold, and swim twenty strokes. He would then put his head under the water, claiming that one hadn't been swimming unless one had been fully under. David Lunan, a new member of the Community, once asked him if he was undertaking the early morning exercise for his physical or his spiritual benefit. "Neither," he replied. "Sheer exhibitionism."

George enjoyed playing the fool at the concerts which he ran for years, sitting at the piano and singing his party pieces. He could be particularly humorous with kids. Tom Bogle, a divinity student helping with the youth camps, remembers a group of children playing in the village street, when George approached with Metropolitan Anthony Bloom and an Anglican bishop. Tom lined the squad up quickly on both sides of the road and got them to salute. Without breaking the flow of the intense conversation, George goose-stepped through the ranks of the children, leaving them all in hysterics! That same summer, when Tom had to summon some laggards from Clydebank, George turned to him, and said, "Listening to you, Bogle, reminds me that St Columba's voice is said to have been audible at the other side of the Sound – maybe that's the only thing you and I have in common with him!"

Many people came to Iona, from different parts of the world, at this time simply to be in contact with George MacLeod (though the great man was a little taken aback to be asked in the cloisters by an American lady where Dr MacLeod was buried). To hear him preach or lecture was a special privilege, and there were many who sought him out for a private word about their own suffering, or vocational struggles. He would have a notice pinned to the sacristy door, asking people who wished to speak to him to sign the list. It was invariably full. He was nonplussed one day to see that his wife had booked him for the afternoon!

The weekly pilgrimage – which was started by George as an attempt to find a suitable devotional quiet day for both craftsmen and minister members of the Community – was open to all on the island, and many would follow Dr MacLeod as he bounded energetically round the six-mile hike. The pilgrimage began at the ancient St Martin's Cross in the Abbey grounds, went south to the Marble Quarry and St Columba's Bay, moved back up the island to the Machair (common grazing ground) for lunch, then northwards to the Hermit's Cell and the top of Dun I – the highest point on the island with a marvellous view of the Inner Hebrides – before finishing in the ancient graveyard of the kings. At each point, George would lead a meditation based on the significance of the stopping place. The Iona pilgrimage was renewing and reinvigorating – island beauty, conversation among people of many nationalities and backgrounds, and uplifting worship combining to make it a memorable experience of physical and spiritual journeying.

The 1950s and 1960s were the times of the great radio and television broadcasts from Iona. George's unique gift for the telling quip or story helped the sermon stay in the mind. Some of these were humorous; he told of a youth camper coming out from the Abbey church saying he liked the service but he didn't think much of the spasms (Psalms)! Another was of an ill-equipped voluntary Abbey guide talking about "The McDonald and Child" at the centre of St Martin's Cross. The quips were usually thought-provoking – "The trouble with extempore prayer is that it is a great strain on the memory", he would say.

George's aphorisms were not extempore, they were practised. When a BBC producer asked him to begin one of his broadcasts in such a way, George responded, "Does that damned man not realize that one of these quips takes me three hours? He thinks they come off the top of my head."

One of the BBC's senior producers, Stanley Pritchard, is in no doubt about George MacLeod's standing as a broadcaster.

"In my thirty years of religious broadcasting," he reflected, "working with thousands of ministers of all denominations, I would put George top of my list of effective communicators. He gave so much time to the preparation of every broadcast, no off-the-cuff for him. Even in his Moderatorial year he set aside special time to prepare for the many broadcasts required of him. Everything that he said on the air was prepared and written down, then in rehearsal he would underline words for emphasis, note pauses and hesitations, mark inflections, until the pages became almost unreadable. Yet the final delivery suggested the spontaneous urgency of one who spoke without notes. His was an art that hid art."

Occasionally during the summer, George would take members of the family in trips across Mull in their old car (which had a diesel engine specially fitted to it for ecological reasons). He delighted to show his son, Maxwell, the old houses of Mull, especially the last inhabited black house. He was appreciative of the Celtic knowledge of the Gaels, and taught the family to respect it.

Some of George's visits to Mull were on Community business. He would walk down to Camas on a disputed right of way. The owners of a hotel at the top of the path had fierce dogs, which quite often frightened off the local salmon fishermen. The wife of the owner would come rushing out with the dogs and a conversation would ensue:

"Ah, Dr MacLeod, how nice to see you. Do come in for a drink."

"No thank you, I'm walking to Camas. This is the road to Camas."

Winds of Change

"Dr MacLeod, please wait. I'm sure my husband wants to speak to you."

"Tell him to walk over to Camas. There's an established road between this house and Camas."

Exit MacLeod, striding grimly down the track.

At the end of each season on the island, George would go alone to St Columba's Shrine to thank God for the summer work, and offer up what lay ahead. On the car journey through Mull, he would sing songs at the top of his voice, obviously relieved to have another summer behind him. His exuberance was powerful. He would insist that everyone in the car would sing one song – a terrifying experience for young students who were being given a lift.

"I've been travelling this road for many years," he would say almost ritualistically between songs, "and I can honestly say that I've never seen the Highlands looking so seraphically beautiful."

The car would be lifted by nets on to the *Lochinvar* steamer. Breakfast on the steamer was a special treat – a full Highland breakfast served by staff who always had a story they were saving specially for Dr MacLeod.

On one occasion the car broke down near Oban, and they had to put up for the night in a croft house. The old lady who owned the house was a great fan of Dr MacLeod's through his broadcasts, and she confided to him that she was worried about her son, who was a bit of a lad-about-town.

"It was quite magical to watch him working on that young man," Maxwell MacLeod remembers. "Every time the kid came into the room with his hat on, Father would flick it off his head and beat him round the shoulders with it, making the young man roar with laughter. They formed an immense bond within hours. Quite simply, Father became a father figure to him within hours, and I remember going to bed with a lamp and hearing them talking long into the night in the room below. It wasn't sermonizing. Father listened with immense sympathy to the young lad saying how the simple croft was dull, and he congratulated the lad on how well he was looking after his mother.

"The following morning the car was fixed, and off we went. The old lady charged us ten shillings for lodgings. The young boy looked like a changed personality, shaking Father by the hand as an equal, and finally receiving a whack on the shoulder with the cap that had been whipped off his head!"

Then home to 4 Park Circus Place, Glasgow. George would work, like his father before him, in the Victorian gentleman's smoky den, pounding away at the typewriter with two fingers. Maxwell remembered his father as not having the same *joi-de-vivre* in Park Circus Place as he did on Iona.

"The crisis rather than the joy of the Iona Community seemed to permeate that room," he recalled.

George was not always a hero in his own household. Lorna used to chide him for not spending enough time with the children – saying that he had more time for Borstal Boys than for his own children. George was shamed by these observations. In a sermon on forgiveness, he remembered an incident involving his daugher, Mary.

"I was busy. I was writing letters. I was self-important. My little daughter was going to school that morning for the first time. She came into my room, in her first school uniform. I was busy. I was writing letters. I said, 'Your tie is not quite straight.' Then I looked at her eyes. She wasn't crying. She was unutterably disappointed. She hadn't come for tie inspection. She had come to show she was going to school for the first time. A terrific day. And I let her down. What is that bit in the Gospel . . . whosoever shall offend against one of these little ones . . . better for a millstone to be tied round his neck and that he be cast into the sea. I ran downstairs. I said all the right things. I crossed the road with her. I went to school with her. I had missed the moment, missed the point. I will always see those eyes. Sometimes when I am very busy. Sometimes when I am writing letters. I am forgiven, but I won't forget."[1]

Maxwell was at Cargilfield, like his father before him – indeed his father was a Governor of the school. When Father came to watch his son dodge the ball at cricket, he had to retire to the car because it reminded him so much of himself at that age.

Father entertained the children while mother disciplined them. Park Circus Place was not always happy for Lorna, since it was now in the midst of a commercial area with no neighbours. George was away a great deal, and she had to handle the family crises, as well as dealing with the incessant stream of tramps at the door.

Lorna put up with it, and with the journeys alone to Iona with two children in the car, because, as she put it, her husband was a very great man, and great men were different. George loved his wife and family and was remorseful when reminded of his neglect, but the hectic life continued.

On Christmas Day, 1959, a third child, Neil David, was born.

"Neil David (he being by adoption, we trust, of the House and Lineage of David) keeps his hands raised in a Celtic benediction which augurs well," the proud father wrote to Penry Jones, who had jokingly suggested the name Noel. "We thought of Nicholas but found, in a dictionary, that he was odd. Noel somehow sticks.

"To my surprise I did not mind whether it was to be a boy or a girl. But on Christmas Eve Lorna announced that if it was a girl she wanted it called *Abigail*. So I prayed hard for a boy, raising at that late hour *the whole Problem of Miracles*, as the SCM would say."

Within a month, George was on his way to America again.

21

Visions of Angels

There can be no resistance to the ruler without resistance to God.

JOHN CALVIN

To which party must Godly persons attach themselves in the case of a religious nobility resisting an idolatrous Sovereign?

JOHN KNOX

When George MacLeod got on the aircraft for a two-month lecture tour, he was glad to leave behind him the controversy over bishops which had continued to dog him.

Brigadier Bernard Fergusson had taken him to task for being "too concerned" with bishops. Describing this as the unkindest cut of all, George said that the Iona Community was divided about the approach to the question.

"As for myself, dear heart," he addressed his doughty opponent, "when the proposals were first canvassed by the Inter-Church Relations Committee of the Church of Scotland, before seeing the light of day, I was the only man on the Committee who articulated the belief that it could not do for Scotland, and urged instead an examination of the South India or North India scheme. In them the validity of our orders are not questioned, all simultaneously submit to a mutual re-ordination for all from each, and the bishops, recovering a pastoral function instead of a Big Business status, are subordinate to the General Assembly who can appoint OR DIS-PENSE WITH such bishops as they have appointed."

George was also involved in public disputation in *The Times* newspaper with the Archbishop of Canterbury. Dr MacLeod claimed that in a previous article Dr Fisher had "elucidated episcopacy as of the essence of the Church" and that this "insistence" would split the Church of England from top to bottom.

In a private letter to Dr MacLeod, the Archbishop said that he had misunderstood what he was trying to say. He said he had pointed out from the ordinal the historic ground on which the Church of England rested its case – that the three-fold ministry of bishop, priest and deacon flowed from apostolic times and had continued ever since: that the ancient churches also supported the same principle: and that all planners of church reunion since 1927 had also accepted the three-fold ministry, chiefly because of the historic link it provided with the Church of the earliest days.

"I concluded *not* that episcopacy was of the essence of the Church, but that it was for the Church of Scotland to show cause why it need no longer be regarded as *requisite for progress* in Church Unity. Knowing the sensitiveness of the Church of Scotland to any suggestion that they are in an inferior position, I declared that the Church of England and the Church of Scotland stand *on an equal footing* in the Church of Christ, quoting St Paul. I could hardly have said more clearly that episcopacy is NOT a *sine qua non* within the Church of Christ."

Saying that there was no reason why Episcopacy and Presbyterianism and Congregationalism could not be synthesized in a united Church, Dr Fisher went on: "The Church of Christ I should like to describe as a circle. It is perfectly easy *inside* that circle to draw squares; and in certain respects the Churches within the Church are separate squares within the one Circle of the Church. Your problem of squaring the circle only arises from your mis-statement of what I had said!

"You say that the problem of elucidating the place of episcopacy would split the Church of England from top to bottom. But we have been openly engaged on the problem with other Churches for many years past and have both learned and taught much in the process. This is a kind of race in which no Church ever wins. Only the Holy Spirit wins. You say that if episcopacy is 'requisite', only one has won the race. Who is that *one*? The Church of England? Or the Anglican Communion? Or the Church of South India? Or the theologians who produced the Anglo-Scottish report? Or who? If only *one* has won the race, perhaps it might after all be the Holy Spirit who has won. At any rate, I said in my letter, there is a *case* for episcopacy so deeply established that it does not need to be insisted upon but only to be examined and re-examined.

"However, the point of this letter is only to make clear to you that you attributed to me a statement that I did not make, and then built your argument on this false foundation. I have no hesitation in signing myself – Your friend and humble Episcopalian, Geoffrey Cantuar."

In his reply, George did not go as far as addressing the Archbishop as "dear heart", but he said it was nice of him to trouble to write a personal letter. He thanked Dr Fisher for clearing up the misunderstanding, and said that if he had written as clearly to *The Times* as he had to him, he would not have written in the way he had!

"Resultingly, if episcopacy could be referred to as one of the requisites in a new triangular shape of things to come, with Presbyterianism and Congregationalism as two other requisites," he wrote craftily, "the whole viewpoint in the North and in English Noncomformity could be revolutionized."

George not only loved to cross swords. This correspondence, like countless others with those of rank, or the merely rancorous, shows again his dogged consistency and incorrigibly Reformed principles.

The visit to the States was as hectic as expected. This time, it was a speaking tour of fifteen universities in Virginia, Missouri, Ohio, Massachusetts, New Jersey, Connecticut and Oklahoma. As usual, there was tremendous interest in what he had to say, and the conversations with students bore fruit in terms of vocations.

He visited his predecessor as royal chaplain, Rev. David Read of Madison Avenue Presbyterian Church, New York. It was through him that George was invited by his famous parishioner, Thomas J. Watson, founder and chairman of IBM, to visit him in his office. At one point during their chat, Mr Watson pressed a button, and a microphone suddenly popped up on his desk. Mr Watson said into it: "Good morning all! I have with me here in my office the Reverend Sir George MacLeod of the Church of Scotland, who I have asked to tell you about the wonderful community he has founded on the Hebridean island of Iona . . ." In every office and factory of IBM throughout the USA, all the workers, blue and white collar, stopped work to listen to George's impromptu talk!

He took the opportunity to go to Union Theological Seminary and look up Douglas and Joyce Alexander, whose wedding ceremony he had conducted. Douglas, who had been warned by the great Professor William Barclay of Glasgow University not to join the Iona Community because half the parishes in Scotland would thereby be closed to him, was something of a "favourite son" of the Iona leader; indeed, George saw in him the beginning of the second generation of Iona Community ministers, and hoped that some day he would be leader of the Community. Douglas had earned full marks as guestmaster during the Queen's visit, and had often been invited by George to share in important moments of the Community's life.

Douglas had had an invitation to do a specialist ministry in the Virgin Islands, and George, who knew the place well, built up a picture of the sun-drenched islands.

"If you decide to go, write to me and tell me what it's like," he said to the younger man, "and at the foot of the letter, submit your resignation as a member of the Iona Community."

He was joking, wasn't he? (When Douglas eventually became minister of Bishopton – George tried to get him to go to Canongate Kirk – the Iona leader wrote to him: "You have a great, and I hope costly, ministry before you.")

Not long after his return from the States, George was embroiled in fresh controversy at the General Assembly of the Church of Scotland. His stunning victory over Central Africa the previous year had caused a strong reaction; it was as if people had woken out of a hypnotic trance to find they had voted against all they held dear. Their feelings were summed up by Brigadier Fergusson: "I wish, fathers and brethren, that I could inject you all – give you an injection against the most glorious eloquence of Dr MacLeod."

The old spellbinder's rhetoric did not work this time: his opponents kept pinching themselves into consciousness to make sure they did not succumb on this occasion. He praised the prime minister's "wind of change" speech, and paid tribute to Mr Iain Macleod, the new Colonial Secretary, whose actions – such as releasing Dr Banda and fellow detainees – had "given a message of hope to the whole continent."

Since Iain Macleod was regarded as a traitor by many in the Conservative Party, this was, perhaps, not the most tactful thing to say.

Dr MacLeod's critics were helped by a speech by Dr R. H. W. Shepherd, a respected missionary from South Africa, who had been peeved because he had been back in Britain for eight months before becoming a member of the committee – and even then it was at his own suggestion.

Moving an amendment which deleted the most radical sections of the report, Dr Shepherd said the Committee's reports were too full of invective, and were extremist propaganda. He then went on to launch a not-very-veiled attack on the convener.

"It does not improve the position that some advocates for the Committee so often profess to be pacifists. Pure-bred pacifism many of us can appreciate. Pure-bred belligerency we can understand. But this unpredigreed mongrel mixture of belligerency and pacifism is, to say the least, extremely confusing."

Dr Shepherd, free of course from the taints of either pacifism or belligerency, moved in for the kill. He criticized George MacLeod's "Someone must speak for the Africans" refrain which provoked a great deal of criticism in the Press after the previous year's assembly.

"It is the true function and privilege of the Church," he said, "to be a reconciling force among all classes of men, and that we can never be if amidst the warring classes we are always espousing the interests of only one, and in our pacifism constantly kicking one another in the shins."

Dr Shepherd's amendment was seconded by the Duke of Hamilton, chairman of the Iona Appeal Trust.

George's view was that when men were oppressed and denied rights because of their colour or race, the establishment of justice was a biblical precondition for reconciliation. In this he was talking theology, not politics, though he was continually accused of "bringing politics into the Church". When he lost the vote, he was deeply disappointed, feeling that the Church was letting the Africans down by speaking in more muted tones.

The Assembly vote gave some small comfort to the beleaguered Sir Roy Welensky, prime minister in the Federal parliament, who argued at the conference on the future of the Federation at Lancaster House in 1960 that a multi-racial system would develop in the course of time. In this view, he hardly had any African support, as the tide of African nationalism became unstoppable.

George provoked fresh controversy with an article in *The Glasgow Herald*, which brought him into conflict with the chairman of his own Appeal Trust.

He had been invited by the *Herald* to write an article celebrating 400 years of the Reformation. What he wrote caused fury among traditional Protestants. His main point was that it was not adequate any longer to try to re-create the Reformation.

"There are those who seem to wish to do so," he wrote. "They long for a Restoration. They would recover the old Confessions;

reinstitute a catechism; rewrite the Tablets, even revert to six-teenth-century architecture. But such a re-creation, superficially laudable, is, in fact, idolatry. Idolatry is not essentially the worship of a statue (in Iona or anywhere else!) Idolatry is essentially the worship of a static God . . . Our God is a God that moves. The paradox of his changelessness is that He is in constant motion. The sixteenth-century Reformers knew this. One of their mottos was 'A Reformed Church is forever to be reformed'. Thus, to be true to them is to be imbued with the same Spirit that informed them. It is, like them, to be concerned only with how to make God living and relevant to one's own age."

Arguing that most reforms had come, not because the Church had wanted them, but because of inexorable pressure from outside, Dr MacLeod said that it was more fruitful to look at the modern environment to see what it was saying than to look at the Reformers' insights and to try to recover them. What was required, he said, was a new doctrine of man, in the face of growing modern technology, and a new doctrine of the unity of mankind in the face of international chaos. This would require to be complemented by unity in the Church, since only the reconciled would be listened to by a world needing reconciliation.

John Knox, he said, was not a denominationalist. He was not a Protestant over against Catholicism: he believed himself to be a Catholic Christian, and regarded Rome as a deviation.

So far, so polemical. Then came the dynamite, as he turned to "that damned bomb".

"As we watch, appalled, its ever-gathering strength and its unimaginable lethal potential, we may come nearest, in terms of our day, to the biggest problem that was theirs – namely, when is it God's purpose that his people should rebel against lawful authority? This for years was John Knox's great agony . . . We all know what his final answer was. Today we claim it was his greatness to rebel and usher in the new day.

"Unless the 'sovereignty of the monstrous regiment of the damned bomb' is annulled soon, may it be that the real celebration of the Reformers will be seen in the witness of those who, for the freedom of men and, indeed, for the continuance of civilization, unilaterally rise up against the possibility of its use? High treason? Yes indeed. And was not Knox a traitor?"

John Knox a traitor! Rise up against the damned bomb! High treason! All in the name of the Reformation!

The number of coronaries over tea and toast is not on record:
certainly a considerable number of people were reduced to incoher-
ent rage by the Very Reverend Chaplain to Her Majesty the Queen,
who seemed to be advocating sedition – and all in the sacred name
of the Protestant Reformation. The Duke of Hamilton's rebuke
was one of the milder ones.

"May I have your assurance that you will not at any time use the
Iona Appeal as a platform for such a line of argument?" he wrote
to Dr MacLeod immediately. "Were this Appeal to become in any
way interpreted as presenting treason as a Christian alternative in
the world of today I am afraid I should no longer be able to
associate myself with it."

George had, on his own admission, a disturbed night before he
penned his reply. It is a classic document. It gets to the heart of
George MacLeod's burning concerns, as he wrestles with a fellow
old school tie man over things that matter deeply to him. If
anything explains George MacLeod's love-hate, embattled relationship with the Scottish religious and political establishment of the
time it is this letter.

He told the Duke that the much-needed reforms in Africa had
often been initiated by Christians, who had been denounced as
Communists by Dr Shepherd and others. Then he went on to the
nuclear arms race:

"The best remark of Assembly Week came neither from the
Queen, nor the Lord High Commissioner nor the Moderator. It
came, as it has so often come in Scottish history, from an auld
buddy in the High Street. She said to the beadle at St Giles: 'It's a'
fine enough: *but the flood is no' runnin' deep enough.*'

"What is the Spirit saying to the Churches? The British Council
of Churches recently had an international commission on the
Church and War today. They concluded the best thing for Britain
was to increase her conventional forces while still manufacturing
the Bomb. Such may be the political answer but, dear God, is that
all the Church has to say at this hour? If so, the Church has lost
Labour, lost the colonies, and lost Western civilization.

"Has the Church nothing to say about non-violence? Has the
Cross nothing to say about it? Or is the Cross just about a personal
transaction? If so, could we stop talking about a Christian West
and just get on with the arms race and have done with it?"

The passionate letter concluded with a plea to the Duke.

"My interpretation may be wrong. I am prepared to listen to any argument by a theologian, a layman, or to any auld buddy in the High Street as to what the alternative CHRISTIAN answer is. I look for it everywhere but cannot find anything that does not boil down to the BCC view as above. Everyone is so conscious of its complete bankruptcy as a church pronouncement that, so to say, while 'non-entity' confronts us, we prefer to discuss whether the Communion Table should be at the end or in the middle of the Church.

"Now to come to the point (and you will be relieved to hear this letter has a point), are you prepared to continue to sponsor this Appeal?

"I do not want you to go out, not because of money but because of you. You are as frustrated by our world as I am. Do you want to have a movement in our midst that will not let this vast issue continue going by default? The one thing that matters is that the Church should speak at the right time. I do not think the time is obvious: else I would not have refused Bertrand Russell.

"I want a movement in the midst that is determined to grapple with the New coming up and that might still carry the main Church with it. The movement is the Iona Community. If that sounds egotistical I don't care a damn. I have prayed for years for a better movement to turn up that would say and do it better. But it just is not here.

"By accident I am its leader. By accident you are an important Sponsor.

"Do you think I have not groaned and grunted for years as to when to say what? I cannot release you from groaning and grunting about what I say and when. I will not make you happy. I am not at all happy myself. No one has a right to be happy. But in the light of what I have written, is it worth your going on groaning and grunting? I sincerely hope it is."

The Duke of Hamilton stayed. Groaning and grunting.

Behind the dispute lay the dramatic rise of the Campaign for Nuclear Disarmament, which caused deep concern among political and military leaders. Founded early in 1958, CND called on the British government to renounce nuclear weapons unilaterally, as an example to other nations. It quickly became a mass movement, able to mobilize thousands of people on to the streets for marches and demonstrations. George was delighted by the rise of the movement, of which he was a founder member.

As with any popular coalition which experiences immediate

success, deep divisions over tactics soon appeared. Many signed-up members were people of moderate political views who simply felt that the nuclear arms race was spiralling dangerously out of control, and a halt was necessary. Others sought more revolutionary goals, and saw the campaign as a way of precipitating fundamental political change in the country.

Those in CND who felt that street marches would achieve little, argued for stronger resistance. The Committee of 100 was set up, consisting of prominent persons who were prepared to cause obstructions at nuclear bases, and generally engage in civil disobedience to highlight the nuclear threat. Bertrand Russell, who had a great admiration for George – "How MacLeod came to where I am, by means of a dour Presbyterianism, I'll never know," he remarked with bewilderment – wrote to him asking him to be one of the main sponsors of the new approach. George declined, not because he was against breaking the law under any circumstance, but because he felt that the spiritual ground had not been prepared, and the tactic would simply cause division. In the meantime, he spoke at rallies and demonstrations with an enthusiasm which did not endear him to many senior churchmen, especially as CND was often labelled as a Communist organization.

Early in 1961, George was back in USA and Canada, this time on a two-month fundraising tour on behalf of the Iona Appeal Trust. He was featured in *Time* magazine, and was followed around by the press, who wanted to know his views on disarmament.

The Duke of Hamilton would not have been pleased by the publicity, but he might have been reassured – or confused – by George's decision to send Maxwell to Gordonstoun public school.

When George was challenged about the decision by his old Tory friend, Peter MacEwen, who asked mischievously if he was sending his son to the local school, George replied: "Good heavens, no. I tried getting him into Winchester, but the queue of Labour peers trying to get their sons in before they destroy the school was too long."

He would always say simply that it was "the done thing" – a strange reply from a man who spent a good part of his life challenging "the done thing".

George did not spend all his time on the streets. The Church Extension work also took up a great deal of his time. He wrote a personal letter to every minister in the Church of Scotland, and enthused the 150 "key men" he had recruited to look after every region. He ran it like a military campaign. His secretary, the Hon. Marista Reith, daughter of Lord Reith, kept tabs on the performances of each congregation, and George himself visited many Prebyteries to drum up support. He communicated the need for new churches in the housing schemes with characteristic enthusiasm.

He also launched what he called "The Laymen's Appeal". Lunches were hosted in big houses, and prominent businessmen were invited to attend. A minister of a church extension charge usually spoke, and George painted the overall picture. Then, before he left town, he wrote a letter to each of the guests asking them to support the Appeal.

The upshot of all the effort was that the Church Extension Committee's debt was completely wiped out by the time George retired as convener at the 1961 General Assembly. Whatever his critics felt – and some didn't know whether to laugh or cry – no one could ever accuse George MacLeod of not giving heart and soul to his beloved national Kirk.

His old friend Archie Craig, Moderator in 1961, was loudly applauded when he said of the retiring convener: "I used to think he had a certain magnetic quality that money flowed to as steel chips flow to a magnet, but I discovered that he has got a passionate love for Scotland, a passionate love for the Church, and an uninhibited and unsparing self-devotion to these purposes."

The Hon. Marista Reith, now married to the Rev. Murray Leishman, recalled the heady days of the Church Extension campaign.

"Church Extension was a very romantic thing at the time," she said. "George could be outrageous. He thrived on aggression, given or received. Before any big meeting, he would pick out those he knew would be most hostile, and it was amusing to see them melt! There would be great guffaws about it afterwards. He knew exactly what he was doing.

"He used to dread the committee meetings at the Church of Scotland headquarters. They were very defeatist. He felt the committee was not just overdrawn in cash, but in belief in the future. Yet he managed to enthuse the key men he had appointed in each region, and they got caught up in his vision. He used to tell them that if Boots the Chemist were to open up a new branch every month, it would be hailed as a miracle of business achievement – yet the Church was doing just that."

Marista got on well with George because, she believes, as daughter of Lord Reith, she was on familiar territory. Both were towering, energetic, authoritarian men of action, who had been rivals from an early age.

"They would never have admitted to the rivalry – they were too much of gentlemen to do that," said Marista, "but it was seething below the surface. They were not close; they were too much alike.

"My father was disconcerted by George. Once, my parents went to stay with George and Lorna on Iona, and my father left on the early ferry in the teeth of a howling gale, with some relief. The storm in the Sound was nothing compared to the storm in Dunsmeorach!

"My father was essentially a pragmatist, not an ideas man. Ideas that had to be debated threw him a bit, and when the sheer force of George MacLeod's character banged up against his, the results were interesting.

"George had a total commitment to the Church, but my father, who had been over-exposed to the Church as a child, sat very loose to it. George wanted him to come to some kind of stated position about it, and the tension rose. My father interpreted it as a threat – moving into an area in which he felt intensely insecure. George cut right through his ambivalence. They were enormous men with huge similarities and acute differences. That is what made the electricity."

George admired the BBC Governor's high standards, but he could see the dark, undesirable effects the tortured and crotchety Calvinist could have on his nearest and dearest. Reith tried to prevent his daughter marrying, and George, who conducted the ceremony, was influential in persuading him to attend the wedding.

The 1961 General Assembly was not an entirely happy time for George MacLeod. Four days before the event, he resigned as convener of the Committee Anent Central Africa because he was not allowed to present a minority report making more radical proposals than the official report offered.

He had been deeply disappointed by the previous year's Assembly decision to cut major parts of the report, and he felt there was a concerted attempt in the committee to muzzle him. His decision to resign caused fury, and one of the committee members, Dr Melville Dinwiddie, made a strong attack upon him, saying that

George MacLeod as convener "had been the problem right from the start". He went on:

"When the purpose of our committee was defined as a watchdog for the Christian angle on affairs in Central Africa and not a prejudiced mouthpiece for one side or the other, our convener registered his disagreement, and wanted to continue to hit the headlines and dramatize the situation. It is for the Assembly to decide whether the committee has presented a reasonably balanced report, and when we remember that the membership includes a former Lord High Commissioner, the wife of another former Lord High Commissioner, an ex-Moderator and two ex-governors of African colonies, one can only conclude that 'We're a' wrong but oor George!'

" . . . The reaction in this country will range from childishness to heroism, but I'm greatly concerned about the effect in Africa . . . If the convener had wanted to increase tension in that part of Africa, he couldn't have found a better way of doing it than by such an unnecessary and irresponsible action."

George might have been flattered by such an exaggerated view of his ability to influence events in Central Africa, but he was unabashed. He strode to the rostrum to propose an addendum to the Committee's report, in the form of an appeal by the General Assembly to white Europeans in Central Africa to demonstrate their awareness of change and thus make possible a "continuance of their great contribution to the common good of any new association in that land." He said Europe was to blame for the mess in Africa, having carved it up, with the Church tagging along. Now they had come to a crevasse, and only the spiritual could bridge it.

" . . . We must plead with the white, but still dominant, minority, on bended knees, in mutual shame plead with the whites to demonstrate their awareness of the radical change in the new environment and thus make possible a new association that still could be a guiding light to all Africa south of the Equator. And thus give the Church time, the whole Church – European and African, Assemblies, hierarchies, convocations – to retool, to fashion its ambulance stretchers into trusses for the bridge which only the spiritual can now create."

His great adversary, Professor James Pitt-Watson, now made his way to the rostrum – to second George MacLeod's addendum!

"I seldom have listened to a speech by Dr MacLeod when I

found myself entirely in agreement with him,' he told the Assembly, "but he always contrives to make me unhappy for my own good."

The result: victory for George MacLeod, and absolute fury among his opponents, especially in the Committee Anent Central Africa.

Was his act of resignation a childish decision? George MacLeod was certainly a stubborn man who liked to get his own way, but he knew the knives had been out for him ever since his unforgettable, unforgivable victory in 1959. He believed deeply that justice for the Africans in Nyasaland was not a fit subject for compromise, nor for a 'balanced' report. Almost all of the report he agreed with, but it did not go far enough and he felt he had to speak. To resign as convener and successfully propose a more radical motion was seen by some as foul play. To others, it was a gamble, bravely and brilliantly achieved – Courage, Brother – for the sake of others in their night's darkness. George's motion was certainly more in tune with what was actually happening in Central Africa, as the Monckton Commission reported that the strength of African feeling was such that the Federation could not be maintained.

George failed to be elected Rector of St Andrews University. He was less than keen initially to stand, and told his sponsor, Tom Bogle, that if he had a chance of winning he would let his name go forward. Tom invited him to meet his committee – "most of whom owed me favours and didn't know him, and he enchanted them with songs, his cape and crook, his vision, his pacifism and his concern about universities" – but he failed to captivate the whole student body. (George's interventions in party political terms were not generally successful. When he spoke in support of Penry Jones's candidacy on the Labour platform at Haddington, he told the local citizenry how marvellous it was they were receiving the Glasgow overspill! It was not a vote winner.)

In the Spring of 1961 he was off again to America, Canada, New Zealand, and Australia, this time on a fund-raising trip on behalf of the Iona Appeal Trust. Since its inception two years previously, the Appeal had gathered in £53,000. The trip brought in another £10,000, with promises of more, and George managed to look up many friends of the Community.

The rebuilding programme on Iona went on apace in 1961 and 1962. The restored Michael Chapel was dedicated by the parish minister, the Rev. Dr David Stiven, who regularly worshipped with the Community. The chapel, on late Celtic foundations, was restored by virtue of gifts from South Africa and Ghana.

The final restoration of the chapel was of great significance for George. In the mid-1950s, before the Community moved out of the Rome Express, George had stood in the washrooms looking out at the chapel ruins – where the rubbish bins stood – observing that it would not be long until the chapel was restored.

"But where then will we keep the bins?' asked Douglas Alexander, shaving beside him.

"You are a Glaswegian," responded George. "Only a Glaswegian could respond like this when we're talking about the recovery of a medieval chapel."

Then George added, "Maybe you're right," and carried on shaving.

Douglas reflected later: "He was saying that maybe, after all, we should be content, because there was still a long way to go. I simply wasn't aware of the extent of his vision – very few people were."

George MacLeod was delighted to have a chapel dedicated to the Archangel Michael, since he believed in the presence of angels. They were a sign, he believed, of the ultimately personal nature of all reality.

"Men do not speak of angels today," he wrote, "but is it not significant that, in common parlance, we have been forced again to speak of *demons?* We begin to chant again 'demonic' of men and of hidden powers. We begin to cringe faithless before powers that cannot be plumbed in the depths beneath or clearly plotted in the heavens above. Equally we begin to fear the unknown in the marvels around us: fearful of atomic principalities that can not only blast a hillside but render dead the embryonic child in the womb of a mother as she walks to work. We are all girt about with powers as frightening if they become our masters as they would bring us light most glorious were they kept our servants."[1]

The ultimate horror for George MacLeod was the notion of a mechanistic, supposedly "neutral" universe being manipulated by amoral technocrats, serviced by unfeeling representatives of a "private", individualistic religion. For him the created order was alive, filled with the Personal. Detached manipulation of the universe was consequently truly demonic and ultimately destructive. His very being cried out against the abuse of the atom to make weapons of unspeakable destruction: he saw it as blasphemy against the holy at the heart of the universe. Those who described George MacLeod's protest against the nuclear arms race as being a matter of politics did not know their man.

He could express it best in the language of poetry and prayer, which he saw as the scientist's true vocabulary when confronted by the awesome universe:

> Invisible we see You, Christ above us,
> With earthly eyes we see above us, clouds or sunshine, grey
>   or bright.
> But with the eye of faith, we know You reign:
>   instinct in the sun ray,
>   speaking in the storm,
>   warming and moving all Creation, Christ above us.

> We do not see all things subject to You.
> But we know that man is made to rise.
> Already exalted, already honoured, even now our citizenship
> is in heaven, Christ above us, invisible we see You.

> Invisible we see You, Christ beneath us.
> With earthly eyes we see beneath us stones and dust
> and dross, fit subjects for the analyst's table.
> But with the eye of faith, we know You uphold.
> In You all things consist and hang together:
>   The very atom is light energy,
>   The grass is vibrant,
>   The rocks pulsate.

> All is in flux; turn but a stone and an angel moves.
> Underneath are the everlasting arms,
> Unknowable we know You, Christ beneath us.[2]

Visions of angels were an integral part of the MacLeod world-view of theology, politics, worship and social action. Soon it was to be the mysterious rippling of carpets.

22

Land of Twist and Twirly

I have a dream today – that freedom will reign from every hill and molehill in Mississippi – from every mountainside, let freedom reign – and when this happens, when we allow freedom to reign, when we let it reign from every state and every city, we will be able to speed the day when all of God's children, black men and white men, Jews and Gentiles, Protestants and Catholics, will be able to join hands and sing in the words of the old Negro spiritual, "Free at last, thank God almighty, we're free at last".

MARTIN LUTHER KING, JUN.

He had black moods but was all for life. Sentiment was subdued in him; astringency and buoyancy were always breaking through.

MICHAEL FOOT ON ANEURIN BEVAN

Question: where was prime minister Harold Macmillan on the day the Profumo scandal finally erupted?

Answer: On Iona, with George MacLeod.

Rumours that the Rt Hon. John Profumo, Secretary of State for War, had been consorting with Christine Keeler, a call girl who had been sharing her favours with a Russian naval attache, had been rumbling since early 1963. In March, Profumo told the House of Commons that the stories were untrue, and he successfully sued two journals for libel.

At the end of May, the prime minister set off for a well-earned holiday in Scotland, handing over his responsibilities to his deputy, R. A. Butler, and noting in his diary, "I am to get only the minimum of telegrams and papers. It should be a real rest."[1]

323

On 4th June, his rest came to an abrupt end. Profumo's confession that day to the Chief Whip that he had lied to the Commons created a dangerous crisis with the potential to bring down the government. The news was communicated to Mr Macmillan in Oban.

"I do not remember ever having been under such a sense of personal strain," the man known as "Supermac" noted in his diary. "Even Suez was 'clean' – about war and politics. This was all dirt."[2]

George MacLeod was called to the telephone. Could he receive the prime minister on Iona? He met Mr Macmillan and his wife, Dorothy, on the jetty – "Snap!" said the prime minister to Calum Macpherson the Abbey clerk of works who, like him, was wearing his Guards tie – and George showed the somewhat distracted Mr Macmillan round the Abbey.

News of the major development in the scandal was beginning to leak out in London. How convenient for the premier to be on a remote sacred island, discussing holy things, well away from reporters whose minds were on lower things!

Mr Macmillan – noticeably tired and down – and his wife had tea at Dunsmeorach, before being seen off the island by George. The Iona leader was amused by the bolshiness of some of the more radical members of the Iona Community who objected to him entertaining a Conservative leader. He said nothing, perhaps because he didn't know of the developing scandal – or perhaps because he did. The enigmatic Macmillan would have been the second last person in the world to reveal such a thing: George MacLeod, the pastor used to keeping his lips sealed on the confidences of the great and the humble, would be the last. At any rate, a framed picture of the prime minister, signed with a gracious salutation, arrived soon afterwards at Dunsmeorach. George enjoyed the irritation of the Community radicals as they winced at the sight of it on his mantelpiece.

There is something touching about the picture of these two men – the Victorian gentleman-clergyman and the Edwardian patrician-politician – walking around the holy island, chatting about Celtic theology, while a very unholy sex scandal was erupting in London. The Profumo affair was symbolic of the tacky side of the sixties, and neither George MacLeod nor Harold Macmillan coped well with that heady decade of political change, personal liberation, "swinging" life styles, and cant. Within five months, the bewildered Macmillan was writing his resignation from his sick bed.

As George MacLeod attempted to read the signs of the rapidly changing times, he saw the death throes of an age, particularly as he looked forward to the celebrations to mark the 1400th anniversary of the landing of St Columba on Iona. Everywhere around him, he found endings.

Scottish letters? At the 1962 Edinburgh Festival, over 1000 people had gathered, within a stone's throw of where Burns sang, Scott wrote and Stevenson studied, to hear a debate among modern Scottish authors.

"Two of the speakers volunteered the information," George MacLeod wrote in disgust, "that they were homosexuals; one seemed to convey that when the Muse deserted him he resorted to heroin; while somehow, as a finale, a jazz strummer took over the microphone and sang a bawdy song about Lady Chatterley. All a straw in the wind, of course. But it is a wind of conviction that has been blowing strong enough for long enough. Folk begin to know that they need expect nothing any longer from Scottish Letters."

Scottish culture?

"Again, there is an end of typically Scottish culture. Let the 1962 Tattoo at the Festival be sufficient token. I confess that at previous Tattoos my pacifism has always been threatened for at least three hours. The skirl of the pipes, the quiet as the Last Post was sounded, the gathering surge of the band as 'Land of Hope and Glory' was taken up by the crowd, combined to create a nostalgia in my being for earlier less complicated days. But not this year! Has even the Army lost its nerve, as to the effect of martial scenes upon the public? For, when the paratroopers' scene came on, and their grim attack on the Castle was portrayed, behold, sudden like, the old Castle was defended by a *platoon of clowns!* Their faces white with flour, lips red with grease paint, these jesters minced their way forward to confront the paratroops! The one martial moment was thus turned into a farce. And, at the end, up went the arc lights, not on a 'sad sinking of the flag, the long day over'. Up went the lights on an audience snaking from their seats to do the twist, forsooth, to the massed bands of Her Majesty's Forces. Land of Hope and Glory gave way to Land of Twist and Twirly.

"It is true that we stood to sing the first two verses of Psalm 100.

It is also true that, after the first night, they had to print off the second verse – as Scotland had forgotten it!'[3]

If this was the war, then Captain MacLeod was losing it. Another post-war reconstruction was disintegrating before his eyes.

The winds of change were reaching hurricane force, blowing away so many of the old markers. What little wind there was was more than just boisterous: in fact, it was impossible to stand upright in it. It was no time for a Victorian gentleman to be out on the streets alone.

The revolutions associated with the sixties – though they had their roots much earlier – were wide ranging and bewildering. The tides were running fast – the auld buddy in the High Street would have been impressed by their depths as she was swept away – and George MacLeod failed to ride them. He was not a sixties man.

The "permissive age", as it was dubbed, represented a constellation of movements and feelings which, however different and even contradictory, created a unified consciousness of change, a sense of the end of an era. The most sensational and most widely publicized change was in sexual mores. The restraints of the post-war era were cast aside: "what feels good" became the principal guide for what was called the "new morality", particularly as the revolutionary birth control pill allowed people to experiment sexually without risk of pregnancy, if not without guilt. The Wolfenden Report had created a climate in which homosexuality could be discussed and practised more openly between consenting adults: it was described more as a condition or an orientation than a sin. The failure of the authorities to prevent the publication of D. H. Lawrence's "Lady Chatterley's Lover", with its explicit sexual descriptions, was regarded as a landmark pointing towards the new moral landscape. Almost anything seemed to be permissible in print, on screen and in personal behaviour.

The sexual revolution was part of a much wider questioning of all authority. This was seen particularly in the universities, where students engaged in highly publicized "sit ins" to demand more participation in running the universities and shaping the curriculum. The impact of television in highlighting and spreading the new and sometimes outrageous "youth culture" was enormous. Student leaders, such as Daniel Cohn-Bendit ("Danny the Red"), became folk heroes, and popular musicians like the Beatles, Joan Baez and Bob Dylan spoke for a new generation. Folk festivals became massive celebrations of the exciting new culture in which all things could be experimented with.

The dramatic rise to power of the youthful John F. Kennedy – "looking like a schoolboy on holiday" was how Macmillan, who got on well with the American president, described him – helped create a political culture in which youthful idealism was king, and the pragmatism of deals worked out by older political hands in the legendary smoke-filled rooms was derided and despised. The "old politics", with its Cold War rhetoric, was blamed for America's growing involvement in the increasingly unpopular war in Vietnam – an especial irony since President Kennedy was deeply implicated in its escalation. As the affluent children of old-fashioned, traditionalist Americans turned against the values of their parents and tuned in to the all-loving rhetoric of hippy "Flower Power", it began to appear as if truth were a generational matter. It was possible to be written off simply by virtue of being not-young.

The new culture had a place for religion – of a kind. The emphasis on "new consciousness" permitted exploration into new religious experiences as well as into drug-induced trances – one "trip" was no more valid than any other. All was relative, only the experiential had something to teach. The mood favoured the cults rather than the traditional mainstream churches, which were seen to be part of the problem rather than part of the solution. Sinless utopianism was in vogue.

The churches themselves were deeply affected by the new climate. As an integral part of the old authority which had lost credibility, they were on the defensive. At a time when only the subjective and the experiential was regarded as having authenticity, the Church's historical theology was at a disadvantage. It was also under more substantial attack from the sharpest philosophy of the day; a considerable number of influential philosophers regarded all metaphysical statements as literally non-sense. The new logical positivists held that only that which was empirically verifiable could be regarded as true. This left a God "out there" who acts in love towards the world as an impossible idea: philosophical "God-talk" became reduced to chatter about the spiritual tendencies of the human rather than conversation about an independently existing divine being.

A key word for the new age was "honesty", meaning the refusal to accept things simply on the basis of authority. At its best, the new trend produced liberation and clarification, at its worst it led to self-righteous humbug. Sin was not abolished simply because people started talking about honesty; in fact the more talk of honesty, the more it was necessary to check out the rhetoric.

When *Honest to God*, by John A. T. Robinson, the Bishop of Woolwich, was published in 1963, it caused a sensation. Its amazing sale of 400,000 copies in Britain alone showed the hunger among lay people for a theology which made sense to them.

Drawing mainly on the works of two theologians, Dietrich Bonhoeffer and Paul Tillich, Bishop Robinson, who had been a popular lecturer on New Testament topics on Iona, argued that it was no longer meaningful to talk of "God out there": God was to be found in the depths. He was, to use Tillich's phrase, "the Ground of our being". Using this key, Robinson redescribed several of the main Christian doctrines.

The reaction among some church people, and people on the fringes of the churches, was one of relief. Many of them had grown up with Sunday School notions of God as an old man in the sky: now a bishop was telling them that they could discard some of the old concepts and still be Christian. Others were furious, accusing the bishop of betraying historic Christianity.

What Robinson was doing was to take the common parlance of theologians and philosophers, and share it with ordinary people. In the process he distorted some of the emphases of both Bonhoeffer and Tillich, but he widened the whole debate about the nature of theology in an explosive way. It highlighted a current debate within the Church: should the Church embrace the secular view of the world, and look for hints of God within it, or should it oppose secularism root and branch?

The question had been addressed by Dietrich Bonhoeffer in his celebrated *Letters and Papers From Prison*, meditations written in the prisoner-of-war camp in which he was incarcerated. Elusive and somewhat fragmentary, the writings talked of the need for a 'religionless Christianity' – a Christianity shorn of many of its traditional trappings. Bonhoeffer himself was a man of profound faith and prayer, with a highly disciplined spiritual life, but he argued that "man come of age" needed to be less dependent. Life was what God was interested in, not religion as such, and it was in the midst of life, and the centre of suffering, that man would find God.

The debate was both exciting and unsettling. The Second Vatican Council, called by Pope John XXIII, added further uncertainty, by seeming to move away from traditional notions of authority and obedience. It was as if the whole religious world were shifting. What was being experienced was what Tillich called "the shaking of the foundations".

If traditional notions of God were called into question, what then of traditional Christian morality? It could not escape re-examination either. Though the traditional Christian ethic was based on love, it was perceived to be rule-bound and obedience based. Fresh scrutiny of the Christian attitude to personal relationships, in the light of the new birth control possibilities, led to debate within the Church about whether Christian sexual ethics required new expression. The secular new morality found its theological counterpart in the emergence of "situation ethics" in which very few things could be described as being sinful themselves – everything depended upon the context.

There is a sense in which none of this was new. Historically, within the Church, there had always been debate about God "out there" and God "in here": about God as external to the world, and God as part of the unitive substance of all things. The best of Christian theology had attempted to hold to both major aspects, believing that the tensions and contradictions and paradoxes were part of the inherent limitation of all language about God. Similarly, the best of Christian ethics had recognized that love and not rules must be pre-eminent: but also that love may be as blind as obedience, and a do-it-yourself ethic fresh for every context was both wearisome and dangerous. In the sixties, the shaking of the theological and ethical foundations was linked to a new, pervasive and sometimes intolerant youth culture, spread almost instantly by the immediate power of the omnipresent television screen.

In a world in which the image rather than the word was dominant, the Church looked like a dinosaur – flat footed, lumbering, obsolete, trapped in its own past. If the new race was for the sure-footed and the swift, the Church was far behind. The Church of Scotland complained to the BBC about the sexual explicitness of some of its programmes, but got little in the way of assurance; indeed one senior BBC official described the complaints as the "baying of hounds". The reign of Lord Reith was well and truly over.

The winds of change were blowing very chill for the churches, which were forced on to the defensive at every turn. The trumpet was making a very uncertain sound, and what squeaky noises it did make seemed to signal reaction or retreat. The Kirk's membership figures tumbled, despite reassuring Moderatorial noises about the Church being in good heart.

A lack of confidence about the Church's message and the forms of its life was like a contagion. Seeing the rapid changes in society around them, many ministers felt the Church to be a reactionary force, a stumbling block in the way of progress. It became a commonplace for clergy to express the view that their congregations, who paid their wages, were not allowing them to exercise a proper ministry and were burdening them with expectations which belonged to a past era. Congregations were in turn bewildered by disillusioned ministers who seemed, unless they had misunderstood them, to mock the very things of God. Quite a number of men left the ministry to go in for social work or other professions, leaving behind them bewildered and hurt congregations.

The sixties' changes had a profound effect on the Iona Community. The assumptions underlying the very foundation of the experiment – confidence in the Church, the ministry and the gospel – were now seriously challenged. It had been assumed that the gospel itself was clear-cut, and that if only the Church, inspired by a renewed and properly trained ministry, could live up to its gospel, the people would come back in and the life of the nation – indeed of the world – would be transformed. Now that the Church was seen as a dinosaur which would have to die in order that something new could evolve, and the ministry was regarded as a frustrating and a conflicted role which no one interested in real social change should even contemplate, there were obvious problems.

It was even worse, now that the very gospel itself was under attack. If talk of a God "out there" was disallowed, what was left of the traditional gospel in which the Creator of the world came to earth in his Son Jesus Christ? With a bit of excision here and there, the figure of Jesus of Nazareth could be made to fit the flower power scene – yes, one might imagine the Jesus of the Sermon on the Mount putting flowers on the barrels of the state troopers' rifles. Theological attention was focused on the historic Jesus of Nazareth, shorn of theological and legendary accretions, but the "quest for the historical Jesus" produced more scraps than substance.

The Iona Community attracted bright, thinking, social activist ministers, who thrust these questions into the heart of the Community's life. Was it possible to believe in a God any more? Why not follow Jesus but jettison the notion of an external God? If God did exist, had he abandoned the Church in favour of pursuing his purposes out in the world? Was the Church not a reactionary body obstructing social progress? Was it not time for an experimental, alternative Church to be established? Had the ministry not become a professional club protecting an obsolete tradition and keeping the results of biblical criticisms from the laity? It was a far cry from the excited debates about training, housing schemes and mission which had absorbed the Community.

The effect of this lack of confidence in the institutional Church and questioning of its gospel – even though it was not shared by all, or even a majority of members – accelerated the already developing shift of the Community's central attention away from the Church and ministerial formation on to international issues. Peace became more important than the renewal of public worship: activism on the streets was more of a burning concern than prayer to a deity who might not be there at all: justice in Africa was more exciting than ministry in Glasgow: industrial relations became a more interesting topic than training for the ministry.

What of the Community's leader in all this? Some things about the spirit of the times appealed to him – particularly the peace movement and the recognition of the central importance of human rights and social justice. He had been fond of quoting Professor John Macmurray's dictum that the main contribution of the Jews to religion was that they did away with it – he was as aware of the corruptions of the Church and the distorting effects of the trappings of religion as anyone. Yet at heart he remained a MacLeod of Fuinary, an Auld Kirk minister who believed wholeheartedly in the stable trinity of gospel, Church and ministry. He was no fundamentalist, biblical or ecclesiastical, and he saw the need for the faith to be reinterpreted and reappropriated by each new generation; but as Norman of the Barony had graciously submitted to the deaf Covenanting lady's imperious demand to "Gang ower the fundamentals", so his grandson recognized the validity of such a request, even in the sixties. There were still fundamentals to gang ower, even if they might have to be re-expressed for a new day. He felt that much of the cultural, political and religious thinking of the time was fundamentally shallow.

There were also fundamentals of human behaviour. He was

appalled by the new permissive sexual ethics, and his reticence in discussing such matters made life difficult for him.

When subjects such as "personal relationships" featured in the youth camp programme, the youth secretary would be summoned to George's office to explain. The first few times, Jim Robertson did all the talking, but as he gained confidence, he adopted the strategy of saying nothing other than to ask exactly what he was concerned about. The meetings soon stopped! George also said that it was unwise to have boys meeting in the girls' dorm for discussion sessions, even though space in the youth camp was at a premium. At concerts, if there was any item which George deemed to be even slightly dubious, he would intervene and send everybody home.

It was, however, more and more difficult for George to impose his will. The Community debates began to weary him: it was all too reminiscent of the SCM talking about "The Problem of God". Was it for this that he had set up the organization – to become a debating chamber reflecting all the sins of the Church? He could not quell the discussion with an imperious wave of the hand – the democratic spirit of the times was such that George's style appeared archaic to some of the young turks. This is not to say that George was not still an inspiring and, indeed, revered figure within the Community and it certainly did not mean that it was a case of the Iona Community versus George MacLeod – the Community was a diverse and highly individualistic group of often argumentative people with different approaches to issues – but the situation had changed in subtle, and sometimes not subtle, ways. George Mac-Leod now not only had his imitators but his mimickers in the Community, and for the first time there were mutterings in the bars about the possibility of a palace revolution.

George was aware that things were not moving his way, and it depressed him. He had on several occasions described himself as, like other men, "a civil war inside – the civil war is between our hopes, which we can't get away from, and our failures, which we can't deny." As an idealist and a somewhat driven man, he was frustrated by the gulf between his dreams and the reality he saw around him. He found it difficult to take time off and relax – there was too much to do, and too little time in which to do it.

When he went on holiday with his family, he would spend the first couple of days sleeping off his exhaustion, and would be in a foul temper until he gradually unwound – then he would be warm and loving and attentive. He could never entirely take his mind off the Iona Community when on holiday: he could be found sitting on the beach, still wearing jacket, shirt and tie, furiously scribbling notes in his Filofax. Reforming the Church, not to say changing the world, was a costly business, demanding total attention and not a few sacrifices, as his family could testify with feeling.

The words which Donald MacLeod wrote of his brother could well be applied to the great Norman's grandson: "Those who knew him only in society, buoyant and witty, overflowing with animal spirits, the very soul of laughter and enjoyment, may feel surprised at the almost morbid self-condemnation and excessive tenderness of conscience which these journals display, still more at the tone of sadness which so frequently pervades them. For while such persons may remember how his merriest talk generally passed impercep-tibly into some graver theme – so naturally, indeed, that the listener could scarcely tell how it was that the conversation had changed its tone – yet only those who knew him very intimately were aware that, although his outer life had so much of apparent abandon, he not only preserved a habit of careful spiritual self-culture, but was often subject to great mental depression, and was ever haunted with a consciousness of the solemnity, if not the sadness, of life.

"In point of fact, much of his self-reproach arose from the earnestness of the conflict which he waged against his own natural tendency to self-indulgence. For if on one side he had deep spiritual affinities and a will firmly resolved on the attainment of holiness, he had on the other a temperament to which both 'the world and the flesh' appealed with tremendous power. His abounding humour and geniality had, as usual, their source in a deeply emotional region; rendering him quickly susceptible to impressions from without, and easily moved by what appealed strongly to his tastes. This rich vein of human feeling which constituted him many-sided and sympathetic, and gave him so much power over others, laid him also open to peculiar trials in his endeavour after a close life with God."[4]

The stress of George's situation, as a somewhat lonely, even if gregarious, man carrying enormous burdens, expressed itself from time to time in pains in his ears – which would cause him to sit holding his head in his hands – and outbreaks of psoriasis. The scaly skin disease affected his hands and feet. The treatment was the application of ointment to the affected areas, and this was lovingly done by Lorna. His feet had to be placed in polythene bags at night, and he often had to wear gloves. He bore this burden stoically most of the time, but his inward agitation occasionally manifested itself in outbursts of frustrated anger.

If George sometimes felt himself to be losing both the civil war within and the theological war outside, he certainly did not show it during the wonderful celebrations to mark the 1400th anniversary of the landing of St Columba on Iona. It was pure Iona theatre, orchestrated and directed by the contempoary Columba himself. The weather in June 1963 was glorious. Various gifts were dedicated, including a public address system for the Abbey, a staff, Bible and a replica of a 6th century Celtic missionary bell for the St Columba Shrine, and a new carved wooden lectern for the Abbey church.

Pentecost Sunday had a strange beginning for George MacLeod. He had been very busy with preparations for the celebrations, and he was surprised to wake up feeling not in the slightest bit tired. He got up at six with the intention of getting on top of the day before events began to crowd in on one another. As he was dressing, he was conscious of a strong wind, alternately moaning and whistling through the house.

"I looked out to sea which seemed calm," he noted. "I looked at nearby trees which seemed still. I then saw the corner of the carpet rippling up and down. I woke my wife who, not unreasonably, while confirming this phenomenon, suggested that someone must have left the front door, or a large window, open. I examined all doors and windows and returned again and shut the door of our room, but the carpet was still rippling like a moving yet somehow static snake. The wind also continued.

"As I crossed toward the Abbey, I was still aware of the wind which somehow was yet not blowing me about. And into my mind came Pentecost with its 'sound as of the rushing of a mighty wind, and it filled the house where they were sitting.' This biblical language precisely described my immediate experiences.

"On becoming thus aware of a modern Pentecost I immediately began to wonder whether I was becoming slightly light-headed with all that had been going on late into the night before and so early in the morning. Was I definitely 'air borne'? – I asked myself – and would I do something silly in the course of the day? That gave way (I still had not covered the few hundred yards to the West door of the Abbey) to the question in myself whether I ever expect anything really overtly spiritual to happen? Do you get me? . . . If hundreds of people came to Iona on Pentecost determined to partake of the Sacrament together – the whole Church – for the first time for centuries . . . If they have all been praying for a great day . . . is it really extraordinary that some*THING* should happen? As Christians in our modern world are we really expecting any-*THING* to happen?"[5]

Pentecost Sunday was memorable. The celebrant was the Rt Rev. Lesslie Newbigin, a Scots Presbyterian who was also a bishop of the Church of South India, and the preacher was Professor James S. Stewart, Moderator of the General Assembly of the Kirk. Bishops and Moderators from Scotland, England, Ireland and Wales, along with leaders of the Baptist, Methodist, Congregational and Greek Orthodox Churches, and of the Salvation Army, the Society of Friends and the Taizé Community in France assisted with the distribution of the elements. The Roman Catholic Church did not participate, but sent fraternal greetings.

The service was remarkable for its degree of unity, and also because it was televised live, beamed by Eurovision to Germany, France, Holland, Denmark, Norway, Sweden and Eire. All of those nations sent their own commentators. The BBC got its expensive equipment on to Iona by means of an army tank landing craft which beached at Martyrs' Bay – the inlet which had in the past received coracles, viking galleys, royal funeral barges and Clyde puffers. George's first act was to take Ronnie Falconer, who was producing the programme, into St Columba's Shrine, to offer up to God all they were about to do.

On St Columba's Day, June 9th, over 1000 pilgrims came by land and sea for an act of dedication. At a simple ceremony at the jetty, the Moderator of the Presbyterian Church in Ireland handed over to the Iona Community the gift of *The Derry*, a Donegal fishing boat.

The arrival of the boat from Ireland went back to the unannounced visit to Iona made some years previously by Dr Eammon de Valera, prime minister of Eire. George MacLeod remembered the visit:

"I attempted to be his guide, not a little embarrassed by the presence of his son, an expert in the High Crosses of Ireland. He courteously corrected me three times in my description of our own.

The premier was charm itself, truly catholic in generous congratulation of our building purpose, but even more delighted by the singing of God's praise upon which he stumbled, when he had expected to enter a dismal, empty fane. I was, he said, to return with him for luncheon on the Corsair, but we were a vigorous community with a closeknit programme and I begged to be excused. 'Then when you next visit Dublin,' he almost commanded, 'you will be my guest.

"'Is there anything I can do for you?' he asked as we passed St Martin's Cross on his departure. He had been so whimsical that I dared an impertinence. 'You can return to us the Book of Kells from Trinity College, Dublin, for was it not wrought here?'

"I saw across his brow a gathering furrow, such as Lloyd George must have known when Republican conversations were at their worst, so I hastily added, 'Of course, you could take away St Martin's Cross in part exchange.' Calm returned to his brow. 'You can have the Book of Kells on one condition – that you bring Iona within the hegemony of the Irish Free State.'

"'Not on your life, sir,' I replied, and he renewed his invitation to Dublin.

When George became Moderator and was due to visit Dublin, he took the Toiseach at his word. He wrote ahead asking if he might pay a 15-minute visit which might be either private or official; if the latter, he would turn up "dressed like a medieval pirate". De Valera insisted it be an official luncheon.

"The hospitality was lavish. Knowing that a speech lay before me, I was content with a simple sherry. Other Scottish delegates were able to enter more, shall we say, into the spirit of the party.

"During one of those pauses that speak louder than words, the entire table could do no other than hear, only too distinctly, a Scottish delegate ask, 'What, Mr Prime Minister, would you say is the main difference between Northern and Southern Ireland?' During the instantaneous and yet immemorial pause that followed this innocent but outrageous sally, a distinct swish was heard outside the window. It was the Liffy turning back on its flow. By way of desperate remedy, I almost shouted, 'Would you ever consider sailing in a curragh with me, sir, from Derry to Iona when we all celebrate the fourteenth centenary of the arrival of St Columba?' The situation was saved as the Premier discoursed most learnedly on the building of curraghs then and now. I assured him I was in earnest, and promised that a friend of mine with a modern yacht could sail in our wake and make transfer possible in the event of a storm.

"'Bring your yacht,' he countered, 'but she can sail ahead of the coracle. In any storm they could transfer to our craft!'"[6]

The only discordant note on St Columba's Day 1963 was a separate pilgrimage and service organized by the Anglican communion, reviving Highland jokes about the Macleans of Duart having their own boat at Noah's flood. The preparations for the service had their lighter moments, though, with the bishops and provosts of the Scottish and English churches arguing among themselves about the form of the service.

"They argued their way through most of the service," recalled Ronnie Falconer, "pausing only to unite when Canterbury sent up his chaplain with some suggestion or other. When the chaplain returned to his master, sitting alone in the chairless nave, Canterbury's sole sign of emotion was a twitching of his famous eyebrows."[7]

George was furious at what he saw as the Anglicans' insensitive behaviour, but contained his rage enough to take part in the service as an ordinary worshipper and receive communion. After all, he had been confirmed as an Anglican at Winchester.

The Columban celebrations of 1963 constituted one of the most exultant high spots of George MacLeod's whole life.

He sensed, however, that there were hard times coming. And he was right.

23

Grace and Granite

*When I give to the poor, they call me a saint. When I
ask why the poor have no food, they call me a
communist.*

DOM HELDER CAMARA

*I think the essence of the Judaic-Christian Faith is
very similar to Playboy.*

HUGH HEFNER

If in doubt, go to America.

Early in 1964, George was back in the States for a two-month
lecture tour, Lorna joining him for the last three weeks.

More lectures, services, vocations. George was at the height of
his popularity, with articles about the Iona rebuilding appearing in
the American newspapers, as well as in the religous journals. He
drew crowds wherever he spoke, and people of all ages sought him
out to seek his advice or spiritual direction. He was regularly meeting
people who had been to Iona to share in his exciting experiment.

He also raised more funds for the final stage of the rebuilding.
He charmed money out of the wealthy Presbyterians of Pittsburg,
though some encounters were unpredictable. One meeting with a
wealthy Presbyterian potential donor in New York was going well,
and George waited with eager anticipation when the man went
upstairs in his opulently furnished apartment to 'get something
very special'. The American proffered not the expected hefty
cheque, but a bottle of Scotch!

America, as usual, thrilled and stimulated him. He was perfectly
happy to be away from Iona for long spells; he was restless, ever
seeking new ideas and fresh vision. And much of what was
happening at home was irritating to him.

Back in Scotland there was the major unresolved problem – what to do with the restored Iona Abbey. George was firm about what he wanted Iona Abbey to become – an "experimental wing" of the Scottish Divinity Colleges. He believed it should be a residential college for the training of clergy, building upon the insights gained over the 26 years life of the Iona Community.

George had a vision of what the Church should be – imaginative yet conservative in its theology, radical in the outworkings of that theology, and uncompromising in its personal ethics. He would prefer it to be pacifist and socialist, though he would tolerate varieties of opinion and practice; it would be a Presbyterian national Church of Scotland with elected bishops who would be directly accountable to Presbyteries and who would be compelled to stand down at the end of their seven-year stint; it would work very closely with other churches; and it would have a form of confessional where people could receive the forgiveness of sins and the laying on of hands. He believed that such a reformed and transformed Church would win the next generation, and he was convinced that ministers could be trained for such a Church in the restored Iona Abbey. He insisted, even in his low moments, that the best years of the Church were still to come.

Though he had supporters for that view within the Iona Community, the reality was that he was losing the war. Such a clear-cut programme did not sit well with the prevailing mood of questioning of gospel, Church and ministry. The focus in the Community had shifted towards the training of the laity – and many members were determined that the restored Abbey, which had been rebuilt by many hands, should not be given over to the training of the clergy. They claimed that to do so would be to turn the clock back. Others simply felt that it was impractical to have a ministerial training college on Iona. Others again argued that one shouldn't go to a classroom any more to learn theology, even on a sacred island – the Community's ministerial training should now take place on the urban front lines.

The debate was further complicated by the reaction against the founder's style, which was perceived to be autocratic. Some of the younger members, who had not been born when the Community was founded, believed that George was out of touch with what was actually happening on the front line. They had much more contact with Ralph Morton than with George, and they were unsympathetic to the MacLeodian black-and-white oratorical style.

The mid-1960s represented a crisis-time for the Iona Community and for its leader. It was decided to deal with the issue of what to do with the restored Abbey by establishing a commission on the future of the Community.

In a paper for the commission, George said that although he agreed that the Community should attempt to provide training for the whole Church, lay and ordained, the training of ordained ministers should still be a priority.

He proposed a three-year training course for divinity students, in which they would spend six months of each year on Iona engaged in theological study, prayer and the leading of worship, all in the context of community, four months in industry, one month in a parish, and one month on holiday. He said that the crisis facing the Church could not be dealt with by seaside missions or furnishing church halls like pubs, hoping that the outsiders would come in. The central challenge, he said, was the deification of the material and the denigration of the sacred, and added: "Christ, the Light and Life of the world, is seen to be imminent in His creation for those who have eyes to see. The answer to scientific humanism is not some flight into the spiritual. It is the recovery and protestation of True Humanism in the light of the Incarnation. We are on the threshold of a new appreciation of the Faith, if we have the courage to enter in."

George believed that the crisis of the times required a new engagement with the material and the spiritual, and that the clergy, as leaders of the Church, should spearhead this new engagement. And what better place to begin again than in the restored Abbey of Iona?

The Community did not agree. In January 1965 it was decided that when the rebuilding was complete, Iona Abbey should be developed as an all-year-round place of meeting, conference and training. Minister members joining the Community would spend part of the summer on Iona, and the rest of the time in Community House. A permanent group would be appointed to staff the Abbey and welcome groups and individuals from a wide variety of backgrounds for retreats and courses on a variety of topics.

George MacLeod had just lost one of the most important battles of his life – and it hurt, because he had been defeated by his beloved Community. Things would never be quite the same again.

*

Grace and Granite

At Pentecost, 1965, a dedication service was held to celebrate the completion of the rebuilding of Iona Abbey. Eight hundred people participated in an open-air televised communion service in the Abbey grounds. Representatives of 16 nations took part in the thanksgiving, though what pleased George more than anything was the presence of a group of 80 people from Govan. David Russell, chairman of the Iona Appeal Trust, whose father had first drawn up plans for the reconstructed Abbey living quarters nearly forty years previously, ceremoniously opened the great door of the new West Range. The crowds poured into the restored cloisters to share their communion bread with strangers – a custom believed to go back to the Celtic era.

George MacLeod, a vigorous 70-year-old, was entitled to take pride in the achievement. One of Europe's most sacred possessions had been imaginatively restored – not just as an interesting museum, but as a living international centre of ecumenical Christian renewal, inspiration and education. The symbolic nature of the rebuilding, begun in times of hostility and war, had inspired many people, and the Iona Community's experiment in training had caught the imagination of the Church – not just in Scotland but in many parts of the world. To see the beautifully restored Abbey, with its simple granite strength against a background of ever-changing colours of sky and sea, was to be reminded once more of the prophecy of St Columba:

> In Iona of my heart, Iona of my love,
> Instead of monks' voices shall be lowing of cattle;
> But ere the world comes to an end,
> Iona shall be as it was.

The restoration also brought into focus Columba's other prophecy about his beloved island:

> Unto this place, small and mean though it be, great homage shall yet be paid, not only by the kings and people of the Scots, but by the rulers of foreign and barbarous nations and their subjects. In great veneration, too, shall it be held by holy men of other churches.

When George had embarked on the vulnerable venture in 1938, committing himself to its leadership for five years, he had no idea

341

of what lay ahead. He certainly never imagined that the rebuilding programme would be extended, and that it would go on for 27 years. He had not anticipated being leader of an ever-expanding community for anything like that time – he had envisaged being in charge of a small-scale training and rebuilding experiment for a few years before returning to parish ministry in Scotland. During those 27 years, many people had given up jobs or plans to help with the venture, and countless lives had been influenced or changed in the process. George had borne the lonely burden of responsibility for raising the funds for the rebuilding, sometimes lying awake at night wondering how the staff would be paid.

While it had been a community venture, the vision, the inspiration and the drive had come from George MacLeod. The Iona Community was his brainchild, albeit now a lusty adult prepared to take on Father in bloody but essentially familial conflict. The Community which argued vociferously with its Founder acknowledged that it owed its existence to him, even when it knew that to claim its own life it had to resist his sometimes overpowering embrace. While the restored living quarters of Iona Abbey testified eloquently to the skill and deep commitment of men like Ian Lindsay, Calum Macpherson and Bill Amos, the rebuilding was not just a sermon in stone on behalf of the living God, but a monument to the grace and the granite of that latter-day Columba, George Fielden MacLeod.

Norman MacLeod, *Caraid nan Gaidheal*, who had wondered aloud more than 150 years previously, as he walked among the ruins of Iona Abbey, whether the island would ever be honoured as it once was, would have been very proud of his great grandson.

If the outer rebuilding was now complete, what next? George was clear: it was what he termed the "inner rebuilding".

"So seen, the Iona Community is still relevant in the new situation," he wrote in a reflection after the Pentecost celebrations. "But if it is to remain significant it must not neglect its original genius (in the strict and not laudatory meaning of that word). The genius of the Community was to act rather than to talk: to have a stab at new liturgical forms and if necessary blunder: actually to lay on hands and conceivably shock: to get thoroughly involved in Africa and mayhap make wrong political choices: to send out scores of 'ordinary church members' to protest the Gospel street by street in corporate mission . . . no less than Roy Welensky goes on paper to claim that it was the Church of Scotland that finished off the Central African Federation!

"If we are to remain significant in the new climate we must not neglect this 'genius'. But by the very nature of the new climate we must pause to consider where we stand in all this 'honest to God' mood. The future significance of the Iona Community depends not on its intellectual interpretation of the present situation but on what action it takes in and through that interpretation . . . Until the Reformed churches *act* again it is quite certain that Rome on the one hand and the Pentecostals on the other will capture the allegiance of such as seek a definite faith for our day."

Looking to the future, George concluded: "Iona can be the home of the New Reformation. But it must recover its genius: keep acting its insights at whatever risk if its insights are to be clarified and the next obedience seen. If as a community, we write at all it can be no more than passing calculations in the sand, to point to the next Obedience."

His theme betrayed his fear that the Iona Community was turning into a discussion group, producing endless papers, commissions and seminars; and that Iona Abbey would become a conference centre rather than a place of training-in-community, a home for well-heeled religious chatterers instead of a training camp for Christian revolutionaries.

The work he enjoyed most on Iona was one-to-one discussions with individuals. Not for him the "non-directive listening" of current pastoral theory: he was blunt and direct.

When Colin Douglas, son of his former assistant Hugh Douglas, was a guide at the Abbey, he and David Beckett (now minister of Greyfriars Kirk) were invited by George to join him for a swim.

"Off he plunged in his green Bermuda shorts into the foaming brine, followed somewhat reluctantly by David and myself," Colin remembered. "As we were drying off afterwards, George asked me if I had given any serious attention to going into the Church, which I confessed I had not. And that, plus being on Iona, was basically my call to the ministry."

Major T. B. Mitford was said to have cadets who, after jumping off a cliff for him, would then wonder at what they had just done. George had a similar kind of authority. He had a New Testament directness about him.

The man who more than most was to see the fruits of George MacLeod's vocational seeds was the Rev. Horace Walker, for many years secretary of the Church of Scotland's Home Board. His verdict is quite unequivocal.

"If I were asked who in my opinion had most influence in my time in bringing young men to consider the ministry as a vocation, I would unquestionably nominate George MacLeod," he said. "For so many he made the Christian faith an exciting adventure.

"When, in the fifties and sixties, we had problems recruiting men for the toughest new housing areas and pioneer mission jobs, it was more often than not that the volunteers for such work came from the ranks of the Community.

"We have had many fine orators and preachers in the Church in my time, but I have never heard any but George who, in the white heat of inspiration, could so fuse and weld together apparently disparate elements and ideas. Often it seemed like spontaneous combustion! Sometimes he overdid it and fantasy was the outcome. But far more often he illuminated old truths and made them new."

George was not simply interested in producing ministers. He would give himself to any who required him. When David Lunan was leading a youth camp, two of the youngsters asked if they could possibly talk with Dr MacLeod. It was the Friday of a hectic Community Week, but George immediately agreed to speak with them at 10 o'clock that evening. David Lunan was invited to join them.

"He talked with them like a father," David remembered, "and eventually it emerged – they found it almost impossible to express themselves, not because they were tongue-tied, but because they didn't know what had happened to them – that they had had a religious experience. Through the services, the beauty of Iona, the discussions and the fun in the camp, perhaps also their own little romance – in a way they couldn't comprehend, God had become real to them."

George went with them into the Abbey church and prayed with them. It was typical that he should make time for two rather confused young people, at the end of such a demanding and exhausting week, and speak to them with such kindness and directness.

Later that evening, nearer midnight, he walked with David a few times round the Abbey, unwinding after the long day. He said to the younger man, "Besides committing our lives to Christ, we have to find the way he wants us to serve Him and to witness to Him. Of course, for us all it's different. For me it's pacifism."

David was to experience George's directness of speech in a different way, when he came in late for a Community meeting. "Lunan, why were you so late?" the leader asked him. "Do you think your time is more important than ours, or do you just like to be noticed?"

George was never very comfortable around women, and there was a lot of bad feeling in the Community among some members' wives, who chafed at the restrictions placed upon them. It could also have its amusing side.

Isabel Martin was leading the youth camp, while her fiancé, Iain Whyte, was joining the Community. Isabel was suffering from camp leader exhaustion, so Iain gallantly said she could sleep for the afternoon on his bed while he went off to build a wall.

"At four o'clock I arrived with a cup of tea," Iain recalled, "to find my beloved bolt upright on the bed in a state of shock. As she was dropping off she was aware of footsteps in the corridor, and a familiar voice coming nearer and nearer. George MacLeod was showing a party of distinguished American ministers over the Abbey! 'And this is where the new men sleep,' he boomed, opening the door of my room. Seeing a reclining female camp leader on the bed he was nonplussed, but all his background of gallantry took over. 'I'm frightfully sorry!' he shouted, and closed the door.

"On hearing this, I had visions of 'We love you, pray for you and send you off the island' treatment. Sure enough, as we filed in for the evening meal, the Leader would not allow me to slip by. 'Come and sit beside me, Iain,' he said, and I sweated blood while the old rogue talked animatedly about peace, the New Reformation in Christ, and everything except women on members' beds! I'm sure it was deliberate, but twelve months later, he sent us a St Martin's Cross for our wedding, and wrote that ours was 'yet another Iona marriage.'"

Much of George's energy went into the peace movement. The momentum of the Campaign for Nuclear Disarmament had been slowed by dissension within the ranks over tactics, but even more importantly by the signing of the Nuclear Test Ban Treaty in 1963. George, who asked the General Assembly of the Kirk to establish a special committee to keep under constant review the theological, ethical and international issues raised by nuclear war, said he thanked God for the signing of the treaty, but found it ominous that millions of people had almost stopped thinking about the perils with a sigh of relief.

His proposal fell by a large majority.

It was in the 1960s and 1970s that George MacLeod established his reputation as a "lost cause" man. The popular legend that George was a lonely loser in the Assembly all his public ministry does not bear examination. He was always a controversial figure, but he experienced signal triumphs – such as the campaign against the Central African Federation, which had collapsed finally in 1963 – as well as dismal defeats.

His peace crusading met with repeated failure, however, and he became like a wilderness Churchill in reverse, warning against the dangers of escalating and ever widening nuclear development. The signing of the Test Ban Treaty was a symbol of the perceived success of negotiations and diplomacy; in fact, the nuclear arms build-up was accelerating, and spreading to new countries. Amid the optimism over negotiated solutions and the putting down of the peace movement as hippy or Communist, George MacLeod was seen as a predictable prophet of doom.

The state of the ecumenical movement also concerned the Iona leader. In 1965, the minister and kirk session of St Giles' Cathedral applied to the Presbytery of Edinburgh for permission to allow the Rev. John Tirrell, an American Episcopalian minister, to administer the sacraments while serving on the staff of St Giles.

The exchange had been set up by the St Giles minister, George's old friend, Dr Harry Whitley, and the controversial American bishop James Pike, who had ordained Tirrell. The move caused great embarrassment to Kenneth Carey, the Episcopal bishop of Edinburgh, and nobody enjoyed that embarrassment more than Harry Whitley.

Carey did not approve of the appointment and had not been consulted; at a time when ecumenical developments were proceeding very delicately, the presence of an Episcopalian clergyman celebrating communion in the High Kirk of Presbyterianism would be explosive. The official Episcopal position was that their communion was open only to members of their church, though some Episcopalian clergy simply disregarded the rule, and offered the bread and wine to members of all churches. Harry Whitley affected not to see what the problem was – either the Episcopalians believed in the ecumenical movement, and in the validity of Church of Scotland ministry and sacraments, or they did not. The St Giles' minister was angered by what he saw as Anglican exclusiveness and pretentiousness, and he was determined not only to test the inter-church waters but to rock the ecumenical boat.

In this he was enthusiastically supported by his mentor, George MacLeod. Having been confirmed as an Anglican at Winchester, George had always had a particular interest in Presbyterian-Episcopalian relations. With his family, he had smarted at the insult to his great uncle, the Rev. Dr Donald MacLeod, who had not been permitted to take part in George's parents' wedding; and the debate over inter-communion in Toc H, which had led to his resignation in 1926, had further soured him. Incidents like the separate Episcopalian pilgrimage to Iona in 1963 added to the irritation, and he bridled at any suggestions of Anglican superiority. In many ways George admired the Anglican Communion, and there was much that he borrowed from its worship and practice. He had many friends and admirers within Anglicanism. The Iona Community had members and Associates who were Episcopalian, and prominent figures from the Church of England visited Iona and shared in the life of the Community.

What he did not admire was what he saw as Anglican equivocation on ecumenical matters. The polite tittle-tattle of ecumenical tea-and-sandwiches was not for him: typically, he wanted action, not more papers. He was fed up with endless rounds of talk while Scotland declined into irreligiosity – it reminded him too much of the SCM (which, now that it had taken on board the current secular theology, he said was no longer either Christian or a Movement). The Tirrell action was right up George's street – let's forget about the diplomatic niceties and put things to the test! Harry Whitley and George MacLeod were like two bulls in an ecumenical china shop, and they enjoyed themselves very much.

Some of the Kirk's ecumenical leaders were appalled at what they felt was a discourtesy, and sent messages of sympathy to Bishop Carey. They accused Whitley and MacLeod of being egotistical wreckers who were setting back the whole ecumenical advance. The tempestuous Harry Whitley, like George MacLeod, had trodden on more than a few toes in his time (indeed, any moves to make him Moderator were quickly blocked) and there were more than a few long knives out for him. Unacceptably murderous thoughts were masked by talk about the Holy Spirit.

The Holy Spirit was also much invoked at the Presbytery meeting, but he must not have made his intentions clear because it ended in a draw – 106 votes each. Many ministers felt that the appointment of Tirrell was a deliberately anti-ecumenical move. The Moderator declined to exercise his casting vote, and the matter was referred to the 1966 General Assembly. The Assembly swiftly and firmly passed the hot potato back to the Presbytery, saying that it was up to the Presbytery to decide.

The celebrated "Tirrell Case" ran and ran, attracting considerable media attention. Professor T. F. Torrance, a leader of the ecumenical party, went down to Cambridge to persuade James Pike to withdraw support, and Canon Hugh Montefiore likewise lobbied the American bishop. The outcome was that the request for Tirrell to celebrate the sacraments was eventually withdrawn.

It is interesting that George MacLeod, who was perceived publicly as an "ecumaniac" favouring bishops in the Kirk and the recovery of "Catholic" practices, was now accused of being an ecumenical wrecker. It was bewildering to many, but there was nothing inconsistent in his position. Yes, he was in favour of bishops – provided they were elected, accountable and had to retire after seven years. Yes, he was in favour of the recovery of certain "Catholic" practices – wasn't the Church of Scotland part of the one, holy, Catholic Church? Yes, he was in favour of the ecumenical movement – provided it was an action-based united missionary movement. But why all the talk about inter-communion, and no action? Why all the talk about validity of others' ministry, but no shared experiments? He literally had no time for the "softly, softly" ecumenical approach. He much preferred the overturning of the tables in the temple to a discussion with the moneylenders about the problems of providing credit in ecclesiastical buildings.

People were also confused about his attitude towards Roman Catholicism. The "driver of the Rome Express" greatly admired many aspects of Roman Catholicism, but he had his reservations.

"You know how vague everything is becoming in Protestantism – as for instance in the recent report on sex and morality," he wrote to one correspondent who took him to task for his pro-Roman views. "The Roman Church still has a strength and a scheme, related to which is their 'solidity in worship'. You are aware that although Scotland has very simple services, in proportion to our size more Scotsmen try to join Freemasonry than in any other country! There is an inherent desire for order, symbol and mystery. That is provided by High Mass in the Roman Church. I certainly agree with you that it does not re-present the simplicity of the primitive church when indeed, in its earliest days people actually brought their loaves of bread from their own cooking and piled them high on the communion table with the obvious meaning that it is the whole of the 'common life' that is taken up by God and transformed.

". . . My own view is that people will always be made differently and some veer towards Quaker simplicity – who have no sacraments at all – and others veer towards an assistance to devotion coming from great colour and music and ordered worship. I am sure that both are well pleasing to the Lord – provided it is 'the heart's aye the part aye that makes us right or wrang'.

"The real problem about Rome to me is not their form of worship or their confessional or their worship of the Virgin Mary, but their (political) claim that their church is the Kingdom of God. We would claim that the Church is the servant of the Kingdom of God. Once you equate the two, then of course you are always trying to build a 'Holy Roman Empire.'"[1]

What about the Protestant churches, though? George admired the Roman Catholic ritual, sense of mystery and discipline, and felt that these things were presently lacking in the Protestant churches. The doctrinal and moral confusion of the time was distressing to a man who had in his lifetime twice seen the kind of post-war reconstruction he wanted crumble in a morass of what looked like self-indulgence.

As always, he was convinced that the Church held the answers to the problems of the age, but only if it lived its radical message. What distressed him most about the Church's own theological and moral confusion was that at a time when people were searching for answers, the Church's message seemed to be only that it was searching too. In a pamphlet he wrote in December, 1966, titled *Nearing the Eleventh Hour*, he expressed the fear that the institutional Church might be too late with its Word.

"The Church today is paralysed with self analysis," he said. "Its mission has become uncertain, its worship, still reverently respected, has lost its zest, even clergy discuss how far they are committed to prayer. From the pulpit the trumpet sounds with an uncertain voice. Bible reading has become duty, and not the daily necessity of the soul. Where the Sociology class rooms are full, the Divinity Halls drop in numbers. In our four Divinity Halls in Scotland, there is now one full-time professor or lecturer for every three of our regular students. We also are at our Eleventh Hour.

"Most assuredly it is not a new preoccupation with the things of

Peace that will revive us. The Bomb is not God's trick to recover His Institutional Church. But a faithful obedience to the Way of the Cross, for the twentieth century, can do no other than take account of our modern plight and see faithlessness as the cause of our secular world.

"Michael must come back into our consciousness (not just our intellects). Angels must become our consciousness again – not floppy damsels in their nighties, but dynamic forces in their serried ranks. It is because we have left 'all that' out that the Faith has become 'background music' and demonic secularism rules our souls.

"By all means let us say that the secular is the realm of God's activity and that He is in and through all things. But realize He has both let loose Satan there, for our disciplining, and that Christ is also there for our salvation. If there is no darkness, there is quite assuredly no Light. The Task is so deep that only a Church with a recovered obedience can hope to cope with it."[2]

The statement was classic MacLeodian rhetoric in the face of a situation which was out of control. At a time when the transcendent God was all but disappearing from public life, and indeed was being pronounced dead even by theologians, George MacLeod's answer was to stress the majesty of God. At a time when sociology was king, and metaphysics had been ruled out of court, George MacLeod talked about angels. At a time when utopias were ten a penny and talk about "sin" was regarded as distasteful and even psychologically damaging, George MacLeod warned about Satan and demonic powers.

It was defiant stuff, because George MacLeod was losing the sixties war. He was becoming more isolated in the Church of Scotland, as he spoke, almost obsessively, about peace at every opportunity. Even in his own Iona Community – with its seminars on the Secular City, Jesus the Man for Others, and the New Morality – he was regarded by not a few as yesterday's great man.

It would take nearly twenty years for him to become again today's great man.

In the meantime, he had some news which would send shock waves through his Community.

24

Church-Work is Slow

*After some short pause, the old knight, turning about
his head twice or thrice to take a survey of this great
metropolis, bid me observe how thick the city was set
with churches, and that there was scarce a single
steeple on this side Temple Bar. 'A most heathenish
sight,' says Sir Roger. 'There is no religion at this end
of the town. The fifty new churches will very much
mend the Prospect; but Church-work is slow, Church-
work is slow.'*

ADDISON'S SIR ROGER DE COVERLEY

*There's more fun at a Glasgow funeral than there is at
an Edinburgh wedding.*

ANON (GLASGOW)

Late on Hogmanay, 1966, George's old diesel-engined Standard
was stopped by the police, who were making random checks for
drunk drivers.

"Your name, sir?" inquired the weary policeman, sniffing the
driver's breath.

"George MacL . . . no, wait a minute," (checks watch with a
grin), "Lord MacLeod."

"Right. Oot the car. If there's one thing I can do withoot the
nicht it's a funny man!"

When members of the Iona Community heard the news on New
Year's day, 1967, they could scarcely believe it: George MacLeod
had resigned as leader of the Iona Community and had accepted a
peerage!

"MacLeod of Iona" ran the headline in the *Daily Express*, but
George deliberately chose not to be named in that obvious way. He
felt that Iona was too important to be associated with any one

351

person's name. He elected to be titled Baron MacLeod of Fuinary, thus identifying himself with his ancestors. (There was immediate controversy about the spelling of Fuinary, some saying it should be "Fiunary". George's reply was that the spelling had varied over the years, and that he was sticking with the spelling chosen by his great-grandfather, the Gaelic scholar.)

The new life peer, who had been made an extra chaplain to the Queen upon his compulsory retirement as royal chaplain on his 70th birthday, wrote to his sovereign:

"This whole development has been the biggest surprise in my life and I feel that I cannot refrain from expressing, however briefly, my great sense of gratitude for the honour you have conferred on me and my household.

"I have never countenanced for a moment those who have called me a prophet. It is good now to have the fullest proof that I cannot be one. Prophets invariably get pelted, whereas I have been promoted!

"You once told me at Balmoral that the Sound of Mull could be lovelier than any part of the Western Isles. I told you then of the Manse of Fuinary, where two of my direct forebears ministered, father and son, for an unbroken 103 years. The manse is now our family holiday home and it appeals to something very deep in me to be allowed to sign myself from now on, George MacLeod of Fuinary, Morvern."

Norman of the Barony could hardly have expressed the matter more felicitously to his sovereign lady.

The Duke of Edinburgh, who had enjoyed many a verbal battle with George about pacifism – on one occasion, the royal equerry sat nervously tapping the table with his fingers as the two men went after each other, no quarter given, with George finally exclaiming, after the Duke had made an equivocal response, "Now you sound like one of these Church of England bishops!" – sent a telegram of congratulations. Unfortunately, it was posted to the empty flat above his, and was handed in to him by the landlord a few weeks later. (George had reluctantly moved house to Edinburgh three years previously. Lorna had never been happy at Park Circus, and had wanted for some time to live in Edinburgh. George preferred the direct bluntness and street humour of the Glaswegians.)

"Imagining it might be from the tailor who made my last suit, suggesting payment, I opened it casually," he told Prince Philip apologetically. "It read – 'Buckingham Palace – DELIGHTED TO SEE YOUR NAME IN THE HONOURS LIST' – and was from yourself.

"I just had to tell you all that, to explain my otherwise gross discourtesy toward your generous gesture toward me. Tomorrow I shall seek the telegraph boy and shall pray all this night that my pacifist convictions will rise to the occasion."

Letters of congratulation poured in from Archbishops, politicians (including Harold Macmillan), university principals, churchmen, and ordinary people. Mervyn Stockwood, by now bishop of Southwark, welcomed him to the House of Lords saying, "It is a terrible declension for us both!". Journalist James Cameron wrote from India to say, "I heard you'd been canonized, or ennobled, but I don't know what to do about it, except to say that I'm sure it isn't enough."

It seemed as if all Scotland had been touched by the news.

Professor David Cairns suggested he should call himself "Baron Rox of Aden": Naomi Mitchison, the novelist, said that the House of Lords was a depressing place, but George would help to make it more cheerful: actor Tom Fleming reminded George that he had often heard him tell the story of a peer of the realm who had a nightmare that he was making a speech in the House of Lords – and woke up to find that he was!

Thus did George MacLeod become the first ever Church of Scotland minister to sit in the House of Lords. The news of the peerage made the international press. Saying that he was the nation's best known living Protestant minister, *Time* magazine described the Iona Community as "one of the century's most influential experiments in Christian living." It reported that the new peer would not be a spokesman for his church in the Lords since, as he said, "I have not been famous for always saying the same thing as the Church of Scotland."

Why did he take the title, after declining to be known as Sir George for so many years? He said jocularly that he did it to make an honest Lady of Lorna!

His main reason was that the offer came at the time when he was considering giving up the leadership of the Iona Community, and was seeking a new role. Having spent a good part of his life urging Christians to become involved in politics, he was now being given the chance to practise what he preached. And the House of Lords would provide a new platform for his peace crusade.

When Labour premier Harold Wilson asked him about going to

the Lords, it was with a view to increasing the number of radical voices in the upper chamber. George's affirmative reply indicated that he would take his place on the cross-benches. Ever his own man.

"This totally unexpected offer did seem to 'chime' with conversations I had already been having with Lorna – and no-one else – about the best way and time of relinquishing the leadership of the Iona Community," he wrote to all members.

He had not even discussed the matter with his deputy, who was as surprised as the other Community members to read the announcement in the newspapers. Ralph was hurt by what he felt was a snub. He would have felt even more hurt had he known that George had confided the news to Douglas Alexander, by then warden of Community House, whom George knew he could trust, and who he wanted to be alerted in order to alleviate the upheaval which would hit the Community and would unsettle Ralph. It certainly was unsettling for Ralph, and worse was to come when George failed to support him in his bid to succeed to the leadership.

Why had George decided to relinquish the leadership of the Community at this time? On one level, it was perfectly understandable. He had never intended to lead the Community for so long: the Community was now well established as a force in the Church: the Abbey rebuilding was now complete: and he was 71 years of age. It is also true to say, however, that the decision about the future use of the Abbey had an effect on the timing of the move. He might have been tempted to stay on to supervise the experiment of using the Abbey as a divinity college, but he knew full well that the prevailing winds were blowing in a different direction. It was time to go.

George indicated that his resignation would take effect from 1st September, 1967. He explained why.

"At the level of pence, I don't want to go out precipitately," he told the Community. "Without going into details of the present state of the finances, it is clear that they stand in the precarious situation more or less normal for the past quarter of a century! As you know, I have been in a position not to draw any salary from the Community since its inception. Without prejudice to the shape of the future structure of the headquarters of the Community, new money must clearly be found if I am to be replaced by a full-time appointment. Further, the considerable potential now presented by Community House in Glasgow urgently requires a full-time additional member of staff there."

The remarkable fact was that in the twenty-nine years of his leadership of the Iona Community, George MacLeod had not received a single penny in wages. He had used the money he had inherited from his parents to pay his own salary. He rarely used his inheritance on himself – it was used to support the things he believed in.

It is one of the ironies and contradictions of the radical Iona Community that it owed its beginning and development not only to donations from a battleship builder, but to the inherited wealth of its founder, leader and driving force. (On several occasions, when there was no money in the kitty, he had signed legal guarantees which could have bankrupted him.) Not only that, the flow of money which came in for the rebuilding programme was not unconnected with the fact that the charismatic founder had one foot firmly in the New Club, Edinburgh, even as the other foot was kicking the Establishment with great gusto. These contradictions were summed up in the title Lord MacLeod of Fuinary – prompted by a Labour prime minister, approved enthusiastically by the Queen, and disapproved of by some of the more left-wing members of the Iona Community.

George also indicated that before he left the leadership he wanted to clarify the recently agreed peace commitment of the Iona Community – a broadly-based commitment to peace and justice which allowed pacifist and non-pacifist to coexist. He indicated that for him, the promotion of pacifism now had the status of a calling.

"I confess that the same 'tap tap' of conviction that I suffered when I 'had to go to Iona' in the Thirties, now apprehends me when I face the Power of Non-Violence in obedience to the Person of Christ – as a major challenge to be explored by the modern Church. No one knows much about the subject (least of all the writer) but an increasing number of people are wanting to know. It cannot just be preached. There must be practice in its portrayal. Come it soon or late, I am convinced that this is what Iona, physically and spiritually, is for.

"Manifestly the Community as such, and as of now, does not subscribe my conviction. All I wish to plead, before personally pulling out, is a recognized place for this conviction within the life of the Community. Can a 'corner of Iona', by the agreement of the whole Community, be used for its deeper study and expression? If not, it seems a pity if this issue has to be laboriously developed elsewhere."

It was this "tap tap" of conviction, in the face of the escalating nuclear arms race, that made George MacLeod an even more uncompromising pacifist in the late 1960s and 1970s. Up till then he had, of course, been well known as a leading pacifist, but he had many other concerns as well. He had always declared vehemently that the Iona Community, like the Church, had room for people of varying convictions on the war issue. He was now becoming more insistent that pacifism was the true gospel response, the "only one way left" for an obedient Church in the midst of a disobedient generation. Pacifism was moving from being one issue to being *the* issue.

At the 1967 General Assembly, he spoke in favour of an unsuccessful motion urging the government to disassociate itself from American policy in Vietnam, and to seek negotiations based on the complete withdrawal of all American and other foreign forces.

Warm and generous tribute was paid to the retiring Iona leader by the Moderator, the Rt Rev. Dr Roy Sanderson, who had first been influenced by George in the direction of the ministry some forty years previously.

"George," he said, "it may seem strange if I address you by name in this way in the General Assembly, but surely there is no greater dignity than that which flows from affection, and it is with affection that you are known throughout the Church of Scotland by your baptismal name. This is a family occasion, and for me the mode of address is appropriate – a family occasion, but you have not always been the good boy of the family. Sometimes by your very exuberance you have caused your mother Church embarrassment, and sometimes you seem to have been an enigma to her, but in her heart of hearts, be assured, she has always been mighty proud.

"It is with affection and pride that the General Assembly would have me thank you most cordially for the leadership you have given to the Iona Community, and for having created the Community at all. At the start, as you well know, there were those who thought it was a mad-cap scheme . . . but you were filled with a three-fold vision.

"You had, first, a vision that younger ministers and artisans would be joined in fellowship, that they might recover in the twentieth century and within the context of the Reformed Church, whose traditions were ever dear to you, something of the tradition of Columba and his community. And, secondly, you had a vision that Iona might become again a place of spiritual refreshment and outgoing power; and to this end you were determined to try and restore the Abbey to its former glory. And thirdly, you had a vision that the members of the Community, having learned to worship and work together, would offer their service wherever it was needed most, particularly in the difficult places and crowded areas.

"Not only this generation but all future generations have been put under a debt to you and your Community. For the rest, the story is written in the lives of men and women and cannot adequately be told. History will give its own verdict, and I have a feeling that even then it will not be wholly free of controversy, but yours has been a leadership that has never waited upon popular applause or been unduly daunted by opposition. Those who have followed you wholeheartedly, and those of us who have enjoyed your friendship and benefited by your influence – and it is over forty years since yours was one of the voices used to call me to the ministry – have, I hope, been able to show you some measure of our gratitude already, but others who have been and remain critical of you would surely also admit that they, too, have been stimulated by you, even though it has been the stimulation of the gadfly! You and the Community you have led have been good for the Church and profitable for the Kingdom of God."

The Moderator's eloquent tribute was received with thunderous applause.

It was a bewildering time for the Iona Community. Even those Community members who had fought him tooth and nail in the love-hate drama of the previous few years found the prospect strange. Fighting Father was one thing: living without Father was quite another.

When the leadership election came, there were two candidates, Ralph Morton and Ian Reid, a former senior army chaplain who had been minister of an Edinburgh housing scheme parish for nearly 20 years. Ian Reid's enabling and pastoral style was much closer to the Ralph Morton model than to the charismatic Mac-Leodian lead-from-the-front mode, and he was certainly no pacifist. The Community wanted a change of leadership style, and Ian Reid had some of Ralph's qualities while being younger and having Scottish parish experience. He won the vote.

George's farewell gift from the Community had already been made – against his will. It had been decided to commission a portrait which would hang in the Abbey buildings. The best Scottish portrait painter of the day, David A. Donaldson, agreed to undertake the work.

The resultant picture of George in his Iona double-breasted navy blue suit and blue shirt and tie was very controversial. It portrayed him as determined to the point of stubborn, distant, powerful, almost arrogant. George did not like it, and Lorna appreciated it even less than Lady Churchill liked the notorious portrait of Sir Winston.

Handing over the portrait, Ralph Morton said: "We have defied George MacLeod. We have insisted on doing something against his will. We have put him at the mercy of an artist."

In acknowledging the gift, an unusually subdued George was less than fulsome. He said that in his life's work he had reflected what other people had given to him: just as his portrait was made up of many brush strokes, so his work had been contributed to by all those present.

Was George so upset about it because as an essentially private public figure, he had to endure a gifted and perceptive artist moving in close to his private "space" in order to make a very public interpretation of his subject's private world? Or was it that David Donaldson, for all his reputation in the salons, was to George's eye too much of a sixties man – twists and twirls in the wrong places, and a compulsion to shock?

Soon it was Ralph Morton's turn to retire, typically keeping his disappointments to himself. George said that his deputy's biggest contribution had been in fashioning the Community pattern when it evolved from being a coterie and became a company.

"I think it is true that in recent years his interpretation of our times has increasingly differed from my own," George acknowledged. "Inevitably, in the nature of the case, within Community circles, mine has received the greater prominence. How galling this could have been to a lesser man than Ralph! How disastrous even, had he been unredeemed. In all vicissitudes, China, Cambridge, Community, it is Ralph's unfailing loyalty that shines through."[1]

Loyalty had also shone through in George's indefatigable secretary, Miss Dalgleish, who took the opportunity to retire after years of hard and committed service.

In his final broadcast service as leader from Iona Abbey, George recalled with thanksgiving the family whom he stumbled upon worshipping in the ruins of the Abbey more than thirty years previously, giving thanks for the fact that their single candle in the darkness had in the course of time been replaced by 100 candles, as people from all nations crowded into the church.

Calling on the whole Church to address the nuclear issue, he concluded his final Iona broadcast with a powerful appeal.

"Only the Christian Church is sufficient to deal with so vast a proposition. It is miles beyond politicians. Only angels can deal with demons. Only Christ can cast out Satan.

"May it be that when the youngest listening at this moment are dead and gone, let alone the older among us, may it be that the new word of peace may come from this island so proverbial of peace? May it be that (for all our blundering in the building of this place these last twenty-nine years), God will use it for his greatest purpose? The new way of power? It was Samuel Johnson sitting in the ruins of Iona nearly two hundred years ago who declared, 'It may be that in the revolution of time, Iona will again become the instructress of the Western regions.'"

George may have been losing the war, but in the midst of his distress about the way things were going, he was lifting his eyes to the horizon of the future – when he would be dead and gone – and, like Columba before him, was looking to the day when Iona would have a word which people would long to hear. At a time of depression about the way the declining Church was going, he was clinging to his deep conviction that the best days of the Church were still to come, and that these best days would somehow be connected with Iona.

Was all this the wishful thinking of a great but disappointed man, projecting his dreams of an ideal, unattainable reconstruction which was slipping further and further from historical view? Was it a whistling in the despairing darkness? Or was it inspired prophecy, the more awesome for having been uttered within that sacred island tradition of dreams and visions?

With these last public words as leader of the Community, George MacLeod stepped out into his own personal wilderness.

In the difficult years which followed, George was a general

without an army. It proved to be a painful experience, and not just for him.

It was very hard for him to let go of his command of the Iona Community. Being a backbencher was never his style. Having led the Community from the front for 29 years, he could not resist the temptation to lead it from the back.

George's activities created problems for the new leader. Ian Reid had a difficult enough job without having endless advice from his illustrious predecessor. (At a reception at Holyrood Palace, the Duke of Edinburgh asked the new leader: "Is George always breathing down your neck?" to which Ian replied, "At least he retired, which is more than Schweitzer did".)

"I felt very insecure when I was appointed leader," Ian Reid recalled. "I knew that the world identified the Community with George. I knew also that the Community at that point wanted a change of leader. I knew that I was no charismatic leader, and that I could not be like George. On the other hand, I had to show that I was leader and not him. Considering his personality, he was exceptionally understanding."

That was a typically generous assessment. George did breathe down his successor's neck, and offered him more advice than he could wish for. As a sensitive, caring and somewhat diffident man who was, by his own admission, somewhat in awe of his distinguished predecessor, Ian undoubtedly suffered through the experience, though he did so with grace and understanding. After all, he owed a great deal to the man who had influenced him in the direction of the ministry and the Iona Community, and whose leadership had inspired him as he laboured for years in one of Edinburgh's less salubrious districts.

Ian Reid not only had the difficulty of living in George's formidable shadow. He had to lead the Community at a time when the Abbey rebuilding programme was over, the Community was no longer a new and exciting experiment, and confidence in the Church and in its message was not high. But further: the fact that the Community owed so much to its founder was now itself a problem. For 29 years the Community had not had to raise money for the rebuilding or find a salary for its leader; as a group which talked a great deal about economics, it now had to face economic realities from which it had been sheltered. Many of its individual members had to struggle financially, but as a corporate entity the Iona Community resembled a privileged child which had grown up secure in the knowledge that Father's allowance would see it through. Any financial worrying had been done on their behalf by Father: now the sleepless nights would have to be shared, and the accounts spread out on the table.

Ian Reid had to create the structures which would allow the Community to survive. It was unspectacular work, lacking glamour, and the new leader's vulnerability was not helped by the fact that George was making high-profile speeches calling for a New Reformation. There was a danger that the Iona Community would be perceived as having lost its vision and excitement now that George MacLeod had retired, and Ian Reid's patient and undemonstrative style certainly contrasted with the founder's flamboyant confidence. The new leader had to cope with George's impatience and frustration over what he saw as the Community's tendency to "blether" rather than to take a firm "line" on issues.

George was often insensitive to Ian Reid's difficult position. He could be alternately caring, mischievous, supportive and bullying. He was in many ways a deeply loyal member of the Community, yet he was incapable of dissembling, and his frustration with the way things were going boiled over. It was not simply that he liked to get his own way, though this was certainly the case. In essence, he felt the time was short, the issues were urgent, and clear and decisive action was needed.

On occasion, George could be obstructive and bloody-minded. Some years previously, he had written a pamphlet for visitors to the Abbey. Its historical material was not always accurate, and Ian asked Tom Graham, a member of the Community with an honours degree in history, to write a new pamphlet. George was furious, and wrote imperiously to Ian saying that he would reprint his pamphlet with his own money, and would leave copies for visitors. He did not do so, but Ian always had to be aware of what the founder was doing in the background.

George would circulate proposals about pacifism to members of the Community without consulting his successor, who was right to be upset by this intolerable behaviour. Ian Reid and the conveners of the Community's committees soon began to have a certain sympathy for the leaders of the Church of Scotland who had railed furiously against a maverick who seemed to be a law to himself!

At the age of 72, the energetic George MacLeod was a man in search of a role. Now that he was free from the running of the Iona Community, his concerns became ever more global, and much less parish and church based. In big demand as a speaker, he concentrated almost exclusively on the themes of pacifism and social justice, and seemed much less interested in the structures of the traditional Church. In a wide-ranging interview in the *British Weekly*, his disillusionment with the ecumenical movement became apparent.

"Forty years ago," he said, "at an ecumenical conference which I attended, the Anglicans said that what stood in the way was the validity of our orders, and this prevented intercommunion. Last week, forty years later, at renewed discussions, they were saying precisely the same thing! I calculate that actual acts of union will slow up. High Anglicans delude themselves that Rome is drawing nearer and will proportionately slow up union with other Protestant denominations lest they spoil their own chances of the larger plum.

"To be sure, let all denominations continue increasingly to intermix in church meetings. This is all to the good. But don't let's forget that Romans, Anglicans and Presbyterians have worked and laughed together cheek by jowl in shipyard, factory, shop and office since the industrial revolution and already get along fine. Indeed, we only separate for our acts of worship. This is at the dictate of incomprehensible formulae of priest and prelate.

"If we would get courageously lost in obedience to Pentecost in the real bankruptcies of our time (war, race and economics) a new dawn would break. We would then see the things that divide us as quite secondary, and comparably easier of solution."

George was still convinced that Iona had a unique role to play in the renewal of the Church, and he was alarmed at proposals to make the island a conservation area.

"The essence of conservation is to *CONSERVE*, and the essence of religion is to *POUR FORTH*," he wrote to a no doubt startled Secretary of State for Scotland.

"Already this last summer more young people were coming to camp unorganized, higgledy-piggledy around the Abbey, in their blue bivouac tents, than we had all summer in our organized Iona youth camps. Some were Roman Catholics asking where High Mass was celebrated, some were living in sin, some were smoking pot. But nearly all were prepared to discuss the Faith by the hour, seeking a new way of life.

"In my opinion, it is only a matter of months before total immersion adult baptisms will be conducted at the old Celtic site, such is the gathering pressure of revolt against secularity.

"Now this is a messy business, and I can well imagine, in a decade, the Ancient Monuments Board – with the best will in the world – but from a distance, advising and *ULTIMATELY DICTATING* how everything can be trimmed up, camps corralled, tents banished, for the benefit, peace and quiet of day trippers (most of whom are disappointed at not finding a pub). The Holy Spirit will flee away for some place of relative freedom, while Iona, in the great day of the new revival, could become the museum piece of the century. This might occur, not because of ill will, but because of the complete impossibility of anyone legislating truly to conserve a holy island, who is not in daily and religious contact with its everyday life."

George's freedom from the burdens of office gave him the opportunity to accept more invitations to speak. He went to New Zealand in September 1967 on a speaking tour on behalf of the International Fellowship of Reconciliation, of which he was president. The Kinross and West Perthshire Constituency Association of the Scottish National Party asked him to consider being their candidate at the next General Election (he declined). To an invitation to go to America in 1968, he replied accepting, saying, "The fact is that in February 1968 I shall be seventy-three years of age, coming up to seventy-four! What my mental processes will be like by then is anybody's guess. I should hate to arrive on a stretcher. On the other hand, I am perfectly well aware that Adenaeur was making a mess of Germany at the age of eighty-eight. But you have been warned."

Lord MacLeod's maiden speech in the House of Lords was in support of a motion to delay implementation of the Labour government's Commonwealth Immigrants Bill, which was designed to stop the influx of Kenyan Asians into Britain. He said that despite all the protestations to the contrary it was a racial issue, and he praised the contribution of Asians to the life of Britain.

He was congratulated by Lord Beaumont of Whitley, who said how pleased all those who were members of the Anglican ministry were to welcome such a distinguished Free Church leader to the House.

"As a theological student I was once listening to a lecture given by the noble Lord," he said, "with every word of which I disagreed. Since then it has taken me some time to realize that I should have agreed with every word that he said then, and I hope that it will take the noble Lord less time to convince your Lordships' House than it took him to convince me."[2]

Their Lordships failed to agree with their new peer, who was no doubt surprised, as a former Moderator of the established Church of Scotland, to be described as a Free Church leader.

Later in the session, he was on his feet to protest against the Russian invasion of Czechoslovakia. Typically, he managed to make it a hymn to non-violence, while the noble Lords sat bemused.

"The old power structures – even the latest – have turned in on themselves. In the ultimate, said Martin Luther King, it is non-violence or non-existence: there will be no existence unless there is non-violence, yet still it is true that it is better to fight injustice than to do nothing. What then of the new fight? The power of non-violence has nothing to do with passivity; it is not withdrawal; it is not pusillanimity. What are the great names of contemporary Christian history? Kagawa in Japan, Luthuli in Africa, Danilo Dolci in Italy, Niemöller in Germany, Martin Luther King in America – every one of them totally committed to non-violence, yet every one of them up to the neck in politics, every one of them in prison at one time or another for being involved." The noble Lords shifted uneasily in the face of this strange, passionate Scottish rhetoric. They carried on as if it hadn't happened.

George had no more success at the 1968 General Assembly of the Church of Scotland when he launched an attack on international financiers who, he said, were running the world. Speaking against the background of continental student revolts against authority, he said young people had become aware that it was bankers, not politicians, who made the key decisions in the world.

"By all means let the General Assembly, in their report on devaluation, call on the people of Britain to work hard and make sacrifices," he cried. "But youth will increasingly ask: 'For whom the work, and for whom the sacrifices?' Is the whole world of global labour just to go on doing just that for the benefit of indifferent Mammon? . . . It is urgent that the whole issue of international monetary finance be independently reviewed.

"Is there anyone still asking: 'But what has this to do with the Church?' OK, let's drop it then. Let's become like the Russian Church which is the poodle of the atheist society at the Kremlin. For the Kremlin says: 'You can look after people's souls, but hands off when it comes to bodies – that's our department.' Don't forget that the Great Parable of Judgment, whether we are to go to heaven or hell, is dependent on what we do about people's bodies, not their spiritual welfare.

"But at a lower key, some may be saying this is for the bankers to get down to. Have you ever queried the bankers? I have. Try the lower echelon of bankers and most of them will say, 'These things are too high for us, we cannot attain unto them', but a small minority will whisper, 'You've got something there, boy; isn't it extraordinarily cold weather for so late in the month of May?'

"Try the upper echelon of bankers. I have. I wrote to the top man of a London bank, a charming man, asking his comments on a similar document to the Haslemere Declaration. He replied that the figures were inaccurate. I immediately asked which figures, but have had no reply.

"They are in training for the job of international bankers. They know what is good for us. Don't consult us, the paltry crowd. But do they know what is good for us? Or are they sowing the seeds of the next war?"

His plea for a review of the role of international financiers fell largely on deaf ears.

"Moderator," said Mr J. Hume, "we are all well used to Lord MacLeod's magnificent oratory, and we appreciate it, but some of us are young enough not to be taken in by it . . ."

What was happening to George MacLeod can best be summed up by a story which he himself told again and again.

A missionary in India with great courage decided to accompany the pagan tribe of his district on the occasion of their annual pagan festival. He marched with them into the forests by night till they came to the point where they paused to go down to the groves for their obscenities and bestialities. At the moment of the pause, he preached the love of God. The young men nearly killed him for his interference, but he returned to his compound unscathed.

The next year he repeated the act and there was lessened tension. For nine consecutive years he repeated his preachment on the great occasion, just before the tribe went down into the dirt. Then he died a natural death. The next year, when the Feast came round, the head of the tribe asked the mission to send someone else – *because it had now become part of the show.*

In the late sixties and seventies, the regular warnings of the old Scottish pacifist warhorse became just that – an essential and predictable part of one of the longest-running and tiredest shows in town.

The sad thing was that the audience, which applauded the elderly missionary thespian before voting almost ritualisitically against him, hardly even seemed to notice that the theatre was steadily emptying.

PART SIX

*

PROPHET
WITH HONOUR

25

Hear the Word of the Lord

And Amaziah said to Amos, "O seer, go, flee away to
the land of Judah, and eat bread there; but never
again prophesy at Bethel, for it is the king's sanctuary,
and it is a temple of the kingdom.

Then Amos answered Amaziah, "I am no prophet,
nor a prophet's son; but I am a herdsman, and a
dresser of sycamore trees, and the Lord took me from
following the flock, and the Lord said to me, 'Go,
prophesy to my people Israel.'
"Now therefore hear the word of the Lord."

AMOS 7, 12–16 (RSV)

If we do not listen to the prophets, we shall have to
listen to Providence

A. C. CRAIG

Sunday May 5, 1968, Athens. It is seven o'clock in the morning.
The sun is shining. Trouble is brewing.

The Very Reverend, the Lord MacLeod of Fuinary is the
designated Church of Scotland's "spiritual leader" on an Inter-
Church Travel cruise to the Mediterranean and the Holy Land.
The group, which includes Lady MacLeod and the three children,
have had an audience with the Pope before going on to Crete,
Rhodes and Cyprus, where they were received by Archbishop
Makarios. After six days in Jerusalem and Tiberias, and a visit to
Ephesus, they disembark at Athens.

George MacLeod has sought and received an assurance from
Canon Arthur Payton, organizer of the trip, that there will be no
official reception with the Metropolitan at the Cathedral of Athens.
He does not want to give any credibility to the Colonels who are

running Greece – they have forcibly ejected the Church's appointed Metropolitan of Athens, and replaced him with their own man. Athens is awash with rumours of detention without trial and cruelty towards members of the political opposition.

Canon Payton breathes a sigh of relief as the last of the coaches takes the remaining members of the party on a sight-seeing tour of Athens. Then Archbishop James, Dean of the Greek Cathedral in London, comes running to say that he has been to see the Metropolitan of Athens, and that he and his bishops will be waiting in the Cathedral at 12 noon to receive them! The Canon decides that he cannot snub the Metropolitan, and he sends messages to six out of the seven groups to turn up at the Cathedral at noon. He gives specific instructions that the group which includes George MacLeod is not to be informed.

In the Cathedral just after noon, the speeches are under way when Canon Payton looks in horror to the west door of the Cathedral. His personal nightmare is unfolding before his eyes. There, striding towards him along the long aisle, is a very determined and angry Lord MacLeod, dressed in colourful tourist shirt. Despite the protestations of Canon Payton and Archbishop James, he insists on speaking. They try to prevent him, but he bursts out loudly: "Is the Archbishop aware of the sufferings of prisoners in this city? Is he aware of the cruelty and torture which is being meted out to innocent people?"

The tension in the Cathedral is unbearable. The Metropolitan of Athens retreats behind the Iconostasis, out of sight, and the rest of the procession melts away in embarrassment. George MacLeod continues to hammer home his point, saying he is disgusted that the Metropolitan and his bishops won't even give an answer to the question, and that they are well aware of what is going on in the city . . .

No one who was there will ever forget that confrontation. Least of all Canon Payton.

"We went away from the Cathedral," he remembered, "not in our usual joyful mood, having had a great ecumenical exchange of singing and praying, but having had an encounter which none of us would ever forget.

"When I got back to the ship in the evening, because we were not sailing until late that night – in fact nearly midnight – I had dinner on shore and was rather late getting back on board. I was very touched when I went to my cabin to find George and Lorna standing in the corridor, waiting to see me. They were so sweet, so apologetic, so upset. But then George showed me some of the papers of Amnesty International with the evidence of what was going on in Athens. I said, 'Oh, George, why didn't you show me that before? This is a vindication for you, and I admire your courage. Thank you for what you have done today. And we will know about this tomorrow.' And he gave us a talk the next day about prisoners of conscience in Greece, and we gave him our full support."

The journey home – taking George MacLeod back just in time to escort the Queen Mother round Iona Abbey – must have been an interesting one.

This little-known awesome confrontation in Athens tells a great deal about the stature of George MacLeod. The episode is reminiscent of the great prophetic encounters of the Old Testament, in which the seer is possessed by a Word which burns within him, and which cannot be contained. On May 5th, 1968, a complex, sometimes egotistical, often heroic twentieth-century Scottish Presbyterian minister became the bearer of the message of the Lord and acted in the great tradition of Amos, Jeremiah and Isaiah. And though George MacLeod would resist the parallel, there is more than an echo of Jesus striding into the Temple and overturning the tables of the money-lenders. It was a classic Word-event, in which the prince is left speechless, his sycophantic courtiers silenced and the embarrassed bystanders addressed at the very core of their being. Time seemed to stand still as the eternal invaded the temporal in a disruptive and uncomfortable moment, transforming Athens Cathedral into a theatre of Palestinian-Greek-Scottish prophecy. Reluctant bystanders suddenly became, whether they liked it or not, participants in a drama which demanded a decision.

George MacLeod strode up that aisle, unconcerned about the danger or even embarrassment to which he was exposing himself, because he knew that an injustice was being perpetrated, and that a cover-up was being acquiesced in – all in the name of a cosy ecumenism in which truth had been made secondary to polite relations. A charade was being enacted in glorious Greek Orthodox costume, while people were being tortured in prisons not far from the ecclesiastical scene. For George MacLeod, a man with a passionate hatred of injustice, the very stones of the Cathedral would have cried out if he had not spoken. He was prepared to endure the wrath of some of his fellow tour members – "The trouble with your father is that he doesn't understand real church politics," spat out one very angry graduate of the ecumenicity-at-all-costs school in the direction of a rather awed Maxwell MacLeod – because he could not have lived with himself if he had remained politely silent.

For that single moment of passionate utterance in Athens Cathedral, much shall surely be forgiven the man.

Passionate speech was also uttered in the theatre of the General Assembly of the Church of Scotland in May 1969, but with less dramatic effect. Once again proposing the setting up of a special commission on nuclear war, he said that if all the starving children in the world were lined up one behind the other, the queue would stretch for 23,000 miles. Britain spent £80 million a year on hunger relief, and £1250 million on armaments.

"What is it we are supposed to be fighting against Russia for?" he cried. "Because of their collective view of men. What do we stand for? Ultimately we stand for the value of human personality, and in the last resort we are still prepared to kill off one million men, women and children, infinitely valuable human personalities, all in the course of a summer morning." Voted down.

The Iona Community also spoke. In 1969, Dr Nancy Brash became the first woman to join the Iona Community, against the wishes of its founder. George argued that the Community had a special task of reaching out to industrial men, and that an all-male community had a better chance of doing that, especially when most congregations were perceived by working men as being women's organizations.

The Community believed the time had come to break the all-male rule and to change the ethos established by its somewhat chauvinistic founder. The following year, new members' wives were permitted to be with their spouses in the Abbey during the joining programme.

The old ramparts were being breached, and George MacLeod was not a happy man. Always courteous and charming towards the opposite sex, the 74-year-old Victorian gentleman had an elevated view of women – in particular roles. He did not see women as inferior – indeed, quite often, the reverse – but he had never been able to allow them out of the nursery and the kitchen and into the theological conference room.

George MacLeod was losing the war on various fronts, but he had one stunning victory in 1969, when he became Lord Rector of Glasgow University, succeeding Lord Reith. He had spoken at the University several times. On one occasion, while conducting a mission to students, he was asked by a cocky young student whether he would be able to take his dog with him to heaven. When the questioner sat down, George drew himself up to his full height, fixed his eye on the student, and said: "Young man, you'll be lucky to get into heaven in your shirt-tails, never mind your damned little pomeranian!"

The Rectorial campaign was a stormy one. George, who was the nominee of the Labour Club and the International Club, was dismissed early on as the one least likely to win the election, on account of his age. He campaigned on a platform of increased student representation, and promised to be a working Rector on behalf of the students.

The Liberal Club, labelling him "Lord MacLeod of Funeral", described him as "a swinging 73–year-old nominated as the representative of youth by a rabidly Presbyterian socialist clique in the University. Lord MacLeod is a prophet of doom, censorship and sexlessness (for others)".

Fifteen students were arrested in street battles on the day of the election. The too-old prophet of doom won handsomely, polling 1293 votes to Lt Col. Colin "Mad Mitch" Mitchell's 861, Daniel Cohn-Bendit's 836, Baroness Elliot's 706, and Mrs Winifred Ewing's 554.

Thus, at an age when many retired men were happily tending the garden or unhappily dealing with the degenerating effects of old age, George MacLeod had a new role as the champion of the young.

As he robed for the Rectorial procession, George approached Professor Murdo Ewan Macdonald, and said, "Murdo Ewan, I hear you do very good impersonations of me." Murdo responded, "Well . . . I . . ."

"Damn you!" chortled the man who often styled himself "Lord MacLeod of Buffoonery", as he strode off.

His rectorial address was rollicking stuff.

As the first minister of the Church of Scotland to hold the rectorship for nearly 300 years, and as the man chosen by Dick Sheppard to be his Assessor three days before the newly elected

Rector's untimely death in 1937, George MacLeod spoke unapologetically about religious matters. He attacked the universities for what he saw as their complicity in research for chemical and biological warfare, and for making science a god.

"We all know the key failure," he said. "It is lack of 'Universitas'. Lack of an all-embracing cult: a magnetic north star. Pluralism pulverizes. Theology, the Queen of the Sciences to which all the others bowed (in the days, for instance, when the Rector had to be a Priest or Parson) has long ago been relegated to the cellar, a veritable Cinderella of the disciplines. This would not be so bad, save that all the other ugly sisters get uglier and uglier. And the ball becomes a cacophony.

"Man, destined to be higher than the angels, has descended lower than the beasts. And it is all because we haven't got a cult, a north star. We are fragmented.

". . . There is only one hope for our society today, be it campus, or town council or the courts at Westminster: to *recover the realization that Christ was a revolutionary*: and make Him our Way again, till we recover the Truth of things."[1]

It had been more than 250 years since the University of Glasgow had heard such an evangelical Rectorial address. Quite a few staff and students did not like its uncompromisingly personal nature. Some who voted for him found as they listened that they had got more than they had bargained for. At a time when "objective" knowledge was glorified, detachment was regarded as the ideal, sociological analysis was on the academic pedestal and religion was regarded as outmoded, George MacLeod had moved into the heart of academia and claimed the central ground for Christ. How distasteful and vulgar! Others again were offended by the radical political content of the Rectorial sermon, which was followed by the inevitable controversy in the correspondence columns of the press.

George appointed Douglas Alexander, by then warden of Community House, as his Assessor. (He used to address his Assessor in letters as "Dear Ass"; Douglas would reply, "Dear Wreck"!). He did so without reference to Ian Reid, who found such discourtesies upsetting. It must also have been galling to see George MacLeod so continually make the headlines.

Impatient with what he saw as the Iona Community's dithering on the issues of war and peace, George decided to start a new movement. Calling it "The New Breakthrough in Christ", he launched it, inevitably, with a pamphlet. Called "The Idea Whose Hour is Come", the pamphlet was a typically MacLeodian mixture of breathless romp through history, cavalier use of scripture, partisan analysis of current events, hurried mis-spellings, question-begging conclusions, and flowing, passionate, inspiring, converting rhetoric. As usual, the end of an age was approaching. As usual, the best years of the Church were yet to come. As usual, the pamphlet closed with an appeal to enlist for the new battle.

George said that the purpose of what he called the NBT was not to create yet another society with annual meetings, constitutional wranglings and more talk about talk, but to appeal to many people in the churches.

"If we really are to embark on the New Warfare," he wrote, "it will not be long before the Church is accused again of being a dangerous force, as she has always been when she has approximated to her true self." The arms race, world hunger, moral decline, the religious vacuum, and the fragmentation of knowledge were all dealt with in the familiar MacLeodian telegrams, in support of the author's contention that the power of non-violence was the idea whose hour was come.

"It is already mightier than armies," he wrote. "Unless the Church embrace it now, folk will turn away from her by the direct act of the living God. The purpose of this paper is to rally those within the Church, of any denomination, to work within their congregations in the pursuit of peace by a committal to Non-Violence Now, the defeat of world poverty and the re-establishment thereby of their personal commitment to common worship, to bible reading and to prayer."

People were invited to sign up and send their names to Community House in Glasgow, where Douglas Alexander was co-ordinating the exercise, and where Professor William Barclay (who had once warned Douglas against joining the Iona Community) was active as a Trustee of the NBT. Willie Barclay was one of the many initially opposed to George MacLeod who came eventually to support him.

The *British Weekly* gave a warm welcome to the "radical septuagenarian's" initiative.

"George MacLeod was 25 years ahead of his time much earlier in his life," said the editorial, "proclaiming ideas in the same sort of torrent of disorganized words for which he was accused of being dangerously left, unrealistic, idealistic and irresponsible.

"The ideas he was then expounding are now accepted, normal and valuable parts of contemporary forward-looking Christian thinking. If the idea of 'An Idea Whose Hour is Come' appears all these things today – dangerously left, unrealistic, idealistic, irresponsible, let history make cautious the cynics, the academics, the cold water 'douchers' who are quick to dismiss and destroy the ideas of the enthusiasts."

Despite the publicity and an impressive list of sponsors in the UK, The New Breakthrough in Christ did not make a great deal of headway – perhaps because it was essentially a postal, signing-on campaign, and was not rooted in the life of a community or an organization.

George MacLeod, by now a Doctor of Letters of Muskingum University, USA, a Doctor of Laws of the Roman Catholic Iona College, New Rochelle, and an Honorary Fellow of Oriel College, Oxford, was establishing a reputation as a man who rode hobby horses to death. Pacifism and international finance were the perpetually recurrent themes, but there were other issues. He flirted for years with the Social Credit philosophy – a monetary theory which advocated various measures to reduce the national debt – and, for a time, the question of soil erosion seemed to find its way into every sermon or address. "What's George on about now?" became the question as, freed from administrative burdens, he had time to allow his mind free rein.

In 1970, his preoccupation was with Britain's proposed entry into the Common Market. It had been vetoed by General de Gaulle in 1963, but was back on the political agenda again. George broke his run of lost votes by persuading the General Assembly of the Church of Scotland to postpone support for the Government's application to join the Common Market until more consideration had been given to the matter.

Protesting about the European surpluses while people starved in Africa, he went on: "What is this thing they want us into? Are we sure it is not a white race consortium, a European sufficiency to let Western big business survive against the ever more frequent erosion from American monopolies? Are we so sure it will not in fact threaten the potentiality of a real inter-racial Commonwealth such as the British Commonwealth might still produce?"

George MacLeod, the man described as the "driver of the Rome Express", then produced a joker from the pack.

"Are you so sure it is for nothing that it is called the Treaty of

376

Rome? You know, don't you, that in the Market in ten years time, there will just be European trade unions from Yugoslavia to the Baltic. There are no longer socialist or secular trade unions left in Italy or France. They are run by the Roman Catholic caucus trade unions and the Communist trade unions.

"Do we want all our young trade unionists in this country in ten years time to choose between the leadership of Rome or the leadership of Communism if they are to play an active and significant part in the interests of industrial workers?"

Many people – including Iona Community members – were embarrassed by what they saw as the crudity of George's anti-Roman Catholic polemic, and distanced themselves from it. They were puzzled by the fact that the man who had done so much for the ecumenical movement in Scotland should sometimes sound like an Orangeman on a bad day. What they did not fully understand was that while George saw himself as both a Catholic Christian and a Reformed Church minister, and while he admired the Roman Catholic Church's spirituality and its moral and doctrinal solidity, he hated what he saw as its exclusiveness at the altar, and he feared its pretensions. It was the Roman Catholic identification of the Church with the Kingdom of God which bothered him, and he saw Holy Roman Empires being built everywhere, particularly in Europe. For a man who was perceived as being pro-Roman Catholic and pro-Communist, he actually subscribed to the conspiracy theory in both cases, and feared what he saw as their imperialism even as he admired their moral seriousness.

There was more rearguard fighting at the 1972 General Assembly, this time on the issue of the Just War. Complaining that the Church was continually "humming and hawing" on the matter, he asked the General Assembly to declare that the doctrine of the Just War was outmoded in the nuclear age, and that the only obedience left for the Church was to embrace pacifism. He said that on a visit to Australia and USA, two weeks previously, he had seen students going to prison for staging a sit-down at Princeton University's military research offices.

"They are being baptized in the ornamental fountains outside the door of the chapel," he said, "because of their determination to declare that they have come over to the Christian side in the Jesus Revolution in prestigious Princeton."

Speaking about the nuclear threat, he went on: "We are demon-possessed – at least I hope we are. I hope it is not as rational creatures that we contemplate using one of our Polarises. Each Polaris contains in its belly the accumulated fire power of all the bombs and explosives used by both sides during the last war, including the Hiroshima bomb and the Nagasaki bomb.

". . . When will we realize that we are the cause of the permissive society? Permitting this madness, we are driving our most sensitive youth to drugs and drink and depravity because they can't stand the prospect. But cheer up, there is a rumour of angels. Youth by the hundred in the USA and youth by the dozen here are giving up the dope and the depravity and embracing Jesus with open arms. This is the new thing coming up. What have we got to say to them? Are they going to be forced to found a church of their own while we drone on?"

The oratory was in vain. He was a predictable part of the show. After the applause, the usual heavy defeat.

"I am always deeply moved and uplifted, I feel I am almost reaching the pearly gates when I listen to Dr MacLeod," said the Rev. Ian Campbell, speaking for many. "But afterwards, when I start trying to fly down to earth, which seems a remote place after being in these pearly regions, I find it is not just an easy business."

George was undoubtedly appreciated much more abroad at this time (though he was nominated for the Chancellorship of Glasgow University, which he failed to get. He was also nominated for the Nobel Peace prize in 1973 by Norman Buchan, MP, backed by Douglas Alexander and Robin Barbour. Nothing came of it). He had drawn big crowds in his speaking tour in USA and Australia just before the General Assembly. He was invited to come back and do a ten-week stint as Turnbull Preacher at Melbourne – "good for the ego" he wrote of the invitation – but turned it down.

Back home, he continued to agonize over the issue of permissiveness. His moral puritanism had not pleased all of the students at Glasgow University. His public lack of sympathy for the "sexual revolution" brought him scorn. Interviewed by the Glasgow University magazine, he said that he would not put forward views he did not agree with. He supported Malcolm Muggeridge, who had resigned as Rector of Edinburgh University rather than put forward liberal proposals on contraception.

"If someone asks me to sign on the dotted line on a moral issue," he said uncompromisingly, "I will not go against my views to represent the students."

His style of oratory did not always go down well either. Some students mimicked his breathy delivery, and he was angry at chapel one day when some divinity students, who had heard his stories before, mouthed his punchlines before he got to them. His style was out of kilter with the times, yet his genuine sympathy with the struggles of young people kept the septuagenarian in touch with many of the students.

George found his time as Rector frustrating in many ways. He had anticipated raising the level of debate and prosecuting constitutional reforms, and had expected it to be an exciting time, amidst a ferment of debate. What he frequently found instead was constitutional bureaucracy, student apathy, and academic parochialism. Although he kept his promise to make himself available to students, travelling through almost every week to sit for hours in a borrowed office, he often returned depressed by the fact that not a single student had visited him.

He was succeeded as Rector by Jimmy Reid, the Communist leader of the Upper Clyde Shipbuilders' work-in. It was interesting that George should be the historical link between the driven, highly moral Lord Reith and the politically radical Jimmy Reid, having as he did a foot in both camps.

He had little success in the House of Lords. He spoke on a number of subjects – the arms race, democracy, charities' law, crofting in Mull, the EEC, the defence estimates, the Middle East, local government, Southern Rhodesia – but he made little headway. His style was wrong for the House of Lords, which was uncomfortable with passionate rhetoric, especially of a religious kind. His introduction of theological argument into the debate on the defence estimates met with glazed eyes on the part of their Lordships. It was a very frustrating time for him, and he generally sat on the cross-benches ("getting crosser and crosser" as he would say).

Knowing that he was spending public money, he was more than usually parsimonious. He tried to find cheap accommodation, sometimes oblivious to the strange goings-on around him. His son, Maxwell, was horrified to find him writing a sermon while lying on a dirty coverlet in a Soho bordello. After that, he usually stayed at the Liberal Club, though he sought out the cheapest places to eat.

In the 1970s, George MacLeod's speeches in the General Assembly of the Church of Scotland and in the House of Lords became more and more rambling and repetitive, sometimes to the point of incoherence. No matter the topic, he could still smuggle the subject of pacifism into the debate, and the end result was boredom and irritation. He could still stir the blood and bring people to the edge of their seats, but the old mental discipline seemed to have deserted him. His speeches became somewhat garrulous trips round the political world given by a seemingly partisan and sometimes misinformed guide.

These were wilderness years, a time when an energetic, gifted man in his late seventies found that he had lost a Community – even as he tried to hang on to it – and was losing an audience as well. It was a frustrating time for an ageing prophet who was now more patronized than honoured, yet who still felt a fire in his bones as he viewed the state of the world.

This frustration did not make him easy to live with. At times he could be querulous and ill-tempered, and his painful psoriasis kept flaring up. Increasing difficulties with his hearing did not help.

"Memory is a strange thing," he wistfully told his son, Maxwell, on one occasion. "Sometimes when I am very tired and hear the door bell ring, my mind half thinks, 'Ah, that will be Father come to take me away from all this busyness, back to 4 Park Circus . . .'"

Yet despite times of tiredness and dispiritedness, he still had tremendous influence on a wide range of people. He strongly supported Richard Demarco, whose Edinburgh art gallery was never far from controversy. Demarco, a brilliant maverick who enjoyed taking risks, was deeply impressed by MacLeod's spiritual vision.

"He is one of the youngest churchmen I have ever met," he said with characteristic eloquence. "He is sexy in a Celtic sense! He defends with all his heart and soul the life of the senses. He makes you want to hitch on to his star.

"He saw through my disguise clearly. I am a failed priest. Art is a language which helps you get through each day, helps you pray. In an irreligious age, we have narrowed down the whole business of what it means to be human. George understood all that, and when I talked about art he knew we were talking about the same kind of thing. He recognized me as a fellow troublemaker. When the gallery ran into trouble, never once did that man flinch or let me down."

Another who was deeply influenced was the Rev. Dr John Vincent, one of the Methodist Church's most gifted leaders. He had first met George on Iona in 1950, and had been greatly influenced by him over the years. He dedicated his book, *Christ and Methodism* to George, who had baptized his daughter, Faith.

When Dr Vincent established his Urban Theological Unit, a training programme in radical urban Christian discipleship, in Sheffield in 1973, George MacLeod was the obvious man to open the new Emmaus House.

"George has always been a great courage-giver to me," John Vincent reflected. "I have often discussed with him things which I was half-afraid of doing, and he would reply, 'Right, get on and do it.' He is an acute judge of others, at least of me. 'He'll have the devil yapping at his heels till the end,' he once said of me.

"He must have many disciples. I suppose I am just one of them. He would never acknowledge being a Master with disciples. His genius was always to enjoy the adulation, provoke the disciple, and then throw him back on his own responsibility."

George continued to visit Iona and speak and preach. Though he would sit at the back of the nave during services, it was not in his nature to be a retiring personality, and when he was on the island people sought him out for advice and spiritual direction. His was inevitably a dominating presence.

The Abbey staff enjoyed the founder's visits, and loved to listen to him talk about the early days of the Community. He was pastor and "father" for many of them over the years. One such was Graeme Cairns, who went up part of each summer for 15 years to act as Abbey guide.

"To me, personally, he was like a father figure," Graeme replied, "and I have cause to be grateful for the many 'confessional' sessions I experienced over the years. I found that on more than one occasion in my life, George MacLeod was the only one I could ask for advice.

"When I use the expression 'father figure' I do not mean to imply that there was any special relationship or that I was different from the countless number of others who no doubt had the same experience as myself. I have always firmly believed that for all his great capacity to communicate immediately with any class or kind of person and for all his magnetism, he was strangely remote. Maybe this is a characteristic of all great men. During the fifteen years that I worked annually at the Abbey for at least one week, I met many people who I admired very much, but there is no one I admire more than George MacLeod."

George also continued to travel to help lads in trouble. On one occasion a woman telephoned to say that her son had been arrested for a stabbing offence in a Glasgow street. She insisted on speaking to George MacLeod, because she believed he was the only one who could help. As it happened, George was in bed with a bad cold, and a storm was blowing up in the Sound; against all advice he got up, dressed and went down to the jetty. He demanded to be taken across to Mull (such crossings were not always easy; Donald Macneill, the Iona ferryman who brooked no challenges to his authority, once put George off the boat for getting on before he had been invited to do so), went down to Glasgow, and returned two days later.

He could be magnificent – and petulant. On one occasion, Graeme Cairns had to lead a tourist group as far away from St Columba's Shrine as possible, because of the raised voices coming from within. George was arguing with John Harvey, the Abbey warden, who wanted to remove two small wooden carved elephants which sat on the floor on either side of the communion table in the shrine. They had been put there by George some years previously, and John wanted to remove them because he considered they had no significance whatsoever in relation to St Columba. George knew that John Harvey was well within his rights, as Abbey warden, and that the reason for the removal was perfectly logical. Nevertheless, George would not concede the point. He picked up the elephants and marched off, red faced with anger, at a furious pace.

By the mid 1970s, George MacLeod was very restless and frustrated. Far from thinking about peaceful retirement, he began to look for a new project into which he could pour his energies.

But what could he find to do?

Make a new experiment of course. Start a new community, in some inspiring location.

Which is why George MacLeod found himself reasserting rather more desperately than usual that the best years of the Church were still to come – as he headed for the ancient homelands of Fuinary.

Where better to make a new start than in "the Garden of Eden without a serpent", as his grandfather Norman had described it?

26

The Fuinary Intention

O must I leave those happy scenes –
See, they spread the flapping sails? –
Adieu, adieu, my native plains;
Farewell, farewell to Fuinary.

DR NORMAN MACLEOD.
"the Highlander's Friend"

And it shall come to pass afterward,
that I will pour out my spirit on all flesh;
your sons and your daughters shall prophesy,
your old men shall dream dreams,
and your young men shall see visions.

JOEL, 2.28 (RSV)

It was a curious scene, this ancient highland Garden of Eden. In brilliant sunshine, at the east bank of the dammed-up river, stood a group of Borstal boys, none of whom were much acquainted with innocence. In the river, at the west bank, stood another delinquent youngster, in bathing trunks. After the creed was said, the boy was totally immersed three times in the waters, then he swam across to join the others.

The man in the waders, the celebrant in the midst of the flood, was none other than the Very Rev. Lord MacLeod of Fuinary.

Why was George MacLeod, in the mid 1970s, dunking Borstal boys in the burn at Fuinary? Why was this elder statesman of the Kirk, who had always stood up for the established Church, creating what looked like an alternative to the Church?

The answer lies in the fact that things were not going the way he wanted, and he knew it. He was much less effective in the General

Assembly, which was as far away from adopting pacifism as ever; and the Iona Community, he felt, had become a debating society which did not know what it wanted. Nor had The New Breakthrough in Christ made the impact he had hoped for.

His disillusionment with the established Church had its roots in the 1960s, when he saw a timid and confused Church seemingly back down in the face of unpleasant realities. He felt the Church should have stood firm on the ground of its historic absolutes, while at the same time forging new alliances with radical young people who were against the political Establishment. He was depressed by what he saw as the Church's doctrinal and moral cave-in, and its refusal to seize the opportunity of walking hand in hand with the new breed of idealistic, politically dissident youth.

His continual theme was that the old ways were not working, and something new would need to happen. He even felt the solutions he himself had proposed in the past were not radical enough to deal with the new situation.

"*Only One Way Left* was written when we were all asleep, thinking that the Labour party really believed in socialism," he had written to Douglas Alexander. "There is a revolution coming good and proper. The race is whether it will be non-violent. There is no hope of that save through Jesus people . . . *We Shall Rebuild* and *Only One Way Left* were leftish trends in a patterned society which we thought was evolutionarily redeemable. It is no longer so."

As George MacLeod moved towards his eighth decade, he realized that his dream of a radically renewed Church, appealing to idealistic and anti-establishment young people, was no nearer to fruition. Why? Because, in his view, the Church itself was the spiritual arm of the very political, military, economic and cultural Establishment which was at the heart of the problem.

And the Iona Community, his chosen vehicle to lead the radical reform, was dithering. He saw it as reflecting the weaknesses of the Church it was seeking to reform.

Where, then, was hope? He found it in the form of the burgeoning Charismatic movement, and the various Jesus-movements which were attracting young people disillusioned by the failure of the sixties' revolutions to deliver a new quality of life.

The rise of the Charismatic movement was a reflection of a prevalent deep hunger for experiential religion. Such signs as speaking in tongues, baptism of the Spirit, and the gifts of healing had largely been the province of the Pentecostal Churches, which had always emphasized the gifts of the Holy Spirit. Now such signs were appearing in the established churches, Protestant and Roman Catholic. The mainline denominations were not sure what to do with the Pentecostal phenomena, since they knew from their own histories how divisive such enthusiasms could be. Yet the evidence of personal renewal in the lives of young people, as well as of a revitalized and powerful corporate worship, could not be gainsaid.

George was excited by the Charismatic movement. It was evangelical without being fundamentalist, it emphasized personal religion and individual discipleship, it was informal yet serious, and it bridged denominational gulfs. In the main, it was theologically sound, without allowing dogma to determine the forms experience should take. He was thrilled to find Protestants and Roman Catholics worshipping and studying the Bible together, and sharing common religious experiences. He appreciated its emphasis on healing and the laying on of hands, as well as on high moral standards and personal renewal. He warmed to the testimonies of long-haired young people who had come off drugs by finding that the "Jesus trip" was more satisfying.

With the retiral of Ian Reid from the leadership in 1974, the Iona Community was looking again at its purposes. George proposed that the Community should appoint an enabler in congregational mission, along Charismatic lines.

Many Community members, resistant to what were seen as the founder's fads and obsessions, were not convinced about his current "line". Anticipating this, he wrote to all members.

"Of course I know there are those in the Community who say, 'Go on with your enthusiasm, George, but don't tie down the Community to any "ism". We want an open-ended, broad-based Community, with you at one end, others at the other, and plenty half-in-between.'

"Well, if that is our decision, I think we should be more honest with the public as to what we are rapidly becoming: namely, a replica of the whole spectrum of the Church at large. For some of us keep the half hour at prayer, and some of us don't. Some of us observe the Economic Witness, and some of us don't. Some are traditionalists and others charismatic, some of us go to Church and some of us don't.

"What is it that we are really focusing – what is our OBJECT for existing as a separate entity within the broad spectrum? What is being taught at the youth camps throughout the summer?

"The traditional Church is no longer viable for our precipitous time . . . Anyway, that is where far-seeing Divinity students in the coming decade will be turning their eyes. To incarnate the New Thing.

"But make no mistake. It will be Cosmic Pentecostalism to the core."

Although George was accused of mounting a new hobby horse, the reality was that it was an old theme of his set to a new Pentecostal tune. He had, in fact, been preaching cosmic pentecostalism since the 1940s, with a breadth of vision unmatched by the Charismatic movement of the 1970s. It is also true to say that the 1970s' enthusiasm for process theology and for the cosmic vision of the brilliant Jesuit scientist and mystic, Teilhard de Chardin, was prefigured in the immediate post-war era by the thinking of that intuitively poetic anti-academic theologian, George MacLeod.

George's charismatic line was also tied in with current concerns for a new lifestyle, linked to ecological issues. The "Lifestyle" movement advocated a simple life for the sake of others, conserving resources and, where possible, avoiding pollution. The stress was on self-sufficiency, and resistance to consumerist philosophies. Again, George was accused of jumping on yet another new bandwagon, but he had been concerned about matters of lifestyle and ecology – though without the fashionable titles – for decades. Indeed, one of his proposals for the future development of the Community had been to establish a market garden on Iona, or alternatively to assist with crofting on Mull.

When the majority of the Iona Community declined his invitation to go down the road he was signposting, he knew that he did not wish to waste more energy in attempting to lead the Community his way.

He felt that he had one more experiment in him. And being George MacLeod, it had to be an embodied experiment.

In one sense, it was ironic that George should seek to make his unorthodox latter-day experiment at the manse of Fuinary. Whatever else they were, the Morvern MacLeods were Establishment men to the core; it is hard to imagine them ever saying that the traditional church could no longer do the job. The notion of searching for alternatives at Fuinary, and the immersing of delinquent youngsters in the river – the baptism taking place without the mandatory period of instruction in the Christian faith and without the presence of representatives of the local congregation – would have seemed like an ecclesiastical nightmare to the High Priest of Morvern. That his great-great-grandson would one day be wearing waders in the river, baptizing notorious youth, would have been incomprehensible to the good Dr John.

The work which George had enjoyed most on Iona and at Camas had been the sessions with Borstal boys. So, for his new beginning – again, he turned naturally to the old constituency which had taught him so much.

The Borstal Camps at Fuinary manse – which George had bought several years previously – were remarkable events in the unknown history of the Church in Scotland. The old house was dilapidated, damp and somewhat spooky. (Lorna hated the place, and enthusiastically declined invitations to spend time there.) It had no electricity, was poorly furnished and equipped, and the old Rayburn cooker was erratic.

The day was structured like the Iona youth camps, with shared meals, worship and work. After breakfast, George preached to the boys, standing under the sycamore tree in the manse garden. He used everyday materials to make his point. For instance, he would pick up a nail from the ground and talk about the nails at the Crucifixion, saying that they might have come from Scotland, which was a source of iron for the Roman Empire. He would also give a talk in the manse living room in the evening. On the first evening, with the boys apprehensive about religion, George made a grand entrance. He marched in and put up a huge poster on the wall – it was a picture of a congregation facing a preacher; in the front row was Jesus, sound asleep! It made a big impression on the young people, who felt free to say what they wanted to "Doctor George".

He had his daily swim in the dammed-up river. One of the boys was so concerned about the old man climbing in that he sawed one of the steading staircases in half and put it into the pool for him!

George had individual conversations with the boys. If they wanted to get something off their chest, he would get them to write it down on a piece of paper, which was then put into a sealed envelope and destroyed. He would say the words of forgiveness and lay on hands as a sign of healing.

The really remarkable thing was the rapport which the elderly preacher had with the Borstal boys.

"I was amazed that somebody of his age was able to communicate so well with the boys," recalled Dave Cooper, one of the staff members. "He got to know all their names, and was always there, laughing and joking with them. He was tuned in, not just to their ways of thinking, but to their language."

Dave Cooper had been asked by George to go to Fuinary in order to teach the boys the technique of Transcendental Meditation, a simple form of relaxation-meditation developed by the Indian mystic, the Maharishi Yogi, whose famous disciples included the members of the Beatles pop group. Dave, who had been a full-time teacher of the method, recalled the conversation he had had with George over a meal at the New Club, and then at Fuinary.

"He was impressed by the fact that Transcendental Meditation was not itself a religious philosophy, and was not in conflict with Christianity. He wanted to find out what was attracting so many people outside the Church, and he felt that young people were going after Indian gurus because the Church missed out the mystical element from its teaching.

"The Borstal camps were very exciting and dynamic. The boys were eager to learn, and to break the habits of their past. They were prepared to listen to George MacLeod."

The image of this elderly Victorian gentleman surrounded by streetwise Scottish youngsters, hanging on his every word, provides a remarkable snapshot of one of the most extraordinary churchmen of his or any generation. He never talked down to the Borstal boys, never altered his accent or modified his views – he was in his element, as he had been in the Pleasance in the 1920s, at Fingalton Mill in the 1930s, in the witness stand for John Gordon and many others in courts up and down the land, and at Iona and Camas ever since. Christ had died for these boys, and if theology could not be made clear for them, then it should not be engaged in at all. This very conventional man was flirting with the unconventional; this gentleman who wouldn't take his tie off was endorsing the ultra-informal Jesus movement, because the old fire still burned in his bones and, like the burning bush, could never be put out.

It was a memorable time for another member of staff, Ann Smith. She had had sight problems over the years, and had been told that if she lost her sight for more than an hour, it would probably be gone for ever.

Ann had not come down for tea, and when Dave Cooper went to

investigate he found her crying, holding her head. She had become blind earlier in the afternoon. Dave ran down to get "Doctor George".

"He was very matter-of-fact about it," he remembered, "almost as if he knew exactly what was going to happen. He asked me to put my hands on her head, and he put his hands on top of mine. He then said a prayer in a loud voice – it was a commanding, almost demanding prayer for her healing.

"The effect was immediate. She shouted 'Oh my God, I can see!' in a broad Glasgow accent, tears streaming down her face. She was incredibly happy. Then George prayed a prayer of gratitude. He told us not to speak of it, as he didn't want to be seen as a healer, with all that went with it.

"I've never seen anything like it. It was totally dramatic and instantaneous, totally wonderful. Something very special happened in that room and I was privileged to be part of it. The beauty of it is that it was all very simple and down to earth."

Ann's sight is still fine. Her cure was by no means the first effected through the ministry of George MacLeod, but he did not want to be diverted from his main task by publicity about healing gifts.

George's dream was to form a new interdenominational community at Fuinary, one which would worship together, receive guests and cultivate the land. He shared that dream with a number of people, some of whom he invited to participate in the experiment.

One who was invited to share in the dream was the Rev. Downing Berners-Wilson with his wife, Veronica. A former chaplain at Eton, he had known George for many years. As Rector of Frant, he often entertained George to dinner parties at his rectory along with the likes of Alec Vidler, Mervyn Stockwood and Michael Mayne, now Dean of Westminster, when the conversation went on till three in the morning.

In 1975, now retired, he received a call from George, asking if he and Veronica would meet him at Oban, cross to Iona then go with him to Fuinary – he had had a dream that they might together plan the future of Fuinary! They met, and managed to get over to Iona, drenched by the driving rain.

"The Community was not in residence," he recalled, "so we went to Shuna – bitterly cold and little to eat. We chopped up a chair to make a fire, and then George said, 'Now, Veronica, we shall be all right,' and out of his pyjamas came a bottle of whisky!"

When they got to Fuinary, George showed them the best bedroom. "That's yours," he said. "Sorry it isn't quite furnished." It had a huge brass bedstead with a rusty base and a sodden mattress, and across the whole room was a hosepipe from which no water could be coaxed!

"We slept (or attempted to) in all our clothes, and about six in the morning I went downstairs to find some water – to be confronted at the front door by a massive figure, looking for all the world like Gandhi in a loin cloth, except he was covered with weeds, leaves and mud! Dear George. 'Where have you been?' I said. 'Bathing in the stream – just the place for a baptism – you should try it!'" They did not stay.

George was beginning to despair, when out of the blue he was contacted by Alec Walker and his wife, Anne, who had heard of his vision. Both were ordained, and had done mission work in Madagascar. After some discussion, they and their five children came up from Oxfordshire to live at Fuinary.

Thus, in July 1975, one month after its founder's eightieth birthday, the dream of the Fuinary Intention took root.

The plan was to move towards being a self-sufficient agricultural community, growing vegetables and fruit, and husbanding goats, hens, ducks and geese. The family and the two others joining them would live very simply, and would invite groups and individuals to come and stay. What was its purpose? George MacLeod summed it up in the inevitable paper.

"The 'alternative society' has become almost a household phrase: denoting a simpler way of life in the West, as a preface to an understanding with the underprivileged Third World. But what it would feel like (as distinct from mere talk about it) is unknown to 95 per cent of people, even of well wishers. Here and there experiments are germinating. What chance of one in the Highland region?

"It is much to be hoped that on the first Sunday of each month, the sacrament might be according to the rite of the Church of Scotland. On the second Sunday, the rite of the Episcopal Church, on the third Sunday the rite of the Roman Catholic Church, always provided that the celebrant on each Sunday asks each and all to partake. On the fourth Sunday, without the elements, there would be a Meeting of the Society of Friends: for the Quakers have always maintained that every daily meal is the table of the Lord."

George's aim was to restore the steading and make it an eating place for groups. He also planned to restore the stable as a chapel. Its west wall would be a great clear glass window, offering a beautiful view over the Sound of Mull. Flanking the window on one side would be the stall of a working pony, beside the stall being the old manger of the Fuinary stable. Along the north wall would be the harness, and the working tools of the community. The Chapel of the Stable it would be. The Incarnation at the heart of the life of the community.

And your old men shall dream dreams. It was a beautiful vision from an eighty-year-old prophet.

Unfortunately, it was to remain a dream, an intention. There was more romance than reality in it. The Walkers lived there for close on two years, but the experiment had to be abandoned. Try as he might, George could not get charitable status for the new project – a necessary qualification for the raising of finance. (When he asked the bureaucrat at the Inland Revenue if the proposal was being turned down because of its religious nature the man replied no: for instance, he had given status to the Iona Community which was not far from Fuinary – had he heard of it?)

Some visitors came: a group of Camphill children; some Rhodesian boys, children of political detainees; a group of homeless men from Glasgow; some volunteers to work on the grounds. But the original intention of becoming self-sufficient through making their own bread, growing vegetables, rearing poultry, milking goats, digging peat and fishing was hopelessly impracticable. There was insufficient arable land, and not enough time to work what was there.

It was beyond George MacLeod's ability to organize the project from Edinburgh at that late stage in his life. The Fuinary Intention was both visionary and illusory at the same time.

But there was always America: back there in 1976, shocking them as usual, enjoying the outrage caused by statements such as "the Kingdom of God on earth is in Mao's China". Back home, his plea to the Kirk to get up a special committee to study nuclear warfare failed as usual by a big majority. He was supported by his old friend Archie Craig, who said of the 82-year-old campaigner: "I find his attitude, and I found his speech today, imprudent, unstatesmanlike, irrational to the pitch of absurdity, and it is for these very reasons that I propose to support the counter-motion; because in these characteristics I surely detect the characteristic attitude of the Sermon on the Mount."

Within the Iona Community, led since 1974 by the Rev. Graeme Brown, a former missionary in Africa, he kept pushing Charismatic and ecological themes. He argued that Camas should become an ecological community exhibiting an alternative lifestyle, with a full-time horticulturalist on the staff. The Fuinary Intention may have collapsed, but he wanted to keep alive the vision. He wrote to his friend, the Secretary of State for the Environment, the Rt Hon. Tony Benn, suggesting that a windmill be installed on Iona. The proposal was turned down on technical grounds.

With questions over the future direction of Community House (which was exhibiting signs of physical wear and tear) George had a further opportunity to spell out his vision of what Iona and Glasgow together should be about – a cradle for radical Christianity, inspired by the Spirit of Pentecost. In his paper, he revealed that he had not let go of his dream of using Iona Abbey as a college for the training of divinity students.

"In all my years as Leader of the Iona Community," he wrote, "my greatest sadness came at a Plenary in Iona one summer when the building was almost complete. How were future new members to be trained when there was no more building to be done? Were they to moon around the island for three months cutting grass and washing the floor of the nave? No. Some of us had a grand alternative: to turn the Abbey into a fifth Divinity Hall . . . But at that summer Plenary we lost the vote for such a transference of purpose for Iona. It was a cruel blow at the time. But it was in God's purpose. It would not have been 'understood' at that time.

"But now EVERYONE sees the crisis of our time. Italy, France, etc., going nationally 'Communist with a human face', and not as slaves of Russia. Everyone sees the Church is out on a limb, when only Christian Comune-ism has the key to a united world. We must become the 'New Society' and not live out an isolated religiosity on the edge of the secular scene . . . Many men will increasingly want to join us in a 'Total' Divinity training as Communism (even with a human face) ceases to satisfy."

In 1977, the Iona Community decided to move from its Clyde Street premises in view of the amount of money needing to be spent on it. It was a difficult decision, causing some division, because Community House had been one of Glasgow's most celebrated meeting places. Its role had been changing, as television had made serious inroads into the fabric of community life. The heyday of "classes" in a city centre location was well and truly over, and political meetings generated little excitement. That era of optimism about the possibilities of radical social and political change – in which the Church had an important part to play – was at an end. The Church was seen to be in decline, no longer attracting men and women who could hold their own intellectually in any company; it was relegated to a private "religious" sphere inhabited by those timid and nostalgic souls who liked that sort of thing.

The decision to abandon 214 Clyde Street, with all its associations, marked the end of an era for the Iona Community. Ralph Morton, its first warden, summed up the feeling:

"It's the end of a chapter, the loss of an old friend. And perhaps worse, it carries hints of failure and defeat. But in our sadness at the loss of a building, it's as well to remember that Community House was more than a building. It was a house where work was done and people met and in which some lived as their home. What made it distinctive was not its position or its architecture, but the life that went on in it."[1]

Ralph died before he had completed the article, his funeral being conducted by his former senior colleague, George MacLeod.

George bombarded Graeme Brown with advice, as he had done Ian Reid. Despite his disillusionment with the Community at times, he recognized that it was still his "family", albeit one which argued with him a great deal, and he remained a loyal, if sometimes infuriated and infuriating, member.

On Iona itself, George was still a star attraction. Harry McShane, the well-known Scottish Communist, who had disputed with George in Govan in the 1930s, paid a visit to the Abbey. He was welcomed at the jetty by his old adversary, with the words, "Harry, I'm delighted to see you for two reasons. One is for yourself. And the other is because I've been on my own peeling spuds for the last two days!"

The picture of these two doughty Scottish octogenarian campaigners peeling potatoes, and reminiscing and arguing together in the restored Iona Abbey for the best part of a week, is a heart-warming one.

George MacLeod

On returning from the island, Harry McShane, George MacLeod and Iain Whyte stopped for a cup of tea in mid-Argyll. Irritated at being recognized as a celebrity by someone in the café, Harry asked the man who approached him if he was a member of the Communist party. The answer was in the affirmative. "Well," said Harry, "let me tell you this. I'm in very bad company. I'm between two Christians. And I've just been to Iona. And my only regret is that it has taken me 84 years to get there. And I'll tell you this. It will do some of the 'party' good to go there."

As they left the rather bemused party member, Harry commented. "That'll be reported back. And they'll all say old Harry has finally gone round the twist!"

George could also still be a menace on Iona, shifting Abbey furniture around at will and making the life of the Abbey warden less than easy.

"Music and Drama Week was particularly fraught," recalled Brian Crosby, Abbey warden in the late 1970s, "as George would prowl around attempting to thwart any desecration of holy places – an enterprise I always found curiously inconsistent with his declared theology. At one point I came across him in the Abbey Church in the process of purging the temple of a rehearsal of one or other of the dramatic pieces. I had to intervene and tell him that I had authorized the rehearsal. George withdrew spluttering, and the dramatists continued rather dejectedly – it was a sad episode. Nevertheless, I rate George as one of the heroes of my life and have always delighted in the man and his marvellous sense of fun."

One amusing incident which Brian remembered well was when, during an evening reception at Dunsmeorach, George grabbed him and told him to come upstairs with him and watch his kettle boil! He had just been given an electric kettle which, it was claimed, would boil in less than a minute. Brian found himself on his knees with George in the bedroom timing this technological miracle which did in fact boil a full kettle in less than sixty seconds!

George was a sucker for gadgets and new technology all his life. He exhibited a boyish open-mouthed enthusiasm for new inventions, which was matched only by his handlessness. The only thing George ever made in his life was a small bookshelf which he had laboriously constructed at Winchester, and which Lorna mistakenly swapped for a gas-filled balloon when a rag-and-bone man called at the house. This swap was undoubtedly a big mistake so far as growth in interpersonal marital relationships was concerned.

The Fuinary Intention

The limit of his practical skills was reached in the putting of plugs onto electric cables. To do this, he would have to be left alone in a room for a while, with specific instructions. If any member of the family entered the room, all that could be heard was deep and loud breathing as Father bent over the task under a strong light, referring to the instructions every minute.

His other major domestic practical project over the years has been the systematic driving of nails into practically every piece of antique furniture in the house, in order to hang things up. Lorna thought the valuable old furniture was in for a reprieve when her husband discovered the latest gadget – adhesive plastic hooks. These he placed all along the inside of the cupboard door. When he had hung all the cups he could find on the hooks, he insisted that all the family come in for a lecture. Standing beside the open cupboard door, he instructed them that in the future, the cups were always to be placed on these hooks. He then, as a final gesture, shut the cupboard door – simultaneously smashing all the cups.

George MacLeod's only other practical achievement during the past fifty years has been the restoration of the living quarters of a medieval cathedral on the island of Iona.

In 1979, Iona was in the news again when the Duke of Argyll announced that he was selling the island in order to pay off death duties. There was a great deal of alarm over who might purchase it, before the Sir Hugh Fraser Foundation stepped in to buy Iona for £1.5 million. The Foundation presented it to the nation in memory of Lord Fraser of Allander, and the Government asked the National Trust for Scotland to be the administering body.

George continued energetically but unsuccessfully to try to persuade the General Assembly and the House of Lords to support his various causes. He attended peace conferences in Prague and Moscow, and wrote, lobbied and petitioned endlessly. He launched Mobilization For Survival in Scotland, and persuaded the Iona Community to write to every minister in the land, seeking support for unilateral disarmament.

He was criticized roundly for his speeches and articles. But then, he had attracted criticism and hostility all his life. Some of that criticism had been vindictive and wounding, but he never became bitter – thanks to the core certainty of grace in his life, not the unfeeling hardness of granite.

Despite his flirting with alternatives in the 1970s, he came back to the old Church of Scotland and the Iona Community as his best hopes. Church of Scotland membership was by now below the million mark for the first time. Since George's term as Moderator in 1957, when he had announced a membership of 1.3 million, the church roll had declined steadily. The number of baptisms had dropped dramatically, and the number of Sunday School pupils had halved. It was clear that the Kirk was no longer recruiting even the children of its own members in any great numbers.

At the end of the day, the venerable MacLeod of Fuinary could do no other than stay with that declining church. He was a churchman through and through, albeit an extraordinary one. Disillusioned now by the quietism of the Charismatic movement and the "Jesus Revolution" which had promised so much, he knew in his heart of hearts, that if his dream of a radically renewed Church were ever to come true, it would have to be incarnated at the local parish level. It was summed up in one of the most searing and beautiful prayers he ever penned, "The Church at Home".[2]

> We bless You, O God, for that church at home,
> Let us remember its frailties.
> It is often too frail for the modern storm,
> is that church at home.
> Too conformist to a world that's dying.
> Too respectable for the drunkard
> or the wretch to feel at home.
> Too keen about its money to accuse an acquisitive society.
> Too concerned about its own internal peace
> to say the scarifying word about the Cross
> as the way of peace for the world.
>
> We ask You, Lord,
> so to invade that church at home
> that it becomes careless of dollars and pounds,
> more careful of drunkards
> more courageous for peace
> more acquisitive of love.
>
> And just because each one of us is that church at home, help
>   us to view again

The Fuinary Intention

our attitude to money in the light of Your poverty,
our attitude to drunkards and the lecherous in the light of
    Your love for them.
our attitude to war in the light of Your so strange way of
    dealing with it.

Lest, when we speak so critically
of the frailty of the church at home,
in our walks we should confront You, Lord Christ,
suddenly at the bend of the road
and not escape Your silent gaze at us
Your silent gaze at each one of us
so clearly saying:

"You are the cause of the frailty of the church at home."

27

International Honours

Listen: somewhere a loom is set beyond moth and rust.
Fall tissue of peace, from the loom,
A single fold of light,
That the just man
May walk at last in a white coat
Among his people.

GEORGE MACKAY BROWN
(In "The Loom of Light")

If I'd known I was going to live this long I'd have
looked after myself better.

GROUCHO MARX (ON HIS NINETIETH BIRTHDAY)

The eighties saw George MacLeod get caught up in further controversy, win a notable victory in the General Assembly with the greatest non-speech of his career, and gain international honours.

When Mrs Pat Welburn, housekeeper at the Abbey, sought to become the second Roman Catholic member of the Iona Community in 1979, there had been a debate in the Community about whether a Roman Catholic could be a member without participating fully in the sacrament. George's view was that the Church of Scotland communion was open to all members of the universal Church, and that if someone did not share fully with fellow members in the sacrament as administered by the Iona Community and authorized by the Church of Scotland, it was difficult to see how that person could be a full member of the Iona Community. Others argued that if the Iona Community was to take the ecumenical movement seriously, it would have to reckon with the discipline of the main churches. The Roman Catholic Church did not offer the bread and wine to Protestant Church members, and did not permit its own members to participate in the sacraments of other churches; consequently Roman Catholics could only partici- pate fully in the Iona Community's celebration by going against the discipline of their church.

Behind the argument lay a debate about the ecumenical move- ment itself. Should Protestants and Roman Catholics meet together for prayer and worship, in the hope that out of that fellowship there would grow one day a united Church with the Lord's Table open to all? Or was the sharing of bread and wine a necessary precondition of joint ecumenical activity?

Protestants and Roman Catholics had been worshipping together in Iona Abbey for many years, and in the freer atmosphere of the 1960s and 1970s, many priests had offered bread and wine to all at celebrations of Mass. Indeed, there was confusion within the Roman Catholic Church itself, as prominent figures such as the charismatic Cardinal Suenens of Belgium and several members of the hierarchy in Holland were known to celebrate open communion. The growth of the Charismatic movement, and of house churches, had been pushing the Roman Catholic Church in new directions, and there was diversity of practice, particularly in parts of Europe and Latin America. Quite often on Iona, visiting priests would simply turn a blind eye when known Protestants came to the altar.

There was a great deal of optimism that such informal practices, quietly shared in different parts of the world, would lead the Roman Catholic Church to change its official position. Within the Iona Community, there was no problem about the position of Roman Catholics who chose to share in the sacrament at the Abbey – but what of someone who wanted to become a full member, yet felt in conscience that she should adhere to the discipline of her Church, while at the same time praying that the rules of the Roman Catholic Church would change?

The majority view which prevailed was that if Pat Welburn were not allowed to join, then the Iona Community would not be dealing with the ecumenical situation as it was in the real world. It was further argued successfully that the Iona Community was not an alternative Church but a movement within the churches, and if genuine growth was to come, the Community would have to respect existing Church disciplines.

For George MacLeod, it was all too reminiscent of the Toc H debates of 1926. He believed deeply that the existing stances of the various Churches was precisely the problem, and unless groups such as the Iona Community were prepared to challenge the status quo nothing would really change. As a Catholic Christian, he was deeply suspicious of what he saw as Roman Catholic imperialism, and he regarded the Vatican's view of the ministry and sacraments of other Churches as profoundly insulting. He also felt it a deep outrage that priests should celebrate Mass in Iona Abbey, of all places, while restricting the bread and wine to Roman Catholic worshippers.

When he heard of a Mass taking place in the Abbey, George would attend and would go forward to receive. On several occasions the celebrant refused him, and he created a public fuss. On one occasion, he persuaded Jim Wilkie, a member of the Iona Community who was on the staff of the British Council of Churches, and who was unaware of his intention, to go with him.

"George was in front of me," he recalled, "and when the priest came to him (a visiting priest from the diocese of London) he refused George the communion, and George began to argue. The priest hastily passed him by, refused me also and gave me some kind of blessing, and moved on.

"I am sure it was even more distressing for the priest than it was for me, and I think George was simply being naughty. However, I can well understand his deep feeling that here in Iona Abbey, his own home really, he was being refused the body and blood of his Lord. During my years in London, I worked very closely with Roman Catholics, and while I had never been given communion by them I understood the laws of their church which made this impossible, and would never have put myself in the situation without his encouragement. On the other hand, reflecting about the whole incident afterwards, I realized that it had made me think much more deeply about our continuing problems over the Eucharist with Roman Catholics."

George's willingness to cause public embarrassment within Iona Abbey was not simply mischievousness or a desire to be centre stage in his "own" Abbey, as some of his critics suggested. They did not understand the extent and depth of his lifelong burning conviction that the sacrament should not be exclusive, and that Iona Abbey of all places should be a centre of open communion. He was not causing embarrassment for controversy's sake – he felt that the very stones would cry out if he himself did not. As a prophet who had little time for the niceties of ecumenical conversations, he had to act out his belief. It was simply not in him to be diplomatic, to state his views in measured terms; here he stood, in Iona Abbey – he could do no other.

The Iona Community's policy of using the Abbey as a place where ecumenical relations could grow quietly and informally was called into question when George said publicly, in an interview in *The Scotsman*, that Roman Catholic priests were inviting all to share in the sacrament at Iona Abbey.

The effect was immediate. A Roman Catholic priest on the staff of the Abbey, who was accustomed to share the bread and wine with Protestant believers, announced at the next Mass that the discipline of the Roman Catholic Church would be adhered to. Graeme Brown felt compelled to intervene: he asked George not to publicize acts of sharing of communion.

The Community's founder was unrepentant. Saying that he had received communion from priests on many occasions, and that several prominent Roman Catholics were known to offer the bread and wine to all believers, he asked: "In the name of all this, what do the Romans mean by the 'law of their Church'? Or is it just a law for the rank and file?

"The fact is that Church relations are in process of change, with some strict ones on top trying to retain the old traditions, with a 'commotion from below' (including priests and bishops) believing there is faith, hope and love, these three, but the greatest of these is love."

When it was announced in 1980 that the Pope would be visiting Scotland in 1982, suggestions were mooted in public that he be invited to Iona. George MacLeod immediately launched a pre-emptive strike in a letter to the Iona Community Council.

"IF the Pope comes to Iona and celebrates High Mass (without asking Protestants to partake), I shall publicly protest against his coming at all.

"Let him come and recognize Anglicans and Presbyterians as part of the Catholic Church by giving them the sacrament of Holy Communion (and so make a permanent gesture in the island that belongs to us ALL). But if he dithers, then don't let him *dither* on Iona. It might well mean the 1981 Moderator to go to Rome to clear it re the Pope. But it might mean a *real* ecumenical achievement through Iona that belongs to us all."

The thought of a high-profile visit by the Pope to one of the most sacred places in Europe was a highly attractive one for the publicity-conscious organizers, but the prospect of a piece of prophetic theatre on the Iona jetty, involving His Holiness John Paul II and a belligerent Lord MacLeod, would have been enough to chill the blood of the most sanguine of bishops. The Pope did not visit Iona.

George MacLeod, the gadfly in the ecumenical ointment, was infuriating for many because he represented the awkward prophetic rather than the patient priestly style in inter-church relations. He was the ghost at the ecumenical dinner party, rather like an uncontrollable child who is always liable to burst in at any moment and shock the guests by asking some very rude personal questions. He asked such questions not because he wanted to be rude – though he did enjoy being rude – but because he felt they had to be asked before the conversation went any further. Many people felt his confrontational style was inappropriate for the delicacies of inter-church relationships; yet even those who thought this way found that his actions made them think more seriously and even more realistically about the matter. Was the old prophet right on this one, as he had been so many times in the past, or was he simply being arrogant and opinionated? Whatever the situation, it was hard to disregard George MacLeod.

George was certainly suspicious of Rome's designs. When his old friend Mervyn Stockwood asked him to nominate Cardinal Hume for the House of Lords – prompted by the Duke of Norfolk, who thought it would be good for a Presbyterian minister to propose a Cardinal – he refused.

"I am informed that Cardinal Hume, like the RC Bishop of Argyll," he wrote to Canon Arthur Payton, "belongs to the stricter Rule in the RC Church. They believe that (with nine million RCs now in the UK and with a dwindling C of E attendance) in two generations they will take over the UK ecclesiastically; and therefore they should give nothing away in the form of denominational recognition."

His old adversary, the Rev. Ian Paisley, could hardly have expressed it better.

George still found it hard to adopt an elder statesman role in the Iona Community. He was unable to resist the temptation to interfere in the running of the Community, and it sometimes appeared like cantankerous meddling. He clashed with the Community's deputy leader, Donald Macdonald, over the terms of his appointment, and over the new man's public suggestion that Jimmy Boyle, who was serving a sentence for murder, should be released on parole to work at Iona Abbey.

At this crisis time, the Iona Community had to ask itself how it should move into the future. It set up reviews of its own purposes and organization, and determined to launch ahead into the next phase.

George MacLeod was not without influence on the next stage. I, the author, had for various reasons, declined to stand for the leadership of the Community in 1981. After the hallowing service of the Community during Community Week in the Abbey that summer, George invited me to his room in the cloisters. When I went in, he locked the door, opened the cupboard, took out a bottle of whisky and poured me an enormous glassful. He asked me to sit down. He then spoke for about ten minutes, telling me why he thought I should accept nomination. Next, he stood up, said it was late (it was after midnight) and said that I should go to bed. He added that I should let him know my decision in a few days, and that he would respect that decision.

I recognize it now as pure MacLeod theatre. Iona Abbey: after midnight: the huge whisky: the words of the 86-year-old prophet addressed with utterly simple and direct conviction. It was impossible not to be deeply touched (or even flattered); impossible not to be energized and affirmed; impossible not to understand why men leapt out of the trenches for him. The voice of the aged seer, uttered in his beloved Iona Abbey, mediated through much whisky, sounded uncannily like the voice of God. Johnnie Walker or Holy Spirit? Three days later, it still seemed like the voice of God. Like Major Mitford's cadets, I jumped over the cliff, wondering half way down what I was doing.

George continued to lobby and harangue the General Assembly on the peace issue, but with no more success than before. His rambling and repetitive speeches were received with respectful applause – and sometimes shuffling of feet – but he did not pull in votes.

"The noble Lord George," the Rev. Ian Renton told the Assembly, "whom most of us even in our conscience have applauded and seldom voted for, has suffered the prophet's doom, the doom of Our Lord, who was also applauded, but for whom in the end nobody voted. We always teach our children about the good Lord and the social prophet Isaiah, but if we as a Church have not taken our divine Lord seriously, then let us at least begin to take the noble Lord George seriously."

In the early 1980s the votes began to be a bit narrower, and the Church and Nation Committee supported moves for a "freeze" on the manufacture of nuclear weapons, but George's out-and-out pacifist motions still did not command great support.

He had little success in the House of Lords, where, in addition to the arms race, he spoke on matters such as the plight of ethnic minorities, and Scottish tourism. His theological meanderings bemused but did not impress the noble Lords.

"The House of Lords was not his particular pasture," observed Lord Soper. "He spoke rarely, and sometimes his oration was more of the last Sunday's sermon than it was on the matter of the day."

This view was backed up by Baroness Elliot of Harwood, the leader of the Scottish Conservative peers.

"On the whole, Parliament wasn't the kind of ideal background he liked," she commented. "He liked talking with small groups of young people in the Iona Community, or large meetings. He was a marvellous preacher."

He was appreciated by some politicians. Tony Benn, who George often said in the 1980s should be prime minister, found him very supportive.

"He linked peace and the environment and humanity's need to live together," he said. "He integrated it all into a view of the world which is not just ban-the-bomb, but something much deeper than that – world development and world hunger. He's got it clear and plain and is prepared to take flak for it.

"At many times in my life I've been under fire, usually for supporting the causes that he supported. He would write and say just a few words of encouragement. I can think of no better epitaph for a man than 'he encouraged us', and George has encouraged us."

George was frustrated not just by his inability to win votes in the Lords and in the General Assembly, but by his own increasing frailty. His deafness was becoming worse, the psoriasis was troublesome, his sight was not good, and he was becoming a bit lame. Deafness was the worst problem for a man who loved conversation. He dealt with it by talking more, and using his set conversational pieces, such as: "Do you know the anagram for Presbyterian? Best in Prayer! And do you know the anagram for Episcopal? Pepsi Cola!" It gave him particular pleasure to tease bishops with these riddles.

His frailty irritated him because he had so much to do. Despite his increasing disabilities, he continued to travel to speak at meetings up and down the country, and when he was at home, he spent his time writing letters on the peace issue, lobbying ministers and preparing speeches and articles. Whenever he shifted the furniture around the room, the family knew that a big speech was in prospect.

As well as pacifism, he spoke on ecological themes and, in fact, became a member of the Ecology Party. Many people thought it was yet another fad, but it was not at all out of keeping with his main concerns. Another of his well-worn themes was that Communism was about to collapse because it could not match human aspirations. Again, he was accused of inconsistency, but he had been predicting the demise of Communism for many years – though he insisted that the Church would not be able to attract the disillusioned without itself being radically transformed.

While he was talking like this, no one could possibly give him seer's credit for predicting Gorbachev's perestroika, the incredible events to come in Eastern Europe, and the rise of the Green Party with all that that meant for British politics.

His doctor suggested that his skin and circulation problems would be helped by a holiday in the sun. Lying on a Mediterranean beach was never George's idea of relaxation – a gruelling speaking tour of America was much more his idea of fun. He grudged the expense of task-free holidays, which he regarded as something of an indulgence. However, in February 1983 Lorna craftily persuaded him to go to visit an old friend Hugh Latham, a Roman Catholic monk who was spending some time at a French Cistercian monastery on a Mediterranean island off the coast of Cannes. Called the Abbaye de Lerins, it was the second-oldest monastery in the West, having been founded in the year 400.

George and Lorna, and Lorna's sister, Ursula, spent a couple of weeks there, partly in the monastery guest quarters, and partly in a little flat overlooking Cannes harbour – not too far away from where George's father and mother had first met on the tennis court nearly 100 years previously.

It was a memorable visit. Lorna and Ursula slipped away to try to break the bank at Monte Carlo; George enjoyed catching up with his old friend. He had first met Hugh Latham in America in 1945, when Hugh was Religion Editor of *Time* magazine. They had met and corresponded over the years.

Hugh had briefed the Abbot and the Austrian president of the Congregation of Cistercians of the Common Observance, to which the Abbey belonged, on the stature of their honoured guest. When George expressed his hope that he might share in communion there, the two Abbots decided that in view of their Christian devotion and achievements, it would be possible to welcome George and his two ladies to the communion rail in the Abbey church of Notre Dame de Lerins.

It was a moving moment, especially as it occurred on the feast day of the Abbey's founder, St Honoratus, under whom St Patrick had studied at Lerins in 411. George delighted to send postcards to many friends, saying that he had just received the bread and wine in the historic Abbey.

The next great ecumenical event in George MacLeod's life was the church leaders' gathering on Iona at Pentecost, 1984. When the Pope had visited Scotland two years previously, he had called on the Churches in Scotland to walk together in pilgrimage, 'hand in hand'. As a follow-up to the Pope's call, the Iona Community invited the leaders of the Scottish churches to come to Iona for a weekend of worship, prayer and study. Pastor Jack Glass and his extreme Protestant followers took over Columba's Cell and barracked the guests as they arrived.

The Archbishop, bishops, Moderators and presidents shared in the normal chores of Iona Abbey life – washing the dishes, preparing and serving the meals, sweeping the refectory – as well as in worship and in Bible study. On Pentecost Sunday, the red-robed preacher in Iona Abbey – wearing a CND badge beside his military medals – was the 89-year-old Lord MacLeod of Fuinary. The televised sermon was vintage MacLeod. It was heard in utter silence as the preacher, who declined to use a microphone, summed up his lifetime's message for the universal Church.

The central core was his perennial theme of the Incarnation as the key to understanding the relationship of the spiritual to the material – the necessity of spiritual embodiment in a world in which there was no such thing as dead matter.

"Jesus said that if we really obeyed him, we would be persecuted," he said. "But no one wants to persecute us. We are the consenting spiritual arm of the ever-worsening secular society to which we belong.

"Everyone knows, of course, that our world is now material. We are ruled by science and not by the spiritual beliefs of yesteryear.

What has gone wrong? And by what form of obedience shall we be transformed? Some say simply we must return to the spiritual. But they are wrong. To find what the matter is, we must deal with matter."

Pleading for the Church to concern itself with world hunger and with politics, George went on to suggest that the Roman Catholic Church could lead all the Churches towards unity. Quoting the Pope's call to the Scottish Churches to walk together on pilgrimage – and knowing that John Paul himself had asked to be briefed on the Iona gathering – he went on:

"What leadership towards unity that is! And from the Pope himself! It surely would be a strange pilgrimage if, as we approached a town at luncheon time, we were to separate and go to two different hotels for a separate meal. No. Fellow pilgrims must eat together."

The sermon concluded with a moving call for the Churches to unite in working to reverse the arms race. The packed congregation well understood that this would be George MacLeod's last sermon in Iona Abbey, and their hearts were touched.

One memorably poignant image from that occasion is that of Lorna MacLeod sitting at the back of the nave, her head bowed in prayer, fearful that her husband was going to collapse and die in the pulpit.

Within three months, Lorna herself was dead.

She had been hostess at a ceilidh held on behalf of the Scottish-Polish Friendship Fund, of which she was chairwoman, when, halfway through her speech, she suddenly collapsed and died.

George was in Inverness at the time, speaking at a meeting. The news was broken to him by his son, Maxwell, who had been with his mother when she died.

It was a severe shock to him. He had not expected to be predeceased by his beloved Lorna, who was 27 years his junior. Her love had supported him through many trials, and his mourning was deepened by his sense of guilt at having left Lorna with the main responsibility for bringing up the family. She had loved him steadfastly, through many crises, ready and willing to pay the domestic price for her husband's greatness as an inspiring public figure. Latterly she had pursued more of her own interests, being rather appalled to discover that even in his dotage George refused to do anything other than sit at the typewriter, if necessary contriving things to do.

Lorna's unorthodoxy had been good for George. She loved to chase fire engines through the street, whooping with delight. She enjoyed a cigar at home. Her conversation was compassionate, witty and sometimes outrageous. She could bring out the playful child in George. On one occasion, after she had pointed out some unkempt teenagers sitting on the pavement with their feet in the gutter, she was amused to find her distinguished husband similarly seated when she went to meet him in a respectable Edinburgh street (just as he had done with Harry Whitley's youngsters sixty years previously).

At first it seemed that the news of Lorna's death could not permeate his being, and although he spent hours each day replying to the hundreds of letters of condolence, he could only assimilate his wife's death bit by bit. At the crowded memorial service, standing erect in his red royal chaplain's cassock, he read the lesson, – 'For you have died, and your life is hid with Christ in God.' Only two weeks previously he had written those words to a young widow and had asked himself, as he wrote them, whether he fully believed them. He certainly did.

In the days following, as the enormity of what had happened was borne in on him, he wept openly, recalling the happy memories. The family had never seen him weep before, and the uncharacteristic open display of emotion was touching for all of them.

Then, typically, he went back to work.

The old soldier's regimented day began at 7 am. By 10 am he had answered all the letters of the day, then he set about writing and lobbying on the peace issue. He coped with bereavement by doing what he had done all his life – work. Many people expected him to give in and die after Lorna's death, but despite his frailty, he worked a ten-hour day in his study, still trying to change the world. He had damage yet to do.

"How are you?" the visitor would greet him.

"Dangerously well," he would reply, asking the visitor's purpose in coming. Simply social calls mystified him. His eye was still on the target.

Even so, he was mellower and more approachable after Lorna's death. His own family found him to be more vulnerable and appreciative. Mary, Maxwell and Neil, who were often infuriated by their father's thrawn independence, cared for him in his somewhat defiant old age with loving attention.

George also spent his lonely time reading the Bible from end to end, expressing horror at the savage tales in the Old Testament. On one occasion, he hobbled in on his sticks to the Church of Scotland bookshop, which was having a big Bible campaign. He went up to one of the assistants and said with a twinkle: "There's a lot of rubbish in the Bible that should be cut out, don't you think?"

On June 15, 1985, Govan Old Parish Church was crowded. Iona Community members processed to the front of the church. George MacLeod, robed, took up his place at the front. It was a service of thanksgiving and celebration, on the theme of peacemaking, to mark George's forthcoming 90th birthday. In the congregation were Govanites who had been inspired by his ministry more than fifty years previously. The whole worship and celebration – including a marvellously emotional yet disciplined speech by George – lasted two and a half hours. Many of the themes and causes of George MacLeod's life were celebrated and offered up to God with thanksgiving. The service was followed by a picnic in a Govan public park.

In a tribute, *The Scotsman* said of George, "Time seems to place him securely among the great living Scots, something less frequently allowed a churchman in these secular days. Even at ninety, George probably remains the Kirk's best preacher, propagandist and controversialist." *The Glasgow Herald* which described him as "one of the greatest living Scots", commented: "In George MacLeod, Scotland has given the world a Christian leader of international standing."

George's infirmity was such that he went around advising people humorously not to live beyond 89 – when a cub reporter asked him what he thought about death, he replied, "On balance, I'm in favour of it" – but his ninth decade was to witness some of his greatest triumphs.

At the General Assembly of the Church of Scotland in May 1986, George proposed an addendum to the main report in the following terms – "As of now this General Assembly declares that no church can accede to the use of nuclear weapons to defend any cause whatever. They call on Her Majesty's government to desist from their use and stop their further development."

The commissioners sat back and waited for the usual MacLeod rhetoric, but he simply stood up and said he was not going to make a speech. This itself was astonishing.

There was further astonishment when G. N. Warnock, George's traditional opponent in these annual set-piece debates, began his speech.

"I have resisted Lord MacLeod's motions on this matter year after year," he said, "but the time has come for me personally to change my stance on this."

Saying that he had been influenced by the powerful effect of a small amount of radiation from the Chernobyl nuclear plant in Russia, he went on: "Twice in my lifetime people have been authorized to murder and maim an enemy. It is not really a situation that we contemplate today. We don't need to arm ourselves against Germany or our old enemy, France. Now if I were – as I was in the last war, with the rank of colonel – if I were ordered to press the button for a first nuclear strike, I would not be prepared to do it. I would shoot myself first."

Was it really happening? The loud applause indicated the extent of the sea change that had been occurring in the Assembly on the nuclear issue. The convener of the Church and Nation Committee accepted George's addendum with a small amendment, and it was carried by a large majority.

It is ironic that the silence of the great orator helped the motion to go through. The Church and Nation Committee had done a great deal of theological work on the nuclear issue, and it had persuaded the Assembly in 1985 that the use and threatened use of nuclear weapons was blasphemous. Those on the committee, including Iona Community members, who had pushed for this position did not always see George as a tactical ally. They felt his rambling, predictable speeches were counter-productive.

After all these weary wilderness years, George MacLeod, in his 91st year, had at last seen victory. When friends and colleagues went to congratulate him, some with tears in their eyes, they found him preoccupied with how to consolidate the decision at the following year's Assembly.

Soon, he was back in America.

The Iona Community had decided to replace the ageing "Rome Express" huts, which had served as a youth camp since the end of the rebuilding, with a purpose-built reconciliation centre for youth and families. It had been decided to call it the MacLeod Centre, in honour of the Founder. £900,000 was required to build the new centre, and an energetic fund-raising campaign – called "Go 90", asking people to raise £1 for every year of George's life – was embarked upon.

George was invited to go to America again to speak and raise funds. There was concern about his health, but he insisted on going, along with his son, Maxwell, who had been appointed Appeal Director for the new centre, and the author.

First stop was Princeton Seminary, where George has spoken many, many times. The hall was packed to hear the old story-teller speak about how the Iona Community was formed. With his lecture written in bold capitals on pieces of cardboard, he mesmerized his audience, several of whom had heard him speak there thirty years previously (telling many of the same stories).

In New York, he told his audience they must deal with the "money boys".

"On Iona, we are trying to learn how to go on loving the money boys and defy the monetary system," he said.

Although George was well received, it was obvious that the Iona Community's US constituency had changed radically since the 1960s. The post-Vietnam mood, the rampant individualism and conservatism, the rise of the "me-generation" and the phenomenal growth of fundamentalist religion had combined to erode the power of liberal American institutions.

The conservative, apocalyptic churches were making the running in Reagan's America. The great generous liberal consensus was gone, fragmented, defensive. Politics seemed to have become a branch of marketing. News management was the order of the day, led by the master hypnotist in the White House. The new word in the air was "disinformation", the deliberate attempt to confuse and distract.

In this image-dominated youth and glamour culture, the 91-year-old wrinkled, lame, George MacLeod seemed an anachronism. The prophetic shouter and proclaimer seemed out of place in the chat-show milieu. Yet, strangely, they crowded into the halls to hear him.

"Lord MacLeod, how have you managed to maintain such a single-minded passion for so many years?" asked a minister.

The question was shouted again in his ear.

"I've maintained this single-minded passion for so many years," he replied, "by being deaf."

411

Then on to the third Harry Emerson Fosdick Convocation in Riverside Church, New York, 1500 pastors from all over the States attending. George MacLeod, the first ever visiting Fosdick professor, who had first walked these streets 65 years previously, was going to be honoured by the Faculty of his beloved Union Theological Seminary.

In making George Fielden MacLeod the ninth holder of the prestigious Union Medal, President Donald Shriver addressed him saying:

"What great cause of church and society in our time has been untouched by your energy, eloquence, compassion, anger and disputatiousness? Who else has more abundantly demonstrated that social justice, church unity and peace among the nations root together in the Gospel of Jesus Christ?

". . . You have been called a 'lost cause' man, but we call you an advocate of ideas whose times have not yet come. How would they ever come without leadership like yours which is willing to be a minority for now in service of a majority to come?

"One of your colleagues has said, 'George is infallible proof that in Scotland the Kirk's nae deid yet. Maybe we don't have enough life to launch a revival, but there's plenty left for a good fight.' And another has said, 'When he prays, he means it'. In you the world has reason to wonder if there exists such a person as a conservative radical evangelical.

"For fighting so many good fights, for prayer that has so often flowed out into transforming life, Union Theological Seminary is grateful to God for you."

George replied that the last time he received a medal it was for killing people.

"The love of power has ruled the world, temporal and ecclesiastical, since the beginning of time," he cried. "The Roman Empire was created by the love of power. The Roman Church got pre-eminence through the love of power. The love of power invaded John Knox in his desire to recover power for the new church.

"Now science has given new meaning to power with nuclear weapons. Thus power has jettisoned morality. So this is indeed the Church's hour. Only one force is sufficient for our day. It is the power of love."

Back home to Prestwick Airport in the drizzle. As ever on his return from America, George was tired but energized. He set off for Edinburgh to open the piles of waiting mail.

The best years of the Church were still to come, he felt as he sat at his desk in Edinburgh writing letters. He must keep up the pressure on the General Assembly.

He must work, and work, and work, and keep himself fit until the summer of 1988, when the Jubilee of the Iona Community would be celebrated, and the new reconciliation centre opened.

For Iona, he hoped, might still be the centre of the New Reformation for which he longed and prayed.

Epilogue

It is now the winter of his divine discontent, February 1990. Eighteen months after his visit to Iona and Fuinary, the old man sits at his desk in Edinburgh, working.

For he did not come back home to die. He came back to write another pamphlet.

As he leans back in his chair, he thinks of all the things that have happened in the course of the year. Some of the things pain him to remember, others bring a rueful smile.

– a group of Church of Scotland supporters of the Conservative Party has been formed to counteract the "left wing" influence in the Kirk, specifically naming Lord MacLeod of Fuinary as villain-in-chief.

– a highly orchestrated but unsuccessful attempt has been made to disband the Church and Nation Committee because it is "too political".

– the Church of Scotland has lost another 15,000 members.

– as a strategy for revival in the 1990s, the churches in Scotland have been urged to run a major centrally organized evangelistic campaign, and to invite Billy Graham to lead it.

– he has returned to Iona, despite his announcement the previous year. He has gone back for Community Week, anxious to keep pacifism on the Community's agenda, and has stayed for the week in the new reconciliation centre which bears his name.

– a Roman Catholic priest has been hallowed as a full member of the Iona Community, for the first time ever.

– Communism has largely collapsed in Eastern Europe and even looks shaky in Russia.

– Nelson Mandela has been freed in South Africa after 27 years in jail.

– and, of course, the Templeton Prize.

The announcement that George MacLeod was to share the £250,000 Templeton Prize for Progress in Religion with Professor

Epilogue

Friedrich von Weizacker delighted his friends and admirers throughout the world. The prize, regarded as the Nobel Prize for Religion, was awarded for outstanding contribution to the development of religion. Previous winners included Mother Teresa of Calcutta and Aleksandr Solzhenitsyn.

George, who had been proposed by his old adversary, Professor Thomas Torrance, at the request of the Iona Community, immediately announced that the money would be divided between the two causes closest to his heart – peace, and feeding the hungry. He went to Buckingham Palace to receive the award from the Duke of Edinburgh, who was given yet another lecture about pacifism. ("Please don't get him started!" said Mary MacLeod to Prince Philip when he began to provoke George good-humouredly.) At the lunch, George told Sir John Templeton, a successful international financier, that something would have to be done about the "money boys" who ran the world. Maxwell MacLeod flew to Tokyo to speak on behalf of his father at the public ceremony celebrating the award.

The Templeton Prize, like the Union Medal, merely confirmed George MacLeod's stature as one of the outstanding international Christians of the twentieth century.

But what had he actually achieved?

He had certainly not halted the decline in membership of the Church of Scotland. It had fallen from one and a half million to 850,000 in the space of his lifetime, and the downward trend looked set to continue. Some people even blamed George MacLeod and his followers for the decline. They had confused politics with religion, said the critics, and in taking over the Kirk they had drained it of its evangelical life blood.

This superficial analysis took no account of either the increasingly secular context of the Church's struggle this century, nor of the actual content of the MacLeodian total gospel. It could be argued with much more plausibility – though without proof – that George MacLeod's exceptional ministry had at least slowed down the Kirk's inexorable decline.

And what of the arms race, against which the old warrior pacifist had railed so often?

The turbulent events of the century provided little encouragement. George MacLeod had witnessed so much tumultuous history in the making in the course of his lifetime: after all, he had been born before the student who had precipitated the First World War by assassinating Archduke Ferdinand on 28th June, 1914.

When George was a boy – when Britain, under Victoria, was the most powerful nation in the world, and when the great religious issue in Scotland was which form of Presbyterianism to adhere to – the Boer War was being fought with Christian civility and ferocity. Baden-Powell, besieged in Mafeking, was surrounded by the enemy. Both sides were not only Christians, but Sabbatarians: it was not the custom, therefore, to kill on a Sunday, so from midnight on Saturday to midnight on Sunday, there was a mutually agreed truce. The Household Cavalry inside Mafeking got so bored that they began to play polo on Sundays. The Boers came to Baden-Powell, protesting about the Sabbath-breaking. The British commander immediately apologized to his enemies and ordered the polo-playing to stop.

The situation, ninety years on, was much less gentlemanly. Even in the more optimistic days of *glasnost* the world's nuclear, chemical and conventional arsenal was of frightening proportions. The reality – despite the new situation in Europe – was that the world was was a very dangerous place. And despite the warnings of the ecological movement over many years, the earth's finite resources were being used and abused in ways which could ultimately spell the end of human life itself.

No wonder George MacLeod was weary as he laid down his pen, momentarily. If this was the war, then he was losing it.

His contribution? Simply to have completed the restoration of Iona Abbey, the "Glory of the West", is itself a wonderful and soul-stirring achievement, for which future generations will surely count him blessed. The sparkle of the Hebridean jewel reaches far beyond the shores of Scotland. The bell of Iona Abbey will summon people in the third millenium after Christ to shape a spirituality and a materiality adequate to a new day, while drawing inspiration from the imaginative resources offered by the historical past. As the world looks for spiritual clues to help make life sustainable in the sometimes frightening historical present and future, the Iona of Columba and MacLeod (for surely their two names can be uttered in tandem) will have telling things to say, even in silence.

Intimately related to the rebuilding, indeed impossible to separate from it, is the creation of the Iona Community. George

Epilogue

MacLeod has ensured that his message will not simply be enshrined in Hebridean stones, but in a living, scattered, vulnerable community, forever seeking new ways to touch the hearts of all. They know his stories off by heart, and while they are shaped by the cunning Celtic spellbinder's tales, they are not bound by them. And it will be difficult – though not impossible – for "George MacLeod fundamentalists" to emerge in the future, because he said so many bewildering things at different times in his multi-dimensional life. Many such fragile community experiments do not survive when their inspirers leave the leadership, and though he learned to let go only with difficulty, his Community has over the years negotiated the far from easy task of living without Father. Despite his apparent authoritarianism, it is to his credit that he attracted tough-minded people who were confident enough to stand up to him. There is no doubt that, even when he found himself on the losing side, that is the way he preferred it to be.

Through the Iona Community, George MacLeod has played a significant part in directing the Church's attention to the inner city areas and the new housing schemes. In this, of course, he was not acting alone, but his stature was such that he could not easily be ignored. He attracted some of the most able men in the Kirk to his standard, and trained them for work in the "difficult places". Not only that, his powerful personality and preaching ability produced a rich harvest of vocations for the Church.

Yet, despite the Iona Community's imaginative and partially successful attempt to forge links with the working classes, the Church in Scotland has not been able to bridge the gulf between itself and the poor. There have been many fine ministers, not necessarily of the MacLeod stamp, who have served poor areas with distinction, and are rightly remembered with reverence, but by and large the gulf remains. To cast it in MacLeodian terms, many men have been sent out to the front, but not a great deal of territory has been conquered. Is it partly because the aristocratic MacLeodian frame of reference has been wrong from the start? If he were beginning again, would he do it differently? (During his last visit to New York, over a whisky at the end of a hard day, he answered this question with a rueful but revealing sigh: "I suppose I've been a West-endy kind of Christian all my life". On another occasion he observed: "I would have been a revolutionary if I had had the courage to live up to my own insights").

His influence on the Church of Scotland is hard to quantify, and will best be assessed fifty years from now. He has certainly been one of its twentieth century giants, a towering personality, yet he has often been in the ecclesiastical wilderness. He has been the Kirk's best known public figure this century and the church leader best equipped to communicate the gospel to the "man in the street" since the days of his grandfather, the great Norman himself; yet he has lost many battles in the Assembly, and his standing in the international Christian community has always been higher than it has been in a Scotland which traditionally likes to give its heroes an emotional going-over every so often (for their own good, of course).

It is certainly true that through his own genius, through the work of others with similar concerns, and through the work of his Community, many of the causes associated with his name are now commonplace in the Church of Scotland. Frequent celebrations of communion, the use of responses, the observances of the Christian Year, and the involvement of the Church in the political life of the nation are now very much part of the fabric of faithfulness in Scotland. It would be ungracious, and indeed untrue, to present these things as the achievement of George MacLeod, but his role as articulate spokesman should not be underestimated either. It is also true to say that though he has now won much of the argument, there are considerable sections of the Kirk where his writ would not run, and where congregations would resist it to the last drop of their minister's blood.

If George MacLeod has fascinated, but not always dominated, the Kirk, and has not managed to halt the decline in numbers despite his gifts – which even his doughtiest opponents would concede are exceptional – he has at the very least made the decline much more interesting. The brilliance of his imaginative vision, his boldness, and his adventurous, swashbuckling style have ensured that the words "Kirk" and "dullness" do not necessarily belong together. Christian Scotland could not go down without a good fight as long as MacLeod was on the scene. He and his community have kept a lot of people in the Church, in the fight, sometimes hanging on to the faith by their fingernails.

In today's worthy, decent, but anxious Church, it is not a failure of faith that is the problem, or a failure of goodness. It is a failure of creative imagination that afflicts and paralyses. It takes real boldness to rethink the old faith in radically new terms, and to stake a claim for the central political, economic and cultural ground for Christ. It takes MacLeodian vision and impertinence. It takes the graciousness that is his, and the granite.

His Celtic intuition and imagination have made his theology exciting. His originality lies in his creative synthesis, his gut sense of things ahead of his time, his beautiful liturgical sense, his imaginative use of language and, above all, in his wedding of belief to action. Men and women followed him not just because of his vision and his charisma, but because they sensed that he would not ask them to take risks he was not prepared to take himself. The mainstream view of the Church in Scotland is that the gospel is both personal and political, and although this stance owes a great deal to many different people, the influence of the articulate leadership of George MacLeod cannot be gainsaid. It is not surprising that those who oppose this view of the gospel should regard him still as the leading heretic.

For many people, George's most notable quality has been his radical political vision wedded to his passionate pacifism. It is for this that he is best known outside the Church. Yet it is in this area that he has been most erratic – sometimes brilliant, other times clichéd. There is undoubtedly a place in the Church for the uncompromising prophetic stance, but he could be less than helpful for people who were seeking to change things through the boring routine of bread-and-butter politics, or who simply wanted to know how it was possible to believe in non-violence while at the same time preventing the Hitlers of the world from massacring the innocents.

The caricature of George as simply a political animal – which his own more outrageous statements sometimes encouraged – takes no account of his tremendous pastoral and priestly commitments and gifts. The primacy of devotion in his own life, his peerless conduct of public worship, and his compassionate yet skilful pastoral care and spiritual direction mark him out as an outstanding minister of the gospel. It is not surprising that his time in Govan was one of the most fulfilling periods of his life. For many people, the true greatness of George MacLeod is to be found in the priestly and pastoral dimensions of his many-faceted life. The most abiding testimony to his great influence may well be the numbers of people, scattered in different parts of the world, who have found forgiveness, healing, direction and vocation through his ministry.

Yet he was a man who required healing himself, and he was aware of it. His drivenness, his impatience, his imperious demands on others, his love of the centre stage, his inability to relax as long as there were new revolutions to plan, his Victorian fear of sexuality, his chauvinism and his intolerance of what he saw as dithering were part of what he himself would term his "unredeemed particles". These shadowy areas caused him remorse, and undoubtedly contributed to his periods of self-doubt and depression. He was too private a person to share these areas of vulnerability with others: that would have seemed like self-indulgence to the man who had always to be the strong pastor for others. These human deficiencies were offset by his generosity of spirit and his genuine humility, but others undoubtedly had to pay the price, however willingly, for his vision. Yet had these parts of his "shadow" not been there, would the living quarters of Iona Abbey not still be in ruins?

Perhaps the key to understanding the heart of George MacLeod is his pre-eminent vision of the material shot through with the spiritual. His refusal to allow a separation makes him a very contemporary figure, even though this theme has been central to his life and thinking all the way back to the 1940s, and indeed beyond that to the decisive Russian Orthodox Easter service in Jerusalem in 1933. This cosmic theology, with its correlated ecological themes, is not natural to Presbyterian thinking, yet such a global spiritual-physical theology, linked to personal devotion and social and political justice, can provide the raw material of spiritual renewal for a generation which is finding that concentration on the material is not enough, and indeed may lead to the eventual switching off of the global life support systems.

It will be ironic but not necessarily surprising if a new generation which feels that the traditional Church and traditional theology have failed it turns to George MacLeod, dynastic churchman, Victorian moralist and social conservative for light to guide it on the pilgrimage into the next Christian millenium. Such is the boldness of his integrated vision and his adventurousness in bodying it forth that this old-fashioned nonagenerian is much more of a guru for the young than many younger people whose stuff seems curiously dated. In all his contradictions, even in his stricken infirmity, MacLeod still speaks powerfully to many seekers.

It is, of course, possible that those who make all the spiritual running in the future will be the cult managers, the merchandisers of privatized religion, the Swami hucksters, the tele-evangelists with the Cadillacs and the welded-on smiles. But those searching for a whole vision rooted in history yet alive with mystery, wishing to integrate the personal, the political and the communal, and above all, wishing to try it out in the flesh, will find this big man of Morvern to be a helpful guide. Because he has travelled this way before them.

He is not a saint, in the conventional sense (though he is in the sense that Columba was – an outrageous, volatile adventurer, taking God at his word). Unless you are a Borstal boy, a down-and-out, or a person in the grip of difficult problems, it is perfectly possible to try his patience. He is a larger-than-life being – large in his vision, large in his sympathies, large in his flaws.

No, not a saint, just a hero.

The old man addresses some more envelopes. He is writing to every minister in Scotland, enclosing a copy of his newly revised pamphlet "An Idea Whose Hour is Come". It is about pacifism, world hunger, and the renewal of the Church. The ministers will, of course, be asked to sign on.

He remembers his grandfather's words:

> Let the road be rough and dreary,
> And its end far out of sight,
> Foot it bravely; strong or weary,
> Trust in God and do the right.

He knows the road can be rough and dreary for the foot soldier of Christ, but as long as there is breath in his frail body he will struggle and hope: for the saving of the world, and even for his own reshaping. His own prayer, used by Iona Community members every day in their personal devotions, says it all for him with typical grit and beauty:

> O Christ, the Master Carpenter, Who, at the last, through wood and nails, purchased our whole salvation, wield well Your tools in the workshop of Your world, so that we, who come rough-hewn to Your bench, may here be fashioned to a truer beauty of Your hand.

He puts down his pen again.
Around him in his study are images drawn from his life story –

pictures of the MacLeods of Fuinary, a cartoon of grandfather Norman being attacked by his enemies, photographs of Iona Abbey before and after the restoration, and the Victorian scroll about duty in his father's handwriting, stamped with the seals of his grandfather and great-grandfather.

Tired and frail, the old gentleman dreams: of a day, perhaps long after he is dead and in his grave, when the world will turn back from the brink of nuclear holocaust, having responded to a word of peace, mysteriously connected with Iona and uttered by a radically reshaped and re-energized Church: of flags of a new dawn appearing: of a new and vibrant age, when the material order will be seen to cradle the spirit.

For, after all, the best years of the Church are still to come: are they not?

Endpiece

As for Scotland! The Church of the future is not here! We ignore
world questions. We squabble like fishwomen over skate and
turbot.

Where is the germ of the Church of the future? In what Church?
In what creed? In what forms of government? It may come from
India, as the first came from the East. But all our old forms are
effete, as old oaks, although young ones may grow out of them.
Neither Calvinism, nor Presbyterianism, nor Thirty-Nine Articles,
nor High Churchism, nor Low Churchism, nor any existing
organization can be the Church of the future! May God give us
patience to wait! It may be a thousand, or three thousand years
yet, ere it comes, but come it will!

– *Norman MacLeod of the Barony*, (final entry in his journal,
June 3, 1872, thirteen days before his death)

Notes

CHAPTER ONE

1. Lord Sands, *Kinlochmoidart's Dirk* (Edinburgh, 1931)
2. Norman MacLeod, *Reminiscences of a Highland Parish* (Alexander Strahan, 1867) p. 109
3. ibid., pp. 123–4
4. *The Scotsman* 3/4/1882
5. Donald MacLeod, *Memoir of Norman MacLeod* (Daldy, Isbister, 1876) Vol. I, p. 36f
6. ibid., p. 30
7. ibid., p. 61
8. ibid., pp. 102–3
9. ibid., p. 7
10. ibid., p. 247
11. ibid., Vol. II, p. 38
12. ibid., pp. 295, 6

CHAPTER TWO

1. Lionel Fielden, *The Natural Bent*, p. 14
2. ibid., p. 12
3. *Scottish Field*, July 1959
4. ibid.

CHAPTER THREE

1. *The Glasgow Herald*, 24/5/17
2. Account by Lt. Puaux to A. Bruce, Reuter's Paris correspondent

CHAPTER FOUR

1. Ronald Falconer, *The Kilt Beneath my Cassock* (Handsel Press, 1978) p. 148
2. *Diaries of Professor W. P. Paterson* (Faith and Life Books), p. 261

Notes

CHAPTER FIVE

1. H. C. Whitley, *Laughter in Heaven*, (Hutchison, 1962), pp. 18–19
2. *The Glasgow Herald*, 24/11/25
3. Tresham Lever, *Clayton of Toc H* (John Murray, 1971), p. 153
4. ibid., p. 156
5. *The Glasgow Herald*, 13/2/26

CHAPTER SIX

1. R. Selby Wright, *Another Home* (Blackwood), p. 23
2. Norman Maclean, *The Years of Fulfilment* (Hodder & Stoughton, 1953) pp. 152–3

CHAPTER SEVEN

1. *Scottish Field*, July 1956
2. BBC Viewpoint film, *Can These Stones Live?* 30/9/64
3. *Speaking the Truth in Love* (SCM 1936), p. 112

CHAPTER EIGHT

1. George F. MacLeod, *Govan Calling* (Methuen, 1934) pp. 99–100
2. ibid., p. 103
3. ibid., p. 105

CHAPTER TEN

1. George F. MacLeod, *Speaking the Truth in Love* (SCM, 1936), pp. 13–14
2. ibid., p. 55
3. Quoted in Iona Cathedral Trustees minutes, September 1934
4. BBC Radio interview, 20/3/73

CHAPTER ELEVEN

1. *Coracle*, October 1938
2. BBC film, *Can These Stones Live?* 1964
3. *Coracle*, October 1938

CHAPTER TWELVE

1. *Coracle*, May 1939
2. *Coracle*, November 1939
3. *Can These Stones Live?*

CHAPTER THIRTEEN

1. Charles Warr, *The Glimmering Landscape* (Hodder & Stoughton, 1960), p. 187
2. Sermon, "God Pays on Time"
3. *Coracle*, June 1942
4. ibid.

CHAPTER FOURTEEN

1. George MacLeod, *We Shall Rebuild* (Iona Community, 1942) pp. 21–2
2. Church and Nation Report, 1943
3. *Coracle*, December 1947
4. Sermon, Iona Abbey, August 1946
5. *Coracle*, May 1945
6. *Coracle*, March 1959
7. *Coracle*, January 1947

CHAPTER FIFTEEN

1. *Coracle*, November 1949
2. ibid.
3. Augustus Muir, *John White* (Hodder & Stoughton, 1958) p. 389

CHAPTER SIXTEEN

1. Falconer, op. cit., p. 155
2. BBC Radio interview, 30/5/89
3. *The Glasgow Herald*, 18/2/50
4. *The Bulletin*, 21/2/50
5. *The Glasgow Herald*, 27/5/50
6. *Forward*, 30/5/50
7. *The Whole Earth Shall Cry Glory* (Wild Goose Publications, 1985)

Notes

CHAPTER SEVENTEEN

1. *British Weekly*, 27/12/51
2. *South Africa Outlook*, 1/4/52
3. *The Scotsman*, 23/5/52
4. George F. MacLeod, *Only One Way Left* (Iona Community, 1956) p. 38

CHAPTER EIGHTEEN

1. *Coracle*, March 1956
2. *The Glasgow Herald*, 1–3 March 1955

CHAPTER NINETEEN

1. *Presbyterian Interdenominational News*, 1957

CHAPTER TWENTY

1. Sermon, Iona Abbey, August 12, 1966

CHAPTER TWENTY-ONE

1. *Coracle*, November 1961
2. *The Whole Earth Shall Cry Glory* (Wild Goose Publications, 1985)

CHAPTER TWENTY-TWO

1. Harold Macmillan, *At the End of the Day* (Macmillan 1973) p. 441
2. ibid., p. 441
3. *Coracle*, November 1962
4. Donald MacLeod, op. cit., pp. 64–5
5. *Coracle*, November 1963
6. *Coracle*, March 1962
7. Falconer, op. cit., pp. 158, 9

CHAPTER TWENTY-THREE

1. Letter to A. B. Govan, 1/11/66
2. George F. MacLeod, *Nearing the Eleventh Hour* (Iona Community, 1966)

George MacLeod

CHAPTER TWENTY-FOUR

1. *Coracle*, December 1965
2. House of Lords index, 29/2/68

CHAPTER TWENTY-FIVE

1. George F. MacLeod, *The Way Ahead*, Rectorial Address, 1969

CHAPTER TWENTY-SIX

1. *Coracle*, October 1977
2. *The Whole Earth Shall Cry Glory* (Wild Goose Publications, 1985)

Bibliography

Baillie, J., *God's Will for Church and Nation* (SCM Press, 1946)

Brown, C., *The Social History of Religion in Scotland* (Methuen, 1987)

Cheyne. A. C. *The Transforming of the Kirk* (Saint Andrew Press, 1983)

Dillistone, F. W., *Charles Raven* (Hodder & Stoughton, 1975)

Drummond, A. L. and Bulloch, J., *The Church in Victorian Scotland* (Saint Andrew Press, 1975)

Falconer, R., *The Kilt Beneath my Cassock* (Handsel Press, 1978)

Ferguson, R., *Chasing the Wild Goose* (Collins, 1988)

Gaskell, P., *Morvern Transformed* (Cambridge University Press, 1968)

Lever, T., *Clayton of Toc H.* (John Murray, 1971)

Maclean, N., *The Years of Fulfilment* (Hodder & Stoughton, 1953)

MacLeod, D., *Memoir of Norman MacLeod* (Daldy, Isbister, 1876)

MacLeod, G. F., *Govan Calling* (Methuen, 1934)

MacLeod, G. F., *Only One Way Left* (Iona Community, 1956)

MacLeod, G. F., *Speaking the Truth in Love* (SCM, 1936)

MacLeod, G. F., *We Shall Rebuild* (Iona Community, 1942)

MacLeod, N., *Reminiscences of a Highland Parish* (Strahan, 1867)

Morton, R., *The Iona Community* (Saint Andrew Press, 1977)

Morton, R., *The Household of Faith* (Iona Community, 1958)

Muir, A., *John White* (Hodder & Stoughton, 1958)

Scott, C., *Dick Sheppard* (Hodder & Stoughton, 1977)

Warr, C., *The Glimmering Landscape* (Hodder & Stoughton, 1960)

Whitley, H. C., *Laughter in Heaven* (Hutchison, 1962)

Wright, R. S., *Another Home* (Blackwood, 1980)

Index

Index

Index

Index

Index